Aweigh of Life

Aweigh of Life

A Memoir and Travel Tales of Seven Years in the South Pacific

Anchors aweigh.
Enjoy the journey

e.d. snow

E.D. Snow

CONTENTS

DISCLAIMER

The following is a travelogue and memoir of my experiences sailing and living in the South Pacific for almost seven years in the 1970s. Though some details come from journal entries made at the time, there are many more events that are strictly from memory and have been reproduced as accurately as a memory of events from forty-five years ago can ensure. Recognizing that perceptions vary, as well as the fact that time is like a mighty river, morphing and altering memories, my rendition and opinions may be different from others. Most names have been changed, some names have been left out completely, and some details have been omitted or altered slightly in order to protect their privacy.

PART I

PART 1

CHAPTER 1

*I sail the ocean depths, not to travel the world, but
because I fell in love with her changing moods.*
—Anthony T. Hincks

An anchor aweigh is one that is just clear of the bottom.

I was never tethered tightly to my family body, nor was I brought close in for nurturing and protection. I felt I was not an essential thing to protect. As a young child, I was tied by a thin string that broke again and again. I tugged hard so they'd know my strength, and they'd see my accomplishments. "Am I good enough now?" Seeing my demands not as a need for recognition but as rebellion, they tied thicker ropes with stronger knots made of stricter rules. But they too frayed quickly, eaten away by the acid anger of an unhappy family. I drifted from home because there was nothing to hold me, and when I was far enough away, I pulled the anchor up completely and stowed it deep inside to put down only if or when I found safe harbor.

Anchor aweigh, I touched that exhilarating freedom of deep waters. I ceased to look for safe harbor. I sought out the storms and mountains, any challenge that proved that I could survive without *them*, an ever-broadening pronoun. I changed course, changed boats, just as tides turned and winds shifted, like moods changing hour by hour, day by day, leaving flotsam floating on receding horizons, never thinking that they would be the pieces I'd gather up one day to find my way home and the reason I left.

For seven years, I sailed the South Pacific, lived in thatched huts, experienced cultures less touched by civilization, and gave birth to my first child on an island of grass-skirted, betel nut-chewing, bare-breasted peoples. Though it's only several yards cut from the bolt of my life, the fabric of who I am fifty years later is woven from the threads of that journey. Reconstructing the journey before it's too worn to repair in my memory, I offer this fabric for you to experience its pattern, its colors, and to feel its texture, its warmth, its roughness, its softness, its courage, its blindness, it's self-deception, and its excitement.

In the spring of 1972, by then well entrenched in the sailing community in Hawai'i, I heard whispers that a boat was looking for crew to sail to the South Pacific. I remember searching out the *Westward Ho* quickly, almost frantic that I might miss the opportunity.

"Hey, I heard there's a boat looking for crew. Do you know where it's moored?"

Eventually someone knew where to steer me.

Joined by my friend Emma, I know I interviewed for the crew position with Jackson and Brian, but I don't remember much about the interview. I went with the confidence that they would indeed want me and my experience. Why wouldn't they? I was twenty-two years old. I was blonde, fit, strong, an experienced sailor. I was intelligent, cute. I had few possessions and nothing or no one to return to. My friend Emma, who had no sailing experience to speak of, also got on as crew. Was it that easy because we were attractive young girls? I have no idea, but it was made clear that no one—meaning Brian—should be expecting any special favors.

Jackson already had a new sweetie, Annie. She was a single mother of a four-year-old son. She'd been working at a restaurant in Honolulu when she met Jackson, only a short few weeks before we joined the crew. Annie was extremely private, and in over two months sailing together, I learned almost nothing about her life. I knew she was a single parent and a waitress. I knew she left her child with her parents who had urged her to go have an adventure.

Recognizing others have their own beliefs, I believe that life is random, with each circumstance creating an unlimited set of choices and responses that exponentially expand the direction of a life's journey. Every previous action, every point of rebellion or acquiescence, each confrontation or circumvention presents a different path. They were looking for crew; the Universe, with its spider web of paths chosen or not chosen, had set up this opportunity. Emma and I applied and got accepted. I remember little of our preparation, only that within a few weeks, five of us sailed south from Kailua-Kona, Hawai'i, heading to the Marquesas: three women and two men.

I had $1,000, which I hoped would last me for at least a year, especially if I stayed on as crew on *Westward Ho*. Jackson was paying for all expenses, even food, which was unusual as usually crew—in cruising circumstances versus a "delivery" job—had to at least pay for their own food. In exchange, our responsibilities included standing watch while sailing as well as sharing cooking and cleaning chores. We'd be expected to do a minimum of boat upkeep, some washing down of decks, polishing some chrome, making the boat sea ready, et cetera. Overall, not a lot required for the privilege of sailing to the South Pacific, all expenses paid.

I was raised with privilege. I was white, with all the privilege afforded whites. My father was a PhD in physiological psychology, author, professor, so I had all the privileges associated with an affluent, educated upbringing. None of that, though, had saved me from years of emotional abuse from which I'd finally escaped at age seventeen. Though I had attempted to meet society's expectations of me, my parents' expectations of me to go to college, settle into a career, bury myself with a mortgage and debt, after a year and a half of university, my very soul had screamed out against the boredom of learning through books instead of experience. There is and was no way I was born to pay bills and die. Two old friends—both previous boyfriends from high school—came to Hawai'i and asked if I wanted to buy a sailboat with them. I escaped the mundane, the expected, the enslavement when I'd made that simple choice four years before. After three deep-water passages from Hawai'i to the Mainland, I was fulfilling the quintessential dream of all, sailing the South Pacific!

The first week out was close to perfect. The boat was stocked full of good food. The weather was beautiful. As the days passed, the night sky changed from the familiar constellations of the northern hemisphere being replaced by new constellations. We watched the Big Dipper get lower and lower on the horizon and the Southern Cross became more prominent as we headed south of the equator. I was, figuratively, standing on the bow of *Life Titanic* with arms spread wide. Unaware I was running from anything or in search of anything, I was living life forward, not looking back, and not worried about the future.

At least in the beginning, each day slid into the next with ease. We ate breakfast and dinner, nibbled in between if we were hungry, and spent the rest of the days lying around in the sun, reading, embroidering, napping, fishing, sleeping, navigating, thinking, having an evening drink, eating.

At sea, I was happiest simply listening to the water lapping the hull or curling in small crested waves. I listened to sunrises coming on the whisper of the wings of an albatross scouring the sea for its morning meal in the early-morning dusk. I felt the wind on my face. The point at which the sea meets the sky became the object of meditation, the earth's third eye. I watched sunsets. I watched sunrises. To this day, I prefer a quiet room, devoid of music where my silent thoughts have space to roam, free from the influence of others' lyrics or interpretations. Though I preferred silence, we also listened to music, and at times it seemed that, whether it was Vivaldi, Bach, Crosby, Stills & Nash, or Joni Mitchell, they too had been at sea when they channeled the tunes or wrote the lyrics.

We stood watches, each taking a three-hour stint at the tiller during the day and a two-hour watch at night. I watched as the sea expressed its moods and told its tales. There were the waves formed by and traveling with the same wind that propelled us forward. There was often a deep cross-swell coming in from a different direction, big, long rolling swells expressed by a gale or storm many hundreds of miles away. Eyes on the horizon, we watched passing squalls move by; we watched the whisper of high mares' tails portending weather changes that might arrive a day later with an onrush of stormy clouds or simply a gray sheet hung above us to block out the sun.

As five people on a small, 50-foot boat in the middle of the ocean would do, we shared our stories to the extent each could be candid. We each had our traumas, our own agendas, our abandonments, and dreams, twisted and colored, rearranged, and represented in different guises. Much like new lovers, it takes time to know someone. Emma and I had had multiple friends in common for several years, but we ourselves had not been real close friends where we'd chummed around with each other much before the time we signed on. Only Brian and Jackson really knew each other well before we set sail. Annie was so private; I learned little of her or her dreams. Though eight years Jackson's senior, she seemed to be truly enamored with him, and I could only imagine the conflicts within her: to follow the heart attached to her child or to follow the heart attached to a man. I could imagine the visceral pressure I would feel if I were to have to make such a decision.

When I heard that there was a sailboat looking for crew to sail to the South Pacific, I wasn't thinking of personality dynamics or interrelationships of people on board. I jumped on board the boat in the same way I jumped into life, head on with few questions asked. Only God, or a sailor, knows what days at sea can do to change one's attitude about an otherwise-wonderful person into someone you never want to see again.

So as the confinement of five people on a small, 50-foot boat in the middle of the ocean would do, we began to find fault in others. In reality and hindsight, nobody was evil or bad; it was just that attitudes and opinions changed. I quickly grew irritated with Annie. We were so different, and I was not yet wise enough to know how to accept differences. I felt that Annie spoke and smiled and treated everyone as if they were a two-year-old child, which I resented. She was the oldest of all of us and a mother too, so maybe she couldn't escape this. But also, of all silly things, I also criticized her lack of excitement, of passion, or laughter. For her, life seemed neutral. This fact alone irritated me. Why? I guess because I didn't know how to be around neutral. I wanted to shake the shit out of her to get a reaction of some sort. I do big, in-the-face, take-it-on, or I do "I'm alone with God; leave me in peace." Emma and I had to remind each other not to be nitpicking the little stuff. After all, we were supposed to be on the trip of a lifetime.

The son of wealthy parents, Jackson had lived a privileged life in Wyoming, spending his high school years in boarding school. Several years before buying *Westward Ho*, he had inherited a large sum of money. I had the distinct feeling that he was in search of this thing called life—or just its meaning. As the days passed, though, in my mind, I grew increasingly critical of his lack of experience instead of commending him for his choice to have bought *Westward Ho* and embark on this adventure. I felt that Jackson was so out of his element. He seemed paranoid and constantly nervous. He leaned heavily on Brian to calm him and assure him that, no, the wind was not going to sink us. With his ill-shaped skinny sticks for legs, undeveloped arms, no chest muscles, his body told a story of a young man who, lacking confidence, had never taken on a challenge. His hair was chin length and always in his eyes, constantly shielding the window into his soul. This too irritated the heck out of me for no logical reason. Other than his brief biography of his privileged life, if he had other secrets, he dissembled them to us. Probably more of a woman thing, but both Emma and I wanted to know his secrets, anything that might have given him definition.

Brian was Jackson's right hand and the spine of the two. I remember little of anything Brian shared other than braggart's tales, which weren't of interest. He was the one with the sailing skill, though, and the navigation skill and the physical strength. In contrast to Jackson's spindly, mousy presentation, Brian was a burly, thick-armed, thickly bearded man, claiming Norwegian descent and some distant relation to Thor Heyerdahl. As Jackson's long-time friend, he might have well been the mastermind behind suggesting to Jackson that buying a sailboat and sailing the South Pacific would be a brilliant thing to do. I never knew.

Though Brian had a steadiness to him and good sailing abilities, he also had a temper. Revealed off and on during our weeks at sea, its full fury unfurled a few days from the Marquesas when the sea turned into a washing machine. Swells came from every angle, north, south, east, west. We rocked and pitched and rolled even when our sails were full. It was a strange schizophrenic sea that was hindering our progress, and Brian's reaction was to stand by the mast screaming, "Fuck you, wind! Fuck you, hawk! Fuck you, ocean!" For several hours, he raged, cursing the untamable forces of nature, like he himself had gone mad. I cower around anger, a bit like a war veteran hearing a backfire. *Gawd, please stop!* I had momentary not-nice thoughts like *I wish a wave would wash him overboard.*

We all had our agendas. Emma and I were simply off for the trip of our life, to experience the South Pacific in all its shades, stories, and unknown paths to be explored with no itinerary or plans. No meaning needed. As Robert Louis Stevenson said, "For my part, I travel not to go anywhere, but to go. I travel for travel's sake. The great affair is to move."

I shouldn't pretend to know anyone's agenda, but I figured Jackson was trying to find some meaning in life. I wasn't wise enough yet to have compassion for the pusillanimous tiny world Jackson lived in, seemingly so wrapped up in fear, so lacking in confidence. It irritated me that he was missing out on this marvelous wedding of the human soul with the endless universe. As attitude is imperfection's filter, my critical judgments ate away at the perfection. In the ignorance of my own youth and my own delusions, my assumption was that my dreams were grander, freer, more valid than their dreams. Oh, those vainglory winds of intrepidity.

The constant in life is that everything changes; nothing remains the same. Things once perfect begin to show flaws or unravel. As the days got hotter and hotter, it melted away pleasantries. The deck was a frying pan; below deck was a sauna. Buckets of saltwater, almost tepid in temperature, washed off the perspiration. Standing naked in a fresh rain squall washed off the salt. If it lasted long enough, with the wind blowing, you could actually get chilled. But rain squalls brought wind, and we came to realize wind freaked out Jackson. Remove one problem or flaw—being too hot—and replace it with another, "The wind is too strong; take down the sails!" when the wind wasn't too strong at all. The warp and weft of attitude got eaten through by a constant exposure to forces one had no control over, exacerbated by the simple impossibility to remove yourself from a small boat at sea.

The doldrums hold those who enter their equatorial waters captive. It can be a tranquil pause, a place to hold the stillness. It will eventually spit you out the other side though less quickly without the use of an engine. Unwilling at first to violate its quiet, still sanctity by turning on a motor to push through the stillness of the doldrums, we wallowed in its glass-smooth waters. At least for a few days. In its impenetrable quiet stillness, bible rays of sun would slice through the liquid blue, diving as deep as it could before being swallowed in the depths. Not a ripple against the hull. Not a breath against the sails. Not a sound. Thoughts also stood still in the awe of the stillness. We'd dive off the boat into that halcyon stillness, breaking into the sea's own tranquil meditation to swim in circles around the boat, playing, cooling off in its depths. Far from any land, it was like slipping into the moment of creation. So much water, so deep. Everywhere. Such freedom.

Not cherished by all though. Annie had slipped into the water on her own with a broad-brimmed hat on and was leisurely dog-paddling around when the tiniest breeze filled the sails. We were quickly hundreds of feet away from her. Her screams of terror brought Jackson bounding up from below. I was at the helm, and though I'd quickly brought the boat around, it was going to take a few tacks to get back to her. Jackson, almost as terrified as Annie, mandated that we start the engine and motor back to get her. I was full of my own bravado, I suppose, thinking it all quite amusing— Emma also—but Annie never saw the humor in it, and Jackson made it clear he didn't appreciate my lighthearted chuckles.

A bit more acid eating away at the human dynamics on *Westward Ho.*

Annie never went swimming out in the middle of the ocean again.

We often trailed a 100-foot line behind the boat in the calmer waters. We'd tie knots in it about every ten feet. When the winds were light, I loved diving off the bowsprit, deep, and coming up to watch the boat sail past. I'd grab the line, drag behind the boat for a bit, and then pull myself back up to the rope ladder hanging from the stern. I was the only one who rejoiced in this antic. Admittedly, I quit doing it shortly after we arrived in the Marquesas, when we experienced hammerhead sharks that would follow us for hours on end. Only then did I realize what a yummy morsel I might have appeared to be trailing behind the boat.

Most nights were beyond the majestic, whether there was a full moon, a quarter moon, or a new moon. Under a full moon, dancing ribbons shimmered across still waters. In rougher waters, whitecaps would explode here, there, disappearing, reappearing, like white paint blotches thrown on a dark canvas. There were stretches of sea that were filled with phosphorescence that mesmerized you with its ghostly glow, peeling off the hull's bow, trailing in the wake behind, dancing in glowing blobs, or outlining porpoises that traveled with us at times at night.

The black depth of a night with no moon was pierced by constellations, holes in the fabric of the night. Remnants of dust in an immense body of life. All the magic. Such an amazing universe unseen by the millions who live in a city or town with its light pollution.

Day or night, my ego quickly diminished to an unseeable speck, with only a glimmer of consciousness holding on to a tenuous moment of shimmering awareness. The floating mite of consciousness simply noticed with awe-filled recognition that I am this tiniest of moments on this immense endless ocean on this granule of a planet that is spinning through an unfathomably deep—and endless—space. And this little planet is itself only one speck in one solar system, which is itself only a piece of dust in a galaxy made up of 2.5 billion solar systems. And that one galaxy is itself only another piece of floating lint in an ocean of another 2.5 billion galaxies. Religions and their notion that humankind is somehow the apex of a God's creation had no hold over me in this diminutive state. The suspension—the eradication—of the perceived importance of human beings on this spinning globe was, to me, the spiritual essence of sailing and being at sea.

The reality of deep-water sailing is that, on most days, there was little to do. Winds were generally steady and required no attention though there were the odd days that the weather required multiple sail changes. First, there'd be light winds, and we had the genoa flying; and then a squall would come, and we'd pull down the genoa and put up a small storm jib. Then switch again. But most days were long days of steady sailing and sun and starry nights.

I'm not sure Jackson ever relaxed enough to appreciate what I experienced. He spent most of his time reading German war novels. He grew more and more restless as the days progressed, whining about how much he wanted to get to land when we still had two weeks to go. It affected all of us, and soon we were all hoping to get to land soon just to escape the human dynamics. Because I was looking for it, of course, to justify my prejudgments, I'm positive I could see Annie and Jackson's honeymoon fade and a growing disenchantment held at bay by a tempered tolerance.

Attitude is everything.

As landfall is the only escape from the confinement of a small boat at sea, we were ready for the salvific power of land, a pause in a sailor's life at sea. We were ready to explore paradise lost.

CHAPTER 2

One's destination is never a place, but a new way of seeing things.
—Henry Miller

At sea, there is only one smell. There aren't even the flavors of sea that you note on land. But just as the petrichor can be smelled before the rain reaches you, we smelled the Marquesas before we saw it. When we approached Tahiti, the smell of flowers came across the breeze before we ever saw land, but the smell of the Marquesas, after it had wafted sixty miles across the ocean, was a musty odor of dried hay and manure and earth. We saw Eiau, the northernmost island of the Marquesian chain, at 11:50 a.m. on April 29.

This was a time before *Lonely Planet* and *Frommers*. Before setting sail, I had known virtually nothing about many of the islands we were to visit. I think I was expecting the turquoise lagoons of Tahiti fame, but the next morning, scooting down the coast on the southeast side of Nuku Hiva, we saw instead a mountain's fingers reaching straight to the sea, dressed in greenery growing to the water's edge, and no turquoise reefs. Nonetheless, the adventure in the South Pacific had begun.

Before sundown, we anchored in Taioha'e Bay, the water-filled mouth of a sunken volcano circled by 4500-foot mountains. Smells of land life drifted across the bay: fresh earth, flowers, smoldering leaves and fires burning, food cooking, the dampness of a forest floor, the fishy smell of a coastal shore. At dawn, a Sunday, we woke to the sound of roosters crowing on the shore and sea birds. Seemingly out of place, a small French naval boat, possibly the one we'd seen the day before, had anchored during the night. The hum of its generators was the only unnatural sound.

We scanned the shore with binoculars.

"Hey, Emma, do you think those are brothels?" I asked, handing her the binoculars. On the front porches of several houses, women were lounging in their bras. We could see women walking with pareos tied at their waists but, again, wearing only bras on their tops.

"No, I think they wear them like our bikini tops," Emma replied after scanning the beach.

Is it marketing or culture that defines how one should wear a piece of clothing, or what is indeed deemed "appropriate"?

As we were gathering up our laundry and sheets and all the salt-damp belongings that needed to be washed, a trading schooner—a rusted, filthy, stinkpot copra boat from Papeete—came in and moored at the dock. That morning, besides the navy vessel and the copra boat, there were seven other cruising yachts in the bay; one was flying a British flag, the rest U.S. flags. There was one other square yellow flag flying besides ours, requesting clearance through Immigration. We stayed on board, settling into the stillness of being at anchor, waiting to be cleared.

We shared the binoculars, checking out the undeveloped quiet village nestled under the coconut trees, waiting for the gendarmes to come and clear us so we could go to shore. We saw a VW bus, a couple cars, and a Datsun truck though I wondered where they'd drive to. Taioha'e was not only Nuku Hiva's administrative center, but it was also the capital of the Marquesas. From our vantage, it consisted of about twenty shacks, the gendarme's station, a small hospital. The blue, red, and white vertical bands of the French flag hung in front of what we deemed to be the port captain or gendarme's house. A horse was tied up outside next to a tennis court, of all things, but we didn't see anyone, and no official came out to our boat.

All the while, I felt the excitement of a child about to enter Disneyland except the scene was not of manmade fun machines. This wasn't Americanized Hawai'i where they paved paradise and put in a parking lot. This was the South Pacific. This was paradise before, I hoped, the white man had ruined too much. I was anxious to get to shore, to begin absorbing it all, a sponge ready to soak up every little nuance, every new cultural tic. I didn't want to be a tourist witnessing a different culture as much as I wanted to embrace their more simplistic lifestyle. I wanted to hold both my desire to experience the old but with a familiarity—to awaken some ancient undefined past residing in me—while at the same time experiencing the wonder of its newness.

It was many years later before I realized that I was in search of simplicity. Besides the degradation of the environment around the world, I blamed civilization and privilege and money and all the complexity it brought for the angry, unloving dysfunctional home I had been raised in. I unconsciously believed that harmony with nature and simplicity would sustain and support loving families. I was young and naïve, a child of the sixties, turning my back on the American way and all its pressure to mold me. I didn't really ratiocinate these thoughts; they just simply always hovered on the edge of what propelled me forward.

No gendarme or Immigration official came out to our boat all day. Being in the very first port of call in a foreign country, we felt we needed to abide by the international rules and stay on board until we were cleared. The next day, May 1, Monday, a man named Keith rowed out to our boat. "Hey, there. You arrived the other night, right? Well, you'll have to go to shore and find the gendarmes, or else they'll let you sit here for weeks without coming to clear you."

Thank God someone told us. We all climbed into the Avon and motored to shore, tying off first near the gendarmerie to find no one. We eventually realized that, being May 1, the international working man's holiday everywhere else in the world except the United States, there was no one—the crew on the copra ship nor government officials—engaged in anything related to work that day.

The five of us set off walking along the one-lane dirt road that edged the bay. A group of eight-year-old boys kicked a soccer ball. Toddlers sat in front yards as their mothers, in bras and pareos, hung out laundry consisting mostly of rows of brightly colored pareos and bras and various sizes of shorts. The beach was not in fact a sandy beach but was comprised of small round stones. With each receding wave, the baseball-sized rocks would clack and rattle, stopping only when the next gentle wave rolled in. Chickens scratched about. Roosters crowed. Skinny dogs wandered in search of some morsel of nutrition. Men sat under covered thatched pavilions, talking, laughing, gazing out to sea. Everyone waved to us, greeted us, smiled at us, welcomed us as we walked the curve of the bay.

We sauntered along the road in front of the shacks under the coconut grove. Up close now, all the houses were simple framed squares, covered with quarter-inch plywood sheathing. Square holes were cut in to form windows; a square of plywood on hinges was propped up by a stick to be dropped close when the storm winds blew or night fell. Few houses were painted, just weathered plywood. Tin roofs. So not wanting to see imperfections in paradise, I was admittedly disappointed not to see thatched huts lining the bay instead. But there was a cleanliness and pride in their yards. Taro patches and rows of ti trees marked off boundaries. The thick, low foliage of the mountain leaned down, reaching into the back side of the houses. Flowers—lilies, irises, bougainvillea, ginger, heliconia—brought color and sweet scents. Small lawns were accentuated by the colorful lava-lavas or pareos hanging in long rows to dry in almost every yard.

Why anyone would opt to give up the coolness, beauty, and function of a thatched house for the scar of plywood and tin, I'll never understand. I saw this substitution replicated throughout parts of the South Pacific. A freegan at heart to this day, it's hard to assimilate the reasons behind "progress." What is wrong with simplicity? With less? Ah, even in my naïveté, I recognized the age-old desire to have what one doesn't have. I wanted all that they were shucking aside; they wanted all that I'd left behind.

There were numerous "pavilions" along the road, consisting of four posts supporting a thatched roof over wooden benches and tables. Since the houses were small, most no bigger than 400 square feet, I envisioned these as community meeting areas. During the day, I mostly saw large-bellied men in shorts, sitting and talking, with an occasional child wandering through to sit on a lap before scurrying off. The weekly market would be held under the biggest pavilion, we were told, on Thursdays. On that day, besides fruits and vegetables, meat would be available. We were forewarned that everyone must wait until the doctor, the governor, and certain other key personages take their pick. Then what is left is sold to everyone else. It was Monday, three days to go.

Signaled by an urge or some prescient knowledge of fish behavior, the men under the pavilions would leave their benches and walk to their canoes on the shore. Picking up their paddles, they pushed off and paddled quietly to their favorite fishing spots along the shoreline out in the bay. Their fishing gear consisted of a bottle around which they had wound their fish line. A stick in the mouth held the hook until it was baited. The weighted, baited hook was tossed into the water, and the bottle spun on the stick like a kite grabbing the wind, letting out the line. Silently and patiently, they rolled the line back on the bottle, rebaited it, tossed it back.

There were no businesses to speak of. We passed two tiny cubbyholes, run by Asians, selling bar soap, sweetened, condensed milk, instant coffee, and a few other items, enough to stack two shelves eight feet long. Near the dock was a copra shed where bales of dried halves of coconut meat waited shipment. Copra was the main moneymaking enterprise throughout the South Pacific. The rusted copra boat would be loaded tomorrow with the island's bounty. Today, though, workers rested.

Chez Maurice Bar et Magazin was the only true capitalistic, moneymaking enterprise in town. We heard the music before we found the bar and store belonging to Maurice McKittrick. When we first entered, on the bar side, eight men were playing guitar and a strange-looking instrument they called a *gerrera*, which sounded like, though didn't look like, a ukulele. Two men kept a fast beat, drumming on the plywood table. Fueled by beer, the music was raucously fun. By the laughter and knowing winks of the eye, the songs were raunchy and off-color.

Keith and his friend Red moseyed in shortly after we'd discovered Chez Maurice's. Red started telling tales of their visit to the southernmost island, Fatu Hiva, where fifty "natives" lived in grass shacks. They told of how, upon dropping anchor in the bay, several canoes had paddled out to meet them, clambering on board their boat laden with presents of fresh-caught fish and fruit. And their ukuleles. Wow. I catch Emma's eyes: *I hope we get there.*

While hearing about Keith and Red's experiences, a British fellow named Jim, about sixty-five, came in. His little thirty-foot sloop was anchored near us. Talking tales, he told us how there had originally been two of them to begin with, but fifteen days out of port, his friend, who was seventy, he said, was lost at sea. He sailed on to the Marquesas by himself. He was a charming old man with eyes that smiled and sparkled, happy with life. I filled up on his stories, which were often prefaced with, "You young whippersnappers might appreciate . . ." He was a grandfather figure I would have loved to have gotten to know better but we never saw again.

Chez Maurice only had three three-foot-square tables. With eight yachties and ten big Marquesian men making music, it was a swinging hot spot. The wall was stacked with cases of Hinano Tahiti beer, the only brand of beer sold, which was served warm. Not too soon after we arrived, the local men started buying Emma and I beers. I was not a beer drinker, but warm beer was worse. I kept slipping my beers to Brian.

We also learned from Keith and Red that two of the lighter-skinned Marquesian singers were in fact the only two gendarmes in town, drunk right along with the rest of the locals. They weren't going to clear us through Immigration today for sure. They were clearly unconcerned that we sat in Maurice's bar without having cleared at all. Ah, sweet initiation into the laissez-faire island life.

There was a wall separating the bar from the store section. For some reason, he had not built a door, but instead a four-foot tall hole had been cut in the wall through which the bar counter passed to the store side of the establishment. Maurice would duck between the two portions of his enterprise as needed, mostly spending his time on the bar side keeping the beer flowing. With the navy ship in town, he was preparing for them, moving cases of warm Hinano Tahiti beer from the store side to stack on the bar counter.

I'm not sure why I put so much attention on Maurice. Possibly because he was an anomaly. He was Taioha'e's only businessman. He was wealthy by Marquesian standards. This was the only bar, the only store that carried even a rudimentary selection of necessities, and the only place to exchange money for travelers. Where he received information concerning the current exchange rates, only he knew. When I questioned him as to how he knew what the exchange rate was, he became livid and almost refused to exchange my money.

"Maurice no cheat anyone! You think Maurice cheat? Then go someplace else."

Of course, there was no other place to go. I was traveling with traveler's checks that needed to be exchanged. In present day, when I travel, I don't even carry American money but simply go to ATM machines and withdraw the currency of that country or pay with a credit card, an idea that only came into existence in 1950 but had definitely not reached the Marquesas yet.

Maurice's father had been in the Royal Navy in World War I and had visited the islands. He had returned after the war, taking an island wife and starting a copra plantation. Maurice's father had lived long enough, before dying in a drowning accident, to instill in Maurice the strange mixture of "brogue and brie" as Maurice described it. Quite often in a dark brooding mulligrubs, it seemed his French heritage outweighed the brogue, or else he simply he didn't like Americans.

Maurice had a massive belly. His chest was always bare; his feet were huge leathered pads like all Polynesians. The day's grime gathered in the crease between his gray-haired chest and his belly. Rivers of sweat would unendingly well up in that crease—I watched—and then trickle down steadily in the humid heat to be absorbed by his aloha-print shorts, baggy and knee length, held closed with a drawstring of hand-twisted coconut fiber. Maurice was insolent to most foreign visitors. I wouldn't have given him much attention but for the fact that he controlled Taioha'e and the visitors to Taioha'e. He decided whom to sell beer to, whom to sell tinned butter and weevilled flour to, and he decided the price.

Everything seemed to irritate him. It was so much what I had not expected nor put into my idealized dream. In my mind, he didn't belong in my movie, my picture of paradise. But he wasn't all shirty. He was loving of his children who would come in behind the bar and climb on his lap with their runny noses and tangled hair. Though he would become silent if you approached to talk, at a distance you could watch him read stories to his young children, half-reading glasses tilted down as he read in the dimness of his kingdom. His young wife of twenty-two years would come and stand at the back doorway. He would always rise and walk to her; her eyes would sparkle with joy and admiration. My watchful eye, soaking it all in, saw the paradox, this irascible nature and the warmer, peaceful side he showed his family.

On that first day, Emma and I both eventually tired of the happy musical island drunks as funny and amusing as they were, and we left to explore more. Though it was all part of our first island experience, we felt we hadn't come to the Marquesas to hang out at a bar. Jackson and Brian, with Annie, apparently happy there was a bar in which they quickly made

themselves at home, stayed behind. We found that the men from the French navy ship had come to shore and rented, it seemed, every horse in town. They were riding them everywhere, through town or urging them along the trails up the mountain leaving town. I felt sorry for the weak-looking small horses though I wouldn't have minded renting one for only 500 francs a day.

We came across Patrice, a French sailor, who was kicking and prodding his horse to move even one step. We took up pulling and tugging on the reins of his horse and eventually got it moving along. We walked with him for quite a while. Emma was a military brat and had spent lengthy parts of her youth overseas, so she spoke French fluently. Though I'd had French in school, I remembered very little, so Emma translated parts of their conversation as we fought away hordes of flies, gnats, mosquitoes, and no-nos.

The invention of television had begun to totally change the landscape of American communities, where people stayed huddled behind walls inside their houses watching a square box. Here there was no television. People were outside, doing chores, walking, or just sitting and watching what went by. Children were always visible, kicking a soccer ball in the dirt road or just involved in imaginative play. Everyone was curious about us and always willing to talk.

We had our own questions of mundane concerns like where to get eggs, which we learned might be difficult to procure because chickens run free, so few people knew where the eggs were laid. Fruit was everywhere in abundance and usually free for the picking: mangoes, papaya, breadfruit, starfruit as well as a lot of orange trees and the tropical grapefruit called pompelmous. Vegetables, as we knew them, were not as prevalent, but within our talks, we learned of a German family on the hill at the end of town where we could buy fresh vegetables. We were also told that if we were to go fishing, we should be aware that a lot of the fish were poisonous to eat.

"How can we tell?"

"Oh, you should ask the villagers," they replied.

Some of the same species are good but one out of fifty might be bad. Not that any of us were avid fishermen, I figured we'd wait for Thursday market.

The Catholic church had its influence. Clearly, families were very large, seeming to have seven or eight or more children. Birth control was

not permitted. Condoms were nonexistent. They would have been—and probably still are—a valuable trading item to carry, along with bullets and fishhooks. But there, women started having children usually by age sixteen, around the age the hormones ran hot and heavy. There were mothers there as young as us, twenty-two to twenty-four years old, who had three or four children already.

On our way back to town, we found freshwater where we could "shower." Under a bare pipe with a tap that came out of a cement wall, Emma and I, in our pareos, turned it on and washed our sweaty, salty bodies down.

Patrice, the French sailor with the stubborn horse, had invited us for lunch on his ship. At 2:00 p.m., he came and fetched Emma and me from *Westward Ho* in a navy skiff. For some reason, I felt we needed to be sneaky coming on board a French navy ship, but Patrice and his buddy paraded us back to their small quarters where they had a nice spread of fresh French bread, pate, fruit, cheeses, and a carafe of wine. Emma translated some, but mostly I just sat and listened to Emma and these two handsome Frenchmen carry on for several hours. They were complete gentlemen the whole time and eventually returned us to our boat.

Two days after arriving, Emma contracted an intestinal ailment severe enough to warrant me, who had limited French but more than anyone else, going to the hospital to seek help one night. The hospital was dark, lit by two kerosene lanterns. Mahina, the nurse in charge of the Taioha'e Hospital, was sleeping on a mat on the floor when I arrived. She rousted quickly upon hearing my soft, "Hello? *Bon soir?*"

She heaved herself up from the floor. Her waist-length hair was pulled up in a Polynesian twist, held with a turtle-shell comb, pulled back from her face, the traditional hairstyle of every woman, from a young child to an old gray-haired woman. Laugh lines ran out from the corner of her eyes and mouth, cutting her cheeks into round bowls. Her nursing uniform consisted of a red and turquoise pareo wrapped around her immensely rotund body, twisted off to close at her breasts.

After I told her that one of our crew had unstoppable diarrhea, she replied speaking softly, slowly in French that many babies were in the hospital with the same sickness. In fact, in the dim light, I could see quite a few forms sleeping on mats on the floor as well as on beds.

She walked into the dispensary and brought out several large bottles of pills. Onto a torn brown-bag piece of paper on top of the examining table, she counted out little piles of different pills, getting confused several times and having to start over. She moved pills around with her fingers, like playing checkers, speaking slowly to me in French the whole time. She hummed quietly throughout. She finally got the pills all straight, ten pills each in three piles. When I asked her what I owed, she replied, "Nothing" with a questioning look as to what a silly question that was.

Medicine was free to whoever needed it. No, she didn't want money. Her eyes twinkled as I thanked her. As I was leaving, I paused to watch her check each of her sick babies and patients, putting a hand to their brows, before she again curled on the floor to sleep. I rowed back into the night to the boat.

Unlike Maurice, Mahina embodied that island joy and love, that nurturing, generous, caring soul of a person that I idealized. This authentic act of caring and generosity was an elixir to my soul. My own family had not shown as much love and caring as this sweet stranger had shown me that night. The simple act of caring. I thought, yes, as it should be, before money ruled the actions of people, there was connection and caring and love.

CHAPTER 3

If you're twenty-two, physically fit, hungry to learn and be
better, I urge you to travel as far and as widely as possible.
Sleep on floors if you have to. Find out how other people live
and eat and cook. Learn from them wherever you go.
—Anthony Bourdain

Jackson, Brian, and Annie seemed content to stay on board the *Westward Ho* and read, and they seemed to have no desire to explore. Emma and I had different plans though. After all, we were in the land of Melville; we were on the very island where Melville had explored and written his book *Typee* over a century before.

I have no memory of formulating our plans to explore the island for a few days. In hindsight, we could have ended up a headline, Hikers Lost on Wilderness Island, as we weren't at all prepared. We had a tent, sleeping bags, some water—about a half-gallon—and a bit of food. Not enough for three days. Unthinkingly or naïvely, I had the faith that we would find food and water when we got to where we were going. Villagers in Taioha'e had told us Taipivai was a three-hour walk away though we never got clear directions from them. Other yachties had told us of day hikes "up that canyon"—finger pointing—or "up that trail," finger pointing. When Jackson brought us to shore, we left it with, "If we aren't back by the end of the fourth day, come and look for us. Notify the gendarmes or whatever."

After all, we were on a small island of 320 square miles. We would certainly end up someplace.

On shore, we met Lloyd. He was about twenty-five years old, a good-looking sandy-haired, not-very-tall man. Dressed in baggy khaki trousers, an old short-sleeved white shirt, and an "Indiana Jones" hat with rim turned down with a feather in the band, he looked like he had long lived the island life. He and his wife, Karen, whom we met later, were charming and easygoing. The two of them had hiked up the saddle for a day and had recommended we start there—pointing—saying we could follow the ridges probably anywhere.

Lloyd had been sent to Costa Rica in the Peace Corps. A buddy of his in the Peace Corps was in the Honduras. At some point, they had begun building a boat that they finished upon getting out of the Peace Corps. Lloyd had since then married Karen, but the three of them sailed from Costa Rica to the Galapagos where his partner got off.

In the circuitous meanderings of storytelling, Lloyd mentioned a man named Dave he had met in Costa Rica. After a bit of description, I realized it was the man I had first met in Cabo San Lucas and Acapulco the year before when I had sailed from Hawai'i to Mexico. Dave had remodeled an Alaskan gillnet boat into a sailing boat when in college and had just begun cruising when I'd met him. I had old journal entries from that sail to Mexico that described my impressions of him as "quite the character; a freelance writer for some kind of magazine, a young—maybe thirty—hippie whose goal was to sail up the Yangtze River."

Lloyd also seemed impressed with his unique flare and style of sailing and related tales of their experiences together in the Galapagos, hiking and diving. He figured that Dave was probably already in the Marquesas by now but "Who knows? Dave was unpredictable."

As island time doesn't grab you and shake you to scurry on, we ended up talking for several hours with Lloyd. His stories pulled me into the cadence and sphere of sailing life, the life of the water gypsies moving slowly or quickly from port to port, reuniting and then parting again.

He told us how, within a half kilometer from the entrance to Taioha'e harbor, their main mast had broken. He was working on rebuilding a new mast out of fir from the island. He was almost finished and hoped to be off to Tahiti in a week or two, where they would reunite with his partner and transfer the boat to him to take wherever he wanted. Lloyd was going to go back to Yale. What a change that would be from cruising and living among the South Sea Islands, I thought, to return to graduate school in New Haven. He had different dreams to fulfill now; for him it was time to walk away from the sailor's life.

We met others who had the opposite story. Having made their marks in society, in academia, in the business world, they took a break to sail a while but found they couldn't return to that life they'd left, such as the professor on the *Keramos* with his wife and son who, on a sabbatical from MIT, decided he'd just keep sailing around the world. Though I never met Bernard Moitissier, he was legendary. In 1968, he would have won the first nonstop, singlehanded round-the-world race, but he couldn't bring himself to return to England and instead kept sailing on to Tahiti. There are those people the sea does not release.

We finally managed to end our talk with Lloyd around two that afternoon, and at his suggestion, we hiked up the lowest saddle at the northeast end of town, carrying sleeping bags, a tent, change of clothes, matches, and food packed into a bright-red backpack, along with a half-gallon of cold chamomile-and-lemon tea. I'm not sure what we were thinking other than the villagers had said Taipivai was only a three-hour walk away (even though unbeknownst to us, we weren't on the path that would get us there in three hours). We were undersupplied and underprepared.

By the time we reached the saddle overlooking Taioha'e, it was clear we hadn't brought enough water. Below us, we could see the red or white corrugated tin roofs and the sailboats in the bay. In the distance, we could hear the faint sounds of dogs barking and roosters crowing. The rest was silence. Of course, we could have turned around and been back down in Taioha'e quickly, but we were off to wander and explore; we were not to be so easily defeated.

Many years later, my brother, who owned a twenty-five-man print shop, was lamenting on how to motivate his employees. Both of my brothers and I were highly motivated individuals. We didn't understand why some people are motivated and how others aren't and what one can do to motivate someone. It was decades later before I realized that what I had categorized as emotional neglect by my father was in fact the fuel that motivated me. A small voice was forever asking, "Do you see me now? Look what I've accomplished. Am I good enough now?"

Quitting was never an option.

We hiked another half-mile north along the ridges before we pitched a tent for the evening. On top of the world, the ocean stretched to the horizon on one side and mountains and valleys on all other sides. The land wasn't jungle at this height but dry rocky slopes covered in shrubs, foot-tall grasses, and ferns. Pure-white doves cooed and soared in the wind currents of the valleys. There were little green and yellow parrots, screeching, flying everywhere. We could hear the kid goats bleating in the ravines below us.

Clouds gathered as the last of the light faded. We ate our can of baked beans, bread, and dried fruit we had brought. I stretched out Emma's rain jacket, tying it to the bushes to form a funnel, hoping to catch some drinking water if it in fact rained. Near the equator, it's dark by 6:00 p.m. year round. We climbed into our two-man nylon tent and, after talking a bit, fell asleep.

I have no idea what time it was when I heard the tapping of rain on the tent. I hauled myself out of the tent to ensure my catchment system was channeling the water into our container. I managed to catch almost a half a canteen of water before the rain stopped. Then the full moon came out, and I beheld a sight I've never forgotten: a full moonbow across Taioha'e Bay. It had only hints of the colors of a rainbow, the arc of an angel's wing visible as it stretched across the bay below. I rustled Emma out of the tent to share this mystical and otherworldly apparition. On top of this mountain, with Taioha'e Bay scooped out below us, on an island hundreds of miles from any place, it was a once-in-a-lifetime experience. Never since have the angels revealed themselves as they did that night.

We set off the next morning at first light. Trying to avoid scaling the rocky pinnacles required to follow some of the ridges, we attempted a lower route. It failed, and we had to backtrack. We walked into a whole hive of yellow jackets. In the end, we were forced to scale the rock walls. Emma was carrying nothing. I carried our one backpack, which kept pulling me backward as I found my footing on the sheer wall. Emma's boots had no traction, and she was forever slipping. We struggled onward. One peak more to go. It must have taken an hour to go thirty feet up. Struggling to pull ourselves up onto a ledge that we thought was unsurmountable and unscalable, we were greeted by goat shit. Of course.

The rest of the way, though being up and down, was comparatively easy going. No rock cliffs to climb. The heat came pressing down on us, and thirst remained our biggest problem. We only had the half container of water I'd captured from the rain, and no water sources were in sight. The hills were covered with guava bushes, which weren't ripe yet, and fern trees. The first fruit we came across was what is called noni in Hawai'i. It smells and tastes much like vomit (though purported to have great medicinal properties), and we couldn't bring ourselves to eat it.

For more than a mile, we tore our way through what smelled like clove bushes, the smell permeating the air. We came across groves of pine trees spotting the mountaintops where we rested, listening to the wind through the needles, gazing off along the coastline. I found it reminiscent of Big Sur; for Emma, it reminded her of her childhood in Spain. We watched a half-inch-long caterpillar eat a leaf the size of a dime in less than thirty seconds. Soon it would lay its eggs and then turn into a chrysalis, morphing. Even if we were out of our element, we could marvel at the never-ending work of nature.

Still thirsty as hell and allowing ourselves only a sip at a time, we finally came across a coconut tree atop the mountain. And mango trees! We were saved! Only one tree was dropping its mangoes. I went scurrying down the mud cliffs, collecting them, throwing them up to Emma. Ripping the thick skins off, we were happy for the moisture, the juicy fruit dripping its sweetness down our arms, leaving us sticky as fly paper but satiated. Still needing more liquid than the mangoes provided, I scaled a forty-foot coconut tree and knocked down four green coconuts, which would have solved our water problem except we didn't have a machete to hack off the top of the nut. It turned into quite an ordeal to open them. I ended up breaking the tip of my knife cutting through the husk of the second one, but with a lot of effort, we were successful in opening them all, and we drank of them till satiated, pouring the remainder into our water jug.

Finally, fully revived and refreshed, we took off on one of the cow trails. We kept the ocean to our right as we hiked, knowing that Taipivai was somewhere along that coastline. We wandered through mud and splotches of cow manure on the paths, into jungle, back out on top of another ridge where we finally caught a clear view of what we figured was Taipivai Bay. We hiked through more bushes that smelled like cloves. Mango trees appeared just about the distance apart that we wanted a mango, some with fruit, some not.

On the top of one ridge, looking back along the path we had just traveled, we saw, in the sheer rock face of a mountain, a large tiki face. Thinking it would have been quite a feat for any man to have carved it into the mountain, I assumed it was just a trick of the light. Then again, maybe not as we discovered that in fact there were tikis not only on this island but also on all the islands we visited in the Marquesian archipelago.

We came across orange trees bearing moist but sour fruit. Coming to a cluster of coffee trees, we sucked on the bitter red berries, thinking we'd suck in some caffeine. I remember thinking it strange that the coffee should be up so high in the middle of nowhere, but the reality was we weren't all that far from Taioha'e or Taipivai. We were just wandering half lost and felt like we were in the middle of nowhere. Coffee was in fact a crop that was raised and exported from the islands as I learned later. Though it was grown there, people preferred to drink instant coffee thick with sugary condensed milk. This so-called progress irritated me.

We finally picked up a good well-defined cow path, which took us inland and lowered us into the valleys where the jungle got thicker and denser. As we came up to higher ground, we would get glimpses of Taipivai Bay in the distance. But there were many deep ravines and mountain ridges yet to go. We got drenched by rainstorms and then baked by the sun as we walked onward. When we smelled smoke, I knew we were getting close to people, and not too soon after its first scent, we came to a valley of coconuts, acres and acres of straight-poled, bushy-headed coconut trees reaching to the sky and dancing with the sun.

In this *Alice in Wonderland* scene, I spied a girl with long blonde pigtails—blonde!—scything weeds. Then we saw another girl a bit older. Both wore torn stained jeans and a hand-me-down T-shirt or blouse. Other children appeared. None seemed too excited with our tramping down from the mountains with a pack on my back in hiking boots. One of the boys, though, did take off bounding across the sun-flickered meadow and climbed a slightly leaning coconut tree. We could hear coconuts dropping to the ground, hollow and firm. The sound of the coconuts dropping must have alerted the pigs because within minutes a large family of pigs came snorting up and over the knoll toward where the boy had run off to.

A solitary one-roomed wood-planked house stood on stilts, protected from the pigs, cows, and goats by a rock wall. A woven mat encased the

railing of the one-chair porch. In the grove there was a small thatched-roof shed off to the right within the yard used for storing and drying coconut meat. To the left was a tin-roofed shelter with a pot of water boiling over a fire. Not too far from the fire was a dead pig, which was being skinned when we first arrived. Monsieur Raphael, the father of these children, left the dead pig and approached us. He wore dirty ragged shorts, a white T-shirt, and a straw hat. With ears that stuck out and crow's feet crackling from the corner of his eyes, the big smile that greeted us was toothless. He was about fifty years old, very firm and in good shape,

The boy, who had scurried away when we first arrived, returned with several green nuts, handing them to his father. Monsieur Raphael slammed the green nuts into a pointed pole wedged in the ground and ripped off the husks. A few well-placed hits of his machete, and in one swift sweep, he sliced open a drinking spout no larger than a quarter. That was my first introduction to the simple way to open a coconut. I wished I'd known of it before I broke my knife blade.

Monsieur Raphael began to offer me the first drink, but as I reached for it, he suddenly gave it to Emma. What I didn't catch was him telling his daughter in French, "Ladies always come first."

For the close to ten miles we probably hiked, I had carried the pack for all but a few hundred yards; I had climbed the tree for the coconuts when we were dying of thirst; I had opened the coconuts; I had slid down the mud to collect the mangoes, and I had balanced Emma across the rivers. I had done all the work, and Emma got the first drink? Only later did I learn that he thought I was a boy, being rather flat-chested, muscled, with my hair tied up under a bandana, and being the one carrying the pack.

As pigs snorted and grunted and little black-and-white piglets ran around top speed amongst the fallen coconut husks, we chatted with Monsieur Raphael and one of the older daughters for a while. Three of the younger girls and two boys sat staring at us, occasionally speaking amongst themselves, waving away clouds of black flies and gnats. Emma was having a bit of difficulty understanding any of their French because, Emma said, it was French with a Marquesian accent, not unlike, possibly, an American listening to Cockney English. But it also could have been because none of them, young or old, had their teeth any longer.

After a bit, Monsieur Raphael and his children pointed toward the path that would take us to Taipivai, hinting at their need to get back to the tasks they had been engaged in, and we set off again on a cow path through the jungle. Coming up onto a ridge, we saw a house whose path to it we had somehow missed, and so we felt we had probably missed the path to Taipivai. At this point, we were discouraged, very hot, and thirsty. My feet were killing me and were starting to blister from walking in wet boots. We were about ready to either walk down to the house to see where we had gone wrong or to pitch camp in the middle of the cow path—the sun was about to go down over the mountain—when suddenly a boy came down from over the hill. We asked, "Est-il cette route a Taipivai?"

"*Oui, oui.*" He pointed up the path from where he had come.

With our spirits back up again, we set off climbing and winding up the path in the direction the boy had indicated. No farther than 300 yards along the path, we heard voices. It was Mr. Raphael and his daughters and sons and five dogs, climbing up through the jungle. The two boys were riding the horses on which was slung the pig, slaughtered and quartered and wrapped in burlap. They too were all off to Taipivai. They offered to take my pack on the horse for me, which I was more than grateful to give them.

Taipivai village soon came into full view. A much more picturesque village than Taioha'e, it was set back from the bay a quarter of a mile. Coconut trees stretched up into the valley, climbing up the backs of the mountains, for as far as the eye could see. A sixty-foot-wide stream cut through the middle, slowing and widening as it edged through the village and eventually dumped into the bay

From our view on top of the mountain, we could see the Catholic church dominating the village as one denomination of church or another is wont to do. Cannibalism had been prevalent in Taipivai as documented in Melville's *Typee* as it had been throughout the Marquesas. I suppose the church's influence to end cannibalism is a good thing, but at that time as I do still today, I had a visceral aversion to religion or missionaries wiping out centuries-old cultures to be replaced with a mythology of a Zeus-like god, life after death, but "only if you believe like we tell you to believe." I don't remember ever hearing my parents discuss church or religion, through osmosis, maybe, or just the luckily infrequent contacts I had with

my father's mother—starched, critical, and zealous—I adopted a disdain for organized religion. As children, we went to church the week before my paternal grandmother came to visit, all as a ploy so that when we went to church *with* her the following week, the pastor could honestly say, "So nice to see you *again*." Ah, the hypocrisy, I thought.

I didn't understand this masquerade until decades later, after my mother died, and in her things was a self-analysis my father had had to do when he was getting his PhD in psychology from Rochester University. In it, he outlined memorable moments in his childhood, what happened, what his reaction was, and how it served to develop his personality. In it, passage after passage, he described his mother having "frequent use for the stick and whip." A fervent member of the Holy Roller Church, she believed everyone was born a sinner; she labored under the delusion that she could beat my father into heaven, I suppose. At the end of each passage where he described a particular behavior and his mother's reaction, he was to analyze how each incident had contributed to his particular psychological traits, most of which were "accentuation of negativism, factors leading to disintegration and neuroticism; acquisition of fighting mechanism as a defense to social inferiority; disintegration and maladjustment disorder; social inferiority as a result of religious affiliation; development of introversion and antisocial tendencies."

Exceptionally brilliant, my father had graduated high school and left home for university at age sixteen. Once away from his mother, he also left the church, but the wounds and scars of his upbringing were deep; he was unable to leave them behind. He turned his focus to psychology; not clinical, mind you, but rat psychology, exploring the physical workings of the brain organ, inserting electrodes in rodents' brains to see which part of the brain governed what function of the body. He ran experiments on conditioning and what the most efficient method of bending a subject to his will was: punishment, positive reinforcement, intermittent reinforcement, mixed reinforcement/punishment. He became renowned in his field. And he became an alcoholic, workaholic, rage-alcoholic man around which we tiptoed on eggshells. As a child, I never saw my father in church, but I absorbed a dislike for church without ever understanding why until decades later.

Would we make the same choices in life if we knew all the secrets hidden from us as children? Secrets that unconsciously mold us to become who we are, secrets that, still unknown to us, drive us away or forward in search of the answers resounding in an echo bell for the question why. At that point in my life, looking down on the dominating Catholic church in Taipivai, I hadn't yet even asked myself why. Why did I choose to sail the oceans, search out the less civilized, the less damaged societies? Why did I have this visceral aversion to religion? Why was I drawn to simple loving women like Mahina and away from people like Maurice? I was simply aware and cognizant that I did.

We went the rest of the way down with Monsieur Raphael and his daughters at their speed, which was close to running down the mountain. They never stuck to the paths but knew all the shortcuts straight down. We were there in ten minutes. Emma and I and the three girls plopped down by the river. Soon another daughter, Claudette, and her friend, a Polynesian, Gabrielle, joined us. Finally, introductions were made; Yasmina, Marie, and Adelle. I took off my bandana and let my hair drop and went to wash in the stream. "Ooh, c'est une fille." (Oh, it's a girl.)

It was then that I realized why Mr. Raphael had not shared the coconut water with me first. I must have looked a sight and acted that much the worse for him to think I was a boy for all that distance. Then they asked if I was Emma's daughter. I got the final laugh with that one.

Though only two years older than me, Emma was more mature in both looks and demeanor, almost matronly in her presentation. Large-busted and more feminine, from her walk to her gentle talk, she was my opposite. She wasn't physically strong; hence, I carried the pack. I pushed against the world, leaping into it through its perceived barriers, rude and resistant; whereas Emma allowed the world to come to her, wrap itself around her, and she received it quietly. Her face often held a smile not unlike the *Mona Lisa*. Though we too had brief squabbles, we were, I felt, a well-melded team, balancing each other out, creating a whole.

The girls were intrigued by us, finding out that we were friends who had sailed together on a boat from Hawai'i. Giving us mangoes and pompelmous to eat as they plied us with questions, they were amazed that we'd camped the night on top of the mountains. In fact, they were amazed that we, two girls alone, had taken the length of time we had to hike to

Taipivai. Why did it take so long? Hadn't we been afraid? Weren't we afraid to sail across the ocean? They were just full of questions, chattering away. Gabrielle and Claudette were much more curious and much friendlier than the other sisters, Gabrielle proudly demonstrating the little bit of English the sisters had taught her in the school.

As it was late in the day, they offered that we could stay at their house. We all paraded down the neat little dirt road, past the clean, neat yards abundant with fruit trees. We were something new and different, and the entourage, mostly of younger children, that followed us grew larger as we walked. The houses in Taipivai were better built than those in Taioha'e. Many had a cement-base structure; all had large porches and planked wood siding instead of sheets of plywood or hardboard. They were generally much larger than those in Taioha'e also though none larger than four small rooms at the most.

As it turned out, Monsieur Raphael was head honcho of Taipivai. He was in charge of the copra plantation, which, from what I gathered, belonged to the Society as it was called: the cooperative of Taipivai. Monsieur Raphael had come from Nice, France, when he was eleven years old. He was of a family of nine boys and three girls. One of his other brothers, as it turned out, was director of the gendarmes in Taioha'e— maybe one of the drunk gendarmes we'd first seen at Chez Maurice. His other brother was head honcho of another valley on the other side of the island. The rest of his family and father lived in Papeete, for whom he wrote us letters of introduction to meet when we arrived in Tahiti, which we never followed up on.

Monsieur Raphael himself had a family of nine girls and four boys. Arriving at the house, the other children, shy and giggling, watched us cautiously as the youngest of them, a little three-year-old girl, clung to her mother's skirts. The mother looked much older than her years though she probably wasn't even forty years old yet. Her oldest was twenty-two, looking close to thirty. Their toothlessness did not lend to a more youthful appearance.

Their hospitality was only the first of a recurring pattern of generosity offered by every islander I met throughout most of the South Pacific. I can't envision a single neighborhood in all of America where I would walk down a street and be surrounded by generous people offering me food and a place

to sleep. Here it was a natural extension of the bounty that nature shared with them. Though we were an exciting diversion for this whole village, I also felt that we were a prize to be displayed because it was Monsieur Raphael's family that had met us first and had the honor and privilege to provide us hospitality. Though they were already fifteen people to feed and house, they offered two strangers a place to sleep and food to eat. We shared dinner with them, which included fresh-cooked pork, taro, and sort of tamale made from bananas, manioc, and coconut cream cooked in banana leaves, a food, we learned, that was made and prepared in a similar fashion throughout the islands.

As night was quickly approaching, they swept out the porch, and one of the girls laid down a mahala mat and told us to put down our blankets. They marveled at our nylon down sleeping bags. Mama sent one of her nine girls off to fetch two pillows encased in aloha prints of *ulu* and hibiscus flowers. They were visibly so excited to have us there, constantly bustling around.

Not completely removed from the more-civilized world, as its tentacles crept in to entice the islanders for more, it happened to be big movie night in town that night at the Catholic mission. They played Wednesday and Sunday nights, usually two movies a night. Monsieur Raphael, I guess being head honcho of the copra plantation, had the only car in town, a Toyota pickup. The two boys sat in front; all the girls, including Emma and I, piled in the back, and Monsieur Raphael drove us *one block* down the street to the mission church's theater, which was nothing more than a cement barn with a tin roof over rows of backless wooden benches. All the girls wanted to sit next to us. Crowded in close, they were talking, whispering, chattering in their Marquesian and French about us. All the young men sat on one side; the *jeunes filles* on the other. The guys kept turning and staring at us as objects of curiosity. For that evening, two young American females were movie stars to them.

The movie blasted on—blasted—and it was all in French. I couldn't understand a word of it. Like a classroom movie in high school, the projector was set up in the middle of the room. The speakers were turned up full blast, maybe to cover up the sound of crying babies and the howling laughter of the younger kids who ran and chased each other about whenever they felt like it. No one had a thought that they should sit still and watch the movie! After all, they were children.

The film would break, and lights would go on; the man would whip out a splicing kit and mend the tape. The children continued to squeal and run about during these breaks. What I now would coin as PTSD flashbacks held in one-second time capsules, I see my father screaming at my mother to shut us up. The squeals of joy and laughter coming from my brothers and I playing out on the lawn interrupted my father's concentration. He was so quick to rage against a child's freedom and happiness. That flash of a time capsule pushed me up to the edge of wanting to tell these children to be quiet, to sit still. Instead, I watched a different version of life expressing itself without reprimands or anger. Maybe because of that, throughout the island, I seldom heard a child cry. I seldom saw children fighting. I never saw parents yelling at their children. I saw kids be kids. Joyful chaos. The film broke numerous times; the scene repeated itself. Joyful chaos.

One of the movies, flecked and streaked, starred Ronald Reagan. When we told the girls that he was now the governor of California, it really got them excited. The last movie was a Three Musketeer movie in color, which seemed to quite tickle them: "C'est jolie, n'est pas?"

"Oui, oui," we would say.

One of the girls, Melanie, was full of questions, asking about my family. When I explained that my parents were divorced, and that my mother lived in Hawai'i and my father in Texas, she couldn't understand. I did not add that my father had left my mother for my mother's sister. As it is, they didn't know divorce, let alone deeper scandals. "No amour?"

It could be that the lifestyle itself didn't stress people to the point of divorce. It could be that everyone was raised similarly, and so they came into relationships and child rearing with the same ideas and principles. It could be that families were large, and there was a lot of help, so no one got stressed and searched for someone to blame. It could be that they were all Catholics. But divorce was not something these people knew about or understood. It was illuminating to recognize the societal agreements I had accepted as normal—broken homes, divorce, greed, possessions, fathers raging at their children, and the stress under which so many Americans lived—were indeed foreign to these beautiful people.

Regardless of or because of the movies that came to this village, this village that only a hundred years previously had accepted cannibalism as a norm, Gabrielle and Claudette expressed their desire to escape, to

go to Papeete. Having visited their grandfather and uncles several times, they preferred it, they said. "Here," they said, "there was no chance to get married. Everyone knows each other since babies. We know everyone too well," they complained though I was thinking this is a good thing. "We have no desire to marry someone who is almost our brother or in some way related to us," they said.

They also revealed that, right then, they had no desire to get married. They didn't want to have kids right away because then "you always have them following after you." I remember thinking, naïvely at the time and definitely sexist at this time, that I thought having children was an island girl's main goal for lack of anything else to do. I certainly wasn't interested in having children—I wasn't even interested in having a relationship, so I guess we weren't all that different. Their wanting to go to Papeete, desiring to escape the confines and expectations of their lifestyle, was the same as me escaping mine. I was searching for simplicity; they were seeking the diversity of a more "civilized" society.

After the movies, Monsieur Raphael drove us the whole block home. Some of the eighteen- and twenty-year-old boys were out serenading with ukuleles on the streets. Walking home to their houses later, they called out *bon soir* into the darkness, just for us. Flirting with the American nymphs that had come to town, the beauty and innocence of the moment was so sweet. Only six days into our first stop in the South Pacific, I was replete with the magic of paradise.

I slept wonderfully all night though some of the loudest roosters I've experienced awoke me at five-thirty when the sky was just becoming light. The little girls, seven-, eight-year-olds, were already awake and spying on us. When they saw us wake up, they ran off giggling. The next I saw them, they were picking up every leaf in the yard by hand. I think they used them in the loo for toilet paper. I saw no toilet paper in the latrine toilet, only a pile of soft pliant leaves.

It seemed that at each house, before school, the same rituals were performed. A seven-year-old girl might have the baby at her hip while the mother or oldest sister stoked the fire, boiling taro or other foods for the day's meal. Five-year-olds were cleaning the yard, sweeping the packed-down earth with homemade twig brooms and picking up every leaf. The men and older teenagers would be out in their canoes fishing. Everyone had a task, and it appeared that the children of each household were raised with similar expectations. You didn't hear children fussing, "I don't waaaaaant to." You seldom heard a baby cry as there was a whole village to love and comfort him. It's this sameness that Claudette and Gabrielle wanted to escape; it was this sameness that I felt brought harmony. I often thought that one of the problems with marriages and relationships in more complex societies was that people were raised in such disparate ways that when they came together as a couple and began raising children, their differences were too great and too ingrained to overcome. I recognize I was not there long enough to truly know if the same problems existed in relationships there as what occurred in American families, but I enjoyed imagining that somewhere in the world, things were different than what I'd experienced.

While at the movies, we had left all our belongings, including cameras, on the porch. All were untouched when we returned. There was no crime. No one tried to hustle us or hassle us; they only made us feel welcome. Discussing this concept with Gabrielle the next morning, she said there was zero percent crime in the Marquesas. Of course. Where would a criminal run to avoid the shame and punishment? What would they need to steal? People had everything they needed.

Asked if there was a lot of crime in America, I said, "Yes, a lot of stealing, killing, raping."

"Why do people steal there? Can't they find work? Do they like jail better?" These were the questions. They couldn't comprehend stealing or crime in general. It became an esoteric sort of discussion. Like divorce, I'd just accepted crime as natural, as part of life in any culture. Here was a culture—or at least these teenage girls on this isolated island—that couldn't comprehend it. It was difficult to try to explain why my parents were divorced. It was difficult to explain why the two of us were sailing and didn't have families of our own. It was difficult to explain capitalism and greed and a people who would do anything for power. We explored these differences in our cultures as best as the language differences permitted.

Since everyone had food, a house, free medical care, what would they steal? Why would they steal? I understood. How could one explain? How did one explain that the very civilization they desired would in fact change their culture, bringing with it commodities that maybe not everyone could afford but everyone wanted; bringing with it the more damaging commodities of sugar and tobacco and beer, creating lifelong addictions, driving people to want more and more, erasing from their memories that they had once had it all. Examining this through the negativistic lens I too often used, it seemed only a matter of time before "progress," the capitalistic mentality that I saw embodied in Maurice McKittrick, would advance like a dark cloud of doom upon these people. Yes, there was in fact a jail in Taioha'e, but it was there primarily for the prisoners that were brought from Papeete, a "more civilized place." Having recently read *Papillon*, I knew the French liked remote islands on which to house their prisoners. Out of sight, out of mind, and so far away that their voices were muted.

Sitting on the porch in the early-morning quiet, we were brought some mangoes by the little girls. I brought out a box of raisins, which they ran off with, sharing them with their brothers and sisters. As they ran off, the next-door lady walked over, curiously asking questions. She offered for us to take a bath at her house. We declined, not feeling quite dirty enough since our showers the night before. "Merci, ca va. Ca va."

She asked us how long we were staying. We told her we would have to leave that day to get back to Taioha'e the way we came. She thought it awfully far to be walking and asked why we didn't take a boat back. "Maybe their father could do some business in Taioha'e today and take you back," she suggested.

Then she left, returning to her house, only to return bringing us two cups of coffee and a warm fresh French baguette from a little bakery somewhere. Somewhere in Taipivai, there was a bakery! The coffee was like hot candy, instant coffee almost white with thick sweetened condensed milk. Without another word, wrapped in her colorful pareo, she smiled and walked back to her house again.

The idea having been planted, when Adele and Claudette arrived a few minutes later, Emma asked if maybe there was a boat going over to Taioha'e. There began a chattering between the three of them. Claudette left to talk to her father.

While we waited, the local gendarme came down to get some of the pig that Monsieur Raphael had brought down the mountain the evening before. Somewhere a radio suddenly started blurting out Rod Stewart's "Maggie May" sung in French by Richard. We told them that was a popular song in

America now. The music comes from a Papeete radio station, we were told, that broadcasts every day from 6:00 to 9:00 a.m. and from 5:00 to 10:00 p.m. As this was being explained, one of the girls returned and told us we should get our things together *now* because we should go to Taioha'e *now* with their father in the boat. Suddenly the slow pace of paradise sped up.

We felt the boat trip was being made for us, but we were grateful. Though I would push through anything under the worst of circumstances—to prove to myself and others that I could—of course I will accept ease and effortless moments if they arose. We went down to the house where we had slept and packed up our things quickly. One of the little girls came with a handful of bananas. We wrapped the bananas, oranges, and mangoes up and set off, six of us, down the road, Emma and I and Monsieur Raphael's four oldest daughters.

I had the thirty-five-pound pack on my back. Because I constantly projected my strength and self-confidence, no one ever offered to help me. Emma carried nothing. As unconsciously as I projected my strength, she projected a fragility that called out to be pampered and helped. The daughters carried her bundles of fruit. Monsieur Raphael led the front. Stopping at Gabrielle's house, she gave us more pompelmous, mangoes, and oranges as she joined the entourage following us down to the boats. We exchanged addresses. "For sure we will write them and maybe send them a French-English dictionary."

I still have their address written in the back of my journal.

We all piled into Monsieur Raphael's little power boat and headed down the river, which widened out, glassy smooth, past the last of the little houses and the coconut trees. The sun was just coming over the eastern hills sheltering the valley, slicing through the trees in a familiar dance of light and shadows. We eventually came to the sandbar that, at low tide, blocked the bay and forced everyone out of the boat to cross over it. Being the royalty they seemed to think we were, they demanded we sit in the boat as Monsieur Raphael, Gabrielle's cousin, and another local pushed us across the sandbar. We headed out into the bay, which was like a deep fjord extending out almost two miles. Up on one of the cliffs, Gabrielle pointed out two tikis, maybe six feet tall, that guarded the entrance to the bay. She said farther up in the valley, there were seven more tikis guarding the valley. Ah, it had been a real tiki I'd seen.

About three-fourths of the way out of the bay, we saw a man rowing his boat. It turned out to be the teacher. His engine had broken returning from Taioha'e. As Gabrielle told us, he lived in Taipivai where he taught school, but for some reason, his wife lived in Taioha'e. He had gone to visit her. So Monsieur Raphael, without hesitation, threw a line, and we towed him back to the mouth of the river.

The remainder of the boat ride back to Taioha'e was uneventful. We stayed close to the cliffs formed by ancient tendrils of volcanic lava dripping to the sea. We could see goats poised on pinnacles of rocks a thousand feet above the ocean. A few large caves were visible. There were very prominent rock structures, arches, and twists in the mountains. Most of the cliffs were a lush green on top before the sheer rock face dropped to the sea. As we neared Taioha'e, Claudette saved a mile by maneuvering the boat through the surge of ten-foot space between Matauapuna and the main island.

Coming into the bay, we pointed out the route we had taken to Taipivai. They pointed to the road that wound its way up the northwest mountains. They said up that road, it was a three-hour walk to Taipivai, just as the villagers of Taioha'e had said. We had taken a day and a half of hiking through the brush, scaling rocks, climbing mountains when we could have walked up a road for three hours! But it was well worth it, in the challenge it presented us, in the exercise we so much needed after thirty days at sea, in the land and country we saw, and the people we met along the way. Gabrielle definitely thought we were crazy—"Vous etes fou" said with a laugh—to have taken the route we did.

Coming in on the boat, we dropped our things off on the *Westward Ho* and gave Monsieur Raphael, Gabrielle, and Claudette the ship's tour. They were intrigued by the compact living space, the miniature galley/kitchen, as they'd never been on a sailboat. Luckily, Jackson, Brian, and Annie weren't on board. When we went to shore, I paid Monsieur Raphael 300 francs for bringing us over, which he gave to Claudette who returned shortly with ice cream and slushes. We then spent the rest of the afternoon talking under the pavilion. Eventually it was time for them to leave. We helped them load their small motorboat up with some lumber and other commodities they were taking back with them. They invited us—insisted—that we come back and visit. We kissed each other's checks and said *au revoir.*

We eventually found our other crew members at Chez Maurice's drinking warm beer. It was quiet, no music playing. Jackson and Brian were caught up in braggart's rights with some other yachties who were visibly uninterested in their swagger but were enjoying the generosity in buying round after round.

CHAPTER 4

What you've done becomes the judge of what you're going to
do especially in other people's minds. When you're traveling,
you are what you are right there and then. People don't have
your past to hold against you. No yesterdays on the road.
　　　　　　　　　　　　　　　—William Least Heat-Moon

There were friends made in every port. Good connections. Fast connections. Bad connections, though not too many of them I think mostly because we were never together long enough to know the bad traits and characteristics of those we met. Those that left the sourest feeling were those I'd sailed with long enough to know our differences were too great to be able to share the same small space for extended periods of time. Not that they were bad people, just that our differences were too great. I too, of course, had my failings though I worked hard to get along with everyone both for my own selfish ends, I suppose, but also, gee, isn't life just better that way? There were new things to experience, new people to meet, new places to go.

The very fact that there was this fluid, moving community of people sharing a commonality was enough to overlook most differences. In this world of sailing, we came together in a port and parted again. Maybe we'd come together in the next port, or it might be months later before we happened to be in the same place at the same time for a day or a week or several weeks. The characters varied.

Chase was a retired navy officer, receiving a generous pension after twenty years of service. In his mid-forties he was traveling leisurely with his wife and teenage son. He was working on a novel at the time for which he later wrote the screenplay for a movie of the same title. When I read the novel years later, I could see all of the characters that had been sailing through those South Pacific Islands that season with the names changed "to protect the innocent." He went on to write the screenplays for several big blockbuster movies.

Peder and Henri were two German men who had been cruising together for several years. Peder was a trapper, he said. They'd spent over a year on the Amazon in Brazil where they had been given a small monkey, Chico, who was still sailing with them on their funny little boat whose bubble hatch reminded me of a submarine, completely airtight. They came over for drinks and talk one night, bringing Chico who delighted in scurrying through our rigging. Jackson wasn't particularly happy about having a monkey on board, but he suffered through it. Oscar, another German sailor, joined us that night too. He had set sail with a dog, but it got swept overboard. Though sailing alone on his boat, Peder, Henri, and Oscar sailed as a team, leaving, entering, and staying in ports together.

We eventually pulled anchor and sailed over to Atuona, the main town on the island of Hiva Oa. There I first met Sjef and Sarah from Belgium who had been cruising for four years on a blue steel-hulled ketch. I was immediately attracted to their rhythm and lifestyle. They were completely subsistence living: hunting their own meats that they dried and canned, gathering all their fruits and vegetables for their crossings and living off the land while in port. Sarah reminded me of the Breck shampoo lady, short wavy haired with extra rosy and healthy cheeks and light-blue eyes that captured your attention.

There were two Frenchmen on board *L-Affranchi*, possibly father and son, and their dog that would stand perfectly erect and still on the rounded bow of an Avon raft going full speed across the bay. The *Red Rose* hailed from New Zealand; they were a young couple with a two-year-old boy. They had left New Zealand six years before for a three-month honeymoon cruise to Fiji. Their plan had been to return to New Zealand, but then they met so many other cruising yachts always enticing them onward, "Ah, come on, we'll meet you in South Africa" or here or there. They were only now heading home, six years later. Their son, David, had been born in South Africa; he was out at sea at eight weeks old.

The *Aries*, a ketch, hailing from Marina del Rey carried five guys, drinking-, smoking-type L.A. guys that wore matching crew shirts with their names on them: Walt, Barry, Dylan, George, and Alan. They were an anomaly, so strange and out of place—preppy, I guess—next to the more-seasoned cruising boats, not that we were seasoned sailors.

Also in Atuona, we met George and Martha, a young couple in their late twenties, hailing from New York. As time passed, in new ports, others were met, all with their dreams and agendas and paths laid out.

As Lloyd had hinted, Dave, whom I had first met a year earlier in Acapulco, was in fact in Atuona Bay on the *Paz del Mar*. He was now sailing with a young Costa Rican woman, Magdalena. I coined her the Midget Nun: she was barely five feet tall. She had actually been in a nunnery for several years before sailing away with Dave. I heard, several years later, that she had continued her adventures, riding across the Sahara on a camel.

As we sailed into Atuona, Dave was actually rowing out to meet us, an exuberance and zeal that I learned was his nature to exhibit. After waiting for us to get anchored and settled, he clambered on board and said he had heard of this boat with three women on board, and he wanted to be the first to greet us. *Okay*, I thought. He rattled on, telling me he remembered meeting me in Acapulco also. I guess just as he had left an impression on me, I apparently had left an impression on him. His interest in me was palpable. And though I found him unique and quirky, funny and intriguing and exuberant, I was not at all interested in a man or relationships throughout any of this time. I only wanted the adventure.

Dave's boat was a freegan's frolic. He was sailing on the cheap. The lines on his boat were a myriad of spliced pieces of rope he'd salvaged, maybe ten- or fifteen-foot lengths spliced together to get a seventy-foot length. Bamboo poles served as a self-steering pole; his awning was pieced together from different castoffs of old fabric, multicolored shades of beige, red, green. He had salvaged an old ten-foot surfboard that he had strapped to his stanchions as a backup "life raft." I never saw him wearing "normal clothes" like a pair of shorts. He wore handmade loincloths or simply a halved pareo. Both Emma and I spent quite a bit of time on Dave's boat, drinking wine, talking tales. He amused me. Animated and opinionated, I found him refreshing. Five-foot-ten and thirty years old, wiry, cute, and funny, his individuality stood out amongst other yachties.

Atuona, Hiva Oa, was where Gauguin had lived and done much of his painting. His grave was there, on a knoll above the town, with Mt. Temeii looming above it, prominent, busty, jagged. Someone pointed out how the first of the morning sun danced on his grave before coming down to the rest of the people; I watched for that each morning, a silly little morning ritual with which I became intrigued for no particular reason than it seemed appropriate to honor his grave in such salutation each morning. His artwork was housed in a museum in Tahiti though, more available to the tourists.

Emma and I did multiple day hikes in the area. Besides visiting Gauguin's grave, we hiked deep into the jungle, finding ruins of ancient villages, small stone tikis, and abandoned rock platforms—*maraes*—covered by vines. We found these places by word of mouth from the other yachties. "Walk up this path, you'll eventually come to . . ." "Go here, and you'll find . . ." These were the years where I learned how to travel on a hint, being nudged here, pushed there, bouncing off of one experience on to the next. There were no travel books to guide us, just stories from fellow travelers. And of course, wherever we walked, we were always invited into local people's homes to share a meal or drink. Always.

Through the sharing of sailor's stories, we were urged to go to Hanamenu, a small bay on the other side of the island. So we did, spending a half a day sailing over. It was indeed exquisitely beautiful. A waterfall fed a crystal-clear pool surrounded by a floral display of anthuriums, maraca gingers, bromeliads, and orchids. Without even thinking to ask that we might be intruding on someone's private property, we slipped into this pool to sit in this paradise. Eventually, still dripping in our wet pareos, we met the solitary family who lived there farther up the valley in a cluster of thatched structures. As usual, they welcomed us in, offering us coffee and fruit, apparently thinking nothing of us enjoying their private waterfall and pool.

Most everywhere we went, people would ask if we had bullets, fishhooks, or condoms. For fear of an uprising, the French didn't allow the local people to have bullets even though many owned rifles. Being a predominantly Catholic country, birth control wasn't permitted. Hooks eventually dulled and rusted away. We hadn't prepared to trade anything, and we had nothing to share. But as they were sharing a meal with us and we were taking in the beauty of their little almost parklike homestead of thatched huts, Dave, Sjef, and Sarah came walking down from the upper valley. They had set off a few days earlier to hike over. Sjef had a rifle with which he had hoped to kill a wild goat. Though there were many, he'd been unsuccessful, but he graciously gave them some of his bullets.

Sailing back over to Atuona two days later, we were followed by six hammerhead sharks for four or five hours. I have a visceral memory of how downright creepy they were. It was after that point I stopped trailing behind the boat, like shark bait, hanging on to a knotted rope.

There was a simple market that opened each morning in Atuona, where fishermen sold fresh-caught fish, fresh langoustine tails, and any local vegetables an industrious farmer grew. Multiple meals shared with other yachties revolved around how much was available in the market. We had meals on board other boats or barbecues on beach shores under the coconut trees, bonfires burning into the night. On shore, we were often joined by locals, usually just the men, who would freely partake of any alcohol that was present. Their contribution was often buckets of *poisson cru*, their lime-marinated raw fish, sometimes a bit too ripe for me to even taste.

It was freeing to be able to get off the boat and go exploring each day or row over to another yacht and share stories and food, but the friction was still palpable on *Westward Ho*. The discontent seemed to fuel Jackson's desire to pull anchor and get to Tahiti. The day before we left Atuona, Dave approached Emma and me and said, "Wait for me in Tahiti. Magdalena is getting off, and you can sail with me," knowing how unhappy we were on the *Westward Ho*.

We said we would. But we didn't.

CHAPTER 5

*If you reject the food, ignore the customs, fear the religion
and avoid the people, you might better stay home.*

—James Michener

At the urgings of others though, we did sail to Fatu Hiva, the island that Red had first described to Emma and me in Taioha'e. Fatu Hiva was later made famous by Thor Heyerdahl. He had lived on Fatu Hiva with his wife in 1937–1938, supposedly doing research, but, he admitted, he was attempting to escape civilization, subsisting in a fashion that almost took his life. Having discovered the tikis on the island, this is where he first developed his theories of pre-Columbian navigation from South America, which culminated in several other books that made him famous, *Kon Tiki* and *Ra*. Though written shortly after his return to Norway, *Fatu Hiva* wasn't published until 1974. Reading it many years after that, I resonated with one of his conclusions: "Progress today can be defined as man's ability to complicate simplicity."

Our arrival in Hana Vave, the Bay of Virgins, even to this day considered one of *the* most beautiful bays in the world, was quickly ruined by the actions of Jackson and Brian. We had prepared and eaten dinner while sailing. After dropping anchor, while washing the dishes, we heard music: ukuleles and some other stringed instrument, drumming on the hulls of canoes, and the rhythmic voices of native song, just as Red had described their experience. Two outriggers pulled alongside and asked if they could come on board. I was so excited, thinking, *Oh, yes, oh, yes*, but of course I had to ask Jackson. His reply was an angry "No! Not now. Tell them we're eating dinner now or something."

Emma told them, "Ah, mes amies, le capitan n'est pas amables. Il dit que maintenant n'est pas bon. Peut'etre deman. Si c'est moi, je dit, oui; mais le capitan dit no."

How rude! Why the hell were they sailing in the South Pacific if not to enjoy these magical moments? Here we were in the most enchanted island of all, Fatu Hiva, anchored in the most overpoweringly beautiful bay yet, outriggers filled with fruit and men making music, paddling all the way out to our boat, a full moon. Wow. And Jackson is below reading German war novels and telling them to go away? What an insult to them, their hospitality, their beautiful tradition of greeting newcomers, their culture of making music, to tell them to come back tomorrow. I was furious. What effrontery to suggest they come back tomorrow. Besides the insult to them, Jackson was depriving us all—me in particular—of this enchanting island experience!

The thoughts raged inside of me: I had been sailing on this boat for over two months, and I still hadn't seen the faintest glint of light come out of his head. He comes to paradise asking for the nearest bar and then stays until the beer runs out! What the hell is he doing in paradise? Or any place like this? Why has he come here? He sits on his boat and reads. Probably he makes believe he's the hero of whatever book he's reading at the moment because, after all, he does nothing that would raise him up to the level of heroism or even a minor sense of accomplishment! He was visibly afraid of sailing in the deep blue sea. He doesn't want to go hiking and see the islands we visit. He doesn't want to meet the people. Everything he puts off until tomorrow. Even with the Polynesians paddling out in their outriggers under the full moon of Hana Vave playing their time-filled music and chants, he says, "Not now. Tomorrow!'" Crazy-making angry thoughts tore like a tornado around in my brain.

It is one of the few "old angers" in my life that can rise up still, forty-five years later, and be viscerally felt; that is how profound that moment was.

They paddled back to shore, I'm sure at least as baffled as Emma and I were. The ugliness, being held back for two months, exploded. Down below decks, even Annie got on Jackson's case because soon he comes up into the cockpit where Emma and I were sitting. "What the fuck is all this shit? I'm suddenly the bad guy? You're coming down on me like I did something wrong?"

"We haven't said a word to you, Jackson," I replied as calmly as I could, because we hadn't.

"Just because this was a bad time, I'm the bad guy?" And then to Emma, "Why do you say you're not *allowed* to have visitors?"

Though we shouldn't have responded, we both started telling him of all the times since we arrived in Taioha'e where Jackson and Brian both made it clear that we were not to invite people on board. Eventually, Emma and I moved up to sit on the bow as far away as we could physically get. Jackson and Annie sat in the cockpit arguing. Even the wind seemed angry, howling down through the valley, tugging at our anchor. *Maybe the god of this valley will rip up our anchor and toss the boat on shore,* I thought. *That would show them.*

As much of a shock as his earlier behavior had been, Jackson actually apologized, probably pressured by Annie. Were amends truly made? Was the tension off? We would make an effort until we could get off the boat. But the magic of that moment of music and sharing aboard our sailboat was gone, and a negative silence filled the space instead.

Emma and I went to shore first thing in the morning and didn't return until nightfall. We explored the tiny village of only a few dozen thatched huts. Everyone we met offered us mangoes, papayas, pompelmous, a stick of sugar cane to gnaw on. We saw young mothers, younger than me, with two or three children already. This was their life.

We came upon a man cranking a "coffee machine," removing the pulp and fruit from coffee beans. People went up into the valley every morning about six and picked the ripe red coffee berries. On returning, they'd put the berries through a hand machine that was simply a spiked cylinder, not unlike a little player piano or music machine that, when turned, squeezed out the beans while the skins and meat caught on the bars and were spit to the other end. The beans were then sorted through by hand, picking out any skins that squeezed through and any broken beans. Then the beans were dumped into old five-gallon oil cans that had been punctured with holes. These were taken down to the creek and the water run through it, washing off the remaining pulp. The beans were then laid out to dry on flat slabs of cement for two days. They had little switches of twigs they used for stirring and turning the drying beans. Big tarps were spread across them if rains came and removed again when the sun came out. Green beans were exported. What they kept and used, they roasted in small batches.

We also came across bananas being dried. Sliced lengthwise, they were laid out on screens. While still moist but chewy, they were wrapped in lengths of banana leaves in bundles about three inches thick, tied off on the ends with coconut fiber. I bought ten of these treats; I have never found nor been able to make a more delicious and flavorful dried banana. I think they would ferment ever so slightly in their wrappings, giving them a unique flavor like brandy-infused banana candy.

We explored up into the valley a bit, along a path that the locals said eventually went to Omoa, a larger village farther east. We decided we'd maybe try to hike over there the next day—if it was okay with Jackson.

The only "store" we saw was a four-by-four-foot square box, four sheets of plywood tacked to a frame. Once a day around midafternoon, someone went and propped up a window to sell the few items they had to sell, plug tobacco, processed sugar, canned sardines, sweetened condensed milk. Most of these people were living on little money, what they got from selling green coffee beans and copra. Paradise gave them the rest except for these products they really didn't need but had learned to crave.

We decided to go to a church service out of curiosity not because I liked churches or religion or needed to go to confession. The Catholic church in Hane Vave was wood planked. It was painted white and motel-turquoise. A laid-rock walk, quite overgrown, meandered toward the bay. There was no priest or minister or appointed religious leader. I loved the fact that the statues of the Mother Mary and Jesus, outside the church, were adorned with leis. A large clam shell, green with moss, held the holy water. I did appreciate the islanders' adaptations.

All the women sat on one side, all the men on the other. I don't know if this was the influence of the church or a cultural thing, but similar to the separation of male and female at the movies in Taipivai, it stood out. Most of the service was comprised of singing, truly heavenly with the Polynesian tones and harmonizing. Reading the words from hymnals that were in the Marquesian language, they sang tunes that weren't necessarily the "correct tune" since no one knew how to read music. "A Closer Walk with Thee" might be sung to the tune of "Mary Had a Little Lamb" for all they cared.

But oh, the singing was beautiful. Eventually, someone from the men's pews stood and walked to the front and spoke for ten minutes after which there was more singing, and then everyone left and went home.

Later in the day, walking on paths away from the village, Emma and I heard men chanting somewhere in the jungle. It was as if they were performing a pagan rite that was not meant to be seen. It resonated more with me than the Catholic church ceremony had, more traditional and sacred, but we didn't intrude.

We did in fact hike to Omoa the next day. We followed the footpath through the jungle, higher up the mountain, and eventually came to Omoa four hours later, another village set in a valley with two tall ranges looming up on either side. Again, as far as the eye could see, coconut trees were planted deep up into the valley, the livelihood of the islanders. Nestled at the mouth of the bay, a creek rushed then meandered then again rushed down through the town. A straight dirt road, marked off by a *menehune* rock wall, cut up the middle.

The church in Omoa was much larger than the one in Hana Vave. The rock-laid path leading to its doors was clean of weeds; the lawn was mowed. It was a white cement church with three ornamental buttressed wings on each side. Moss and mildew grew extensively on the windward side. The red tile roof seemed so foreign next to the rusted tin on all the shacks. Though the island was first sighted in 1595, missionaries didn't arrive before the mid-1800s. Here, as throughout the Marquesas, they would have been met by cannibals, and they surely preached, "Thou shalt not eat your fellow human beings."

As the muscles of our legs were still trembling from the descent into town, we sat down to watch an outrigger execute passage through the six-foot surf that was crashing on the rocks. For at least ten minutes, the man and his family sat patiently, motoring back and forth on the outskirts of the surf break until suddenly, seeing an opening, he gunned his engine and rode in perfectly on the back of a wave. As soon as the wave broke, he pulled his engine up, and the suction of the wave brought the boat into shore, not a drop of water spilling into the boat. It was beautifully executed as it would be by people in harmony with the rhythms of the sea. As it turned out, we had seen them in Hana Vave shortly before we left. They waved to us in recognition, a tiny amazement on their faces that we had actually made it. Hungry and a little thirsty, we ambled up the lane into town.

We saw a little boy—*happa-haole* (part white)—that we had also seen two days previously in Hana Vave. He also recognized us and was whispering to his friends about us. A couple of them ran off, and within a few minutes, the children who were not in school were sneaking out to peer at us, again the center of attention in this isolated village. A much bigger village than Hane Vave (which had probably no more than fifty residents), Omoa had a four-room school down by the bay, neatly fenced off, with a large mowed lawn surrounding it. Woven bamboo shutters were propped open with sticks. It became clear that children went to school in shifts according to their ages. The kids that were now at school played soldier during a recess: The lead boy held a white flag with a small red cross aloft. All the others marched in a straight line behind him. Then they broke apart, darting off in all directions, and before we knew it, we were in the middle of a cowboy-and-Indian battle. They used pistol-shaped sticks as guns, constantly glancing back at us for approval. I note it simply because it seemed (in my mind that was consciously or unconsciously searching for a perfected paradise) out of place that they would know this game.

Interestingly, no one approached us with fruit or coconuts or any sort of hospitality that we had witnessed before. The local store consisted of three short shelves with some soap, a couple cans of sardines, and sweetened condensed milk. Nothing to buy.

We had learned that this island was particularly famous for making tapa. We asked the lady tending the store if there was any tapa cloth we could buy. "*Peut etre*," and with that, she locked up her four-by-four store, and off we went cutting through the flowered foot paths and people's lawns. We came to a salmon-colored house, looking recently painted. Entering, we saw there was a young woman with Sophia Loren eyes. She had a really nice figure, unusual to see amongst Polynesian women older than twenty, revealed by a pareo tied low on her hips and wearing a colored bra. A heavyset woman was also there, working on a tapa hat. "Sophia" summoned a man from a back room, who came out with a paint brush in his hand. Though we could tell the man knew French, he spoke only in Marquesian, and "Sophia" translated everything into French for Emma.

Even today, Fatu Hiva, particularly Omoa, is famous for their tapa cloth. It was their clothing and blankets and ceremonial wear before the white man brought cotton. It is made from pounding the bark of the banyan, breadfruit, and/or paper mulberry trees into thin sheets. Gluing together the lengths of sheets with arrowroot paste to attain lengths as long as twenty feet or as small as three-foot square, they are then hand-painted with geometric or nature designs.

As it turns out they had just sold most of their tapa wares. To whom I'm not sure. My thought is someone on the copra boats must buy it up and take it to Tahiti. They had one large piece of red tapa, maybe seven by four feet finished. They wanted 6,000 francs for it, which worked out to about 70 dollars. It wasn't worth it to me even if I had that kind of money on me, which I didn't. In the back room, he had one other piece of white tapa, almost finished. They wanted about 17 dollars for that. It was really beautiful. He said he'd bring it to Hana Vave in the morning if we wanted it.

Then he brought out one of the hand-carved wooden swords, an item I'd seen in Taipivai. It was exquisite. It looked used, not polished like others I'd seen before. It was the only one he had left. Both Emma and I wanted it. We explained this to him. He said it would take two days to make one. Monday morning, 800 francs each. Not knowing for sure if we'd even still be here, we said yes: If he could bring over two swords and the white tapa on Monday morning, that would be great.

Business dealings over, we talked. They chuckled that it had taken us four and a half hours to come the distance. It takes them two hours. But like they said, they are used to it. They were curious about our sailing trip. When we explained we were three women and two men on board, they asked us if we didn't want a Marquesian man, then laughed hard.

It was after one by then. Feeling lazy and not really wanting to hike back, we asked if there were any boats that could take us back to Hana Vave. They offered to take us over in a boat for 500 francs for both of us. Sure, that's nothing! For a fifteen-minute boat ride back. "Okay, we go now."

Therese, the gal who ran the store (and the sister of the fat woman who made the tapa) walked with us down to the bay. She asked Emma, very seriously this time, if we didn't want to take a Marquesian with us. Did we want a Marquesian? We were puzzled. Was Emma understanding this correctly? "Oh, no, we don't really have room for one on the boat."

"Oh, no, here. Have a Marquesian here."

Emma was scared to offend her but replied, "No, it's not possible," she explained. "Our passports and visas don't allow us to stay long."

"Oh, that's okay. Have a Marquesian for a little while."

It was an odd conversation. Why was she being so insistent? Stay long enough to "love 'em and leave 'em"? But as we waited for the men to get the boat out, we made note of the blonde hair around town. Out of the corner of her mouth so none of the kids could hear her, Therese said that several of them have American or European fathers—hit-and-run affairs. She smiled.

Years later, I read that the sexual mores of Marquesians (and Tahitians) astounded the first white men when they arrived. Ships' logs spoke of the women of quite young age offering sexual favors. Maybe it was an instinctive move to bring in new DNA, but it was unusual enough to be noted by the early sailors who first visited. Though the church had a stronghold on some aspects of people's lives, it seemed a bit more difficult for them to instill the "sin of sex" on these people. Sexuality wasn't hidden as it is in our culture. Most families all slept together in the same room, where children could/would or did witness their parents' sexual behavior. It was evident in how young women were when they had their first child. Their dances, the *tamure* and hula, were very sexually suggestive in nature.

But being invited to share their Marquesian men?

The boat that would take us to Hana Vave was on shore and needed to be brought out past the breakers and then to the dock to pick us up. Even at the dock, the waves surged dangerously. We chatted, waiting on the dock, for almost twenty minutes before there was a lull in the larger swells. Two men rowed with all their might to get the boat out past the surf line and then came around to the remnants of the loading dock that was awash with crashing swells. We were pondering the safety of boarding the boat at that point, but we could see little alternative.

While we were waiting for the boat to make it to the dock and after being unsuccessful in arranging a Marquesian tryst for either Emma or me, Therese then—again to our dismay—tried to give us her three-year-old daughter with full faith that we'd take good care of her and that her daughter would have a better life than she would in Omoa, Fatu Hiva.

We were stunned. Strange. When we politely declined, she then began to apologize up and down for not having fed us when we first got into town as if that was the reason why we were declining to take her daughter. She felt very bad about her lack of hospitality, she said. I began to believe the woman was mentally unstable. After apologizing for not giving us something to eat or drink, she again asked for us to take her little girl. Hmm. "No, no, we don't want to take your little girl with us."

Finally, the men got the motorboat over to the dock, and we bid her farewell, leaving her with her daughter standing on the wave-tossed dock. Fifteen minutes later, we were back in Hana Vave. The men scrambled on board the boat as soon as we arrived without being invited, to Jackson's chagrin, but we gave them a quick tour and told them we'd see them Monday. We paid them and they left.

Listening to the music of Vivaldi, Bach, and Mozart on the deck that evening, under the stars and a moon that outlined the promontories that protected the valley of Hana Vave, I wondered how these artists had captured so perfectly in their music something never seen or touched, its strength, its gentleness, its magic. But they had. Even in his deaf, quiet world, clearly Beethoven had been here before.

Turning off the manmade music, I sat in silence. As the full moon rose above the tikis standing tall on the fingers of cliffs, I listened to the wind grow stronger in the trees on shore. The anchor chain rumbled as we swung on our moorage. A cloud blocked the moon, and soon I heard the rain first slapping against the jungle and then against the water, and as it reached us, I ducked below, and it pounded drum beats on the cabin roof.

We left before Monday came, sailing on to Tahiti.

CHAPTER 6

The shoe that fits one person pinches another; there
is no recipe for living that suits all cases.

—Carl Jung

We arrived in Papeete, Tahiti, on June 16. It was a bustling, hustling, noisy town. A city, a shipping port. The large ships on the docks discharged an oil sheen across the waters as noisy cranes worked day and night. It was a shock after being in the tranquil islands of the Marquesas. Traffic buzzed up and down the main drag with Tahitian girls sitting side-saddle on mopeds. On the quay, we anchored stern to, rubber bumper to rubber bumper with other cruising yachts and more permanent fixtures, yachts that seem to have been there for a long time. The noise pierced my sanity.

There were lots of others yachts in the harbor. *Blue Wings* was there from Kona, Hawai'i. *Serenade* was a fifty-foot old wooden double-ended ketch hailing from Santa Monica. Mel was the owner; he was a retired shop teacher from the community college in Santa Monica, about sixty-five years old. His sailing partner, Ben, was half his age. It turned out Ben had done some outsource work for my father's publishing company years before. Small world. Lloyd and Karen on *The Hobbit* had made it over from Nuku Hiva, but we were told they had just left to sail over to Moorea while waiting for their partner. The *Sea Dancer* was moored several spaces down from us.

There was a ninety-one-foot black ketch from Cannes called the *Ventura*. According to the black man from the Barbados, Francois, who took care of her, the boat had been captured by pirates off the coast of

Thailand several years before; after stripping it down of everything, it was set loose again. Eventually someone brought it to Tahiti where it's been ever since. Francois, the only black man I ever met sailing, was quite the woman charmer. He talked me into modeling some swimwear. I was one of several young women hired for the professional photo shoot for which I was to be paid. I found myself in the uncomfortable position of having him reach into my bikini top to hoist up my small breasts to make them more prominent. I quit and left.

Among numerous other boats, *Denebola* was in the harbor also, hailing from Honolulu; there were rumors that it was really the infamous *Charade* that had been stolen several years before. More seasoned sailors came but did not linger long in Papeete; it was a port of call to go through customs and get supplies, do a mail run, and they were gone.

One boat had two young men on board, brothers, who were under investigation because supposedly both of their parents had died at sea; stories swirled like a water spout as to whether there was foul play. They claimed they had kept the bodies on board, hoping they'd come across someone at sea, but they eventually were decomposing too rapidly, and they had slipped them over the side.

Ivo, a young Dutchman, arrived on his little sloop *Vlaag*, sixteen feet long! He had no engine, and he brought the boat in to the quay by lying up on the bow, paddling his boat with his arms as if he was on a surfboard. He was a bubbling, carefree young pied piper—truly—playing the most glorious silver flute, seemingly all the time, his music drifting across the harbor every evening.

Unlike the time we spent in the Marquesas, hiking, walking on shore in the villages, spending time primarily with the island people, life in Papeete circled primarily around the other yachties. Our few weeks there involved a bit too much drinking and partying, a vortex into which I too got caught. Though I was desiring the simple undeveloped island life, I think we were a bit like hikers on the Appalachian Trail who got close to town, enjoying a bit of city life, eating in restaurants, drinking, partying. In Papeete, there was always someone who could play a good guitar, so there were many evenings spent on one yacht or another, playing music, sharing meals. With boats tied stern to at the quay, it was easy to gather groups together, waving someone on board, "Hey, come on board. Have a beer."

Emma and I spent as little time aboard *Westward Ho* as possible, enjoying the company of others while we were searching for another boat to get onto. A bunch of us went to watch *Lawrence of Arabia* in a local theater. Ten years old and dubbed into French, it was its own cultural experience. We hitchhiked or took buses out of Papeete to experience the sandy beaches, like Point Venus, the place where Captain Cook had built a small fort to enclose his astronomical instruments 200 years before, but the beaches were crowded with French tourists. After visiting Gauguin's grave in Atuona, it was a must that we visit the Gauguin Museum in its lovely setting on the opposite end of the island from Papeete. Stone tikis and relics from the Marquesas were set amongst the lawns and tropical gardens through which you meandered between open-air buildings holding many of Gauguin's paintings as well as factoids of Polynesian life.

Overall, Papeete itself was a dirty ferro-concrete smudge, with cars and scooters zooming about, spewing exhaust and noise into the air. There were televisions and radios blaring. As one would expect with greater means for earning a living, the homes were nicer homes, and there seemed to be less visual poverty. There were a few attractive Tahitian girls that we met hanging down by the boats, I'm sure in hopes of meeting foreign men. Several befriended Emma and me, inviting us to their family home outside of Papeete where we spent several days as their guests.

Outside of Papeete, life was a bit simpler and quieter, with homes having their banana and taro patches, a spit of subsistence existence still visible, but being so easily connected to the central hub of Papeete with paved roads, none of the island of Tahiti held the enchanting simple life that the Marquesas had offered up to us.

I was privileged to see the infamous Quinn's Bar, which closed the year after, replaced with a big shopping center. It was probably the most famous bar in all of the South Pacific, famous for its onion beer, rowdy fights, and its one nasty toilet. It was a visible part of the night life of Papeete not far from where the yachts were moored. Michener and James Norton Hall of *Mutiny on the Bounty* fame all made Quinn's a frequent stop. What I remembered most was my introduction to *mahus* who stood out front flirting. In order to have someone do the domestic chores delegated to women, these were young men that were raised as girls in homes where too many boys, and no girls, had been born. Though often heterosexual, they had quite effeminate traits. I was intrigued by this culturally accepted situation, which I witnessed again on other islands, most notably Samoa.

We were desperate to get off of *Westward Ho.* Annie, too, voiced her unhappiness and her desire to return to Hawai'i. Jackson's disconnect became more profound as Annie's discontent became more visible. Brian's angry rages seemed to be more frequent. It took Emma and I, sticking together, a week before we found a boat that would take us on as crew.

The good yacht *Sheila* was an older forty-five-foot ketch from England that already had three Englishmen—Jason, Justin, and the owner, Colin— and a funny American, Geoff, who played a concertina. A forty-five-foot boat with four people is already crowded; it seemed a bit crazy to squeeze two more people on board—maybe they thought there'd be some romance involved inviting two beautiful young women on board.

In the beginning, we were so happy to be off *Westward Ho* and on the *Sheila.* My journal is full of praise for these delightful and charming Englishmen with their cute accents and their funny mannerisms. American Geoff was a stand-up comic, keeping us in stitches all the time.

I don't remember why, but we ended up sailing to Moorea on *Westward Ho* before switching boats. My vague memory is that Annie, too, was leaving, and this was going to be the last hoorah, and Jackson and Brian wanted us to come. As desperate as we were to get off of that boat and again I'm not sure why, we acquiesced and sailed to Moorea with them, spending a week there before they paid for us to fly back over to Papeete where we joined *Sheila.* I must admit it was exceptionally beautiful to fly over the islands and turquoise lagoons in a small plane, seeing it from that vantage point.

We never waited for Dave on *Paz del Mar.*

A week after getting on board *Sheila*, we sailed from Papeete to the island of Hua Hini. We were *now* truly in paradise. This was the South Pacific I had imagined, though of course I had no complaints about our experiences in the Marquesas. We anchored in crystal-clear lagoons of multishades of blue, rimmed with powder-fine white-sand beaches. The first morning there, barely after the sun had peeked over the horizon, I quietly slipped into the glassy-smooth, turquoise waters with not a breath stirring. Fifty feet below, as clear as looking through a window, I could see the anchor line traced across the sand, fish swimming by and colorful coral patches inviting exploration. This was so different from the Marquesas where the water had been deep and dark with no white-sand beaches. It was so peaceful to be away from the noise and stench of Papeete. The crow of roosters would be the only sound coming from land as smoke from early-morning cook fires traced paths into the blue sky.

Instead of climbing through muddy jungle paths up mountains, we spent days snorkeling and diving along the reefs for shells and fish. Our experience in the Marquesas was enchanting with its simplicity, still relatively untouched by civilization, which I resonated with, but the Society Islands (the group of islands generically called Tahiti) were the poster board of island paradise that I had envisioned when I set sail from Hawai'i. Moorea and Hua Hini, Raiatea and Ta'aha were beyond exquisite, not just in their sights but energetically. Like meeting a lover, I was content to sit quietly in its arms, resting. I was morphing, dropping off a fabric of my persona that had climbed the hills to Taipivai, who judged others' dreams not to be as valuable as my dream. I took on a gentler, quieter pace, enjoying each moment.

The fellows on the *Sheila* were adventurous, and we all, together, spent days diving and hiking and exploring different areas of different islands. A whole different pace and rhythm filled our days. We dove regularly near our anchorage, bringing up speared fish, large tridacna clams, and once with a lot of luck, a good-sized octopus that took a lot of pounding to soften enough to be palatable. It was so pleasant to finally be sailing with people who were also embracing the adventure, the newness of different cultures, people with whom we weren't scared to voice our opinions or express our thoughts, where we didn't have to listen to someone cussing at the top of their lungs or complaining of an acid stomach while pounding down straight Scotch.

On July 5, we arrived on the "mystical island" of Bora Bora. The island is surrounded by an amazingly large reef that extends out several miles within which there were dozens of motus, little beach-lined islands, each covered with coconut palms for copra production. Though I felt an excitement to be in this renowned exotic place, my impressions were mixed. Yes, she was a majestic island with twin peaks towering over the fingers of land that slithered out to frolic in the surrounding reef. The coconut trees of both the island and the motus brushed the sky, reaching for the endless parade of white clouds traveling on the breath of the trade winds. The white line of breakers crashing against the outside edge of the distant reef was artistry that tickled the soul. Yes, it was visibly paradise. But there was a fly in the ointment. That lover's energy I felt on Moorea, Ta'aha, and Hua Hini seemed to have entered a divorce phase.

I perceived a distinct negative energy permeating Bora Bora that I didn't expect and quite baffled me, especially after the generosity and beauty of the peoples of the Marquesas. I felt that I was in the Paris of the South Pacific, filled with the Parisian haughty rudeness. I attributed it to capitalism and the tourist trade—my fallback criticism for so much—having cut its edge into their generous lifestyle. You did not hear the resounding echoes of *Iaurana* or see the toothless smiles. My impression was that Chinese merchants controlled most of the stores and markets, markets that were quite modern and well-stocked, but they could not be bothered to greet you or even acknowledge that you'd walked into their store. They had sour faces and negative attitudes. I had the distinct feeling that they did not even want you on "their" island.

Besides the negative attitude, the cost of everything on Bora Bora was excruciatingly expensive. Cabbage was 85 cents a pound; tomatoes were 60 cents a pound; eggs $1.30 a dozen. These prices were three times what they were in the United States in 1972; I've paid less for the same foods in present day, at least seasonally. Where we had been getting limes for free on every other island, we were paying almost 80 cents a pound for them here. No one gave us free fruit. I wasn't there to sponge off of people, but . . . what? Paradise lost?

We had anchored in front of an American-owned "yacht hotel" called the Oa (meaning *happy*). The owner encouraged all the yachties to use his pier, giving them availability to the dock showers, all to encourage them to come drink at his bar, which they did. As evidence of the "civilized world" encroaching quickly, Walt Disney was making a film of a local native boy who is destined to be the king but is afraid of the water. They had built a couple huge oceangoing outrigger canoes for the movie scenes; we hobnobbed a bit with the crew and got to play on the outriggers one afternoon. Though the Oa was, the owner claimed, struggling along as a business, it had been lucky enough to have had six of its eight thatched bungalows, sitting out on stilts in the bay, rented by the filming crew.

A party atmosphere among the yachts was gathering momentum as French Polynesia prepared for Bastille Day, July 14. The *Bellyrub* arrived with Rich and Terry on board. *Serenade* sailed in, and another yacht, the yellow *Lady*, with Bill and Heather, arrived. We had great get-togethers in the bay at Bora Bora, four or five dinghies from other yachts tied up behind *Sheila*, or *Bellyrub*, or *Lady* feasting on clams and octopus simmered in coconut milk, fresh-caught fish fried on little hibachi barbecue pits on the stern. There was a rhythm and camaraderie developing with the other yachts with stories shared of islands visited, islands yet to be visited, all of which we had missed out on *Westward Ho* with their snobbish attitude.

We rented bicycles and struggled on thirty-mile bike trips, up and over passes to view scenes of grandeur encompassing the barrier reefs and other islands in the distance. Everywhere we pedaled, the islanders prepared for the Bastille Day festivities. Even the smallest of villages were constructing thatched pavilions for the upcoming partying. Though unrest was growing between Tahitians and their French colonizer, like most cultures, everyone liked a good party.

But alas, shifting winds brought shifting attitudes. For two days, black, black clouds loomed big like bullies. Gale winds blew as one squall after another hit us. We reset the anchor, playing out more chain, and set another anchor for security. The reef's blues changed hues, subtle or vibrant, as the clouds moved across and threw themselves at the peaks of Bora Bora. We all hunkered below deck for two days as the rains poured, playing cards, trying not to cook because of the oppressive heat below deck.

In the cramped quarters, once again, we found that our newfound cheery crew was in fact not as perfect as we first thought. Colin, the owner of the boat, revealed a very moody side that was difficult to understand or deal with. Emma and I were in agreement that they had horrible eating habits—an English trait, I'm sure—where an eight-ounce can of beef and kidney stew was shared amongst the six of us with a huge pile of white potatoes or rice. Never any vegetables. We were in heaven when we had fresh-caught fish, but the lack of vegetables started grating on Emma and me.

It shouldn't have really been a concern to us whether they wanted fresh salads or not except that we were all part of a schedule where each day was one person's cook day. We were to all share in the expense of food. Emma and I, of course, wanted to cook healthy, nutritious meals that included fresh fruits and fresh salads; their meals consisted of a small portion of meat and huge piles of starch and zero vegetables. They started complaining about what we cooked; we started complaining about what they cooked. They didn't want to have to pay for our salads. Our differences started to become much more noticeable, especially after two days of being confined to below decks during the gale.

Other yachts arrived in time for Bastille Day. A diversion and shift in energy occurred when *Maya* sailed in, a Canadian yacht with four good-looking and fun-loving boogying men on board. As soon as the skies returned to blue, Emma and I were away from the *Sheila* as much as we could be, usually hanging out with the men on *Maya* and admittedly partying a little too heartily. Drinking in port is not an adventure, and not an exploration of roads less traveled. Though I was a twenty-two-year-old bikini-clad young woman, there was always that voice that sat on my shoulder saying, "Hey, I didn't come to paradise to party."

We sailed away from Bora Bora right after Bastille Day on to the Cook Islands. Arriving in Rarotonga, we were able to moor at the docks instead of anchoring out in the harbor. After a week's passage from Bora Bora, upon first arriving, Emma and I prepared to set off to explore the small town. This being the first English-speaking island group we'd been in, Colin asked us to check in the local stores to see if they had treacle or Marmite. I'd never heard of such things, and I thought these blimey Englishmen were playing a joke on us and just wanted us to make fools of ourselves asking for such oddly named things. As it turns out, treacle and Marmite do very definitely exist for all those in the world so inclined to eat such foods. I found treacle exceptionally yummy, a thick, thick sugar syrup; I never developed a taste for Marmite. But the three Englishmen on board *Sheila* had found their heaven.

On our reconnaissance scouting, we found the post office and the local "yacht club," where the yachties could hang out, have a drink, get fresh showers, eat a meal, gather and share stories. It was an unpretentious open-aired, half-walled concrete building with a thatched roof several blocks away from the water. Some of the local New Zealand government workers would also regularly stop in for drinks. Most seemed to love it when new folks sailed in with new stories. For them, it was better than a new movie coming to town. (Though much larger and more populated than Taipivai, there was no movie theater on the island.)

As Emma and I explored the town, we passed a white church whose roof had caved in. At that time, the sun was shining, and bright rays of light streaked down on to the rubble below. The door was open; some of the windows were broken, some not. What lay within the church was everything that must have been at one time a beautiful vibrant center of missionary teaching: wooden pews, now tumbled or broken, a piano, hymnals, sheet music, all lying untouched but for the rubble of a collapsed roof and collapsing walls. The walls that remained standing were white and looked almost freshly painted but were getting overgrown with vines inside and out.

We walked inside. Talking quietly between us, a bit baffled as to why this church was sitting in ruins like this, we inspected the once lovely old upright piano; its strings were broken and rusted; the legs of the piano bench were broken. There were silver flutes and a trumpet lying tossed in the mess. Music stands lay twisted under rocks and piles of roofing tiles and rubble. More hymnals. Bleached-out remnants of sheet music blown into the corners.

As we stood there, we became cognizant of someone standing outside staring at us. We exited the church and asked them, "What happened here?"

The three teenaged girls that were watching us did not respond. As we approached them, they started to back up.

I repeated my question, "Hey, what happened to this church? Why is everything just lying here?"

The girls backed up farther before one said, "It's cursed."

"What do you mean?" Emma asked.

They were hesitant to say anything. And then one blurted out, "And now you're cursed too," taking yet another step farther back.

"Well, wait," I said. "Tell us how. What?"

After a bit of prodding, the girls told us how the Christians, when they'd first come to Rarotonga, built their church on top of the Maori marae or *pa* that had stood as the center of the people's worship for centuries. It was a sacred place, having been imbued with *tapu mana*—or spiritual power—through centuries of holy rituals and sacrifices and ceremonies performed on the raised rock platform. When the Christian missionaries came, they purposefully built their churches on top of these religious sites to both symbolically and physically conquer the pagan religion and replace it with the majesty of the Church of England. Many churches throughout the South Pacific still remained on sites of tapu maraes, but this one had not fared so well.

The tapu mana of the *akini* (the sacred power of the chiefs) of Rarotonga was strong; the church was cursed because it had been built on one of their sacred maraes. Not believing in curses and pagan beliefs, the Christian church leaders blamed its first destruction on natural disaster. They rebuilt it; it was destroyed again. Apparently at some time in the not-too-distant past, it was again rebuilt on the same site. When destroyed yet another time, it was never rebuilt, and it stood as it was.

"The Maori gods' curse destroyed it, and it will destroy whoever sets foot in that sacred space. Now you have been cursed. You will die within two days," one girl told us with a mixture of fear and anger. They hurried away.

On returning to the boat, I couldn't admit to anyone that I had believed her. As Emma shared the details of our reconnaissance trip with our fellow crewmembers, I went to my bunk and found that indeed my throat was beginning to tighten, and it was getting more difficult to breathe. I took my pulse, and my heart was beating out of control. I wanted to call out for help, but I thought, *What can they do? It's a curse. I'm dying.*

Suddenly someone jumped from the dock onto the deck of the boat with a loud thump right above my head. It jarred me out of my obsession that I couldn't breathe and that I was indeed dying. I was cognizant enough to notice that, *Hmm, well, now I can breathe just fine.* I realized the power of thought. At least in this instance, the great power of the white man overcame the curse!

Though the slow cadence of sameness permeated days of sailing and life on land, there was also the random event that we'd get caught in the middle of. In Rarotonga, we were suddenly swept up in the Independence Day Parade. I missed out on some of the initial planning that had occurred over drinks at the yacht club one night where all the crew on *Lycklig, Maya, Sheila, Serenade*, among others—French and Belgian, Swedish, Canadian, and American—had decided they would build a float and participate in the Cook Islands' eighth anniversary of independence from New Zealand control.

I had earlier in the day met a young New Zealand man who offered to give me a tour of the island on his motorcycle. After a day of sightseeing, we sat on the western shore and watched the sun set, talking and talking. After a late dinner, I ended up sleeping at his house. When we woke in the morning, he asked if I'd like to take some LSD, a drug I'd experienced many times but had not taken in several years. He suggested we "drop some" (wherever did that term come from?), and then we'd take off to some beautiful spot on the island for the day.

We dropped the acid and drove back to the harbor for me to change and get a few items. As it turns out, everyone was scurrying about building this float to enter the parade. Two large sturdy poles had been obtained, and the men were busy securing an eight-foot-long plywood dinghy to them. The LSD was starting to come on, but I didn't want anyone to know. I was called into action by Emma to gather flowers and greens to decorate this float with. In the end, I had to tell Emma my mind-expanding situation, especially after she saw me staring at one hibiscus flower for fifteen minutes before I picked it. The Kiwi watched from a distance for a while, smiling and laughing at me, and then eventually left me for the day as I got swept up and away in the parade.

Emma was the parade princess who got to sit in the dinghy, dripping with flowers, hoisted on to the shoulders of the ten strongest men, five a side. I was just as glad to not be the center of attention in the state of mind I was in. The rest of us "marched" along on either side of this float while Emma waved her figure-eight princess wave. Geoff played his concertina accordion, providing our parade music. Henri, a five-foot-tall Frenchman, blew a beautiful finger trumpet through his thumbs for accompaniment in between walking on a handstand for many yards at a time to the excitement and joy of the Rarotongans, young and old. I was in my own world, smiling and enjoying the wonderful insanity of it all. The twenty or so yachties wore life jackets, captain's hats over long nightshirts, or whatever other costume dress they could conjure up. We actually won a prize though I can't remember what it was for: "the best foreign entry"? Ha. I know we brought a fun and unique perspective to what would have been an otherwise-typical, probably-quite-boring very-small-town celebratory parade. And because of my state of mind, it was definitely the most unique of experiences, one that I would have never anticipated happening.

There are yachties that stay longer, go slower as sailors like Dave and Sjef and Sarah did, but we moved on shortly afterward, sailing over to Aitutaki, a small "almost" atoll about 160 miles from Rarotonga. Four hundred feet tall at the center of the main island from volcanic origins, the rest was truly an atoll, a ring-shaped reef surrounding coral-formed islands. The passage through the reef was fairly shallow and required timing to coincide with high tide for some of the boats, like *Sheila* that drew more than eight feet. We actually hit bottom briefly sailing in but were able to free ourselves by tightening our mainsail and forcing the boat to heel, freeing the keel. *Serenade*, who had followed shortly afterward, never made it inside the reef but anchored just outside.

It was while we were on Aitutaki that the fair Englishmen of *Sheila* tired of Emma and me—as we had also tired of them—and they asked us to leave. The next lucky winners to welcome Emma and I aboard was *Serenade* on which Emma and I sailed happily and contentedly for five more months. They ended up being the finest of traveling companions.

CHAPTER 7

The pessimist complains about the wind; the optimist
expects it to change; the realist adjusts the sails.
—William Arthur Ward

Serenade was a lovely older wooden fifty-foot double-ended ketch. The cost of our passage, as on *Sheila*, was to contribute to the food stores, but unlike on *Sheila*, they appreciated Emma and my culinary expertise. We slipped into a domestic sort of role, Emma and I being the cooks, the men washing up. Overall, the cadence and energy of cruising changed for the better. Though Mel was the owner and skipper, it was a group decision as to where we might sail to next.

Our first stop after sailing from Aitutaki was Palmerston Atoll, an island atoll of unique history. As the story was told to us by its inhabitants, all descendants of William Marster, in about 1860, William Marster had been dropped off on the atoll with the task to plant coconuts. Coconuts were not indigenous to all the islands or atolls at that time, and both French and British sailing ships took on this task of planting the coconuts for two reasons: One was to provide food and water in the case of a shipwrecked refugee washing up on their shores. The bigger picture, though, was financial—establishing copra plantations throughout the South Pacific.

According to the descendants living there, the ship forgot to come back and get William Marster. Some said the ship captain had died, leaving no record of having dropped him off. Others claimed it was a simple oversight. In either case, it was over six years before a ship passed and took the lone man off the island. He first went to Aitutaki and married a woman, and having embraced his life on Palmerston, he returned with her and started a family. According to these descendants, Marster left two other times, returning each time with another wife. At that point in 1972, they claimed there were now over 5,000 descendants of William Marster living throughout the islands, New Zealand, and Australia. Since Palmerston consisted of the same gene pool, I assume offspring needed to leave to find spouses.

In 1888, William Marster filed claim to the island as his possession though there were others who contested the legality of this, which makes for interesting reading of its history, none of which the islanders conveyed to us at the time. What they did convey was the social setup of the atoll. Each island was broken into thirds, one section per wife and her offspring (Marster sired twenty-three children altogether). The descendants of each wife possessed a designated third of the atoll to maintain or on which to live. Of the numerous islands making up the atoll, each family had their one-third to tend to, which mostly consisted of harvesting the copra crop.

The passage into the inner lagoon was easily accessible. When we dropped anchor, we were quickly surrounded with canoes, and after setting anchor and squaring away the boat, we went to shore to meet this large extended family. It was the first wife's family that dominated and had the privilege of providing us the island generosity. It was through them we learned their unique history and domestic situation. We settled around a large table with the elders while young children slowly fanned us with banana leaves to keep away the flies and other bugs while we ate and talked. This was the only island in the South Pacific whose native tongue was only English; no Polynesian was spoken. More than their social setup, the thing that seemed most incredible to me is that at some point, several decades before, someone had brought a large pipe organ to the island and housed it in a large thatched church. I never heard anyone play it.

We were invited the next day to join them in their regular activity. In multiple large outriggers, as large as twenty-five feet, the islanders took off paddling across the lagoon, which, at its widest point was about seven miles across. We first paddled toward Cooks, then over to Primrose, and eventually toward Birds Island in these canoes. Some people went onto the islands to tend to the copra; the rest entered the water, leaving their canoes behind tethered to a coral head as the men speared parrotfish and the women collected cowry shells that they would later dry and make into necklaces.

Wearing blouses and pareos in waist-deep water, they walked in the clear water, reaching up to their shoulders to collect the shells that they dropped into woven baskets on their shoulders. They laughed and chatted nonstop. Emma and I were walking with them, collecting the shells for them also, but I kept my eyes on the area around the men who were trailing strings of bloody parrotfish behind them while ten-year-old boys with five-foot sticks beat off the reef sharks that circled. Reef sharks aren't usually much larger than two to three feet and really didn't pose a threat to us larger humans, but I found it a bit disconcerting to have so many circling the bloody fish.

The lagoon seemed to have quite a few large turtles. We asked if they ate them, and interestingly we were told no; whoever was the head of the island had deemed them to be too few in number to keep killing them, and there was a moratorium on killing them. This was 1972, but I remember being very impressed with their foresight.

As the tide rose and eventually got too deep, we piled back into the canoes and paddled back to the main island and village of Palmerston where we partook of a fantastic fish fry, taro cooked with bananas and coconut cream wrapped in banana leaves, and an alcoholic beverage made from fermented fresh-squeezed orange juice. As night fell, many of the younger men came onboard *Serenade* with their guitars and ukuleles. Continuing to drink the yeasty orange home brew, they made music till midnight on the deck of our boat under the stars in the lagoon of this small tropical atoll.

We woke up with wicked hangovers from that orange brew. The taste alone should have warned us. The yeast used was basic bread yeast added to orange juice, sugar, and water. We spent another day recuperating, lying in the sun, swimming in the turquoise lagoons, reminding ourselves to avoid yeasty fermented orange juice forevermore.

Leaving Palmerston, we unanimously decided to sail to Niue, a strange tabletop plateau of land—one of the world's largest coral islands—that jutted out of the Pacific with no relationship to any place else. En route there, Mel, perusing the pilot books, found that there was a reef called

Beveridge Reef that could be found at low tide, about halfway between Palmerston and Niue. We were in complete agreement that we should try to find it even though, or especially because, it was hard to find and in the middle of nowhere. I absolutely loved the adventurousness of Mel and Ben.

Long before GPS, these were the years where sun sights were taken with a sextant to locate your spot on our floating orb. Mel began taking shots, plotting them on the chart, and saying, "Hmm, we should be seeing this reef soon."

Another sight taken, another, "Hmm, we should be seeing it soon."

Water, water everywhere but not a reef to be seen. Our first warning that we were indeed close was when a fish struck our fishing line.

As was rigged on most sailboats, a fishing line trailed behind the boat at all times; the line was rigged to a looped length of surgical tubing that would take up the first jolt of a strike, with an attached bell signaling us that a fish was on the hook. The bell jiggled violently. As I was excitedly pulling in one line, a fish took the other line. I found half a barracuda on my line. When Ben pulled in the other line, he found only the head of a fish. Both had been taken by feeding sharks. The abundance of fish and sharks was our first signal that we were close to this yet-unseen reef.

But we still couldn't see a reef, which began to make us nervous for fear that we would find it only too late. Mel kept taking sightings and reporting that we should see it at any time. Both Ben and I were up in the rigging, looking out in all directions of the ocean. Ben finally saw what looked to be waves forming and gently breaking in a line in the distance. As we sailed closer, we could see the turquoise of the lagoon. The tide kept lowering as we got closer and sailed along its now-very-visible six-mile length toward the horseshoe opening at one end. We dropped the sails and motored through the mouth and into a lagoon of turquoise water, a consistent thirty-five feet deep. Ben stayed in the rigging to watch for coral heads as we motored the six miles back to the head of the lagoon where we dropped anchor.

After setting the anchor, Ben, Emma, and I jumped into the dinghy and rowed over to the surrounding coral reef, which was only about two feet deep by that time. We saw an overabundance of large tridacna clams, six-eight inches long, as well as the langoustines poking their antennae out of hidden holes. Ben had a spear gun with which he speared several fish while Emma and I collected clams. In less than fifteen minutes, we had a feast, and we headed back to the boat followed now, we noticed, by about twenty reef sharks.

As Emma and I were cooking up this feast, steaming the clams and little lobster tails and frying the fish—all of which was too much food for us to eat and we really shouldn't have taken so much, but having no refrigeration, it would be better cooked than not—the wind started to pick up. The sky was still blue, but the wind was enough to have Mel check the marine weather band for a weather report. What we discovered was there was a big gale blowing our way. Plotting it out, the brunt of it would be upon us in four or five hours. Though it was Mel's boat and his final decision, we all decided it would be best just to wait out the gale at anchor there in the lagoon of Beveridge Reef. We laid out another long length of anchor chain on the main anchor, and then Ben and I set two more anchors at forty-five degrees, rowing them each out in the dinghy. Clambering back onboard with the wind growing steadily and finally the ominous black clouds of the pending storm rushing in from the horizon, we pulled the dinghy on board and secured it, and we battened down the hatches and went below.

For four days, we rode out this gale anchored in that lagoon in the middle of nowhere in the Pacific Ocean. It was truly a bizarre experience, never experienced by any other sailor I've met. The wind howled, the rigging clanked. Rain came in sheets. We had no land references to look out to through the portholes to know whether our anchors were dragging, so periodically one or the other of us would pull open the turtle hatch of the companionway and stick our heads out into the wind and rain, trying to verify our position to the reef, which itself wasn't necessarily visible, but at least during the daylight hours, the churned-up lighter-colored turquoise water of the lagoon verified we were holding strong.

Unlike on the other boats where confinement brought discontent, we spent those four days below playing cribbage, reading, eating, and having wonderful conversations. I don't know why it is that we all got along so well. Maybe I had finally settled in a bit, getting more into a rhythm that wasn't pushing out against life so much, always trying to prove myself. Maybe it was as simple as being amongst people that were just simply nice people, who I felt didn't judge me or expect me to be different than I was or that I felt I had to prove myself to them. Maybe it's because the decisions made were inclusive; I wasn't just a crewmember responding to a superior's orders but a member of a group making group decisions.

So we perused the pilot books, looking at where we might go after Niue. Niue was west of the Cook Islands, east of Tonga, and south of the Samoan islands, so would we go north to Samoa or directly east to Tonga?

When the gale finally let up, and the blue skies returned, we continued on to Nuie, a brief two-day sail. Nothing very attractive held us there for long. One of the first images I remember was I saw two children walking crippled on the sides, almost the tops of their feet. It was so painful to watch, and I asked someone about them. They were born clubfoot, but having no doctors, their feet were never fixed. She added that not too long beforehand in a time she remembered, they used to throw deformed children over the cliff into the sea. I have no idea if this was true, but it shocked me to hear it as it shocked me to see the crippled children then, and it's one of the things I always think about when I think of our brief stop on Niue. There is uranium on the island as well as naturally occurring mercury; I questioned the reports that say there are no adverse effects due to this.

The second memory I have is of poisonous sea snakes. On the shore near our anchorage, children frolicked off the rocks, leaping into the water, diving, playing. We weren't too far from them, and during one of my swims to cool off, I snorkeled toward them only to be shocked by a huge number—I'd say several hundred—of striped snakes swarming in the water where they were swimming. They assured me, with no apparent fear, that they *were* very poisonous. I went back to the boat.

The third memory of Nuie was the limestone caves of which there are quite a few on the coral island. They were quite extensive with stalagmites and stalactites, all of which seemed out of place on this plateau in the middle of the ocean. They are one of the tourist attractions for modern travelers visiting the island.

Red Rose, Kuan Yin, Maya, and *Bebinka* sailed in and gave us news of Aitutaki. One interesting piece of news was that *Sheila* had gotten into some sort of trouble there—rumors were that someone had taken the Immigration officer's daughter to bed—and they were being fined $1 a day for each day they remained. Wow. Except they couldn't get out of the pass until there was a spring tide high enough to set them free.

In the end, not feeling a big draw or much attraction to Nuie, and the anchorage being very poor, we left after a few days and sailed south to Tonga, about 330 miles away. Though Tonga consists of over 160 islands spread over about 290 square miles, we only went to Vava'u, anchoring at its main town of Neiafu. We had arrived on a Saturday evening. As soon as we'd finished breakfast Sunday morning, Emma and I bundled up the laundry and rowed to shore. We were in our typical garb, bikinis with our lower half wrapped in pareos. As we left the dinghy and started walking with our laundry, we were quickly approached by the police. They wore white shirts tucked into black skirts with six-inch-wide woven belts, a *ta'ovala* or *kafa*. They informed us we were under arrest.

"What? For what?" we asked. They explained that we were dressed improperly (in bikini tops showing our midriffs), and that we were not allowed to do work on Sundays. No activities other than going to church, singing hymns, eating with your family or friends, or walking quietly were permitted on Sunday. The Church of England had a stronghold on this island kingdom, and we were definitely breaking the norms of modesty, dressed as we were and attempting to do our laundry.

We humbly pled our innocence, talking ourselves out of going to jail that day by pleading ignorance of their mores and with promises to return to our boat and not leave until Monday. Though I would have loved to have protested, I of course acquiesced to the age-old adage that when in Rome, do as the Romans do. We did leave the boat later that day, though, dressed appropriately and wandered around and through the residential communities. Indeed, we heard a lot of hymns being sung, and we witnessed many a person walking solemnly along the roads with their hands behind their back as well as groups of Tongan families sitting around, eating, talking.

It wasn't only on Sundays that we needed to dress modestly. Having seldom used anything but bikinis and pareos, we dug out T-shirts, and instead of halved, we wore our pareos long to the ankle so as not to offend anyone. In our wanderings the previous day, we had found a beautiful stream that entered large caverns where the next day, in the cool shade of the cave, children were diving and swimming. Women were on the downside of the cavern washing clothes, so we joined them, scrubbing, sudsing, and rinsing our sheets, pareos, towels, and bikinis. After taking them back to the boat to hang from the rigging, we again went to shore to explore.

To arrive at Neiafu, we had meandered through a passage that was lined with many small islands, almost giving us a sense of being in a fjord. But as we came around a point and came upon Neiafu, we were struck by an ugly conglomeration of storage sheds, corrugated tin shacks, a rickety wharf, and some rather English-looking four-story buildings of green brick. The most impressive structures were the churches.

Many of the men wore black or dark blue lava-lava skirts, like the policemen we'd met the day before, with white shirts, each wrapped with the woven *ta'avala*. We also noticed women, and some men, wearing woven mats that were belted on well above the waistline to below the knees. It looked almost like they'd wrapped themselves in one of their floor mats. Some wore pieces of tapa cloth in the same manner. We were told that this traditional dress—the mats or tapa—is worn with respect. No one can see the king unless they are so attired, or he or she would be imprisoned.

When Mel had gone to shore to clear customs, a man had given him a nice cowry shell, informing him that he would now be his "agent." Quite the hustlers. I remember quite a few children, if not outright begging, at least trying to sell us something at a "bargain price." I found this both interesting, because it seemed out of place, and annoying. We were also approached by industrious young men offering to take us out cave diving. I had already come to the realization that I was running out of my precious $1,000 I'd started with months before. Otherwise, that was definitely an offer I would have liked to do. In the week that we were there, Mel's agent, the cowry man, came regularly, bringing boxes of vegetables to sell us. They seemed cheap enough though I think we could have gotten them cheaper. He took Emma and me to his house one day, a house about twenty-foot square, where his wife was weaving *ta'avalas* and making cowry necklaces. Both Emma and I bought a *ta'avala*, paying him $5. His hustling paid off as the average Tongan at that time was lucky to make about $1.20 a day.

The most memorable event of our week in Tonga was witnessing the beginning and the end of a whale hunt. The beginning was watching a large thirty-foot open boat motor out of the bay one morning with about ten men on board. It was peculiar seeing such a large open boat, but I didn't think much of it until it returned around 2:00 p.m. towing a small whale. It was only then that I noticed a harpoon mounted on the bow. They towed the whale to the wide boat ramp where the village people were already coming down to the shore. The rope, still attached to the harpoon that lay lodged in the whale, was thrown to some men on the shore, and they hooked it up to a motorized wench near a building and began to pull the twenty-foot whale up onto the boat ramp. Once completely out of the water, men surrounded the whale, and standing knee deep in intestines that were thicker than their legs, they started carving it up. As rivers of blood drained into the bay, villagers threw large slabs of meat into five-gallon buckets to carry to their homes. A few trucks appeared and filled up their back beds, possibly to take to people in more distant villages or maybe to a large freezer some place in town. We were asked if we wanted some whale meat, but we all declined. By the time it was dark, there was little left of the whale. The only forgiveness I could find for these people to have killed one of these magnificent creatures is that they truly used it all. Life does eat life in one form another after all.

On my first crossing from Hawai'i to the Mainland, I was awakened around 11:00 p.m. one night to hurry onto deck. Next to us, not five feet from our side, was a whale at least the length of our boat, forty-five feet. Though it was dark, we could see the phosphorescent outline of the gentle creature as it cruised along with us. We could smell the fishy stench of its blowhole breath. It left when dawn came. That was my first up-close-and-personal love affair with the huge creatures. Porpoises, though smaller, incited the same deep almost-aching love, a desire to be their best friend and travel with them forever. Any sense of my humanness fell away in their presence. I felt a stronger heart and mind connection to them than with any member of the human race. I say that honestly.

I made note that every place we went, the local folks had their drug, whether it was kava, betel nut, or fermented brews made from the nectar of the flower of coconut sprays or orange juice. In Tonga, the drug was kava. Related to the pepper plant that gives us black-and-white pepper, its root is crushed—in one way or another—mixed with water, usually, and then drunk ceremonially. It produces a calming effect. In Tonga, we were told that traditionally kava was prepared by virgin girls chewing the root and spitting their saliva into a bowl, which is then drunk ceremonially. I was never in a position to be offered a bowl of spit to drink. But our private agent, the cowry man, brought kava to the boat one day and showed us how to pound it, squeeze water through it, and drink it with a ceremony similar to Fiji and other islands. I felt no effect from the muddy-tasting brew.

It rained a lot while we were in Tonga, curtailing a lot of exploration, but Emma and I were blessed with being led to a small village, Okoa, which was actually its own little island connected by a bridge. Fifty thatched huts sat picturesquely on neat hedged lawns. Two teenage girls led us to a large cement building where all the married women spent all day weaving mats, four women to a mat. One mat, called a *fala*, was being woven with eighth-inch strands of *pandanus* while *papas* were woven with half-inch strips. A *fala* could take four women weaving every day, except Sundays of course, one month to make. Only married women were allowed to weave; girls not yet married had the duties of preparing food for the married women and taking care of the younger children. We were told the people were preparing for their king's visit in two weeks. He was coming for the opening of a hotel and airport, and the people would give him presents of tapas, wood carvings, mats, baskets, and kava. Of course, I wondered what a king does if all sixty thousand of his people give him these presents regularly. Does he store them in a shed or redistribute them?

Whether it was the crippling hold of the Church of England on its inhabitants and visitors or the realization for all of us that our money supplies were dwindling, we decided not to explore farther or go to Nuku'alofa where the king resided at the capital. A week later, we were heading northwest toward Samoa.

It was a week of erratic winds, rain, gales, no wind, and then I remember waking to see the island through a heavy haze. The water was mirror smooth except for an eight-foot rolling swell. We were barely moving. The sun was bearing down hot already, pressing down on us in the stillness. After an exciting breakfast of pancakes, Mel's favorite, we all started pulling out our mattresses and blankets and towels onto deck to dry out.

That lasted about one hour before we saw the ominous blackness on the horizon nearing quickly with the white-capped wind line. It was a good wind though not strong enough to consider reefing the main. It was blowing from the west, directly from the direction to which we wanted to sail, so we were on a close tack. The rain was refreshing, and we were all standing in it to cool off and wash the sweat from our bodies. Through his fogged glasses, Mel noticed a small rip in the mainsail. Almost talking to himself, he asked me whether I thought it would hold.

I replied, "A stitch in time saves nine," adding that I doubted it would hold.

He replied, "Well, I'll watch it." Watch it he did as the whole main split in half.

A sailboat at sea without a main to steady it with an eight-foot swell coming from the wrong direction is not pleasant. Rocking and pitching, we pulled down the torn sail and started the motor. Below decks, the roaring engine created even more heat. But one of the things that made sailing on the *Serenade* so perfect is no matter what disaster presented itself, no one, even Mel, gave a shit. We adapted. We just went with the flow.

Twenty-four hours later we motored into American Samoa. The first impression was the huge amount of pollution and stench from the ships and the canneries. Japanese fishing boats lined the north side of the harbor where Starkist and Van Camps canneries dumped fish scraps, offal, and oil into the water, and the ships pumped their bilges. It was sad to watch this cancer eating up paradise.

Pago Pago harbor is naturally very beautiful, 1,500- to 2,000-foot mountains completely enveloping a bent-finger harbor created, like Taioha'e, by a sunken volcano. One could imagine its beauty before the fish canneries and ships polluted it. Though there was one nicely designed Polynesian hotel at one end, most of the homes lining the bay were wood or cement with rusted tin roofs. Things felt dirty. It had a tired energy to me.

It wasn't just *my* expectations that were toppled; none of us resonated with American Samoa. The people weren't as friendly as we had experienced in the other islands. Without any concrete reasoning other than my own prejudices, I believed their lack of friendliness was because it was an American territory fed by American capitalism where social generosity was tossed out. Then again, even early missionaries reflected on the warrior nature of Samoans, so it could have been an innate cultural issue. I recognize I shouldn't disparage a whole culture—and I'm not—because of a brief and restricted stay. I'm positive, if I'm honest, that if the nasty, smelly tuna canneries and ships and that whole aspect of commercialization hadn't been the first thing I saw—and smelled and heard—my attitude might have been different, and my perceptions altered. Again and again, give me nature and simplicity. Give me the societies that live in harmony instead of those societies that support man's desire to conquer and alter his natural environment to serve greedy desires.

Of course, I'm not naïve enough to not praise many aspects of the onward-marching progress of humanity: improvements in everything from clean water to wastewater treatment, to medical advancements, to refrigeration, and some aspects of transportation. I search for the balance, believing it can be achieved if power and greed did not reign so strong.

Interestingly, American Samoa was the first place that we had experienced theft. It was minor, some cash stolen from Emma's bag. We had taken the aerial tram to the top of Mt. Avala above the harbor, giving us exquisite views. A twelve- or thirteen-year-old girl had attached herself to us when we arrived at the top, walking with us as we enjoyed the incredible views. I remember feeling a bit uncomfortable with her tagging along. Why was she on top there to begin with? There were no villages or houses near. Emma's radar apparently wasn't on or tuned to the same frequency. For some reason, she had left her bag unattended at one point, and the girl got into it, stole some money, and disappeared, probably to attach herself to the next unsuspecting tourist. We never saw her again.

We hadn't experienced theft or even considered it on previous islands. The only other time I experienced theft was in yet another American territory, Ponape, several years later, where our boat, unattended in the harbor, was totally ransacked. Medicines, including morphine suppositories, as well as our rifles and ammunition were stolen. Was theft an American sickness? Like the girls in Taipivai asked, "Why do people steal there? Can't they find work? Do they like jail better?" Was it coincidence or the degradation caused by the capitalistic connection?

We stayed in Pago Pago long enough to get the mainsail repaired which luckily didn't take too long. As soon as the sail was repaired, we chose to sail over to Samoa—also referred to as British Samoa or Western Samoa—to the island of Upolu. Though the islands are only 100 miles apart, the cultures are night and day. *Lycklig*, the Swedish boat, and *Restless* were at anchor when we arrived. They were quick to praise the island for its beauty and less-spoiled culture. The *fa'a Samoa*, or traditional Samoan way, is alive and well to this day. It was a slow, peaceful, clean island. The villages were picturesque. Apia, the main town and village, was inviting, clean, friendly. Most of the houses outside of Apia were *fales*, open-walled thatched structures that had woven covers to drop down during storms or night. Communal living and sharing were strongly evident, and the Polynesian smile and generosity we had first witnessed in the Marquesas and through most of the Society Islands were again shared freely.

Most of the islands were so small you could drive around them in an hour if you had a car, so unless some unique event snagged us to stay longer, we came, stayed usually three days, filled our tanks with water and bought any fresh supplies we could find, and moved on. The excitement to explore and hike that I'd experienced in the Marquesas and parts of Moorea and Bora Bora had lessened. I was morphing a bit, maturing maybe and changing with the experience. Of course, the terrain had changed too, being more like the Hawai'i I knew well and had sailed away from, not as populated or developed for sure but with the same texture and feel of coconut-lined white beaches, frangipani, turquoise lagoons. I had quieted into a bit more of a seasoned sailor. Maybe it was the camaraderie found on the *Serenade* where there wasn't this constant need to escape, but I absorbed the different pace with ease. It fit me not to stay too long in a place once explored and absorbed; it was okay to move on. I also loved being at sea at least as much if not more than arriving at a new island to explore.

On *Serenade*, Mel was open to any suggestion as to where we might sail to and explore. The four of us seemed to have adopted one mind where the urge to move on or to stay caused no strain on any of us. It was Mel's boat, and he was the skipper and in control, but he never dictated any schedule for any of us. He was married and had left his wife behind in Santa Monica because she didn't like to sail. She had acquiesced that he could go for a year. He smiled and said he was going to take that literally: he would go for a year and then spend a year coming back. He was in no hurry. He was moving at a pace that was comfortable for him and for us.

But as we were like one mind, we found we were all in a similar situation: we were all running low on money, including Mel, and we needed to get somewhere where we could work, ideally New Zealand. Because we could, we sailed over to two off-the-track islands of Wallis and Futuna, back into the territory of islands controlled by the French. Again, we stayed a few days—we came, we saw, we went—and then continued on to Fiji.

CHAPTER 8

Life is a series of natural and spontaneous changes. Don't resist them; that only creates sorrow. Let reality be reality. Let things flow naturally forward in whatever way they like.

—Lao Tzu

It seems, at times, daydreaming is not encouraged in our everyday society; it's not permitted to lose ourselves in thought. If we daydream in class, our teacher says we're not paying attention. If we daydream at work, we are reprimanded and maybe even fired. If we sit in a meadow with our friend, they want to know what is wrong if we don't talk. But the sea is the daydreamer's throne, watching the soul dance with the wind gods, the sky god, the sun god, the ocean gods. I could sit effortlessly without guilt, without reprimand in the ethereal space of the mind, allowing fluid thoughts to flow through and never take root for hours. Unknown to me at the time, the passage to Fiji was my last dance with the sea, my last big daydream, for several years.

The best anchorage for yachts would be within the confines of Mosquito Island by the VouSiga Hotel. A bit away from the bustle of Suva, the hotel itself was very friendly to the yachts who anchored there, allowing dinghy tie-ups and availability of water on the dock where we would go daily to shower in our bikinis under a hose, giving the tourists an eyeful.

Lycklig, Maya, Simaric, Restless, Salty, Physalia, Fancy V, and *Margaritha Tripp* were already anchored there as well as the *Valkyrie*, a sixty-one-foot pay-to-sale ketch, run by a thirty-year-old woman—Tugboat

Annie we called her. We hadn't seen Roger and the others of *Maya* since Niue. Emma was happy to see them; though she wasn't sharing much, there seemed to be a romance happening. Knowing we'd be forever moving on, it was reasonable to keep things close to the chest, I suppose.

Suva was a bustling city with a large Indian population. The smell of curries permeated the marketplace, and for pennies, we could get a steaming bowl of rice and vegetable curry. Indians had originally been brought to Fiji in the late 1800s as indentured servants. After such policies were ended in 1916, many decided to stay; some were forced to stay. Their population grew close to half of the total population of Fiji. As the brief visitors that we were, I was simply a witness to two distinct cultures living and working side by side. I was often told (and it appeared to be a truth) that Fijians were not industrious people, so it was the Indians who ran the shops and did much of the hard labor. Eventually, as was happening throughout the islands of the South Pacific, there was unrest. In other island groups, the unrest was focused on wanting independence from their colonizing powers. In Fiji though, the unrest was related to a racist apartheid that rose up to suppress the Indian population. Uprisings began to occur in the late 1980s with the Fijians trying to take back their land from Indians. Luckily, we saw none of that in 1972.

There was a monstrous open-air market in Suva where you could buy tapa cloth, wooden bowls, and other carvings as well as vegetables and fruits. Fresh fish, meats, and chicken hung in the heat with the stall keeper shooing away the flies. There were tables of kava root, which sold at different prices because of its quality. Someone had told us of a Fijian tradition that if you come into a village and present the chief with kava root as a gift, they were indebted to treat you as a guest. In the days of sharing stories, Roger and Peter on *Maya* and Emma and I decided it would be quite the adventure to hike across Viti Levu from Suva to Nadi. It's about 110 miles by road, but we were going to hike across the highlands, and—wanting to experience the traditional ways—we carried only water and the finest quality kava root.

I recorded few details in my journals about the trip. I have absolutely no idea to this day how we knew where to start, what footpaths we would take, how we were navigating. But for ten days, we hiked up mountains, across fields, sometimes down roads briefly before a local would redirect us to turn on to some path. We hiked past dry rice fields where Indian men were winnowing chaff, flicking a semi-flat basket into the air just enough to have the wind catch the chaff and remove it. The same expert move was repeated until the grain was clean after which it was poured into a sack. The flat basket was again refilled and the motion repeated.

We entered small villages of ten or fifteen thatched huts built around a common center. Their houses were much bigger than many of the thatched dwellings we'd seen in other parts of the South Pacific. They reminded me more of photos I'd seen of African huts, thick thatched roofs of bundled grasses, not woven fronds, that hung low over short walls with only a doorway to enter, no window openings. We attracted immediate attention upon entering a village, surrounded instantly by children, and eventually approached by adults. We asked for the elder of each village to whom we presented our kava root. We were welcomed into their homes. We were given tea and something small to eat, maybe a piece of boiled taro root or a bowl of rice; if it was only noon, we would fill our water containers, and we would keep walking. When it was evening, we were welcomed in the same way, given food, and a mat to sleep on for the night. We were a diversion from their everyday activities in these remote villages where there were seldom, if ever, white people who visited, especially coming on foot bearing gifts of kava. I fully recognized, with a minor level of guilt, that we were wealthy and had so much more than these people, and they clearly didn't have a lot, and yet they shared freely with us, strangers from a strange land.

In the ten days, there were no jungles; the land was quite dry for as far as the eye could see. I don't know if it had been defoliated of its timber a century before, like so many places throughout the South Pacific, even into New Zealand, or if this was its natural state. We did seem to find water in streams easily though. In hindsight, I think we were lucky not to have gotten some water-borne disease. Again, as in the Marquesas, there really wasn't much danger of getting lost as any path ended up leading to some small village in one direction or another or to the ocean.

Upon entering one village, all its people were preparing for a traditional wedding. We were invited to stay for the wedding, which we did. It was an all-day affair, starting with chanting and singing in one hut, feasts, more chanting, and then the ceremony. The bride and groom stood out, draped in long leis and with white powder—flour or talcum—making large crosses in their tightly curled afros. After the actual ceremony, of which I don't remember much except that it seemed a mixture of Christian and Fijian rites, a feast followed. Food was mounded in the middle of a long woven mat on the floor. We sat cross-legged on the ground on either side. Banana leaves served as our plates; we all ate with our fingers.

After the feast, it was time to prepare the kava root. Luckily no virgin was chewing and spitting kava here. Similar to what the cowry man had shown us, here the kava was pounded—uniquely in old munitions shells left over from World War II. I have no knowledge of the caliber of these shells, but they were about eight to ten inches wide by almost two feet in length.

Most islands had seen the white man's wars at one point or another, and these remnants remained as a reminder. In some places, the war machine was still at work: In the Tuomotus, southeast of Tahiti, the French were actively detonating nuclear bombs during the time we were sailing. In Rarotonga, we had met a Greenpeace boat who had recently returned from protesting the bomb testing. They had been rammed by a French navy ship in an attempt to keep them away from the test site. The crew on the Greenpeace boat had been taking photos to share with the world. The French had boarded their boat specifically to take the film, but they avoided having the film confiscated by having one of the women on board hide the film in her vagina. In retrospect, the navy ship we'd seen in Taioha'e may well have been taking some R&R from patrolling the Tuamotus.

Back in the mountains of Fiji though, multiple people were pounding kava in the old shell casings. The rhythmic thumping could be heard throughout the village. After mashing the kava to a twisted fibrous mess, water was poured through the mashed roots repeatedly, wringing and squeezing the root mass as they slowly filled a large wooden bowl with the dirty-looking water. A lot of kava was being prepared for the evening ceremonies, which took place in several different places.

In the large pavilion where we ended up, a circle of about twenty people, us included, sat around one large thirty-inch-diameter wooden bowl. One man would dip in a half coconut shell and pass the liquid around, each taking their turn drinking. Ceremonially, you would hold the cup before you, bow your head, say "Matha, matha, matha" three times, and then drink it in one fell swoop, passing it back to be refilled.

It tasted basically like mud. This went on and on for many hours into the night. People would fall asleep, wake up, and drink some more. Some got talkative for a bit, and then they too would fall asleep for a while. Though I was drinking as much as everyone else, again I felt no effect from it; mostly I needed to pee a lot. We too ended up sleeping on the floor that night amongst the wedding revelers until morning when we were graciously fed before we carried on our hike.

Finally arriving in Nadi, we found a cheap guest house to stay in that night. Outside in a coconut grove, we watched a fire-dance ceremony. It was mostly local people walking the hot coals as a tourist attraction, but a few tourists ran across them also. I was offered the opportunity but declined. Instead, exhausted, I remember enjoying the first soft bed I'd had in ten days.

It was in Nadi that we heard that a hurricane was forming and heading toward Fiji. It had only fifty-mile-per-hour winds at that point, and it was possible it would just burn itself out. Emma, the two Kiwis Roger and Peter, and I started hitchhiking back to Suva. A ten-yard dump truck carrying giant orange pumpkins finally stopped for us. We climbed on top and sat high above the cab on top of these pumpkins for the all-day trip back to Suva.

At this point, I knew I wasn't returning to the States. I didn't have enough money for a plane ticket, number one. I had less than $100 left. But I could not conceive of returning to that world where people repeated their lives in the same way every day to keep "civilization" propped up and humming along toward its destruction. The gypsy sailing blood was coursing through my veins. The plan at this point was I would sail with *Serenade* to New Zealand where the boat would stay for the hurricane season before carrying on. My goal was to get to New Zealand where I could get work and earn enough money to keep sailing. We had originally been planning on setting sail for New Zealand a few days after we got back from our hike. But the forming of Hurricane Bebe altered our plans.

Before we left, I wanted to buy a tapa since I'd never gotten one in the Marquesas or Tonga. There were several vendors selling them in the large open-air market where we'd bought the kava root. While some shopkeepers were boarding up windows and hurricane warnings were flying, I headed downtown. I found I wasn't the only one as I ran into the crew from *Lycklig*, *Restless*, *Salty*, and others. The air was filled with electricity and rumors: Ellice and Gilbert Islands were being hit with 120-mile-per-hour winds, but the weather reports suggested it would miss Suva, going to the west of it. One sailor reported that the local radio was reporting only fifty-miles-per-hour winds for fear of panicking the people, but the yacht club was getting reliable warnings of 120 miles per hour. Everyone had different reports. You would leave a person after excitedly sharing the warnings, run into a different group reporting a completely different forecast, and then bump into the original group of people again and receive a completely new set of warnings. We were like ants meeting other ants, antennae waving, sharing information, and then scurrying on.

Finally returning to the VouSiga where *Serenade* was anchored, I found Ben, for some reason, skunk drunk at the bar. The bar was filling quickly, though with more bubbling yachtsmen, most of them being dismissive, saying, "It's not going to be bad" or feeling it was just not imminent enough to be worried about. In spite of their apparent nonchalance, there was a palpable nervousness in the air. Even I felt an anticipation edging on anxiety just from the nervousness of all the others. I had no boat to lose and seriously doubted my life to be endangered, but the energy was high. Admittedly, I thrive on catastrophic situations; I did as a child and I still do. Though I don't want to see people injured or hurt or for them to suffer losses, I was actually hoping for this hurricane to hit us hard for the excitement of it, the experience of riding out a hurricane.

Pondering why I have such thoughts, why I feed off of not necessarily catastrophes but hard times, part of the reason I believe is because I'm fully present during an emergency. I'm completely focused and alert. My mind quits comparing and criticizing and judging but instead gets very pointedly focused on the impending task at hand. It also might be a bit like war veterans who are more prone to become addicted to gambling. They came out alive again and again, surviving on the adrenaline rush of the moment; back in civilian life, they have no identity without feeling that adrenaline, which they trigger when they go all in, blowing their last penny.

I didn't experience adrenaline rushes, but a part of me, a voice from childhood, silently roared, "Hey, watch me survive this. Can you see me now?"

On the edge of a cliff, I resented cautionary warnings. Through repeated moments of perilous behavior, my parents eventually gave up, letting me be except, damn it, that wasn't really what I was acting out for. What I really wanted was for them to acknowledge me, to say, "Great job." I guess the reasoning is irrelevant. I know I was excited about the pending storm and not at all fearful.

Emma and I managed to stumble Ben to the dinghy and get him back onboard *Serenade* where he passed out for several hours. While Bebe was still a day away, we held the tension at bay, waiting, checking the marine band weather reports. As the wind continued to increase, *Maya* Dan rowed over to borrow our motor to help chase down *Salty*'s dinghy that had broken loose. Ben, sobered up enough and needing to feel useful, I guess, took off with Dan for several hours in what was a fruitless search.

Tuesday morning broke with dark foreboding skies, intermittently pouring rain, and winds gusting to forty miles per hour. About nine o'clock, Emma and I hailed one of the dinghies of one of the big fishing boats as they headed for shore. We took showers, drank a couple tea and brandies, ordered some fresh fish and eggs to hold us through the hurricane, and talked with others. The VouSiga was completely prepared, its windows boarded up, the dining room tables and chairs moved back away, jokingly to allow a few yachts safer anchorage. We saw Jason from the *Red Rose* who, along with *Bebinka*, *Physalia*, and a couple other boats, had taken refuge up a river a few miles down, tied down by a spider web of lines to the mangroves. They were stocking up on beer.

We were all worrying about *Sea Dancer* who had been anchored at the Fijian Hotel west of Sigatoka. The last communication with them over the marine band radio said they were dragging and were evacuating to the Fijian Hotel. People buzzed about the bar, the anxiety and tension rising. Some were getting drunk. We figured we might need to have our wits about us, so we eventually caught a ride back out to *Serenade* with one of the hotel's speedboats run by a couple Fijians who had been speeding about, helping out where they could.

Around noon, the *Valkyrie* began dragging and was assisted by the salvage boat *Salimar*. She had been on the edge of the opening into Mosquito Bay, a less-protected place, and had dragged in 50-mile-per-hour winds, not a hopeful sign. They towed *Valkyrie* farther in to the moorage where we were moored at Mosquito Island, but there was no room for another boat, and everyone, including Mel, shooed them on. Finally, *Salimar* took her out and behind the motu where the barges and trading schooners were anchored after which we all settled down to watch and wait. The radio came on regularly, updating the information every two or three hours as the information was relayed from Wellington. In the afternoon, it reported it would pass over Nadi and Sigatoka and would miss Suva, but we still waited, checking our anchors and our positions in relation to the other boats. The winds continued to grow stronger: fifty, sixty, and seventy miles per hour. Without wearing foul-weather gear, the rain was like bee stings.

We were one of the lucky ones because we already had established our anchorage when we had first arrived. When it became clear the hurricane was going to have some impact, we had set five anchors out, which took even more space away from the ability of another boat to drop anchor there. Other boats too set every anchor with as much chain and line as they had, taking caution to avoid being on top of another's anchor and chain. Who knows what that spider web of anchor lines looked like down there though people did their best to secure themselves without causing problems for others. Laying out so much line didn't allow for many boats to anchor securely, and the latecomers weren't allowed in.

About four o'clock, *Valkyrie* began shooting flares as she again was dragging across the bay. Apparently, she didn't have a lot of anchoring gear. Three good anchors are a minimum to carry; five is optimal. We watched from where we were. At times, you couldn't see her as sheets of rain drove across the water. The two VouSiga speedboats flew out to help them, one of them eventually returning to get *Salimar*'s assistance. I would note that the assistance was not without a fee. Any of the rescue tugs working would demand the promise to pay 10 percent of the value of their boat before they would assist. And they collected as they could. Later, when I was visiting the yacht harbor in Auckland, a man approached and asked if I'd seen a certain boat in the harbor. I said, "Oh, yes, it's right down there," pointing.

It turned out, they were the collection agency coming to collect that 10 percent value promised.

As it grew dark, it appeared everyone else was holding well. The wind howled; the rain blanketed the shore and mountains. A line of people leaned on the railing of the deck at the VouSiga, watching. Heads popped up out of hatches to check their anchor lines and position. On board *Serenade*, we ate a good dinner of fresh fried fish, brown rice, and salad and then returned to watching and waiting. The noise of the wind and rain was deafening; we could barely hear each other on board when we talked. The wind grabbed any sound and carried it away. The bay had turned a thick mud color; the capping waves churned a dirty, frothy brown. We were as prepared as we could be to ride out the worst hurricane to hit Fiji in twenty years, a hurricane that, in the end, killed twenty-eight people and left thousands homeless.

As it darkened, we realized electricity was out on shore, giving us no stable lights to line ourselves up with. We noted our relationship to masthead lights from other boats and shadows of boats, the outline of the VouSiga Hotel, other barely discerned landmarks, and the mountains that occasionally revealed their shadows against the blackened clouds. At 7:30 p.m., a new Wellington forecast reported the eye fifteen miles from Nadi heading southeast toward us. The winds grew stronger, the rain heavier, the sky black with night.

For hours, flares lit up the sky, bright red, hanging in the sky before being thrown back out to sea by the wind. It was indiscernible from which boats they had come. We were helpless to help, barely in control of our own predicament let alone someone else's. We knew how much anchor and chain we had out, that the bottom was eighteen inches of mud over slate. We also knew there were fools out there, maybe with a seventy-pound anchor down on rope, not even chain. Chain is tantamount to a good anchor holding. Maybe that's all *Valkyrie* had; what stupidity if so. She would be a lovely old boat to lose. More flares. What can we do? Nothing.

I seldom saw Mel get upset, but he started screaming curses at *Salimar*, the rescue tugboat, as they were recklessly running too close to our mooring lines as they surged out to help another boat. Nine-thirty report, the eye was over Central Viti Levu and expected to be on the southeast coast at midnight. Translation: the eye would pass right over us at midnight. Steady-blowing 120-mile-an-hour winds! Could we withstand 120-mile-per-hour winds? What will happen if people start dragging?

We attacked the stinging rain, clinging to the lifelines and rigging lest the wind blow us overboard, checking for chafing. Mel was visibly worried; he suddenly looked old. We were surprised to hear a loud thumping on our hull at the water line and a voice twelve octaves too high screaming, "Ve are drragging! Ve are drragging! Vhat should ve do? Any minute now ve heet you!"

A man had actually swum over to our boat to pound on the hull. We hauled him onboard.

"Well, would you like to tie off to us?"

"Yes. Yes. Thet ees vhat I vant to know."

Mel told him he could tie off to us unless we started dragging because of him. Knowing how stressed Mel was, I was impressed with his generosity and aid to this less-fortunate fellow sailor. So we tied a line to the little Swede, and he jumped back in the water and swam back to the boat except he could barely swim. Whether it was that he was wearing a long-sleeved shirt or the fact that he couldn't swim well or the fact that he was attempting to swim against the driving wind and rain, I was concerned he'd drown on his way back to his boat. But he made it back to his dinghy, which he climbed into, almost sinking it. I positioned bumpers alongside our boat; they wanted to fly horizontally instead of hang vertically. The Swede loosened his anchor line, allowing his boat to come alongside us. Taking a line from his bow cleat to our stern, we tied it off firmly and then eased him past us until he was astern of us.

From our vantage point, bundled in foul-weather gear with rain deafening us as it pounded on the canvas dog house, we watched that little Swedish boat heel forty-five degrees with gusts and start sailing toward us only to fall off abruptly, come up tight on his line, and swerve to the other direction. In this fashion, the little boat zigzagged behind us as the winds grew stronger. If I had been him on that little thirty-foot fiberglass sloop, I wouldn't have been able to rest below, but the Swede kept going below, popping up every five or ten minutes to ask if everything was still all right. A thumb's-up and a wave assured him, and we returned to our waiting and watching.

The winds began to swing more east-northeast from the west-northwest that had prevailed. The sky continued to be blood red with flares being shot off from behind one of the motus. Except for the wind blowing them back out to sea, I thought some of the flares were bound to land in our cockpit. *Fancy V*, belonging to a forty-five-year-old long-haired Bob, broke its mooring, snapping a five-ton mooring block in half and dragging. It had collided with *Lycklig*. We focused our high-beam flashlights in their direction as Arvid and Theo tried to push the boat away from them. Bob must have thought he was securely tied off to a permanent mooring block; he was one of the few sailors not on board his boat riding out the storm. *Lycklig* let more scope out on their anchor lines, drifting back away from the boat, hoping *Fancy V* would free itself. When it didn't, they figured the mooring block was well entangled in their anchor lines. If it were to drag more, it would take them too. They were prepared to cut *Fancy*'s anchor chain and let it adrift if they had to. In the end, neither boat dragged.

Back to circling the harbor with our light trying to assess our position in relation to other boats. Other lights off other boats were doing the same. More flares lit up the sky.

Then suddenly at 11:25 p.m., the wind and rain stopped. We were in the eye. No wind. So quiet. The sky cleared. The moon and stars came out and shined down brightly. The silence almost hurt after the racket of the wind. Everyone was suddenly leaping in their dinghies to reset and/or untangle their numerous anchors accordingly. We had five anchors to pull, row to the opposite direction, and set down one by one. It was quite a feat. Though the wind would not be as strong as the frontal attack, it would still be significant when it started blowing in from the opposite direction. We had about an hour to reset anchors and resituate.

The full moon shone down as dinghies were put in the water. You'd hear the thud of its occupants clambering in, the oars being set in oarlocks. Two to a boat in most cases, pulling themselves along the side of the boat to the bow, grabbing one of the secondary anchor lines, and slowly bringing it up into the dinghy. Taking it back to the boat, doing the same with the next, bringing in the anchors all except for the main anchor. As the wind started to increase from the other direction, the boats swung on that anchor, and then one by one, the second, third, and fourth anchors were rowed out and dropped.

It was a focused endeavor of a group of people working in unison, each taking care of their own but helping others when necessary like ants rebuilding a crushed ant mound. Lights scanned the waters, focusing where deemed to be needed. Voices came across the water from folks on the dock of the hotel as well as other boats asking how everyone was doing, asking for cigarettes, asking if someone had some whiskey to share. The almost-full moon and a sky full of brilliant stars glistened down on us. The worst was over.

The next morning, forty- to fifty-mile-per-hour winds were still blowing but diminishing, with spots of blue sky breaking through. Bird song coming from the motus seemed exceptionally shrill and clear after the racket of the wind and rain. The big cargo and fishing boats that survived their moorage out by the motu, outside the protection of Mosquito Island, untangled their anchors and moved out, either back to Suva Harbor or to the aid of stranded ships. A large old wooden schooner, belonging to the salvage boat *Salimar* and purportedly having been the private yacht of the queen of Tonga at one time lay on the reef, her hull reportedly filled. The *Salimar* had been busier saving other boats.

There were several power boats swamped near shore and on the reefs, and we could see the mast from a small day-sailor sticking up out of the water at the far end of the bay. It appeared a few of the yachts had lost their dinghies, but other than this, general surveillance proved little damage to those in our immediate vicinity. We heard the 109-foot three-masted schooner *Rebel* was on the reef in the Yasawas, and the *Fletcher Christian*, a boat of similar build, which had been used as a charter boat, had sunk completely. The Rewa River was twenty feet above its banks and the town of Nadi, where we had been just a few days before, was five feet underwater. I wondered how *Red Rose*, *Bebinka*, and *Physalia* had fared tied to the mangroves upriver. There was extensive damage in the Yasawas, an archipelago of islands making up the northwestern edge of Fiji, with 95 percent of the homes destroyed and 64 percent of the trees down. The mountains had buffered some of the force on the Suva side; as we walked along the mud-strewn streets, we viewed a lot of fallen branches, twigs, and leaves but little other damage.

Downtown Suva was closed up except for Morris Hedstrom and Burns Philip groceries, which were staying open till noon. The post office was open though. I was surprised. I sent off telegrams informing family back in the States I was okay. Otherwise, Suva looked like a ghost town, all boarded up with only a few people on the branch-strewn streets. The marketplace, usually bulging with people and taxis and buses, was empty. Many of the little Indian pushcart sweet stands, chained to utility poles, were tipped over, their roofs blown off. We quickly toured the deserted city, stopped in at the twenty-cent curry place, and headed back to the VouSiga Hotel where, fueled by booze, people compared stories, which mostly consisted of the fears and thoughts they'd felt as the hurricane bore down on them. While at the bar, one of the yachties rowed over excitedly to announce they'd just communicated with *Sea Dancer*, the boat that had been caught in Sigatoka; the boat had hung on its last anchor throughout, and "it was still there in the morning." We all cheered. Must have been a bit how those folks felt when they saw that "the flag was still there."

When *Sea Dancer* sailed into Mosquito Bay by the VouSiga a couple days later, there was not a drop of paint on the forward side of the hull; the wind and water had blasted it completely down to the wood. Theirs was the most exciting story of all. After three anchors had broken, they figured they needed to abandon the boat. As they were trying to get into their dinghy, it flipped them out in the wind. They ended up swimming to shore. Having to walk along the beach against the wind to get to the closest shelter, their bare legs were bloodied from being sandblasted as the wind drove the sand into their shins. They stayed the night in a local hotel, expecting their boat to be gone in the morning, but the last anchor had held by some miracle. People bought rounds, and more rounds were bought.

The *Serenade* weathered the storm with no damage done at all. Though I got my wish to want to experience just what I experienced, I was in awe of its power and humbled by the damage done to quite large vessels who hadn't had the good protection and anchorage that we had been lucky to have first. I felt good that we'd been able to help the Swede, for surely his little boat would have been pummeled on the shore. I felt a surge of camaraderie for everyone working together, our hearts beating together, working as one, sharing the same moment, helping each other make it through when help was needed. Most of us had stayed with our boats; there was only the *Fancy V* that had no one on board to tend it, but even she made it through thanks to *Lycklig*. It had been one of those moments that tested your fortitude, your heart, your presence to be in the moment.

Hurricane season came early and caught a lot of sailors off guard. It had been our intent to leave soon after Emma and I returned from the hike, but the hurricane delayed us. As soon as things had stabilized and shops opened again, we went about stocking up and preparing to sail to Auckland, New Zealand, which we did, but the journey was short lived.

Two days after setting sail from Suva to Auckland, New Zealand, we broke our backstay, almost losing our mast. We had a full main up and a large jib and had been moving at a good clip when *boing*. Below eating breakfast, we jammed the companionway all trying to rush topsides at once. The main mast was leaning forward dangerously. As quickly as we could, we got the main and jib sail dropped. Assessing the cause, we found that the backstay fitting had cracked and broke at the base of the turnbuckle. The bumpkin was dragging in the water and the backstay flipping wildly through the air. We managed to capture the backstay, tie it off with a two-purchase block and tackle and secure it to the boom crutch and track bar. At first, Mel announced we'd motor our way to New Caledonia, 600 miles away. This was the one time where there was disagreement. After a vote, Mel was overruled, and we turned toward Fiji, limping back the 150 miles with shortened sails. At that point, Mel decided he would be wintering in Fiji.

His announcement was a bit of a "Shit, what now?" moment for me. I needed to get to New Zealand and work. After helping supply the boat for the trip to New Zealand as well as wasting some money in celebratory hurricane drinks and buying the tapa, I had $75 to my name. This would have been more than sufficient to get me to New Zealand for free on *Serenade* where I would have been able to stay on while I found some work to do, earned some money, and then carried on sailing. *That* had been the plan, a plan that had crystalized while sailing with *Serenade*. I was having the time of my life, and I felt the journey had just begun. All the random pieces had been falling into perfect place all these months until this moment. Suddenly I was scurrying for a new plan.

From months of an existence where I literally was floating along, going wherever and however the waters of life took me, I was suddenly having to shift my energy into survival mode. I picked up that cloak and wore it as easily as I had worn the gypsy cloak. I started brainstorming. In the six days since the end of the hurricane, since we'd left and sailed back to harbor, most of the other boats that had also planned to winter in New Zealand had already left. My options of getting out of Suva on a sailboat were very limited.

As with all challenges, I rose to meet it, which in this case began by networking and talking with folks. Several other yachties, including two young men, Jeff from Seattle and Dermot from Slough, England, informed me that they were going to take a cruise ship, the *Oriana*, from Suva to Auckland in two days. That became my most viable option though it would take close to the last of my money. Because there were several others buying passage, we developed a plan to smuggle me on board, a plan which got squelched the day after. Since I knew I had to get to New Zealand to work, I had been removed from *Serenade*'s crew list, and Immigration demanded that I produce a ticket out of the country. Though I went through several contortions with Immigration to avoid having to purchase a ticket, in the end, I was forced to spend $69 for a one-way ticket.

Two days later, I said farewell to Emma with whom I'd been sailing for nine months and Mel and Ben who were such delightful souls and travel companions, and I took my few possessions and caught the *Oriana* to Auckland. It was a two-day passage. Instead of floating across the Pacific, my energy, perspective, and goal was now getting to New Zealand, finding a place to sleep while I found work, trying to survive on less than $10 until I did. Instead of quietly floating across the Pacific, this cruise liner seemingly sped through the water. Viewing the water from so high up felt different than being so one with it in a small boat. Maybe it was the higher angle, but the water wasn't as pretty as it was on a sailboat. Though it was the same ocean, it was impersonal, a dark blue metallic color without heart. A definite shift in attitude.

I felt disappointed in myself that I was taking this ship the last leg to New Zealand, like I was less of a hero, less of an adventurer, less of a sailor, all sorts of self-deprecating thoughts along those lines. But reality was reality. After purchasing passage on the *Oriana*, I had six one-dollar bills in my pocket. On the two-day trip to New Zealand, I talked with Jeff and Dermot. Though it had been a part of our earlier discussions, I shared my worry about my lack of money, not sure how quickly I'd find work, where I would stay while finding work, all those sorts of survival questions. They insisted that I not worry about money right away but instead join them for a while. They were going to rent a car and explore the country. If I'd like to join them, I was very welcome, and they would pay for everything. Though difficult for me to accept charity, it would allow me an opportunity to figure out what I was doing, so I accepted.

While sitting in the ship's library perusing a book I'd found, an older gentleman and I struck up a conversation. He was fascinated with the fact that I had been sailing for the past nine months on what seemed to him to be such tiny little boats. When asking me what my plans were, I explained, "Well, the first thing I need to do is get a job because I only have $5 or $6 left."

After chatting for a while and upon leaving, he offered me twenty New Zealand pounds to help out.

"Oh, gosh, no. But thank you." I refused the handout.

A few hours before we arrived in Auckland, I ran into him—he clearly seemed to have been seeking me out—and he was very insistent that I look at a certain book in the library before I leave, telling me I'd find it interesting. I did, and in it was a twenty-pound note. I took the money then.

Upon arriving in Auckland, Jeff and Dermot rented a car, and we set off exploring the North Island. Meandering up the east coast, we stopped at beach towns, Ruakaka, and north through Whangarei. I so distinctly remember being appalled at the food offered and served in restaurants: sandwiches made of canned SpaghettiOs on white bread or canned asparagus on white bread. Ugh. That was the standard fare back then. We camped on beaches and meandered north. In Kawakawa, we turned off the main highway and turned toward the Bay of Islands, Opua, and Russell, where a lot of sailboats anchored. Though their tentative plans were to eventually return to their home countries, the sailor's itch was still there, and we were all looking.

Continuing up through Whangaroa toward Mangonui, we stopped near Houhora to get a milkshake. There we met Urion Edwards, aka Bear, a man of big build, mop of hair, thick beard, with the saddest eyes. Not that he was sad; it was just that the physical shape of his eyes made him look so sad. He was twenty-five years old and a fisherman, with a small twenty-two-foot boat with which he long-lined for snapper.

He invited us to sleep at his house that night, which was a small one-room shack on five acres of land with an outhouse and fifty-gallon barrels for washing that he kept full by pulling up buckets from a well. He had a ten-by-ten smokehouse near a row of locust, cedar, and wattle trees in which he hung fish to smoke and dry, which he would sell later for way more than he sold his daily catch of fish to the packers. Bear offered for us to spend a second night if we wanted, so as he went off fishing the next day, we spent the rest of the day exploring all the way up to the northern tip at Point Reinga, returning for another evening of making music and talking.

Bear offered for me to work for him fishing if I cared to. He could pay me, he said, two cents a pound for everything that was caught and sold, and I could stay at his shack. I told him I'd consider it. For now, I'd travel a bit more with Jeff and Dermot. Before we left, he gave us several addresses of friends in Auckland and south of Auckland in Hamilton, claiming we could go and introduce ourselves and crash at their houses. New Zealanders, we discovered, were as open and generous as many of the South Sea islanders. Such a natural way to move through the world, sharing and giving shelter to travelers.

Two years before, I'd sailed with several friends from Hawai'i to Santa Cruz. Jack and Irene, two of them, had since moved to New Zealand and bought 100 acres of land. I had a basic generic address as Broadwood, Hokianga, 300 miles from Auckland. I hadn't known whether I would have the opportunity to see them at all, but now it seemed they were on our route, and Jeff and Dermot were game to search them out.

We found Broadwood without problem. It took us another half a day to actually find Jack and Irene. Folks at the Broadwood Store were familiar with them coming in to buy soap or kerosene every few months, but they didn't really know where they lived. It was, "Out Pawarenga way somewhere." Whenever we saw someone, which was infrequent on the rural road, it was the same response, "Ah, yeah, mate, they're out Pawarenga way, but I don't know exactly where."

Eventually, we found someone who told us to look for a foot swing bridge and "then follow the path."

"Where's the swing bridge?"

They'd point farther down the one-lane dirt road.

Eventually we found the swing bridge, fourteen miles out from Broadwood, though nobody really knew exactly where they lived beyond that, but "follow the path." There turned out to be numerous paths. The one we chose followed the Rotokakahi River around instead of heading up over a 500-foot hill. Walking up from the tree-lined river, we came upon a meadow that opened up into gardens where we found Jack, in a homemade leather breech cloth, working in the garden. What a surprise for both of us: that we'd actually found him with such poor directions and that he was living this lifestyle. I'd had no clue. He, of course, was just as surprised to see me as we hadn't been in contact for well over a year.

We stayed for two days, sleeping on the floor of their small thatched hut, which consisted of one main room with a loft where Jack and Irene slept with their eighteen-month-old towheaded daughter, Aihe. The thatched hut, resting in rolling hills waving with long swaying grasses, was terraced with Irene's flower and herb gardens, parading mint, comfrey, thyme, dill, borage, and more. A low-reaching porch covered the entrance into the small house. A foot-stomped dirt floor was covered with thick, soft sheepskins and two large winter-coat cow hides. An eighteen-inch high table with a huge vase of flowers on it was surrounded with cushions on which we sat while Irene fixed tea. A spinning wheel and a box of sheared wool sat in the corner. A wood-burning oven cook stove sat recessed in the middle of the back wall opposite the door. Irene picked through a pile of cut wood and kindling to feed into the small gaping mouth of the stove.

An enamel sink was set into a bench of rough boards beneath which sat dishes and stores of dried beans, potatoes, and other staples hidden by colorful but earthy-toned curtains, adding color to the soft shadings of the brown thatched walls. Ladders led up to the two lofts at either end, one being Jack and Irene's bed, the other for storage. There was another small room being used for storage of clothes, linens, and food stores, separated by a woven nikau wall; this later became my room while I was building my house.

We sat cross-legged around their small table. Jeff and Dermot were asking question after question, "How do you cure the hides?"

"Make a paste of kerosene and alum and rub it in, stretch it tight in the sun for two or three days, then scrape off the excess."

"How do you catch the eels?"

"Well, I have a wire trap with an inverted cone opening. Put in meat or fish scraps and put it in the river with the mouth downstream. You can make a good one out of plaited flax or vine though, like the old Maoris."

I fell in love with what they were doing. Love at first sight. Shunning civilization and development, I had been searching only for simplicity. Other than soap and kerosene, some flour, salt, and a few other items, they were completely subsistence farming. They had a milking cow for milk, cream, butter, cottage cheese, and cheese, a garden where vegetables could be grown year-round in the temperate climate that seldom got frost; they had chickens for eggs. They had sheep from which Irene spun wool and wove it into warm fabrics. Jack cured the hides of sheep for rugs on the dirt floor, and, stripped of the wool, he made moccasins and leather clothes. Without electricity and refrigeration, meat was brined, salted, smoked, dried, or given away to neighbors. They invited me (and Jeff and Dermot too) to stay if I wished to find a corner of their land and build a thatched hut.

I still needed to earn some money though, so after two nights, we parted and headed south. In Auckland, we did in fact look up Bear's friends who did invite us to stay there. Dermot and Jeff eventually carried on touring New Zealand while I stayed to find a job. After two days of walking miles around the town, I landed a job as a transcriptionist in a law office.

Though I'd been typing since I was eight years old, I only lasted a week before I was fired. I'd had two problems. One is I couldn't understand their accent. An attorney was dictating, "This is case 123 bah 421."

What the heck is bah? I thought, *Okay, there are a lot of sheep in this country, but* . . . I'd back it up, listen again, and finally I'd bring in another secretary. "I'm sorry, what the heck is he saying?"

She'd repeat it exactly the same way, "123 bah 421."

"Yes, that's what I heard. Um, could you please write it out for me?"

"123/421."

Oh, a slash or oblique. Hmm, okay. *Barrrrrrrr* with an *R*.

That problem solved, the second problem I had was I could not retrain my fingers to spell the English spelling for words like *center/centre, harbor/harbour*, et cetera. I was typing on typewriters, not a computer. I was asked to leave after a week. I think I earned $25 for the week.

I'd been sleeping on the floor in the corner of one of the rooms of Bear's friends. I returned that afternoon and tried to give them a few dollars for giving me a place to crash, which they refused. The next day, I headed back north to Mangonui to take up Bear on his offer to fish. I left early the next morning hitchhiking, with the supreme luck of getting a ride the whole way. No one had telephones. I was waiting for Bear when he came home from fishing.

I spent four or five weeks fishing with Bear. Going out early each morning, we'd bait the hooks and lay out the long lines and then bring the boat back around to pull the line back in again. It reminded me of my early years in Maryland on the tributaries of the Little Choptank River, one of the few warm and loving memories I hold of my childhood where my brothers and I would go out with our father in a twelve-foot runabout, laying crab trot lines. There, we twisted a slice of salted eel into a three-ply rope every three feet for a half-mile line. Laying it out with buoys on each end, we'd pull the line across the runabout with a hand net held out for the crabs to drop in as they came up out of the water.

Long-lining for snapper was similar except the line had hooks every six feet and the fish wouldn't drop off into a net below them. As we brought them into the boat, Bear taught me how to jam a half-inch-thick stick into their mouths and, with a twist, release the hook from the fish's mouth, tossing the fish into the holding bins. It was dirty work, wet, smelly, and dangerous with so many hooks. Lines would get tangled which Bear was patient and so efficient in untangling. There were days when we caught few fish; other days we were almost overloaded—a twenty-two-foot boat is not very large. Each day, we'd return to the docks and wait in line behind much bigger boats—sixty and eighty feet—to offload. They'd weigh out our catch and pay Bear on the spot; he gave me my two cents' worth—two cents a pound.

Every couple of days, we'd bring to his house a hundred pounds of snapper or trevally, which we'd clean, cut in half, brine for a day, and then hang in his smokehouse to cure. He sold his smoked fish to neighbors as well as in the local stores and restaurants, a profitable side enterprise for him. Several nights before I was to quit, having earned a whopping $100 after weeks of work—all of which I was able to save as Bear provided me a place to live and food to eat—Bear had filled his smokehouse with a fresh batch of brined fish, stoked his smoky fire to smolder through the night, and we went to bed. A bright light in my window awoke me in the night. His smokehouse was in flames. I screamed at Bear to wake up. We both ran out into the night to watch flames devouring his smokehouse with over a hundred pounds of fish going up in smoke.

Bear had that row of fifty-five-gallon drums as water catchments. As futile as it might have been, we grabbed buckets and attempted to put out the flames. Between the fifty-five-gallon drums and the smokehouse, though, was a wire that stretched between his house and some trees that Bear used as a clothesline. In the darkness of the night, running full blast with a bucket of water to throw on the flames, I ran into that wire with my neck with such force it threw me backward. Luckily it didn't sever my neck. In the end, with his smokehouse completely engulfed, we tossed water on the wattle trees to keep them from catching fire. This is the way life seems to be sometimes: right when you think you're getting ahead, something happens to set you back a step. Life happens.

PART II

PART II

CHAPTER 1

There is a pleasure in the pathless woods,
There is a rapture on the lonely shore,
There is society, where none intrudes,
By the deep sea, and music in its roar:
I love not man the less, but Nature more

—Lord Byron

When I was nineteen, after my first deep-water passage from Hawai'i to the Mainland in which I fell deeply in love with long-distance sailing, I purchased the twenty-four-foot gaff-rigged cutter *Wanderer II* with the sole intention of sailing around the world by myself. What came with the boat were the sails of course, an anchor and chain of course, and a two-burner propane stove. There were facing Naugahyde-covered settee seats that served as berths, barely wide enough for my shoulders. *And,* the Universe doing all that it could to shift my way of thinking even further outside the expectations of society, there were two books, P. D. Ouspenski's *In Search of the Miraculous* and Yogananda's *Autobiography of a Yogi.* I spent the next year slowly and laboriously poring through *In Search of the Miraculous*, Ouspenski's account of George Gurdjieff's teachings.

The profundity of this astounds me to this day. Why these books? Why these books left behind on a small twenty-four-foot sailboat for a nineteen-year-old young woman to discover? Ouspenski's book introduced me to a realm of esoteric thought that has hovered in the background of my life ever since, leading me eventually, decades later, to a Buddhist practice. It taught me to watch myself watching myself. Still too young with life's desires taunting me, not yet ready to or cognizant of why I should, I definitely forgot to watch myself more often than I remembered, and I easily slipped back into the delusions of life.

One metaphor Ouspenski presented of Gurdjieff's teachings was to visualize life as a cacophony of scales being played out—do, re, mi, fa, so, la, ti, do—a hum of scales expanding in all directions, flying endlessly in time and space: the continuous and invisible energy of life creating itself. In visualizing the twists and turns my life has taken, it's easy for me to see the breaks in each scale, the weakness that exists between mi and fa, and between ti and do where no sharp/flat note resides. It was at these points that one could slip on to a scale emanating in a slightly different direction if one didn't stay awake and pay attention. And again. And again until one could actually end up finding himself going in the opposite direction without consciously making any decision whatsoever.

After a year of owning the *Wanderer II*, I realized that, though I was a great sailor, I had taken on more than I could handle in owning my own sailboat. Literally the day after I sold the *Wanderer II*, I was invited to sail with the *Aum*, a beamy forty-five-foot ketch, to Santa Cruz. Besides the owner, the other crewmembers were Jack and Irene. Do-re-mi-fa-so-la-ti-do. That was how the music played out back then.

Now though I thought my journey was to sail the South Pacific and farther, I found myself on a completely different path. The opportunity to sail on *Westward Ho* had set me off in one direction; each change of boats, change of circumstances, altered the course ever so slightly. There were hurricanes and a broken back stay on *Serenade*, requiring the boat to return to Fiji. Another point was getting passage on the *Oriana*, after which Dermot and Jeff took me in tow, exploring New Zealand, which definitely allowed me to visit Jack and Irene when maybe I would have otherwise never stopped in to say hi.

With each alteration of my course, with each change, I came to realize that I was in fact content to stop sailing. My plan of getting a job to make more money so I could keep sailing was no longer in my repertoire of life's chords being played out. I was still on an adventure, just a different adventure, a different path than what I'd planned when I left Hawai'i. And yet I felt like I'd arrived at my purpose, that all the sailing beforehand had simply introduced me and prepared me for arriving at that point to live that life of subsistence in a remote corner of New Zealand.

Traveling on a sailboat, its own home away from home, eases the weariness that comes with always being on the move. But it doesn't alleviate that idea that you're always arriving and never really coming to rest. Even in civilization, forever pursuing the great agreed-upon dream, everyone continues striding forward, seeking more, seeking better but never ever stopping to savor and be in this moment. The whole of modern civilization was trapped in that circular maze. Working a job to earn money to provide for housing and food did not have the same in-the-moment presence of subsistence living, growing, raising, gathering, and harvesting the food, living in structures that nature provided. It was this reality that I was seeking when I first arrived in the Marquesas. So maybe I wasn't off course at all that I had arrived at exactly the lifestyle that I was seeking while sailing.

I returned to Jack and Irene's land with my precious $100 plus. Jack had a few rules, the main one being no machinery permitted, so no chainsaws, no rototillers, no cars, no boats. I would need to build my own little house. I would share in the garden work and its bounties, and I'd help in whatever other ways he needed, which involved milking the cow, helping with shearing the sheep, and other animal husbandry. I had no qualms about any of it. I was excited to learn all that I could.

I lived with them in their small shack while I built my own house, which took about a month. Jack showed me the best place to get long straight tea tree poles several miles away. I'd hike over with my machete, cut them, and carry back as many as I could each trip, probably sixty to eighty pounds of poles per trip. It took eight trips altogether to get enough long poles. I remember getting severe carpal tunnel carrying them on my shoulder, where I could barely hold a cup of tea or a fork for several weeks afterward. I could have carried less, but it would have meant more trips.

Jack showed me how to weave the nikau fronds (New Zealand's only palm tree) into mats. There is a quite easy knack of climbing any palm tree, which I was quite good at, where you place your feet on opposing sides of the trunk, knees splayed outward, a bit like an electrical linesman climbing a telephone pole with their cleats except it was just my bare feet. There are people who use tension ropes between their feet, but I just climbed barefoot.

Working my way up a tree, I would cut as many good fronds as I could, leaving enough to sustain the tree for further growth. Cutting fronds one day, I couldn't get the angle to cut right handed, so I switched to my left hand, and from the other side of the trunk, I swung at this frond, which cut nicely, but the machete carried downward and severely cut my right leg above my knee. I limped over to Jack and Irene's. They happened to have a suture kit, and Irene sutured up my leg *sans* Novocain.

There was a cattail or *raupo* swamp on their property. Before I'd begun collecting nikau fronds, I had cut most of the cattails and had laid them out to dry nearby. After they were dry, I bundled them into three- to four-inch bundles, tying them tightly every ten inches with thin strips from the local flax plant. (This same strong, durable flax plant was the main fiber for weaving baskets or *ketes*.) There was a deserted house about five miles away that I got permission to take one of the windows from, which, with the help of Jack, we carried back down the road the five miles. Once I had all my palm fronds woven, my cattails bound up, the tea tree poles on site and my window, Jack then helped me build the little A-frame house. We used some nails, but most of the tea tree poles were bound together with baling wire to create the A-frame structure. The woven mats were layered from bottom to top, tied on with flax strings as were the cattail bundles, which I tied in vertically to create the two end walls of the A-frame.

I had a window and a door on one end. Somewhere Jack had found a small old cookstove with a six-inch firebox as well as the necessary stovepipe to hook into the stove, the pipe extending up through the thatched roof. In hindsight, like many things I did during those years, I'm amazed my roof never caught fire. I built a bed frame out of tea tree poles on which I put old cured sheepskins I was given. My biggest decoration was the tapa cloth I had bought in Fiji, which I put above my bed to keep debris from the thatched roof from falling on me. The hard-packed floor was also covered with cured sheepskins, which, every few days I had to take outside to dry as they would absorb the moisture from the ground.

After my little hut was built, I lived alone, quite contentedly, along the banks of the slow-moving Rotokakahi River. Besides Jack and Irene and their daughter, there were two others that also lived on the land. Pole (a nickname derived from his surname of Pollard) lived up in a canyon in his thatched *whare*. Though living an alternative lifestyle, he was in fact a schoolteacher. Five days a week, he'd traipse down the mountain in gum boots, raggedy clothes, and an oil slicker and, behind a tree, change into a three-piece tweed suit and catch the bus to Broadwood to teach school. He'd return on the school bus, change back into his gum boots and oil slicker—or shorts and T-shirt, depending on the weather—and return to his hut high in the canyon and play guitar and sing to his vegetables and write poetry. Pole had been born in England and had grown up partly in Canada and partly in the United States. But this was the lifestyle he'd chosen. Several years later, Pole eventually moved to Adelaide, Australia, where he taught English as a second language, continued to farm, and write.

Another American that I only knew as Leonard lived in something more akin to a lean-to farther into the forest on the property. Though I think he lived there the entire twenty-one months I did, I seldom saw him and barely knew him. He had a degree from Stanford University but preferred instead the simplicity of a land that supported him without the need of money. He ultimately did leave and rejoin civilization as most of us did eventually and was an English teacher for thirty-plus years in New Zealand.

Life fell into a comfortable rhythm. I milked the cow once a day. In the winter months, Jack assigned me the mornings when it was cold and miserable. In the summers, I had the evening milking. I saw Irene most days when I would deliver the milk after milking. We poured it off into quart canning jars. I took a quart home each day, letting it sit until the cream rose to the top, which was often almost a quarter of the jar. After pouring it off into a separate jar, I made my own butter by simply shaking the jar until the cream separated from the buttermilk. If I didn't use all the milk, it curdled naturally. I drained off the whey and ate fresh cottage cheese. When the cow was producing extra milk and we all had extra cottage cheese, we drained it further in cheesecloth, pressed it in a homemade cheese press for several days, and then hung it to form hard cheese. Admittedly, it was never very good, not ever having the proper bacteria, but it was rewarding to have made it.

It seemed a completely natural segue from sailing and experiencing the islands of the South Pacific to now finding myself living in my own thatched hut. Yes, New Zealand wasn't the tropical islands, but it was that less-civilized, simpler lifestyle that I'd witnessed and felt drawn to through my travels. It was a simple life of subsistence, and I truly loved it. I was challenged by its hardships and rejoiced in all my achievements.

I loved being alone too. Though I didn't realize it for many decades, I'm a natural introvert. I recharge my soul and am rejuvenated in the silence of my own thoughts. For the almost two years I lived in New Zealand, they were the happiest years of my life I think mainly because I was so content to be by myself. I didn't have to contend with the idiosyncrasies of other individuals though Gurdjieff's "chord shifts" were unknowingly happening in the background to eventually sneak up and announce yet a different mind-set. But that was much later.

I loved the challenge of subsistence living, so there was never a dull minute. There was much to be learned, and there was always something that needed to be done, whether the simple garden tasks of weeding or planting, milking the cow, washing laundry by hand in the stream, docking sheep, cleaning and scraping a sheepskin down and preparing it for tanning with a mixture of alum and kerosene. Jack taught me how to set snares though I never caught anything. We collected meadow mushrooms, and when the blackberries were in season, we hiked several miles over to pick gallons of them, some of which we made into jams, a lot of which we made into blackberry wine. With no machinery, everything took time, whether walking for miles to gather mushrooms or blackberries or tea tree poles, or hand-hoeing a garden.

I learned about local wild foods and how to prepare them. Besides the everyday species of plantain, dock, purslane, dandelion, wild roses, poke, different cresses, wild onions, and wild carrots, there were numerous plants indigenous only to New Zealand for harvesting. Jack slowly taught me to identify the *karaka* kernels and the *tarairi*, both producing edible fruit the size of olives or grapes. Both had kernels that were poisonous unless treated, which meant boiling for at least ten hours (though not necessarily continuously). I marvel at how the Maoris, or any other indigenous person, learned what was edible or, if poisonous, how to treat it to make it edible. The *karaka* and *tarairi* were the main indigenous foods I collected and ate regularly. But the *tawa* and *hinau* trees, the *makomako*, the *kare-ao*, the *porokaiwhiri*, *patotara*, and others also produced edible fruit. The tea tree itself, besides its now-known medicinal properties, was so named by Captain Cook because of its small tea-sized leaves they used to make tea.

A "million-dollar salad" is made from the heart of the nikau tree, so named because a ten-meter tall tree must be cut down and destroyed just to retrieve the small palm heart. Without killing the tree, one can harvest the flower sprays from the nikau, which are also quite edible. The *ti-kouka*, or cabbage tree, the world's largest lily, grew throughout. We ate the tender leaf bases like eating artichoke leaves. Besides being a food source, its leaves were used for making clothing by the early Maoris. We gathered fiddleheads, a somewhat slimy substitute for a potato, from the large tree fern. This, as well as other plants, also had medicinal value from drawing out infections to reducing pain. We ate the young shoots of the cattail or *raupo*. Flax is another member of the lily family. Besides its six-foot-long swordlike leaves used as both building and weaving material, its flowers produced a very sweet nectar. I had so much to learn, and Jack was a willing teacher.

The horses and cows were on the other side of the hill toward the swing bridge. An almost-daily task in the summer months consisted of collecting horse manure in the fields and carrying it in burlap sacks back over the hill for the garden. Once a month, at spring tide, when the low tide would be the lowest, we'd saddle up the horses and ride ten miles out to the coast on a trail high above the mouth of the Pawarenga/Rotokakahi River where we'd spend the day collecting mussels. Filling up split sacks, we'd return and steam them up and feast on them till gone. We also had a round throw net that we'd use to catch mullet that came up the river, which I got pretty good at throwing. Besides mullet, we trapped eels, which gave me the creeps to cook because even when long dead, they jumped and twisted in the frying pan when cooking them though they were quite good, a bit like pork.

We lived in a Maori community. We were an enigma to the Maori families who lived there because we were living like the Maoris had for centuries but no longer did. Though thinking us odd for our lifestyle, we did have good relationships with the families closest to us. We'd help other farmers buck hay bales when it was haying time, chase loose cattle if needed. Both Jack and Irene were sponges in learning the old Maori ways, many of them almost forgotten. In particular, Irene and I would visit the elder women, some of the last who still knew the old ways of Maori weaving. We learned to make Maori *ketes*, woven handbags. We learned how to safely strip the lace bark trees for its fine material for other more delicate weavings. They taught us where to find and how to prepare natural bush dyes. Back then, it was just part of our life. I practiced making *ketes*, thinking it might be a way to make money by selling them though I never got good enough or quick enough. Decades later, Irene, having embraced and learned the Maori ways well, though a *pakeha* or white man, was hired to teach these old methods to young Maoris who were reclaiming their heritage.

I helped to shear the sheep. I learned to spin wool, coming to love its rhythmic solitude and the magic of taking these fibers and turning them into yarn. I eventually built a loom across the space of my bed where, for almost a month, I had to climb into my bed over the end. I dyed the wool with bush dyes gathered from different barks and plants to give me golds and different shades of brown, and I wove a poncho that I have even today.

Days dripped into days, sped through weeks, became months, showing me spring, summer, and the colds of winter. Each day, each season, brought new things to learn, new challenges, new rhythms to embrace: the burgeoning outdoor activity of springtime and summer, the quiet nesting in the short cold days of winter, where weaving and knitting and reading trumped the days' hours.

One of my challenges during that time was to quit smoking cigarettes. Raised in a household hanging thick with secondary smoke, I began smoking at age fifteen. I'd struggled off and on through the years to quit. Besides its obvious health issues, being as strapped as I was for money, the last thing I needed to be spending money on was tobacco. Determined to quit, every time I had an urge to smoke, which was about every twenty minutes, I went outside with my ax and chopped four- to six-inch thick tea tree poles into sixteen-inch lengths for firewood. After three days, I had a good supply of firewood, and I no longer had the urge for a cigarette. I never smoked again.

Jack and Irene had a black lab mutt named Ratu that would keep me company until a neighbor gave me a little puppy of my own. I had her for about two months before I found her dead one morning. I never knew what killed her, but I was absolutely devastated when she died. I was shocked by how grieved I was. I sat on a hillside all day sobbing by myself, feeling so alone. One of my impenetrable walls had cracked, and for the first time, I fell through into a depth of loneliness I never before had experienced. I wasn't just mourning this puppy's brief life; I suddenly felt excruciatingly lonely. I remember it as clearly as if I were reliving it this very day because it was such an uncomfortable and unfamiliar feeling. Loneliness?

I took two trips on my own while I lived in Hokianga though I have little memory about why or where I was going. The first one was just days after losing this puppy. I know now, having learned many years later, that how I dealt with emotional pain was I traveled. Change your place. Go someplace new where you have to figure out where you're staying or how you're getting there or how to speak the language. Change of scenery, that's all it takes to remove any emotional burden whatsoever.

For whatever reason, I wrote little in my journals during the time I lived in New Zealand. The etching of the decades leaves me devoid of the finer details of that time. I hitchhiked to Auckland. There I got on a train to go south. I remember getting off the train about halfway to Wellington. This is what absolutely kills me is how spotty the memory is. A young man met me at the station; we rode on his motorcycle for thirty miles through frost-covered fields at sixty miles an hour toward the west coast somewhere. With all other details gone, the ghost of memory that remains is how freezing cold I was while scrunched up behind him in that early-morning cold. I can't remember where I went, why I went there, who he was, what we did, or when I returned. When I got back to my home though, I was no longer lonely or sad. Such was the power of travel to change my focus.

Another time, for some other reason that I also cannot remember, I set off hitchhiking again. This time I was picked up by two men whom I do remember, Michael King and Barry Barclay, with whom I got to explore quite a bit of the North Island, learning a plethora of information about Maoris as they were doing a documentary on Maori culture. Wherever it was I was going wasn't important that I arrived because I ended up traveling with Michael and Barry for more than a week. They had prearranged interviews set up in various Maori communities; I soaked it all in. The most poignant memory was while we were in a Maori pa, interviewing some elders, word arrived that someone had died, and we needed to leave. As they gathered up their video and recording equipment, women had already started arriving and were standing at the beginning of the path up to the pa. They'd begun keening. By the time we left, there were five or six women standing, wailing, the most eerie long-drawn-out peals of sorrow, a river of grief upon which the deceased could travel their last great journey.

Michael explained that as people arrived from all over, the women would stand in two lines and keen; the men would walk up to the pa between the wailing women. When everyone arrived, for three days, day and night, people would feast and eat, stand and tell stories of the deceased. After three days, their grief replaced with all the good stories and the soul of the deceased carried forth to the Maori gods, they would leave.

Just four years older than me, Michael was at the beginning of an illustrious and honored career as a historian in which he wrote or edited over thirty books during his lifetime. He was well known and respected for his knowledge of Maori history and culture even though he himself was a pakeha. Barry, part Maori and part white, was also at the beginning of his career as a New Zealand filmmaker. I didn't know I was traveling with such fame at the time. Once again, they were two wonderful gentlemen who took me under their wing for a bit and showed me more of New Zealand through the eyes of the Maori people.

The $100 I had earned long-lining lasted quite a while, almost a year. The only thing I really needed to buy was kerosene for my lantern, hard bar soap for laundry and washing, flour, and salt. I bought a five-gallon tin of black tea for $5. I also bought a five-gallon tin can of Manuka honey (from the tea tree) for $10. I was shocked to see that same honey now sells in health food stores of America for $30 for just a few ounces as it's being touted as having all sorts of health benefits, the most common being as an antibacterial agent that can treat wounds and burns. I ate it by the spoonful back then, going through five gallons in six months.

There was an elderly white man living alone in a rather rundown house on the adjoining property. The stream that bordered our two properties was filled with watercress, so I used to hike over there occasionally to gather it, which is how I finally met him when he approached me one day. He was unstable on his feet, walking with a cane across the uneven ground. After talking by the stream, he invited me back to his house. Though the house was rundown with cracked pink paint on the clapboard siding and old wooden windows that were difficult to open or close, the inside was neat and tidy. The wood floor appeared waxed and clean. It surprised me that he was such a very neat and tidy old man.

He fixed me a cup of tea, plying me with questions about where I'd come from, what I was doing, how I was living. And then he suggested that he'd like to have a companion accompany him on excursions in his car, and would I like to do that, and he'd pay me a bit for it. He was almost seventy years old, I'd say, and relatively frail. I really didn't have a lot of familiarity with being around old people, frail people, and that was my biggest concern, was that I felt awkward around him. More than the money, I acquiesced to accompany him as a way to see a bit more of the area.

Over several months, five or six times, I arrived at his house early, and we'd set off in his car. He had me drive, which made me a bit nervous because it's right-hand steering on the left-hand side of the roads down there. Further, I hadn't owned or driven a car since I left home at seventeen. When I had last lived in Honolulu, I rode a ten-speed all over town, obeying few traffic rules. But off we went. He had a map out on his lap and would direct me. I remember we ended up by bodies of water most times, places over on Hokianga Bay, near Kokukoku, and Panguru. We'd usually end up in some quiet isolated place.

I always felt a bit creeped out with this man whose name I can't even remember, but I felt he was harmless and really just craved the companionship. He was well read, and I remember we had very engaging conversations. I see in my mind's eye now, two people, an old lonely man and a now bush woman, having brisk conversation, sometimes outside, sometimes just sitting in the man's car, facing a bay with both doors wide open, often spending all day like that.

Sailors were always exchanging books, and I had while sailing read *Tropic of Cancer* and *Tropic of Capricorn*. On long rainy, stormy days that kept me in my thatched hut by the fire, I also read a lot. I specifically remember reading several Henry Miller books, specifically *Sexus*, *Nexus*, and *Plexus* there in New Zealand, and I was pondering, *Now, where did I get those books from?* As I started writing this book and referencing my time in Hokianga, speaking of the dark cold months of winter and the books I read, I start remembering these little things like this man of whom I had not thought even once in all these years.

I remembered that he'd lent them to me, and upon remembering that, all these memories popped back in about him, even down to the bit of discomfort I always felt around him. Though always the gentleman, I felt he was some closet pervert though he never did anything overt to prove out my thoughts. He'd bring a picnic; we'd eat, talk, and I'd drive back again. Then I wouldn't see him for a week or more, and then I'd return a book, borrow another, and then I'd drive him somewhere again. Then one day he wasn't there, and neither were his things. A neat, little old lonely man in a shambling pink house in the middle of a green New Zealand pasture by a year-round stream, paying me $5 each time to drive him around and be his companion, lending me books, sharing good conversation, and then he was gone, and no one knew to where or why. I originally wasn't going to write much about my time living in Hokianga, thinking it was just a slow-moving twenty-one months of my life where I lived in harmony with nature, and there was nothing that really happened. But out of the tickle of "where did I get that book?" memories like this have drifted back out of time's elusive grasp.

I had taken on the nickname of Patu shortly after I arrived there. Pronounced *pah'-tu*, in Maori it can generically mean a club or, as a verb, it can mean to beat, hit, strike, or subdue. I didn't learn until many years later that I had been a legend as "a kung fu American superwoman living in the bush like old-time Maoris. Stay away and respect her." Though I didn't have a big focus on having a boyfriend or man during my time there, I had always wondered why the handsome single young men never visited me. Hmm.

But my nickname also served me well. As my money was running out, one of our Maori neighbors whom I'd helped buck hay said he'd heard of a farmer four or five miles on the other side of Broadway who needed seven acres of tea tree cut. He chuckled, "There's two Kiwi blokes that started but couldn't finish it. I bet you can show them up, eh, Patu?"

Heck, yeah, I thought. *Of course. Why not?*

There being no phones, I rode a beautiful Morgan trotter the twenty miles to the farmer's property, carrying a bedroll and tarp, some flour and salt and a frying pan (for my daily meal of flat bread over a fire), an ax and slasher and a sharpener, prepared to go to work on the assumption I would be hired. After meeting the farmer, he said he'd give me a try, showed me where I could pitch the tent, what he wanted cut, and left me be. I slept in a lean-to on his land miles from nowhere. What I was cutting was a wall of secondary growth comprised of two- to six-inch thick tea tree trunks, sixteen to twenty feet tall, standing five to six inches apart. Tea tree, a hardwood and the source of that wonderful Manuka honey, is often the first secondary growth that comes in after a clear-cut.

I pitched a campsite and went to work. The slasher is wonderful instrument. On the end of a long thick handle is a twelve-inch blade slightly less curved than a half moon that's sharpened on both the inside curve and the outside curve. Each side had its purpose and advantage but worked well with most anything under two inches thick. The ax was for the rest.

I was steadily working, getting about an acre done a day. On the fourth day of working, the ax, which I kept sharp enough to shave the hair on my arms, slipped as I pulled it out of being wedged in a trunk, and it landed deep in my shin. I wrapped up my leg, got on my horse, and rode the four or five miles to Broadwood where Pole's sister, Wendy, also a schoolteacher and a young mother, lived. Being fifty to sixty miles from any type of medical care, she sewed me up with dental floss and an embroidery needle, and I went back to work.

Silly me, but blood poisoning set in the next day (why wouldn't it with the unsanitary conditions in which I was working and sweating away—oh, yes, and the method with which I'd sewed up the wound?), so back on the horse to Broadwood I rode where the secretary at the local school phoned a visiting nurse who drove miles out to administer me penicillin. After a course of penicillin and allowing the wound to heal properly, several weeks later, I went back and finished my job. Unbeknownst to me, though, the farmer—or nurse, somebody—had put in a workers' comp claim for the injury, and a month later, I received a $150 check for my time off work. So $49 for clear-cutting seven acres of hard tea tree plus $150, I was rich!

My mom came to visit me while I lived in Pawarenga on Jack and Irene's property. I hitchhiked to Auckland and met her at the airport. She rented a car and drove back up to Pawarenga and stayed for a few days. I come across pictures of her hauling bundles of firewood down the hill and of her sitting weaving fronds for something I was building. I have a picture of her in her bathrobe inside of my thatched hut, ready to go to sleep on my bed of sheepskins while I slept on sheepskins on the floor. What a trooper she was. She lived on the thirteenth floor of a condominium in Honolulu with wall-to-wall white carpets and a view of Diamond Head, but here she was appreciating my lifestyle—well, enduring it at any rate.

We eventually set off to explore New Zealand. In her rental car, we toured in comfort and with an open sense of adventure, winding our way along both sides of the north part of the North Island from the beauty of Hokianga Bay area of Kohukohu, across to Rawene, and out to Omapere, and then over to the Bay of Islands, and finding our way south through Auckland, Hamilton, Rotorua, Turangi, and down to Wellington. We took the Picton Ferry across to the South Island and carried on through Christchurch and eventually all the way down to Queenstown where, just to top off the luxury in which I was traveling with my mom, she bought tickets to fly into Milford Sound and stay at a then-remote hotel, accessible only by this plane. One more unique prize of the trip was that on the way there, the plane landed on a glacier where we ten passengers got to play until we tired.

Milford Sound is like the Norwegian fjords. Maybe even more breathtaking. When we checked into the historic isolated old hotel, the man in front of me turned out to be Daniel Ellsberg of the *Pentagon Paper* fame. Upon hearing his name, I said, "Are you *the* Daniel Ellsberg?"

And his reply was, "My God, even in the middle of nowhere I get no rest!" with a bit of a laugh.

I had actually been quite isolated from world news since I'd left the States in 1972. In fact, I didn't hear the whole story about Nixon and Watergate until years later when I returned to the States. Not being privy to the daily news stories as they unfolded, I didn't know much of the story until I watched *All the President's Men*. But I had heard of Daniel Ellsberg before I'd left. He was hero proportion, and there he stood before me. The next day, we found ourselves sharing the foredeck of a fjord boat cruising the sound. As we enjoyed the astounding beauty of Milford Sound, he offered me an open tin of little white pills. He leaned over and quietly said, "LSD?"

I looked at him quizzically as that was the last thing I would have expected him to say or do, and he nodded seriously. I took one. It was a super peppermint. His face broke with a relaxed laughter. Joke was on me. Good for him.

It was a good trip with my mother. Most of the trip was done on her terms in her style by car with comfortable hotels and good restaurants. I didn't complain as I did enjoy the luxuries while they lasted. Eventually we drove back up to Auckland, searching out any small places of interest we'd missed. After almost a month, my mom flew back to Hawai'i, to her white-carpeted condominium and her volunteer work at the Red Cross, and I hitchhiked back to my thatched hut, rustic lifestyle, and aloneness.

After my mother left, life returned to normal, continuing the daily tasks that revolved mostly around food production, working in the garden, milking, collecting eggs, heading to the coast, lying naked down on the river. I helped Jack shear his sheep. I spun more wool and knitted socks and hats. I decided I'd expand my little thatched hut and add on an extension where I would put my bed. I collected more tea tree poles and nikau fronds, weaving them into mats. When I had all the materials ready, I broke through a section of roof and extended out another A-frame structure. I was building a mansion for sure.

That year, there had been quite a drought that was affecting the cattle farmers. One young farmer, Monty, running a multigeneration family farm, was complaining about too many wild geese that were on his property, eating the precious grass his cattle and dairy cows needed. Though willing to kill them all, he invited us over to his farm to go on what was literally a wild-goose chase. It was a lot of work but an absolutely hilarious hoot chasing geese around his field. Jack and I eventually caught fourteen of them. Though it seemed cruel to me, we tied their feet together and then tied the feet of two birds together, and hung them over a long tea tree pole, one on each side. With the pole on each of our shoulders, we walked the six miles back to our property with fourteen geese hanging upside down over the pole—well over a hundred pounds' worth of weight. We put them in a pen until we had acclimated them to our property after which they were free to roam.

We had mail service. It was always a treat to get letters from home, from my mom most particularly as she conveyed the most news regularly. My older brother and his wife would write periodically, my brother often querying—teasing, criticizing(?), I'm not sure what—why I was living the lifestyle I was, and what was wrong with marriage and the great American dream? He gave me advice not to "get too far out there as it might be too hard to return to civilization."

I of course questioned at times why I was different, why I didn't want what everybody else wanted, what had made me so different. But I accepted what was logical, that there was no way I was born to pay bills and die. It terrified me to think of living like my brothers and the rest of the folks in the United States, working to get money instead of simply working for the basics needed of food and shelter. The longer I continued to live the alternate lifestyle I was living, the saner and more real it seemed to be to me, not my brothers' lifestyles. Now, forty-five years later, the environmental demise of this whole earth screams that we all, every one of us, need to return to a simpler way. Luckily for me, it continues to be a lifestyle I continued to embrace through the years.

I had had no interest to search out a relationship while I had been sailing though there had definitely been flirtations going on at times between a few of those handsome sailor boys. For me, at that time, I was only focused on the adventure, not on looking for a life mate. There were occasional visitors who would come, stay a few days or a week, and leave. Being in the same isolated living situation, Pole and I even attempted to establish a friendly mutual-satisfaction club, but we did not have the chemistry to make it work. I felt I had everything I had ever wanted. Though never a pressing thought, it did rest in the back of my mind that it would be wonderful to have a man to share my subsistence existence with. I figured it would happen when it happened, and I accepted that it obviously wasn't going to happen quickly, living in one of the more isolated parts of New Zealand in a thatched hut and with the name of Patu.

CHAPTER 2

*For far too long we have been seduced into walking a path that
did not lead us to ourselves. For far too long we have said yes
when we wanted to say no. And for far too long we have said no
when we desperately wanted to say yes . . . When we don't listen to
our intuition, we abandon our souls. And we abandon our souls
because we are afraid if we don't, others will abandon us.*

—Terry Tempest Williams

About a month after my mother left, I was surprised when I received a
letter from Dave, the man on *Paz del Mar* that had asked me to wait for him
in Tahiti. I can't remember how he made the connection, a friend of a friend
of a friend, but he had finally gotten my mother's address who forwarded
his letter to me. At this point, it had been two years since I'd last seen him
or had any contact with him. He was in Fiji at the time, after spending time
in Samoa and Wallis and Futuna. Besides a bubbling, cheerful catchup
of his travels, as our letters went back and forth, I became aware that he
was enamored with me, as archaic of a word that might be. At first, he
suggested he might send me money to catch a cruise ship back up to Fiji to
sail with him for a few months to see how we got along. For lack of money,
that idea fizzled out, and he eventually made plans to sail to New Zealand.

As I was saying, I wasn't really looking for a man, but it would be nice.
And here was someone actually chasing me across the Pacific.

We wrote each other three or four times a week. I had my little Olivetti
portable typewriter—having been typing since I was eight, a typewriter,

119

and now a laptop, was always an essential extension of my body. I typed on paper-thin aerograms, ending the letter only when I had squeezed every word onto every edge of the paper. Dave wrote funny letters on onion skin paper onto which he'd paste cutout photos from magazines and draw silly cartoons with expressive balloons. His letters tickled me. They made me laugh just as he had back in Atuona. We shared our thoughts and began formulating dreams.

Only looking back do I realize how completely out of touch I was with myself. Though believing I was content in myself, Dave's interest filled an empty place in my life. His letters filled me up. *That* was our courtship: two months of letter writing where thoughts and behaviors are manicured and presented in their best possible light, with no faults or arguments capable of being revealed. Somewhere in that process, I convinced myself we had fallen in love. Back and forth, back and forth until his last letter was sent from Fiji saying he was setting sail and he expected to be in Paihia, Bay of Islands, by June 3. He said he'd contact me when he arrived.

I didn't wait for him to contact me mostly because I couldn't figure out how that would occur. We had no telephone. Most of the community had no electricity. I decided to hitchhike over and meet him, knowing full well that any prediction of the arrival of a sailboat was completely up to the weather and wind. It took me almost eight hours to get there. I walked halfway to Broadwood before I finally got picked up and got into Broadwood. I walked several miles out of Broadwood before a semitruck picked me up and got me to Mangamuka. Whenever I hear a semi shifting gears from a dead stop, my memory often goes to that truck decades earlier as I remember the driver showed me in the intricacies of the layers of shifting.

A middle-aged businessman finally picked me up and took me to Paihia. After actually driving me down to the harbor to see if Dave's boat had in fact arrived, which it hadn't, he offered to let me stay in his small apartment. He seemed genuinely nice. I accepted. He took me out for some fish and chips, and then, returning to his apartment, we chatted for a while. As trusting as I was, I was a bit shocked when he made his advances. I let him know I wasn't interested, that I was there specifically to meet up with my boyfriend. I ended up having to actually push him away. Because I was the type of girl who would be hitchhiking, he figured I would be receptive to his advances. He said that. What gives men the right to think that way? I almost left to sleep somewhere in the darkness. I was feeling a bit stupid to have assumed Dave would actually arrive when he said he would and that I might in fact be in a bit of a predicament as to sleeping arrangements, but the man got his head back together and left me alone the rest of the evening and was quite apologetic the next morning.

In the morning, I walked down to the harbor and, amazingly, there was Dave's boat at anchor. I hooted and yelled from shore, and finally hearing me, he rowed in to get me. What should have been a happy greeting was in fact a criticism that I had come to meet him, "I told you I'd contact you when I got here. Why are you here?"

I shrugged this off because of my excitement of seeing him. In fact, the timing had worked out perfectly, and because I knew, as I explained to him, there would have been virtually no way for him to get in touch with me, and it would have been difficult for him to find his way to Pawarenga without my help, I had decided to risk coming anyhow. His response should have been a red flag, but I never saw it.

His boat was a mess. We spent two days cleaning it and making order of it before setting out to hitchhike back to my hut, which I was excited to share with him. We got his dinghy safely stored and headed up to the main road where Dave proceeded to put his bag down and sit. I said, "What are you doing?"

He replied, "Well, I'm waiting for a car. You don't think we'll walk the whole way, do you?"

Though it had taken me a whole day to hitchhike there—it was only fifty-five miles away by the shortest route—I was a bit taken aback because I would never consider just sitting by the side of the road waiting for someone to pick me up. At least make an effort, I think, and hope that in fact we don't have to walk fifty-five miles. But I sat down next to him and put my thumb out when cars drove by.

We made it to Broadwood by midafternoon. I informed him that my house was fourteen miles from there, and it was a crapshoot as to whether in fact a car might drive by as there weren't many cars that drove the road to Pawarenga. We began walking down Pawarenga Road with Dave grumbling off and on and not being particularly interested in the things I was pointing out. Luck would have it though, that Monty, from the wild-goose chase, came jaunting down the road in his old truck. He ended up giving us a ride the rest of the way.

I see everything now so much more clearly than I saw it forty-five years ago, though back then, my brain never processed it. I had worn an armor of strength since early childhood to protect me, wrapped in a myth that had served me well, but at this point, having dreamed myself into some idealized romantic relationship, my armor failed. All through my correspondence with Dave, I had been working under the assumption that he was coming to New Zealand to live there with me, to be part of Jack and Irene's little commune, as free of the capitalistic world of money as possible. I had adopted this lifestyle with zeal. Though Dave was definitely not attached to the moneymaking lifestyle, he was not enamored with my subsistence lifestyle at all. Though we talked briefly about building a bigger and better house than what I was living in, Dave eventually made it clear he had no enthusiasm for any of what I was doing. It all involved more work than he was willing to put into it. He thought Jack's no-machinery rule was ridiculous. It became clear that Dave was unwilling to abide by any other man's rules. The weather was harsh; it was too cold. He wanted to sail away, and he eventually convinced me to leave.

When I began writing this travelogue, what leapt to the forefront of my memories were only the beautiful stories, the adventurous stories, the big picture. I was a dancing dandelion seed puff, blowing with the wind, up, up, dipping down, free as could be. The world was mine. I was confident, fearless, focused, and excited about whatever came my way. I was on a continuous adventure of my choosing to go where I wanted, stay, move on, change course.

Then the wind-blown seed got snagged in a bush, stuck, attached to something, someone—stuck.

Decades later, again living alone, not answering to anyone, I can easily feel into the memories of living in Pawarenga, feeling my contentment in being alone and having a sense of being complete. "I had had everything I wanted living in New Zealand except a man to share it with." That is a statement I've shared with many people when I tell my tales. I just would have liked to have had a man to share in the adventure of subsistence farming, living in a thatched hut, growing, harvesting, hunting our food. I had thought that's why Dave was coming to New Zealand.

As Kierkegaard wrote, "Life can only be understood backwards, but it must be lived forwards." I had no understanding of it at the time, but I suffered from (I believe)—and still suffer from (I believe)—a reactive attachment disorder that made it difficult to have healthy relationships. I'd successfully masked any of its symptoms because of my traveling lifestyle. I had so many of the classic symptoms of detachment (oh, so strong and independent), withdrawal from connections (my solitude was the only place I was content), inability to maintain relationships (fleeting, short-lived boyfriends for years), inability to show affection, resistance to giving or receiving love despite craving it, control and anger issues, and inability to really grasp emotions, *and* a tendency to cling to the first person who showed attention. Hmm.

From the moment I met Dave in Paihia, I was aware of but did not heed that we differed in our approach to the world. I embraced working hard for what I wanted; Dave did not have the same work ethic. I often believed he felt the world owed him, that his job was simply to receive. I did not or could not heed the growing awareness that we were puzzle pieces that belonged to different puzzles, and no matter how hard we tried, we'd never be able to put the pieces together to make the picture on my box—nor the picture he wanted.

Dave wanted to have children. He was obsessed with family. That was his purpose in life, it seemed. I had never had any desire to have children. I'm devoid of many concrete memories of the months Dave spent in New Zealand before we finally left. I physically *feel* today, writing this, the thick wall that encased those emotions that were pounding, leaping up, and screaming—but not heeded: "I don't want to have children. I don't want to leave New Zealand and my lifestyle here. I don't want the same things you want."

I was deaf to those silent cries. Within a month, it was clear he didn't want to stay there, and though these memories are rooted in me that I didn't want what he wanted, he convinced me I should leave with him. It was almost like it was a foregone conclusion, and there was nothing to discuss. It was like I was sleepwalking.

If I had been the outsider looking in, I would have said, "Wake up, woman. What the hell do you think you're doing? You don't want to sail away with this man."

And yet I did. I acquiesced like my mother had acquiesced to my father's dictates. In spite of the thousands of miles sailed, I had not escaped my dysfunctional upbringing. I was making a man the center of my life, following *his* decisions, *his* dictates, *his* wants, and not listening to mine at all. I bounced against this wall I'd constructed, silently screaming at myself to just say it, just speak it, just let my feelings be known. I didn't. Give me a hurricane to live through, put my life in physical danger, but when it comes to me simply saying, "No, that's not what I want to do," I couldn't do it.

I thought of an Emerson quote I'd read when I was sixteen: "Every man alone is sincere. At the entrance of a second person, hypocrisy begins. We parry and fend the approach of our fellow man by compliments, by gossip, by amusements, by affairs. We cover up our thought from him under a hundred folds."

When I'd sailed from Hawai'i in my solitariness, in my aloneness, I'd touched a sense of power, and a momentum developed that propelled me forth. I'd found a place of belonging that made me feel complete while being alone. I did not know I needed to remain alone to hold on to my wholeness and maintain my sincerity. After all, they, as well as all of society, all of nature, suggested that I must partner, but my parents never taught me the basics of making that successful. What they taught me was I'm not loveable. But ha! They were wrong: Dave loved me!

Reading the synopsis of novels, it seems they invariably revolve around discovering a family secret. It was a decade later before I learned my family secret, that ah-ha that brought into focus why I was who I was, why I pursued the freedom of travel, why I would not, in fact, listen to my gut and express the feelings that were screaming to be expressed. In my thirties, my mother finally shared the truth of my first six weeks of my life. "You know," she started, "a nanny was in charge of you when you were first born. I didn't hold you for the first six weeks of your life."

"What? Why not?" I asked. I remember exactly where I was sitting, at the table in the house on Second Street in Oregon City. "Why not?" I asked again. I remember exactly the feeling that gripped me.

My mother was visiting, and why she decided out of the blue to start talking about this subject I don't know other than her conscience must have been bothering her. "Your father felt that you should have a nanny take care of you."

"Why? Was something wrong with you?"

"No," my mother responded, "your father felt it was best. He wanted to establish a routine with you where you'd sleep all night right away and learn to not be a fussy child."

A knowing settled in as the screenplay of my birth took form through her telling: Just as we paint pictures in our mind of words we read on a page, through her telling, I saw my mother in labor, waiting by a door. I don't know that this is at all what happened, but in that knowing, this is the scene that played across my mind's eye. Though dressed warmly against the cold December morning, her coat would not close over her gravid belly. She waited while her husband, my father, spoke to the nanny. Dressed in his signature clip-on bow tie, brown tweed sports jacket over which he wore a wool trench coat, he stood before the nanny with his worn brown briefcase in his left hand as he addressed her briefly, "You will be able to reach me at my office though I will be teaching classes most the day, but my secretary should be there. I will call you or inform you of the birth when I know such information. In the meantime, you're now familiar with Robbie's routine, so . . ." He trailed off as he himself was not that familiar with his one-and-a-half-year-old's routine as that was not his domain.

The nanny, Mrs. O'Malley, stood stiffly and respectfully before my father. Her tightly permed gray hair was trapped lightly under a hairnet. Plump, her bosom rested on the belly bulging out from her dark blue tiny-flowered dress; the beginning of jowls blended with her double chin, which wiggled ever so slightly when she spoke. "I have the bassinet ready in my quarters. I believe I am prepared."

Her quarters was a small room near the back of the house, off the kitchen. At the turn of the century, it too was the servant's quarters.

The exchange was short as my father needed to get to Johns Hopkins to teach his graduate class in physiological psychology. He was feeling rushed, not knowing how long it would take to drop his wife off at the hospital and get her situated. He turned toward my mother waiting at the door; she bent her knees slightly to pick up her small suitcase. "Tell Robbie I'll be home soon with a baby brother or baby sister," she said.

Mrs. O'Malley just nodded, not altering her stern gaze that was critical that my father did not take the suitcase from the missus as a gentleman should.

My mother hid her dislike for the woman, a woman her husband had chosen to help out. My father held open the door as my mother waddled out.

They were not far from the hospital, a ten-minute drive and on the way to the university. He parked in front and walked my mother to the front desk, informing them that she was in labor. The nurse in her starched uniform and nurse's cap pinned to her short curled hair called for an orderly to bring a wheelchair. My father kept checking his watch. It was almost seven-thirty; his first class started at eight, and he still needed to park and get to his lecture hall. As soon as the wheelchair arrived and my mom was situated in it, he perfunctorily gave her a quick kiss on the cheek and said, "I'll try to call and check in during a break," and he left in their green '48 Studebaker.

Situated in a room with three other women in different stages of labor, with the help of the orderly, my mother put away her belongings in a small dresser, put on her nightgown, and reclined in her bed for the long wait. When the labor began to become too uncomfortable around noon, a nurse gave her some pain meds to keep her comfortable. A bit later, they gave her more, putting her into the twilight sleep of childbirth still prevalent in 1949.

My mother told me she doesn't remember anything about my actual birth. I swear that I do though anyone would argue it's just my vivid imagination. As my mother tells me her side of the story of my birth, I feel the pressure of me squeezing down that dark, dark birth canal. And then I see a flashing view of a dark head crowning, then breaking free with hands wrenching and tugging at the cord wrapped around the baby's neck. Another brief flash of the cord smashing the nose as it's pulled over my scrunched-up, angry newborn's face. Another flashed image, the head is manipulated, twisted slightly, and suddenly the body plops out. A masked and robed doctor grabs the baby by the feet, lifting it up, and spanks it hard on its slimy red bottom.

I relive my entry into the world. Though sluggish from the morphine that had just moments before flowed through my veins, my hands jerk out, reaching, clawing for some sort of security before I'm suddenly wrapped tightly where then I can't move at all, not even a little bit. Trapped.

My mother sleeps after my birth, still heavily drugged. Eventually, she's wheeled back into her room where two of the other three women are also sleeping off their morphine and scopolamine deliveries. I see my baby body be wheeled into a glassed-in nursery with bright lights glaring, and slowly—my imagination now really filling in the blanks—I hear loud screams filling the room, screams of babies wanting comfort and love and food.

In the darkness of the theater of my birth, where imagination can make anything happen, I watch a baby's spirit hover over its body, wondering if she really wanted to drop into it and reside and take on that life's existence. Through her eyes, I watch a man walk down the hall, approaching a long glass window that looks into the nursery. His eyes finally catch the name tag, "Snow Girl," and come to rest on the baby lying screaming, red in the face, in the bassinet. I see myself as that baby seeing the fear in my father's face, not the fear that comes with bodily harm, but the kind of fear that comes from the heart. I saw the heart of this man who knew he didn't have any love to give.

Sitting in the darkness of my mother's truth finally being revealed, finally filling in the cracks and crevices of my life, I ache and cry for that baby as my first six weeks pass in which my mother never came to my cries. I see me being brought home and handed over to stern Mrs. O'Malley. The learned psychologist, believing in the theories of B. F. Skinner, had ordered Mrs. O'Malley not to spoil that baby, me. He admonished his wife, my mother, not to interfere with Mrs. O'Malley. My mother obeyed him. I see Mrs. O'Malley keeping the door closed to my mother. "On the dot of eight, noon, four, and eight, you shall feed her, change her, and put her down. Do not coddle her."

Mrs. O'Malley complied. Neither my mother nor father—nor Mrs. O'Malley—held me or loved me for those first six weeks.

My mother finished telling me the story by saying, "You screamed nonstop for six weeks. And," she added, "you never stopped screaming."

"Well, what do you think, Mom? What did you think my reaction would be when my own mother didn't hold me?"

She apologized of course. I felt she needed to apologize for her whole life though for never ever standing up to my father, for never standing up for me. But I finally understood a lot about my life and the decisions I'd made—or not been able to make.

At that point in time, in New Zealand, I didn't know this story of abandonment. I had no insight into why sailing the ocean had become such a magnet for me or why living in my thatched hut in Pawarenga had attracted me. I leaned toward and craved simplicity, I think, because I felt that striving for things—education, money, houses, possessions, all the things my parents had had—is what steals away the heart. I had a smoldering belief that if people lived simply in a gatherer's society that everyone would work together, that family could remain strong. I had no understanding of my inability to know my own feelings or understand why I couldn't hear or heed my heart's demands.

Of course, it's all much more complex than that. Each person's life is much more complex than that. Perspectives change too, determined by what we want and what we don't have. We move toward what we think we want—the freedom of sailing, the quiet life of subsistence living—not knowing we're trying to put the pieces of multiple puzzles together into one picture. Exactly how many different puzzles had been thrown together in this box called life?

I spent years trying to fit Dave's blue sky into my blue ocean. It was decades before I realized too many puzzles were jumbled together, and I started tossing out the pieces that didn't fit into my picture. And then as pieces like those containing the nanny and my absent mother were brought out of a completely hidden puzzle box, my own completed picture began to come into view, helping me to make sense of that fateful time in New Zealand when I should have said no but I didn't know how.

I was born five years too early for my father to have learned the now-renowned wire monkey/cloth monkey, maternal separation, dependency needs, and isolation experiments of Harry Harlow, which concluded that babies need love and soft tactual contact to thrive. Acknowledging this deep sense of abandonment at birth helped explain my complete inability at that moment in my life to tell Dave no, that I didn't want the things he wanted. He had chased me across the Pacific. How could I tell him I didn't want to leave with him? Being well trained from birth—I was responsible for my father's anger and my mother's tears of course—I felt more responsible for his feelings than my own. The message I received as a baby and for the subsequent years of hearing angry, hateful fights in my household was clear that I was not worthy. But my gosh, here is someone who loves me! I'd better grab hold of this and cling tight. It's irrelevant what I feel.

One other issue that took a bit of time to resolve before we sailed away was that six months after I'd arrived in New Zealand, my visa was going to expire. Into the alternative hippie community, word went out in search of someone who might want to marry me. A friend of a friend of a friend stepped forth, and we were married before a justice in an unremembered small town. What I do remember is I didn't even know his last name when we walked up the courthouse steps. We kissed like newlyweds and then parted, and I had had no contact with him since. But Dave needed me to divorce him, so the search began. Because divorce in New Zealand really took a toll on the man in my perception, forcing him to give up three-fourths of his earnings to his ex-wife, my "husband" Bill was not coming forth. I told friends to tell friends to tell friends that I wanted nothing from him, just a divorce. Eventually he was found, and I paid an attorney to draw up divorce papers.

Two years after arriving in New Zealand, I bade farewell to Jack and Irene, to Pole, and his sister Wendy. Dave and I hitchhiked back to Paihia. We had almost no money at that point, but Dave was able to procure some work at a boat repair haul-out facility for a couple weeks. I spent most of my time on the boat with no means of heating it in the bleak New Zealand winter while he worked.

I started writing in a new journal again. In the very first pages of the new book, I reflect on whether I had made the right decision, even then not being able to be completely honest with my feelings. I recognized that Dave and I had little in common. They were big things, too. It wasn't at all his intent to live in a thatched hut and slosh through mud in the breaking dawn to milk a cow in order to have milk with his morning tea or to bathe in the cold river running past my house. I wanted to stay in my thatched hut subsistence farming and had wanted him to share that with me; he wanted to sail back to the South Pacific. I believed in walking and making an effort; I believed he felt that others would take care of him. He wanted children; I had no big maternal urge whatsoever. Just as Jackson and Annie had their agendas, Dave's agenda was to take me away with him, sailing back north to the warm South Pacific waters. We had not had a meeting of the minds from the very start. Though I actually sought the advice of Jack and Irene, Pole, and Wendy, I ultimately did not heed it.

When I'd first set foot on New Zealand soil, I never conceived that I'd end up living the lifestyle that I had for twenty-one months. My plans had been to work and earn money, find another sailboat, and keep sailing. But I came to rest and was sincerely satisfied and so content that I never conceived that I'd ever leave. But the one constant in life is everything changes; nothing stays the same.

We—Dave and I—left Opua, New Zealand, to sail north on August 21, 1974, away from my thatched hut and a lifestyle I'd lived for short of two years. Though I enjoyed living by myself, the truth is I also had an equally strong call to return to a sailor's life. Sailing had brought me to Hokianga; it had deposited me on the shores of New Zealand to have had the rustic survival experiences I'd enjoyed. It beckoned me with more lessons to learn. It was the echo of the sea, of both the tumultuous power as well as the serenity of the ocean that called me back and completely overshadowed any of the forewarnings and storm flags. Though courageous in the face of the worst storm, I had no ability at that point in my life to stand up for myself.

Buoyant and bubbling memories pushed and shoved away doubts. Even forty-five years later, the days and weeks where my spirit inhabited a time-space continuum that held no thoughts or judgments, no worries, no future, no past, these memories are part of my soul. To this day, just the thought of sailing returns me to the experience of the sea touching the horizon, blending with the sky to become one. How could I resist that?

PART III

CHAPTER 1

Life is a succession of lessons which must be lived to be understood.
—Helen Keller

After a day of motoring out of Opua in the Bay of Islands into a calm, windless sea, the slight breeze picked up enough for us to set the sails and turn off the engine and fall into silence, the only sound being the hull sibilantly slicing through the still ocean. Out of sight of land, in that silence, I resided briefly in the thought that, yes, I had made the right decision. Again, my ego quickly diminished to an unseeable speck. To feel so at peace with such a sense of diminutive existence for me was and is bliss. It's a state of consciousness that's easily maintained for many long hours under sail. All doubts caught the breeze and gently flew away.

During the idle days of watching the sea, the waves, the clouds, the horizon, and reading the pilot book, we decided we'd try to sail for the island of Walpole, a small and uninhabited French island, 180 kilometers east of New Caledonia in the South Pacific. Although it is geographically part of the Loyalty Islands, administratively it belongs to the Île des Pins municipality of New Caledonia. British Captain Butler discovered the island in 1794 and named it after his ship *Walpole*. The island had been inhabited in the past, but in modern times (up to this writing), it was only visited by scientific naturalist research missions. Though uninhabited islands were on our sights to visit, upon arriving, it usually became clear as to why they had remained uninhabited.

It was the night of September 1 that we figured we should spot Walpole the next morning. We had a nice southwest breeze blowing and were gently moving along at 2.5–3 knots (3 knots is 3.45 miles an hour). The sky was brilliant with stars in spite of the full moon. Dave slept out on deck to be extra safe.

The Westward Ho had been the only sailboat on which we actually stood watch all the time. On all other boats, we stood watch only if we were near shipping lanes or close enough to landfall that there would be more chance of running into other vessels or the chance of hitting a reef or land. Standing night watch was torturous, always a struggle to stay awake because the movement of the boat itself was a rocking cradle's, constantly beckoning you to dreamland.

We didn't steer the boat by hand unless we were maneuvering through a pass or close to land masses in which we were needing to make quick changes in direction. The tiller was tied off and the sails were set, which kept the boat steering on that course in relationship to the direction of the wind. At night, we'd go below and sleep. Though there were two berths in the bow of the boat, each night, we would drop the table down to rest on supports between the two settee seats, pull the cushions down to make a full mattress in the space, and throw a sheet on it. We kept a compass by our head that, if we awoke in the night, we'd check to see if we were still on the course we meant to be on. If the wind had shifted, one or both of us would go topside and reset the sails to bring us back to our desired course. In the cockpit at night, on the moonlit globe of the sea, you see nothing but the expanse; you hear nothing but the lap of water against the hull or the sound of an occasional wave gently cresting on its own in the distance. It's the silence of three crickets in a field or the whisper of a breeze in pine needles at night. It's a sight of no depth, just the bare curved line of the earth touching the sky. Oh, what beautiful bliss.

Upon awakening at 7:00 a.m., there sat Walpole on the near horizon about twelve miles to the southwest of us. Dave had already reset the sails as close as possible into the direction of the wind, which was blowing directly from Walpole. Somehow, we'd passed it to the west during the night though we'd been steering well northeast. Pilot books also set forth information about ocean currents. As there was no notation of strong currents in the area, we were a little baffled as to why we'd missed the island by such a distance. We would probably end up sailing five times that twelve miles just tacking, zigzagging, back and forth to get back there. The sigh of sailing.

While tacking back toward Walpole, we had the diversion of catching our first fish since leaving New Zealand, a barracuda. Though our boat was well stocked with staples, fresh fish was always a treat. We were stocked at all times with months' worth of dried beans and rice, canned butter, and canned cheese (the brand name of both spelled with a capital *Y* for *Yuk*). We always left port with lots of onions, garlic, and fresh limes or lemons, which kept well. Cabbage kept well under a wet burlap sack in the shade on the deck, but most other fresh food products didn't survive the heat and humidity for long without refrigeration, which we did not have. We had alfalfa seeds and mung beans, and usually had four jars at different stages of sprout, so that provided a fresh green sprout salad most days.

Also, when we first left a port, if they were available, we'd get the freshest eggs we could—sometimes going directly to the egg farm—and Vaseline each egg thoroughly, sealing its pores. This would keep the egg fresh much longer in the ninety- to hundred-degree heat below decks on the boat. After two weeks, I'd start floating the eggs before I cooked them. Most of them at that point would still sit on the bottom of the bowl of water but on their pointed ends. Once they were floating more than halfway to the top, they were tossed overboard to float or sink.

But catching a fresh fish was always a treat. We would eat as much of it fresh as we could: a little sashimi dipped in wasabi and soy, sautéing some and cutting up enough to fill a stew pot and cook. What couldn't be cooked we started to slice as thinly as possible and laid the strips out on old stove racks we'd accumulated to be used as drying racks. When finally dried as tough as beef jerky, we'd store them in gallon containers. The absolute best way to eat it, rather than just chewing it like beef jerky or reconstituting it in a stewlike mixture, was to fry it quickly in oil. In just a few quick minutes, it was done and had the texture, if not quite the taste, of fresh crisp bacon, barely tasting like fish.

While filleting and slicing and cooking the barracuda, we continued on our long tack for Walpole. The sky was blue; it was sunny and warm. Finally, at sundown, we tacked and settled in to stand yet another night of watch. I took first watch and thought I'd be a martyr and stand at least until 2:00 a.m. I managed to while away three hours, finishing reading *Memoirs of a Shy Pornographer* by the light of the moon and the kerosene night lantern (which served as our running lights to give other vessels a hint of our presence). Today, forty-five years later, I have no memory of the book, and I actually had to Google it, wondering if I was truly reading a pornographic novel while trying to stay awake in our attempt to reach Walpole Island.

As with most islands, there are often layers of feeding banks near the land where fish are more abundant. Our two fish lines were eighth-inch heavy test line with a four-inch hook nestled into a beveled wedge of white plastic tube that served as the lure. Nothing fancy but certainly efficient. As on *Serenade*, near its attachment to our poop-deck railings, we inserted a two-foot-long length of surgical tubing and a bell. The surgical tubing would take up the immediate tug of a striking fish, ringing the bell. We always kept leather gloves tucked safely in the cockpit to quickly grab, put on, and start hauling in the fighting fish.

An hour after Dave relieved my midnight watch, Dave woke me up to announce he'd just caught a twenty-five-pound yellow-fin tuna. I'm not sure why he had to wake me to tell me as it would have to wait till morning to be filleted, cooked, and/or sliced to dry. With two big fish in a row, it was time to pull in our lines and quit fishing.

At seven, a full twenty-four hours after first seeing Walpole twelve miles away, it was time to tack again. Another brilliant sunny day. The blue of the sky sought its union with the edge of the sea but could not completely conquer it as the sea grabbed and stole its light, taking it deeper, leaving the sea a shade richer. It took us most of the day to get within two miles of Walpole at which time we finally started up the old chugging engine to motor-sail in. I hate engines. I hate the sound, and most particularly, I hate the smell of the diesel. But I also wanted to get to this elusive island.

As we approached Walpole, Dave was up in the rigging looking for rocks or dangers. On the tiller, I was more nervous about our predicament than I had ever experienced in my thousands of miles of sailing. Looking for an anchorage as described in the pilot book, we were approaching a sheer 300-foot-tall wall of rock being pummeled violently by waves. We were only a football field away from these cliffs, motoring in slowly with Dave in the rigging.

We finally spotted the place marked on the chart as the only anchorage available, a recess in the sheer cliffs above which stood the skeletal wooden-framed remains of several houses or sheds. Coming closer, we saw the remains of a wharf: several posts embedded in the lava rock at the base of the cliffs. No shore or beach or anything that appeared reasonable for landing a dinghy. No one was standing onshore to greet us as they would on any inhabited island. The last time the island was inhabited, according to the pilot book, was 1945—maybe just a war-time outlook. A very lonely outlook for sure, certainly not a prosperous or inviting place to entice anyone to stay.

But the pilot book, our Bible at sea, said, "This is the anchorage." At some point, the engine was put in neutral and we were just ghosting forward on momentum. Though the sails were still set, they hung empty in the lee of the cliffs where the wind didn't blow. In the lee of the cliffs, we were drifting, drifting toward a lava rock wall heaving up out of the dark waters of the sea. The engine was chugging quietly (still in neutral) while Dave, down from the rigging now, up on the bow, was throwing a lead line, searching for a depth in which to anchor. "We're getting too close. Do you want me to turn?" I yell from the cockpit.

Dave, dropping the lead line again, yelled back, "I'll tell you when to put the tiller hard over."

I could feel his tension. So I was waiting and waiting, my stomach spinning, my teeth gritting. Pulling in the lead line, he again sent it flying. And again.

The black cliff loomed out of the sea. The sea water was still deep blue, not the lighter blue that comes with anchorages. Finally, out of my own nervousness, feeling in my gut the lead line would not find ground, I put the tiller hard over. No response. Just as that reality sunk into my stomach with a gripping terror, Dave yelled at me, "Put the tiller hard over!"

Not seeing the bow swing, he turned to ensure I'd done it, and I shrugged my hands in a sign of helplessness. "It is hard over! But it's not responding."

My eyes were on the cliffs. He suddenly screamed, "The engine!" which we both had forgotten was in neutral. I was frozen. I didn't know whether to put the engine forward or reverse because I didn't know nor did I want the responsibility for deciding whether there was enough room for us to make the turn going forward. But Dave, flying back to the cockpit, slammed it into forward, and with the tiller still hard over, we made the turn and cleared the cliffs by a matter of yards.

Dave started screaming at me, "Why didn't you tell me the tiller was hard over?"

I don't do well when people scream at me; too many years of watching my father rage at my mother often culminating in my mother's black eyes. Nothing I said would have ameliorated the adrenaline rush of the near-miss that fed his angry outburst. The issue wasn't what I did or when I did it but the fact that we'd almost wrecked the boat on a rocky isolated, remote island in the middle of nowhere where no one would have probably ever found us because it is not an island anyone goes to and because we never quite knew where we were going so our destination was unknown.

We did find another spot to drop the anchor a little way farther down. Dave threw in the hook, and we dropped all the sails. I sat nervously thinking it was just all much too scary, all too precarious of an anchorage. Thousands of frigate birds drifted on the up-currents of the wind near the cliffs. I watched while fully aware of my nervousness about the anchorage. After a short and reasonable discussion, the engine was turned on, the anchor came up again, and we pushed out away from the lee of the island to catch the edge of the breeze. With a warm breeze over our shoulder, we set the sails to pick up that southwest-southerly wind. Cutting the engine left us again in the silence of only the hull caressing the water as we sailed into a truly majestic sunset, almost a gift prize for making the good effort. We left Walpole for someone else to visit—maybe just the naturalists' research missions.

We came. We left. We never made landfall.

With no need to stand watch as we sailed well away from the cliffs of Walpole, we dropped the table and made up our sleeping berth. Unless it became an ordeal like our attempt to reach Walpole, we would head to New Caledonia. The weather for the following days was glorious, each morning breaking sunny and blue. At that moment, I was indeed happy to have given up the wet, cold gray winter in New Zealand. At that moment, I had no regrets.

After three crossings from Hawai'i to the mainland States and then many thousands of miles sailed from Hawai'i through the Marquesas, Society Islands, Cook Islands, Fiji, Samoa, Tonga, and others, I had never learned to navigate. I hadn't had a reason to. This time, though, the need to learn navigation was truly a matter of life and death. For the first time, there were only two of us on board, and if something were to happen to Dave, whether it be sickness or the eternal swim, I would need to bring the vessel into port. Of course, in this day and age, forty-plus years later, few sailors know how to navigate with a sextant and plot it on a chart; they all use GPS, never conceiving that the world of electronics could end with a massive solar flare or equipment malfunction.

It took me two days to be confident with the sextant and plot the course. Dave commended me that indeed I had learned well. Thankfully. I dead reckoned that we were a little too far north of the Havannah entrance, so we altered course to 250 and sailed along on a good beam reach. My first shot with the sextant put us about twenty miles off of Dave's, almost at Mare Island, Loyalties. The noon sight should have put us off of Pine Island though it was an hour later before we saw land, but absolutely nothing appeared to be Pine Island according to descriptions and drawings in the pilot book. Two more sights later—we were sure the sights were good—brought the troubling thought that something was seriously wrong with our navigation. We knew there was land ahead, but the descriptions in the pilot book didn't coincide with any of it.

Dave got irritated and frustrated that the sights weren't plotting properly. Neither of us could understand why his navigation was off. I couldn't give him the answer—yet—as I was only just learning to navigate. But I decided to work out the noon sights for the day before and the day after, and that's when I discovered that we'd been working out the sights on the wrong day ever since crossing the date line. We were working our sights for a day ahead. Jeez. How Dave had gotten to New Zealand was *mmm*. Being a day off only puts you off twenty miles. Oh, well, twenty miles just means a reef or an island to run into. No biggy. Twenty miles off is why we almost missed Walpole.

Having discovered the problem, we saw all points began to line up—Cape Queen Charlotte and Guemba Peak and Junie Island and Ven

Island—and the reality that we would be reaching Havannah Passage at about ten o'clock. In the night.

For all the storms I'd sailed through, I was cognizant that I was very nervous about going in at dark. Dave was optimistically cool and confident. I tried to feed on Dave's confidence as the *Paz del Mar* moved through the black waters toward the range lights that we could see fifteen to twenty miles away. The moon came up no longer full but still generously sharing its light, reflecting off the ocean, providing a smudge of a shadow of the land, giving me a bit more confidence. The three range lights, though far away, were easy to line up, the Port Yati light coming in clearly. As we neared the pass, it became evident that we had a flood tide with us, luckily because otherwise, even with the engine throbbing, we would have made no headway against a four- or five-knot ebb tide.

We were moving fast, making twelve or thirteen miles in an hour, which was astounding for the pudgy *Paz del Mar*, which would peak at about five knots tops. The flood tide pulled us along as the sea rushed to fill the reef-encircled lagoons and inlets. The sound of the water on the hull was transformed into a strange rushing sound that I'd never heard in all my years of sailing; not the normal sound of water against bow but just the sound of a lot of water reverberating from all directions, like thousands of little voices tickling the hull. A running swell made it hard to steer with the flood tide angling counter to the range lights. It required physical work and mental concentration to stay lined up with the lights to keep us in the channel. I was steering most of the time while Dave peered through the binoculars and took sightings on the lights and islands. No highway markers, no streetlights. Not too unlike the disorienting experience of driving at night in the streaming white blur of a snowstorm with the snow burying center lines, fog lines, and other highway markings. It was reassuring when a small tanker passed us, hinting there was a plenty wide channel.

We had only the stars in the sky, a waning moon, and three range lights to keep in line as we whooshed through the darkness under the ghost of sails and a throbbing engine. When Dave would take over steering, I'd be making coffee or reading the pilot book concerning the passage, looking for any descriptions that might help let us know exactly where we might be and where our hoped-for anchorage was. I reassured myself that the almost-full moon provided enough light. We could see the breakers and the cliffs pretty well as we moved through the passage even without binoculars though distances were what was deceptive. I knew our anchorage was still somewhere past those range lights.

Our navigation was left completely up to our eyes and clock, compass and pilot book. The book said there was supposed to be a light around the corner, pointing out the end of a drying reef, and a light on the opposite side of Prony Bay. We could see what looked like a light in the far distance, though Dave wasn't convinced it was really the far light but thought instead it was the nearer one off Eastroads Bay. We eventually saw a white tower nearer to us. Timing our approach to this white structure against our compass convinced Dave it was indeed the nearer light that had gone out.

I had not been able to relax this whole time coming in through that rushing passage. I was irritated because I was so tired. It was 2:30 a.m. at this point. We'd been hyper vigilantly sailing through this pass for over four hours, with not one second to relax. I was also very frustrated and stressed because Dave was depending on me for the detailed information from the pilot book. I had to point out that "there were islands somewhere within the bay or that there was this danger and that danger."

And he would want specifics. "Where?"

And not knowing exactly where we were, I would have to hypothesize, "I don't know! Maybe 500 yards from here!" a response with which he was never satisfied. What else could I say? We were traveling in the dark in a place I'd never been. Though I understood we were both tense, I didn't appreciate his criticism of my lack of clairvoyance besides the fact that my upbringing had made me supersensitive to any hint that I might not be perfect.

Near the white tower, we dropped all the sails, and with Dave hanging on the lower ratlines with the binoculars, we proceeded to motor in blindly, I nervously on the tiller ready to swing the boat away from any reef he might suddenly see. And then, luck with us—and the flood tide and full moon—just as the tail of the constellation Scorpio lined up perfectly with the range lights, we saw another sailboat quietly anchored near the shore, announcing there was safe anchorage just ahead. Because Dave's sun sign was Scorpio, he deemed this providential.

Anchor down. Engine quiet.

Peace. No motor. No water rushing against and with the hull.

No stress. Silence.

Safe. Well done. We weathered it good.

Asleep at 4:30 a.m.

On September 7, 1974, we awoke to sunshine and a perfect warmth—finally—in a quiet anchor of two to four fathoms at Eastroads Anchorage, Prony Bay, Nouvelle Caledonie. We were surrounded by not jungle but a strangely eroded yet pleasing scenery: rounded hills behind which conical peaks bosomed up to two thousand to three thousand feet. The greenery, from a distance, was a frosty gray-green, cut and accentuated with scars of iron-red slips. Most of the growth was scrubby, short, sloping right down to the water. Only short spots of narrow white beach showed, trimmed by ironwoods and pine trees growing alongside coconut and *tiare* trees. The sweet, sweet perfume of the tropical flora swirled and danced across the glassy bay, cleansing, caressing.

I sat on the deck, catching up in my journal, writing about how we had attempted to go halfway to somewhere. Walpole Island. That had been our vague destination, a small possibly uninhabited island that we finally reached after a two-day ordeal and then left immediately—where we almost made landfall. If we'd never gone, we would have never known what was there. We would have never seen the cliffs from feet away. We would have never known if that might have been an island we could have made home.

We feasted on fried dried fish, the last of the fresh eggs whipped into a cheese omelet (made with Yuk-brand cheese), biscuits, canned tomato juice. The other boat had pulled anchor earlier, and we were alone in this bay, with the coned mountains, red iron slips of land, dusty-green scrub, coconuts, and palms.

CHAPTER 2

*I am sure it is everyone's experience, as it has been mine, that any
discovery we make about ourselves or the meaning of life is never
like a scientific discovery, a coming upon something entirely new
and unsuspected; it is rather, the coming to conscious recognition of
something, which we really knew all the time but, because we were
unwilling to formulate it correctly, we did not hitherto know we knew.*

—W. H. Auden

New Caledonia was not the prettiest of islands. Though our anchorage
at Prony Bay seemed like a tropical heaven after leaving the cold grayness
of New Zealand's winter, the gray-green shrubbery and deep-carved red
slits visible on the hills and mountains continued to be the dull painted
backdrop as we continued eighty-one kilometers farther in to Noumea, the
only city on Grand Terre, the main island of the archipelago. Dry, eroded,
sparsely vegetated, Grand Terre was referred to by the locals—rather
appropriately—as Le Caillou, "the rock." I didn't say it then, but now, years
later, it was a place to which I never wish to return. It was a poor start to
my "return to paradise."

When we arrived in Noumea, we anchored at the yacht club where we
could easily fill our tanks with water, have an easy site to come to shore
with our dinghy, hobnob with other yachties, sneak in to take cold showers.
But being a funky laundry-flying cruising boat not quite up to a yacht club's
standard, in less than three weeks, we were very impolitely told that we had

overstayed our moorage and that if we didn't leave immediately, the yacht club would confiscate our boat. Hmm, "Welcome to paradise?"

The area around Noumea is a network of bays and inlets. We moved the boat to an anchorage in Moselle Bay where the scenery was even uglier, consisting of New Caledonia's largest floating crane and the local prison, all situated on an uninteresting eroded, unvegetated, lifeless spit of land save for three coconut trees, one fir tree, one dead something or other, and a sprinkling of grass. This bit of ugliness, connected by a dirt causeway, attached itself to the industrial section of Noumea. A large nickel plant was psychedelically spewing red, white, and green smoke so thickly that one couldn't see the gray-green scrubby mountains behind. The industrial district merged into the main business district, which was constructed of old and new maintained and dilapidated structures, none of which had any architectural imagination in their construction or historical or romantic qualities.

Captain Cook had first sighted (and named) New Caledonia in 1774. The first settlement wasn't established until 1851 by the British trader James Paddon, but France annexed the island within three years under orders of Napoleon III to keep it out of the hands of the British. In 1864, France began to establish penal colonies to which, until about 1897, France sent over 22,000 criminals and political prisoners, its location being a perfect place to keep political opponents far from France. Prisoners, even after release, were forced to remain on the island in order to help increase its population, a population that had been reduced mostly by disease brought by the Europeans.

Nickel—and gold and copper—was discovered around the 1870s. The French engaged in blackbirding—tricking indigenous people from other islands onto ships and bringing them to New Caledonia against their will—to mine the ore and to strip the hills of its teak and sandalwood forests. For whatever reason, they didn't permit the local people to work there. Because of the remote location, instead of hauling the ore back to France, nickel smelters were built, the offspring of which I witnessed spewing pollution into the air. The strip-mining and displaced rock from the smelters ravaged the landscape.

How and why did we end up in such a ugly god-awful place when we were sailing to paradise? The island had a mean and ugly history that permeated my soul, much of which I didn't know at the time, but I could feel it, and evidenced by the blemished landscape and spewing industry, I could see it.

Cities and towns come into existence as centers of economic trade, followed by or in conjunction with missionaries, both of which usurp the power and rights of indigenous peoples. None of these conquerors ever had the best interest of the people in mind but instead only their own power, greed, or deluded beliefs that they used to take away the soul of a people. I know many people who love cities and all they have to offer: the nightlife, the theater, the shops. Many of those same people are afraid and fearful or bored in nature. To me, a city—any big city—is a cancerous necrosis fed by that strain of human that takes and takes and takes with an endless greed. A strong opinion I know. If the city were cut off from the rest of the world, the people would perish because all that concrete will not sustain life. They might put in parks or plant flowers by their windowsill, but a city of concrete cannot sustain life.

But here we were, anchored in Moselle Bay, an ugly dirty environment hovered over by a prison, looking across the water to an ugly dirty city and a nickel smelter. But we were here. Why? Before the time of Google and travel books, we didn't know what it would be like until we arrived.

Though admittedly I hadn't earned a lot of money while living in New Zealand, I had always had what I wanted. Our arrival in New Caledonia was the beginning of a new norm—that we arrived in every port without a dime to our name. Having just disparaged the money economy, I admit that though we didn't need money (at least immediately), we wanted some (just a little) to buy a soda, something cold, or a bottle of wine, to buy fresh vegetables from the market, or to treat ourselves to a meal. The only things we *needed* money for was, at the very least, kerosene for our lanterns, which we used to read and cook by in the evenings. We needed money to buy propane with which to cook. While we still had an engine or even a portable generator, we needed money to buy fuel. We needed soap for laundry and detergent for dishes. The list was very short because we had a home, the boat, and there was no rent or mortgage payments. Water was free, either from docks in ports or from rain catchment. This was a time before cell phones and GPS and the internet: a simpler and cheaper time.

Twenty days after arriving in New Caledonia, two days after dropping anchor in Moselle Bay after leaving the yacht club, we still had no money. Not even able to buy a soda, I went to the hospital, arriving just in time before the doors closed at 11:00 a.m. for lunch, to donate a pint of my blood for 1,200 French Pacific francs.

This was an act of desperation. I don't like needles.

Soft, thickly padded, comfortable reclining couches were provided in which to relax. An armrest for the arm—now strapped down—poked through a hole in a partition where, on the other side, sat the assistant with her needles and bottles and swabs and papers. A giant thick needle—at least as big as my artery as far as I was concerned—was inserted into my vein and taped down. Pretty red blood proceeded to flow into a container set on a not-very-sanitary-looking table.

As I was lying there wondering whether I was going to faint, I checked out the room: a few mosquitoes rested here and there about the walls; bits of dust and scraps of lint had collected in the corners. Then my wandering eyes spotted the trash bins. *Well,* I think, *at least they're fifteen feet away from me on the other side of the room.* The lid was open as it literally couldn't be closed because of all the old needles and tubes and bloody cottons dripping out of it. I began thinking of infections and hepatitis. I began to worry about how long before the jar would be filled with my blood so I could leave. I kept looking at the fingers of my hand to see if they were turning white from lack of blood or blue or whatever color they should turn before they drop off. The technician wasn't around. What if she forgot about me, and the blood just kept pumping into the bottle, and it overflowed?

Funny, the paranoid thoughts one can conjure up in such a situation. But she did return, filling up a few small bottles, clamping off the hose, and finally removing the giant needle from my arm. I went out to the desk, signed a few papers, and was handed my 1,200 francs. Walking back out into the sunshine, I kept checking myself to see if I would faint, but I remembered the curse in Rarotonga; if I thought too hard that I would faint, I probably would.

I hitched a ride back to the yacht club to retrieve a cookbook I had lent to the yacht *Intrepid,* a lovely seventy-foot schooner owned by a young American man, Joe. I then walked over to the beach where I ran into Jacques, the miniature Frenchman, and his American girlfriend, Ginny (who stood eight inches taller than him). We ended up having lunch—which for the French always includes a lot of red wine—and talked about babies and abortions and marriages and blood types and infections and garlic and collecting rocks in the mountains. And we drank more wine.

For me, something akin to terrifying happened that afternoon. It was during that afternoon of walking and talking and eating and drinking that I had a profound shift in my attitude. The red flags and the little irksome differences between Dave and me hit me stone cold in my heart. I fell into a deep hole realizing that I had made a horrible mistake in leaving New Zealand to sail with Dave. All the little inklings and red flags I'd had from the day I met him in Paihia rushed to the forefront of my mind. I came face to face with the sure knowledge that I did not love him, that at times I barely liked him. He was a good man in all respects, a kind man, a generous man, a handsome man, an intelligent, a funny man. But between the two of us, we both were too scarred, too injured from our individual childhoods to have any functional skills—most notably good, honest communication skills—to be able to have a stable, healthy relationship.

In fact, I will leave him out of any hint of the blame equation. *I* was too injured. *I* lacked the communication skills. I was responsible for *my* inability to be in a functional, loving relationship.

But why now have this realization after I'd left everything behind in New Zealand?

In the world in which I was raised, it was almost brutally instilled that I was responsible for another person's feelings. Tears of sorrow or anguish or giggles of laughter, either one, could send my father into a rage, and my mother suffered his wrath if she could not keep us children quiet. I was responsible for every fight my parents had, for all the sorrow of my mother and the anger and frustration of my father. Whatever I was to do, it should be in relation to what I anticipated my father wanted. What *I* wanted was impossible to discern, just an unformed wispy, ghost thing that sat on the edges of my life since my first days. When there was any hint of my having my own needs or wants, it appeared only as a disconcerting thought, something disheveled and almost unrecognizable, usually guised in what I *didn't want*. At times, like this moment, it was terrifying to come face to face with what I didn't want. It was complete ownership, for that brief moment, of my own wants and feelings, none of which I had ever communicated to Dave.

My conundrum was I recognized that, having no money, I felt I had no way to leave him. Yes, there was the option of contacting my mother and asking her to send me money not so I could return to the States—that was the last thing I wanted to do—but so that I could fly back to New Zealand, to Whenuapua, Pawarenga, to my thatched hut and subsistence living, and my aloneness. But I knew I could not and would not do that because I was a prideful woman. I resolved to hunker down, shoulder my burden, and hope that just as quickly as this negative thought had entered, it would leave and be replaced with joy, with happiness, with contentment, with hope, with commitment. With love.

So I returned to the yacht club where I snuck in and took a cleansing, though cold, shower, checked our empty mailbox at general delivery, and went to buy a few items with my hard-earned money. I walked and wandered until I could no longer avoid returning to the boat. Thoughts circled, drifted off, and came back in, recircling again. On. Off. On. Off like a naughty child playing with the switch, on, off, on, off.

Hints in my journal entries pointed to a budding awareness—only a glimmer—that I craved my time alone. Because I'd always leapt into life and adventures and was quick to tell stories, I had always thought of myself as an extrovert. But in fact, I recharged by being alone, which is the key element of an introvert. Was I naturally an introvert, or had I learned to be an introvert because I was never conflicted when I lived alone? It was only my feelings that I needed to deal with. Did I want to be alone as it was the only way I could get what I wanted? Possibly. Probably. But did it matter? I was in the situation I was in—and at that time still without the ability to communicate my wants—and I felt there was nothing I could do about it. It was indeed many more years of gathering up the past before I had any understanding of the dynamic forces that were the engine propelling me on this adventure. It's astounding to look back at myself then, but it was what it was. For that moment, I felt I had only the choice to move forward.

Obviously living in the tiny space of a thirty-foot sailboat did not allow me the space I needed to recharge. When I couldn't escape, walls of resentment grew like a mold. Even at moorage, where I could leave the boat, I resented the fact that to be alone, I needed to leave. Dave, on the other hand, thrived on contact with people, seeming to attach to them like a frog's feet to glass. I was relieved when Dave would choose to leave the boat and leave me alone. I'd row him to shore and return to write, read, sit on the deck, and just gaze out at whatever scenery was before me.

There were many good days because the constant is that life is always changing. I believed completely that I had no choice but to make the best of it. I acquiesced to a level of despair and found ways to tolerate it that I called happiness. Oh, and Dave loved me. My gosh, he chased me for two years. How could I let *him* down?

But change always comes. On. Off. On. Change of focus, change of moods, change of action.

I had heard rumors that a glass-bottomed tour boat, *Follies Bergeres*, was looking for a crewperson who could also act as a French interpreter. Though I'd had six years of French, five in elementary and middle school, and another in college, I remembered little. I stopped by the French yacht *Tranquille* to see if Michel would accompany me to help me apply for the job. Though Michel had to interpret for me, somehow I got hired: two days a week, maybe more. The wages were poor, 1,000 francs a day, about $10 for the entire day. I was assured that I'd do very little: clean up a bit, take the wheel when necessary, tell the tourists what we were doing, help prepare their lunches. And I'd get to take home all the leftover food every day: pate, baguettes, fruit. I would start the next day.

On that first day at my new job, Maurice Taxier had me help him build picnic benches. I had expected to be working on his boat with tourists, not building picnic tables. Working in a concrete shed/warehouse next to the docks, Maurice displayed a very short temper and was soon yelling at me in French to hand him a screwdriver or a screw or a chisel. I could not understand him because, first, I couldn't remember my French, but in reality, I never learned terms for construction tools in school French! Give me a break! But after several hours of miming and screaming, the picnic benches were completed, and Maurice finally turned his attention to the job for which I thought I'd been hired.

He wanted to practice taking his eighty-foot-long glass-bottomed catamaran boat away from the dock and returning, practicing mooring it. We cast off, motored a short distance out into the harbor, and then returned, backing the *Follies Bergeres* stern-to. I jumped off with the mooring line and whipped it around the mooring cleat as was my custom in bringing any boat to dock. Maurice yelled something at me that I didn't understand. I looked at him questioningly. He yelled again. I looked at him with exasperation. Then he screamed at me, and I got so angry at him I threw the mooring line off into the water and started to walk away, to quit when he yelled, *"Merci, merci!"* I guess that's what he'd been requesting me to do. Not a good start.

He settled down after that as we became familiar with each other. Other than his frustrated, angry outbursts at me in the beginning, he turned out to be a sweet, congenial old man. I doubt that he'd expected a blonde twenty-four-year-old American girl to apply for the job, but in the end, he took a liking to me in a grandfatherly way. He was tan and fit for being seventy, but I could see, and he complained, that his back hurt and his joints were sore. I eventually learned he was dying from leukemia. Our relationship was mutually beneficial. He needed my English and my strength and agility, though I never felt I really did all that much for it, and I needed the meager 1,000 francs a day.

My spirits lifted when I got the job on *Follies Bergeres*. I got away from Dave, and I was earning money, loosening my sense of dependence on him. Though I was around people every day, they were different each day. That's the On switch for me: change. If I could change the environment, change the people I'm around, it changed my focus. Maurice had few expectations of me, and other than the first day when he got so frustrated and angry with me, I always felt respected and appreciated. He was an intelligent man, and once my French came back to me enough to carry on conversations, it was such a joy to spend afternoons talking with him.

At least two days a week, sometimes four days a week, as he had tourists to fill his boat, we took the *Follies Bergeres* out to one of the atolls off the coast of Grand Terre. I'd help the tourists board, find seats, hand out life jackets that they could wear or not. Most of the tourists were from Australia or New Zealand. I explained to them the schedule and routine for the day, and then we'd set off motoring out of Dumbea Bay, about eight or ten miles to a series of atolls within the barrier reef. We would motor slowly over the coral reefs, the clear turquoise water filled with colorful coral and reef fish mesmerizing the tourists viewing through the glass bottom.

We'd eventually anchor on the atoll, beaching the stern of the catamaran to offload the tourists. I let the guests know they were free to explore the island for about an hour, and yes, they were permitted to climb up into the lighthouse, but they should be back within the hour for lunch. While they were off exploring, Maurice and I would set about preparing a French lunch of pate, sliced meats and cheeses, fresh French baguettes, radishes (the suggested method of eating was to dip them in soft butter), and fruit. On the one table, I set out ceramic dishware and utensils, the food, and of course carafes of French red table wine, constantly replenished from a five-gallon glass jug; people were free to drink as much as they liked.

The guests, sometimes as many as forty, and Maurice and I would fill our plates and glasses and find a coconut log to sit on. Talk and laughter would fill the air as we all ate together. Most tourists were fascinated with the fact that I was an American sailing on a sailboat and working in New Caledonia, and there'd always be discussion around that topic. Afterward, the tourists were free to snorkel, sunbathe, or do whatever they wanted for the next two hours. (Many took naps after all that wine.) As Maurice would relax, I'd wash up all the dishes in the ocean water on the edge of the beach, using the white sand to scrub off the food scraps that small fish would dart in to grab. After putting the dishes away on the boat and ensuring the atoll was clean as how we found it, Maurice and I would sit and talk for the next two hours.

By the end of my two-and-a-half months working on the *Follies Bergeres*, I was having long fairly fluent conversations in French with Maurice. It was during those long talks, covering topics of money and tourism to philosophy, that I learned that he was suffering from leukemia. That explained his seeming lethargy and inability to concentrate. Often when I'd first arrive to work, he'd still be sleeping in his small cabin on the boat, and I'd have to roust him out.

About six weeks after beginning work for Maurice, Dave had an opportunity to do some work over in the Baie de Numbo where there was a boatyard and dry dock. We decided to move the *Paz del Mar* over to anchor there as it would be simpler for him to get to work every day though it made it very difficult for me to get back around to Moselle Bay and Noumea to work with Maurice. I was about to tell Maurice that I would need to quit working for him simply for the reason of being too far away when he informed me that he would be going to New Zealand in a month for chemotherapy and radiation treatment for his leukemia. He was apologizing to me for not being able to keep me working after he left; I couldn't bear to leave him then, knowing how much I really was helping him just get through one day at a time of taking his tourists out.

I don't remember and I did not record in my journals how I got from Baie de Numbo to Baie de Moselle each morning for the next month. I hitchhiked a lot in those years, so I assume that's what I did. Though Papeete, Tahiti, had buses, it's possible there were "chicken buses" making the ten-mile route, but I don't remember taking one. But I continued to work for Maurice for another month, which ended up timely coinciding with Dave finishing up his work with Gabin Marques and our departure.

Gabin was a very, very handsome Frenchman who ran the dry dock in Baie de Numbo, away from ugly industrial Moselle Bay and the Noumea area. He lived happily in an island plantation-style house near his boat works with the fattest and most physically unattractive of women. We spent many an evening on his wraparound porch with the both of them. She was jolly and happy all the time and a fantastic cook. They displayed true affection for each other. Possibly recognizing a question that he figured was in the back of people's mind about what an unlikely match this was, he did not hesitate to tell us that he had had several previous marriages with very attractive women who all ended up cheating on him and divorcing him, taking half his money. His present wife may be ugly, he said, but she was sweet and wonderful and loyal and a great cook—and she knew she had a really good deal, and nobody else would want her. And he loved her, he added.

The transmission was going out on the boat's engine. We talked about getting it fixed—*if* we could get it fixed, *if* we had the *money* or could get the parts to get it fixed. Dave could keep working probably indefinitely with Gabin who had an endless stream of boats coming in to dry dock. Though Maurice would be gone a month, he said his plans were to come back to *Follies Bergeres* after chemo, and I would be able to go back to work for him. Though work and the social life revolving around other yachties who came and went made the days in New Caledonia more enjoyable, it still remained a place that we didn't want to stay for a long period of time.

In the end, Dave and I agreed that, one, we would sail on, and two—though the engine had saved us from slamming into the sheer walls of Walpole Island—what made the most sense was to get rid of the engine.

It would free up a lot of space. It would alleviate the cost of buying fuel, getting it fixed when broken, and the stench of running the engine. We thought we'd be able to sell the engine for a lot, but in the end, it hadn't sold yet when we were ready to leave. We left the engine with Monsieur Gabin Marques to sell for us. Maybe someday when we're needing it the most, we'd get $300 in the mail.

We decided to make giant oars and oarlocks. The two of us could row, or one of us could scull when it was necessary to maneuver with no wind. Since a child on the creeks and rivers of Maryland, I loved to row. And I loved simplicity.

Life continued in the outer world too. My brother sent me pictures of my faithful dog I'd left behind almost four years ago when I set sail from Hawai'i with enough money to be gone a year. I got a letter saying that my paternal aunt had died of cancer. I got another letter announcing that my paternal grandfather had died. Oh, how I'd loved him. He was so warm and loving. He always gave us $2 bills each time he came to visit. Reading the letter, I realized I had not seen him—gosh, I think—since I was maybe twelve years old! Why was that? I thought.

For some reason, my father had not been in contact with his own father for a decade. I learned later that my Grandpa Sam had been found alone, very ill, almost dead, in a squalid Florida apartment. Someone had searched out and finally contacted my father. Around that same time, my maternal grandmother and her sister had gotten too old to live on their own, so my father's remedy to a nursing home was he bought a small duplex in Texas and put the three of them in one side and a full-time nurse in the other. I heard that my paternal Grandpa Sam and my most wonderful maternal Grandma B fell in love in that apartment. They would have been the perfect match, such sweet, gentle, loving people.

I thought of that $2 bill. I remember so clearly driving to town in our green 1954 Plymouth station wagon ready to spend that $2. My parents insisted, "No, you must save it. You can't spend it."

I threw it out the window of the car in a tantrum. "If I can't spend it, why have it?" At seven years old, I didn't understand the concept of saving, but at twenty-four, I had definitely become a frugal skinflint, recognizing the need to spend money wisely, another major difference between Dave and me.

I wondered why my dad hadn't stayed in touch with his father. Even to this day, I wonder why. Other than if I were to make assumptions, it was because my grandfather was a gentle, loving man without much education, and my father was an intense, angry man wrapped up in the contortions of his PhD and notoriety in his field. My paternal grandmother was a witch in my eyes. I had never liked her and dreaded when she'd come to our house as children, oftentimes to babysit us for a week while my parents went to a convention for experimental psychologists. Grandma Snow, we called her, not even some endearing Nana or Grammy E but the stiff name of Grandma Snow. She was a religious zealot with a judgmental attitude that started with the fact that, in her mind, we were born sinners. When I was eight, while she was watching us one week, I'd fallen and broken my wrist. She never took me to the doctor, insisting I was simply a crybaby. The break had been in my growth plate, which never set quite right even after my mom finally got me to the doctor. What did that say about my father that, for some reason, had kept his mother in our lives but not his father?

The news and letters brought the past to the present and then into the past again. Time moved as quickly as squalls rushing forward and moving on.

We got our twenty-foot-long rowing oars built; we painted them red to match the hull and strapped them to the stanchions. Dave finished up work for Gabin at the dry dock. The momentum of leaving slowly gained speed, and the departure date slowly came into better focus. I searched out the Seventh-Day Adventist mission in Noumea and restocked our beans and rice. Dried beans were not a staple part of an islander's diet, but Seventh-Day Adventists, being vegans, always had beans, and there were Seventh-Day Adventist missions everywhere. I bought other nonperishables, canned tomatoes and tomato paste, canned corn and beans, canned butter, and canned cheese, parsing our money carefully. We'd get fresh eggs and veggies the day before we planned to leave.

CHAPTER 3

Change the way you look at things and the things you look at change.
—Wayne W. Dyer

We "sailed" out of Baie de Numbo on December 18 en route to the Chesterfields. There was no wind. None. Inky smooth sea. But it was a joyous and fun exit. Joe tied us alongside *Intrepid* and escorted us out under his motor. Gabin Marques from the dry dock and his son, along with Leo, the Belgian, and Robert of *Taboo* and Pierre, the schoolteacher, accompanied them. Robert, we learned later, was lost at sea. Before he'd left the States, he had prepared for his solo sail by having an appendectomy. In spite of taking that precaution against the most unlikely of events, the irony was that he ended up falling overboard as his boat was later found floating with no one on board.

Joe gave us a bottle of rum. Leo gave us a bottle of Scotch. Then Robert a bottle of champagne. So along with the five bottles of gifted wine (five gallons), *Paz del Mar* was ready to rock and roll.

A light breath began to blow. We finally cast off the line attaching us to Mama Elephant *Intrepid*, but Gabin ended up on board with us for Joe to pick up later. Somehow, we got out of Numbo—the wind was there to help us—but I think the tide was on the ebb. We used "Ever Prosperity"—our new oars—for a bit but quit after declaring it to be too hot to exert that much energy. We slowly floundered along at a knot.

Joe, after sailing slowly full sail around the bay in *Intrepid*, finally moseyed back to take Gabin off the boat. He sailed circles around us like

155

he promised to do, with us taking pictures of her—what a beautiful boat. We gave him our camera. Snap, click, snap: *Paz del Mar* recorded for history. He scooted alongside again retrieving our camera, and then Joe went ahead to Vitoe Pass, the one we'd go out to if we made it before dark. Otherwise, we'd be anchoring at the last atoll.

Around 2:00 p.m., nearing the atoll, with the wind having finally freshened, Joe tacked back, passing us. Everyone was in jubilant spirits. As the seventy-foot sleek *Intrepid* sliced by us, we yelled to Joe, "Let's see your fish!"

"Let's see yours first," he answered to which Dave bent into the cockpit and pulled up the tazar we'd caught earlier. He threw it back into the cockpit to pick it up again, faking the catch of two, boasting the excellence of his tube lure. Dave had a sense of humor, one thing that had first impressed me.

Joe didn't show us his fish but sped by under full sail. The *Paz del Mar* did not *speed* anywhere other than maybe our entrance through the Havannah Passage three months earlier. The sky was crystal blue, the water competing and flaunting her blue against the sky. We were playing like children, all laughing. *Intrepid* tacked around again, catching up to us easily with Joe strutting up to the foredeck. "Okay, you wanna see our fish?" at which Gabin's son, with his dark, flashing, piercing eyes, held up a tazar by the gills of equal size to ours. A kick of its tail told us they'd lucked out and just caught it.

They tacked again, speeding by the slow shallow-drafted, wide-bottom *Paz del Mar*, but this time with hands waving goodbye. Drifting farther away on the breeze, the wind carried the joyful calls of "Have a good trip. Good luck! Don't let your meat loaf! See you round like a donut!"

The smiles were now tinged with a bit of sadness. They had been good friends, filling days and evenings with food and tales. We'd grown close, as close as it might be in a sailor's life; no one knew when we'd see each other again.

As a post-note, Dave, the more social creature than I, stayed in touch with Joe through the years. Both Joe and *Intrepid* are still in New Caledonia forty-five years later. Dave stayed in touch with a few other sailors over the years, but I never did. In many ways, they were simply part of the scenery experienced, and once gone—unless photos had captured their face, their boat—the memory got blurry and faded over the horizon of time. The two people I stayed in touch with through the years were Irene from Pawarenga and Wendy, Pole's sister.

Because of lack of sleep from the party we'd enjoyed the night before, Dave pretty quickly fell asleep against the cabin bulkhead. I didn't let him sleep long before the breakers on the barrier reef grew clearer on the horizon. I could see bottom clearly though I knew it was still fifty to sixty feet deep. I needed another set of eyes to watch for the Vitoe marker that was our exit from the inner bay. We finally verified its position, and about an hour later, we were out the pass with a long rolling swell announcing the deep sea.

A baby shark, two and a half feet long, struck the line. Dave cut its mouth to get the hook out without bringing him on board. Fifteen minutes later, something much bigger, probably a bigger shark, struck the other tube lure so hard, it snapped the line before we had a chance to start pulling. Once we were well settled into our rhythm, I went below to get some sleep, leaving Dave on deck to snooze at standing watch until we were well away from land. I woke up a couple of times to check on him, finally ending up taking over watch at 2:00 a.m.

The petrels and molly hawks came, doing their early-morning fishing ritual, gliding noiselessly across the rippled glass of the sulky morning ocean, pivoting on the tips of their wings as they slid into their turns. The gliding shadows of these dark-gray/black early-morning fishermen were barely discernible against the predawn sky of the same color. The sky was bored, gray and clouded over as if in a bit of a bad mood though a star appeared to announce that a change in the weather would come.

I had watched the birds for a while—or felt them almost like a blind man senses someone close—but I must have dozed off, awakening to the sun, blue sky, and a kiss from Dave who, without a word, immediately ducked below again. For that one silent moment, all was perfect. At sea, far from land, where our relationship to the cosmos was clearly so diminutive, the relationship between Dave and I was always more peaceful because the sea enveloped us; it had the power to hypnotize us, soften us, and erase the little battles of the egos that appeared in relation to land. Being on the sea was our unified goal; differences that I created in my mind dissolved.

The tiller was tied off, and the boat steered steadily in relation to the set of the sails. Again, the rhythm of the ocean was reestablished, preparing food, eating, washing dishes in the cockpit, reading, sleeping, eating, washing dishes again, staring out at sea, and reading some more. I've never permitted myself to read endlessly like I did in those days of sailing. But at sea, truly, there's little else to do—other than the endless meditation—under the beautiful blue skies on the blue ocean with a steady breeze silently propelling the boat along. When we got to port—at least before we left port—we traded books with the other boats; someone always had something new that we hadn't read. And the variety was amazingly stimulating, from Henry Miller's *Tropic of Cancer* to T. E. Lawrence's *Seven Pillars of Wisdom* to dime-store westerns.

Far, far from land, birds followed us, disappearing and then reappearing after scouring the sea. It never ceased to amaze me to see the albatross or petrels so far from shore, days, weeks from any land. But this was their world, always scouring the sea for food.

Days out from Numbo, we came across a school of maybe 200 baby yellow-fin tuna, all about three to four inches long. They continued to follow us for two days, staying in the shade of the boat, some meandering away from the school to feed but always returning to the protection of the Mother *Paz del Mar*. Something larger in the food chain would send these little guys scurrying frantically before they'd return again. Twice, large flocks of birds came from nowhere, attracted by similar schools of fish. We'd watch and listen to the circle of life as tens of these birds dove into the schools, gulping them down as they walked the water in their takeoff.

We spent Christmas Day at sea, a perfect day with light winds pushing us at about three knots with the drifter and main up, gently, quietly rocking downwind. Drank a little wine. Dave gave me a Mako shark's tooth on a bit of cord. And I got a dishwasher for Christmas! I couldn't believe how long it would last, but he was still washing dishes the next day. He was often so sweet.

Just like the swells, the hours and days rolled one into another. There was nothing to enter in my journal as the revelations brought into blurry vision in Noumea had been carried away by the wind or burned up by the sun, leaving only the banalities of the time-slipping summary of doldrum days on the Coral Sea: fishing, sleeping, navigating, thinking, having an evening drink, eating, listening to Vivaldi, Bach, Schumann, Beethoven—their music was written for sailing. Again, I focused on the third eye of the earth, where the horizon meets the sea.

We stayed attuned to the international mariner's Weather Channel, checking regularly for any turbulence like gale-force storms that might be brewing, especially if the swells or clouds portended a change. You could run away from a hurricane or gale if you had warning of it coming, hook around it, and pick up its tail winds for an extra-fast fun sail to your original destination. The Nimbus weather satellites had only been first launched a decade before in the '60s. Before those satellites, the sailors had no warning. Nowadays, forty-five years later, sailing is a high-tech undertaking with satellite Internet, satellite phones, GPS, and hundreds of weather satellites circling the globe, bringing astounding accuracy to any forecast.

Though we were monitoring the Weather Channel periodically for the bigger storms, a passing squall could bring dangerous wind and lots of rain but seldom lasted more than a half an hour. You could see it as this dark gray, what, cylindrical rain cloud stealing a slice from the blue sky, its own little, miniature storm in the middle of the ocean. If we were getting low on water in our water tanks and wanted to try to catch some rain, we'd head for the squall, but because often the wind might require us to reef or drop sails, we would avoid them if we could. Though less frequent, there were white squalls too.

A white squall has no dark cloud to announce its gale-force wind, but if you're watching the sea, you see it coming like an invisible monster in a sci-fi movie. They're exceptionally dangerous because they're unseen. On the *Westward Ho*, while sailing to the Marquesas, we almost lost our mast by one. I was lying on the deck sunbathing. Annie was at the tiller when a white squall hit us with such force, heeling the boat over so hard and so fast almost completely on its side. I was thrown into the lifelines. Annie, the most inexperienced of everyone on board, hung on to the tiller and just started screaming, not knowing what to do. I was clambering aft on the deck as best I could, trying to reach the cleat and wench to release the mainsail and jib sail when Brian flew up through the hatch and got there first. Releasing the sails, we righted quickly, the sails left to fly and flap wildly as the wind blew sixty miles an hour for another three or four minutes before it passed. It was a crazy, jarring experience even for me. Brian gave Annie and Jackson a lesson on watching the sea for the turbulent white caps that would always announce a white squall on a blue sunny day. That was the only white squall I ever experienced in many thousands of miles and many days of sailing.

But of the hundreds of other squalls I saw or sailed through, there were two other memorable ones. One squall that we came upon almost took over the whole horizon on our starboard side. Unless we tacked to completely avoid it, we were going to come really close to it if not sail through it. We chose to not tack. As we got closer, we noticed porpoises racing toward the squall, and as we got closer yet, we saw what appeared to be at least a hundred porpoises running the edge of the squall, leaping and churning up the waters. As we got closer yet, we saw what looked like a mile-long school of tuna—which is what the porpoises were feeding on—that were feeding on a monstrous school of smaller fish. All this was happening on the outer edge of this squall. Only fifty yards from us, we skirted this oceanic feeding frenzy occurring between our boat and the squall for at least a half hour.

The other memorable time concerning squalls occurred as we were approaching the Great Barrier Reef off of Australia. As we now no longer had an engine, having left it with Gabin in New Caledonia, we were very much at the mercy of the winds and the currents. I didn't journal the details, so it was not recorded where we first came within sight and sound of the Great Barrier Reef, but we were forced to sail north along its edge for several days before we reached Grafton Pass, the entrance to Cairns, Queensland.

The sky was, as usual, a brilliant blue; we could see the turquoise highlights and an occasional breaker marking the edge of the reef several miles to our west. There were squalls several miles apart dotting our whole path. Within every squall we could see lightning striking. I was terrified. I felt fear—absolute, uncontrollable fear. Way more fear than I'd felt looking at the cliffs of Walpole Island.

Dave and I had a screaming fight. I was, I will admit, out of control, screaming that we absolutely had to hang battery cables from the rigging into the ocean so that if that lightning, ever so attracted to our mast reaching into the sky, chose to strike at us, at least it would not blow out the bottom of the boat and leave us floating in the shark-infested waters off the reef if we were to survive the strike. Somewhere I had gleaned that this was a viable solution to such a situation. Dave's retort was that attaching those battery cables to the rigging would in fact better attract the lightning; we were safer to just hope the lightning wouldn't hit us. As we entered the squall line, I went below and curled up and cried, confident that I would die. I didn't want to see the lightning bolt when it hit us.

Obviously, we survived to tell the story. On January 7, 1975, as the dawn mellowed into yellows and wiped the blackness from the covering cupola above, my heavy lids began to lift from near sleep. I wasn't quite asleep but definitely starting to nod off. I was supposed to be standing watch, but oh-but-oh, night watches were so difficult, staring into a void of blackness. So close to the Great Barrier Reef for days, we had had to stand watch. Needing our best visual acuity, we couldn't read by a light to keep ourselves awake. It was unsafe even to keep the radio on or music playing for very long as it was too easy to drown out the ominous telltale rumble of the waves crashing on a reef. So you sit in the blackness, head moving quickly from one star to another, one point of focus to another to prevent the lids from fluttering and finally closing over those oh-so tired, bloodshot eyes.

The sun was at my back as we sailed into the long, twenty-plus-mile pass to Cairns through Grafton Pass. Cairns sits at the mouth of the Trinity River in a part of the world that has a twenty-one-foot tide. Thankfully again, we must have had a flood tide as we had in New Caledonia as the passage was quick and without incident.

CHAPTER 4

*Develop an interest in life as you see it; the people, things, literature,
music—the world is so rich, simply throbbing with rich treasures,
beautiful souls and interesting people. Forget yourself.*
—Henry Miller

One of the downsides of sailing was the fear of leaving your boat
unattended for any stretch of time for fear of a wind shift that might come
up quickly and cause your anchor to drag or break free. Michel's boat,
Tranquille, was lost a year later to such a circumstance. I'm not sure why
Dave and I decided to take a road trip; I didn't record any reason in my
journals. Maybe because we still had a bit of money left over from New
Caledonia, so we didn't have to immediately find some form of work. Maybe
somebody we met said, "Oh, you should go to Cooktown." Or just because.
Just because we needed to touch land, smell the earth, get away from the
confines of the small boat. Or because we needed to explore a little bit of
the uniqueness of the Australian outback and a trip to Cooktown seemed
a reasonably short and safe trip to make. I don't recall why we chose to go
to Cooktown, but eleven days after arriving in Cairns, we set off. The tale
told was in the journey, not the destination as it turned out.

According to Google Maps at my fingertips today, Cooktown is 203
miles from Cairns, and supposedly, a three-hour-and-fifty-eight-minute trip
by car. (The road is now paved.) After a day of hitchhiking from Cairns, we
arrived in Mt. Carbine, Australia, seventy-eight miles away. Mt. Carbine
consisted of the Wolfram Hotel, a mine, termite castles, wind wheels,

and space. Two days later, we were still there, residing in the deserted dilapidated post office where, inside, we had pitched our mosquito-netted tent. The porch provided shade, the River Manganese (or Mitchell River as it's called now), down the road a bit, provided our site for washing, and the fields were for our relief. Each day, we sat on an overturned oil can, waiting for that telltale rumble of a semi or a four-wheel vehicle to come down the rutted, eroded road to take us to Cooktown. We waited, Dave and I. There had not been even one car in two days after we had originally arrived.

For its diminutive size (population ninety-one in 2007), Mt. Carbine was not an uninteresting place. It was a regular barnyard, the sounds at least. There were the roosters, some with the cracked voice of age, some with the cracking voice of youth, cocking their doodles for their hens. The hens cackled out their eggs. The turkeys strutted and gobbled, always seeming to announce themselves ensemble.

I sat and watched. Two bulls were roaming about, giving out their frustrated lamentations of horniness. Dogs barked. Distempered puppies whined. The continuous clanking of the cowbell announced the whereabouts of Alvin's small herd of shorthorns that moved about across the unfenced fields. Butcher birds sounded of church bells and dominated the flying musicians comprised of pigeons and thrushes, starlings and kookaburras. Eight horses, heads low in the heat, ambled by, curious of the figures sitting by the side of the road but uncomprehending of their plight. The sun got hotter. We saw no one save a sixteen-year-old boy on his motorcycle. He cruised up and down the road, across the fields, drowning out the more pleasant sounds.

Sitting on a plateau in a virtual wasteland, Dave and I listened to the sounds of Mt. Carbine and watched the little things that happened. It was much like being at sea where there was nothing but ocean and the sky but so many things occurring: the changes of the wind, changes in swells giving warnings of faraway storms, changes in clouds, porpoises greeting us and moving on, birds resting on our mizzen boom.

In the valley of the St. George River, rocked and treed mountains punching up into the sky, two Americans waited in Mt. Carbine, viewing its desolate existence, waited for something to happen. The largest wolframite mine in Australia (so said the locals) had left its scars evident in the razed mountains, now flat hills, which had been devoured to mine the wolframite.

The crushing and sorting shed, log encasements, mounds of discarded soil, and smatterings of working machines dwarfed the disintegrating bone-brown post office.

The Wolfram Hotel set alone on the other side of the road and comprised the rest of the town. Covered in vines and post plants, it looked like a grandmother's house with an extra-long porch when empty of the drunks. Most of the beer was consumed out on the long porch that fronted the whole establishment. Even with ceiling fans turning, the inside was excruciatingly saunic.

Jemma and Alvin owned the Wolfram Hotel though never were the two of them there at the same time. Alvin seemed a pleasant man though insecure. He was balding, at least in his sixties, with watery blue eyes that were always flushed red from too much sun and drink. The stories surrounding the couple were shared by several different folk. Supposedly Alvin was camp, as the Aussies say, and kept a boyfriend in Cairns. Because of this discovery, Jemma had kicked him out to live in a house down the street with his herd of cows,

But Jemma was herself a legend. As the story went, she'd run the pub there for fifteen years, considering the mining men *her* men, sometimes completely refusing to serve an outsider. "Ah, it's all right, lass, she treats all the women the same," one of the regulars assured me when I'd made a comment about the apparent wickedness in her soul.

Supposedly she was once a brothel madam for whatever excuse that might have been for her present demeanor. She was simply a very unhappy woman who landed in this desolate town, and anyone who cared to drink at the bar was stuck with her. The energy of her mood swings could have powered a rocket launch.

Of the miners, there were those that hardly set foot in the pub, who had their wives and families at home, living hidden in the undulations of the high desert. Then there were those, the majority, who hardly left the pub to go home. They worked the mines six days a week and drank the rest of the time. The bar stayed open for as long as there was someone to drink. There was no peace officer about to enforce the ten-o'clock closing hour in effect in Australia. Besides Jemma, I was the only woman I saw in the pub.

Friday night we listened to the rowdy, drunken outback gibberish from our tent pitched under the porch of the post office. All the regulars were letting loose. Finally, we joined them: Tommy, the mayor, born and raised in Mt. Carbine, forty-three, fat, drunk from morning till night. He was the mayor, someone said, because he was the only one fool enough not to have left town. Terry was the wolframite dynamiter. Supposedly Les was at one time a Mormon preacher though, clearly, he had left the fold as evidenced by his high alcohol consumption. There were more lonely drunken faces too, shouting us drinks and asking, "Where are you from? Overseas? Yeah, I have a friend from overseas. You might know him."

The innocence and naïvety of these men working in isolation were both sad and humorous.

Another morning and we were still sitting by the rutted road. Across the way the wind wheels turned in the fields, drawing up the artesian water. The mud stumps of the termite hills, four- to five-foot-high castles of red mud, spotted the fields. Dave, exploring while I waited for a car that never came, kicked over one termite mound and watched them for a while before he finally relieved me of my watch for cars so I could engross myself in watching the termites scurrying to rebuild their homes.

As the sun reached its zenith, American Bob (as everyone called him) ambled up the road, introducing himself, and invited us to his house for dinner if we were still there, which we were. Bob was middle aged, fat, jovial, much like Burl Ives in both bearded appearance and texture of voice. His wife, Joyce, was plump, blonde, outspoken, a Colorado woman.

The evening at their house was chaotic. They had six children of their own plus an adopted Navajo Indian daughter and an East Indian son. Their house looked like they just moved in with boxes stacked everywhere inside and out though they said they'd lived there four years. I never got an answer as to what brought Bob and Joyce to this high Australian desert land other than Bob said it was a good place "to build a houseboat for his family." Question mark?

That evening, visitors came and went, everyone taking in stride what I suspect was a standard state of affairs. There always seems to be an air of jovial chaos surrounding homes with large families. I was enjoying watching all the people sitting around the table under a huge mango tree hung with lanterns and empty wine bottles. Yes, hung with empty wine bottles.

Joyce had prepared a two-foot-wide pot of spaghetti to serve some twenty people that lived and were visiting there. First, she cleared the dogs' dishes off the top of the table. Without wanting to sound stupid, I asked why the dogs couldn't eat on the ground. Joyce explained that the toads were deadly poisonous, and if they jumped into the dogs' dishes or water, that's all it would take to kill the dogs, so they had trained the dogs to eat on the table. The cattle and horses and other animals that roamed freely didn't die apparently because they're too big. The English had brought the toads in from India a hundred years ago to control the insect population, not expecting them to multiply so fast. "Now, they're a real pest," Joyce said. "There's roads farther out that you can't see the dirt for the smashed toad bodies."

Saturday afternoon, I saw my first streaker, those legendary exhibitionists who were gaining notoriety for taking off all their clothes in public places to run through crowds of people stark naked. While being shouted drinks at the Wolfram Hotel, Joe became Mt. Carbine's first streaker. Joe worked the mines—of course since that's the only reason to be in Mt. Carbine. His face looked like someone pulled down one side—just enough for my eyes to strain to adjust to the lopsidedness of it. One eye and half his mouth all sat a half-inch lower than the other side of his face. It was not grotesque, just very noticeable. He was not ugly, just lopsided. I didn't know the term then, but I'm pretty sure he was suffering from Bell's palsy.

Joe was short and a drunk—the only two adjectives that fit together for Joe other than the Bell's palsied face—and he was already drunk when we decided to abandon our seats on the road to get a beer at the pub. I watched Joe stagger to his car, drive a short way up the road, turn around, and come to a stop. I saw him pulling his shirt over his head behind the opened door, and I pondered what he was doing when the door closed, and he commenced, to cheers, to run down the road past the pub stark naked, lifting and stretching his legs, pumping his arms, his penis slapping his thighs from side to side.

We were all laughing and announcing a streaker when Old Jemma came running out, putting her hair in place—the old horse—only to catch view of old Joe's arse, which somehow she was quick to identify, a fact to be related to the latecomers. Nudge, nudge. "Of course Jemma can tell one ass from another."

We were still in Mt. Carbine Monday. Still under the cool shelter of the post office, breakfast cooking on the primus. Once again, we packed our bags in anticipation of the possibility of some vehicle coming to take us to Cooktown. We waited patiently, though listlessly, for someone, anyone to come along.

The miners were back at the mine.

Jemma's bar was quiet, a ghost-town saloon.

An old Yugoslavian drunk stumbled up the road just after the sun. His car and trailer were broken down on the other side of the Manganese River Bridge. No one to help him. He thought the outback people strange, he said, not to lend a helping hand. I had no patience for drunks either, so I silently concurred with the lack of help.

While he was complaining, a Chevy Impala, the first car in three days, drove up and stopped. A youngish long-haired man got out, talked with the old drunken Slav, and took him back to his car. Joe the Yardsman— not the streaker—sauntered over to me and informed me that the young longhair was going to Cooktown because he had been through earlier, three weeks before, trying to make it, but the St. George River was too high. I guess there are so few cars that come through Mt. Carbine that someone would remember a fact like that.

I told Dave who was again rummaging around in a dump heap, looking for discarded bottles of some vintage and value. He stopped his rummaging and headed down the road to the Yugoslavian's car. Three hours later, Dave and the longhair walked back up the road. The three of us went into the Wolfram Hotel, had a beer in the quiet solitude of an empty pub, and then packed our things in the back of the longhair's car, and drove down the rutted road to Cooktown.

Thirty miles later, on reaching the Reedys St. George River, the longhair—Ron was his name—stopped his car and waded out into the swiftly running river through which we needed to drive. In spite of the fact that the water came to his waist—seemingly too deep to attempt crossing in a sedan—he came back, reached into his glove compartment, took out a roll of duct tape, and sealed the doors of the car shut as if this was an everyday maneuver traveling down an Australia road. He then removed the fan belt from the radiator. "So as not to spray water on the distributor and plugs," he explained matter-of-factly to us, and the three of us got in the car by climbing through the windows and drove smoothly down into the water. Ron gunned his engine and drove till the water was halfway up to the windows at which point the engine died.

"Well, I thought I would make it. Oh, well, shit. Let's pan for gold. Somebody will be along eventually."

At this point, four days had passed. Now we sat virtually in the middle of nowhere. Just like at sea though, we hadn't—up to that point—felt in a hurry. But at that point, I was losing my patience and sense of adventure. Four days since we'd left Cairns. Now we were totally out in the middle of nowhere surrounded by mean kangaroos (which I never did see but if I had, they were for sure mean), ten-foot-high ant hills, and snakes that killed in two minutes. While Dave unloaded our packs from a flooding back seat, Ron removed a couple of pans from the trunk of his car, which was awash with water, and proceeded to give us a lesson on how to pan for gold while telling us stories of the gold rush that happened about the time of the California Gold Rush.

The sun lowered past midafternoon, and I was thinking "eventually" would never arrive when in fact it bullied its way to its fulfillment just as we were thinking to pitch a tent on high ground for the night.

It took us ten hours to drive that next 140 miles to Cooktown. That was quicker than we traveled across 140 miles of ocean in most cases, generally traveling no more than four knots an hour, but I felt a horseless carriage would have been quicker. The rutted, potholed dirt road was so deeply eroded that if our wheels stayed in the tracks, we would have taken out the oil pan. I wouldn't have driven over thirty, but Ron was averaging fifty after we finally got out of the Reedys St. George, that first crossing where we were stuck for three hours with water running through the engine and filling up the inside of the car. Very stuck. Distributor wet, battery dead. Seats wet.

After passing our time panning for gold, a four-wheel drive did in fact come along and attempted to pull us out. Since the engine would not start, we were first pulled backward. In the process of doing that, the steering arm on one of the front wheels got reversed. With a lot of hot and dirty banging and pounding, Ron and Dave got the wheel readjusted. It still took a bit more to get across that river. We borrowed the battery off the Land Rover and got the car started again, but the engine again drowned out in the deep water. Trying to pull the dead weight, the tow rope broke, and again, the car sat in the deepest part of the river. I was feeling disheartened and frustrated when unexpectedly—miraculously—a semitruck, coming from Cooktown, arrived. Then another car came from our original direction. Having not seen a car in days, it seemed like a virtual traffic jam out on the Reedys St. George in the middle of nowhere. But with now five men pushing and the Land Rover pulling, we got the car to the other side. Finally.

Of course, the other car made it through the crossing with no problem! Jay, the driver of that vehicle, ended up driving in tandem with us to Cooktown. On the second crossing, he punctured a hole in his gas tank, but luckily, he had some epoxy to fix it. (At this point, I had a list of survival gear for the Australian bush: snake-bite kit, duct tape, and epoxy.) On the third crossing, we got stuck again, bogged in the sand. Jay pulled us out, and then on we rambled and jumbled down the road.

In the end, getting to Cooktown was a letdown even though it was a change from forever being confined to a sailboat. The adventure was in getting there. Of course, because it's Australia, there was a list of pubs visited on the way. Palmer River Café and Pub was the setting of the biggest gold rush in the world. We had a couple drinks, looked at the relics and preserved snakes and spiders and carried on. Lakeland Downs came into view, a 190-square-mile fertile valley, the folded concern of a $13 million man who happened to pick the wrong people to manage and work this rich piece of land. Bankrupt, he had his land being sold off by his creditors bit by bit.

We stopped at the legendary, iconic Lion's Den, built in 1875, at seven-thirty, not bailing out till almost eleven, getting drunk on brandy (the boys on beer of course). The four of us sat on one side, and the proprietor's son, maybe thirty to thirty-five years old, sat on the other, getting soused on rum. My first impression of him was as an Aussie Okie hillbilly backwoodsman, but in our three and a half hours of conversing, he proved, even through his Australian drawl, to be an intelligent self-learned man. And then there was my Dave, who somehow had become the authority on the movements of the Australian crocodile, a scene that was quite comic.

As I said, Cooktown wasn't much to behold, a sleepy nothing little town. Even today, forty years later, it only boasts a population of two thousand people. Located on the mouth of the Endeavor River, the most northerly town on the east coast of Australia, it was named after Captain Cook beached his ship *Endeavor* there in 1770 for repairs. It became a supply port for the Palmer River goldfields in 1873. After the gold rush petered out, it again fell quietly asleep.

Ron took us fifteen miles out of town to swim in a deep stream that crossed the road and then back into town where he "shouted" us drinks and dinner at the Sovereign Hotel. That night at the pub, we met another couple, Jim and Judy D., with whom we ended up staying at their house for a few more days. They had a simple, easy setup consisting of two tin sheds adjoined by a porch, surrounded by small mini gardens growing capsicum, tomatoes, herbs, potatoes, corn. In the small world of folks living alternative lifestyles, they ended up knowing some of the people who lived in the area of North Hokianga where I had lived.

In the end though, there was nothing of account to relate about Cooktown. Actually, as life should be, it was the process of getting there that was the journey, not the goal itself. A long ordeal to get there with a disappointing outcome. The heat was oppressive. The folks we met certainly brought color to the adventure, most being interesting characters. There were times for sure that I was wishing I wasn't at their mercy, sitting listening to their overblown dreams that, from the brief time I'd known them, I was confident would never materialize. I just watched. But I was grateful for their generosity.

Four days later, we had a long but relatively uneventful return trip back to Cairns, returning with both Jay and Ron. I have no memory of why Jay was now traveling with us; maybe the gas tank leak proved too bad to make the trip back, and I'm sure there would have been no way to get it fixed in Cooktown. I'm not even sure why Ron was going back to Cairns already or why he had gone to Cooktown in the first place. But in any event, Ray, Dave, and Ron sat in the front. I was relegated to the back with Ray's dog Tripper who was usually half sitting on me and the baggage.

What does that say about me? What does that say about Aussie chivalry? Germaine Greer was an Australian woman who started the women's lib movement, and I now knew why. There were pubs I wasn't allowed into, being a woman. There were pubs where I was served beer through a small hole on the outside of the building with the Aborigines who also weren't allowed inside while the men drank inside. I kid you not. Even in the pubs I was permitted to enter, I was usually greeted by the scowls of men who definitely were conveying that they didn't appreciate me entering their domain.

On our return, the Reedys St. George River crossing went smoothly though the engine died in the middle of the second crossing. Meanwhile, a grader had filled in the first crossing with stone, making it a shallow easy passover. On down the dusty dirt road we sped, bouncing and swerving around the ruts. We overheated once. We blew out a right rear tire on a hill, but after a bit of trouble changing it, putting on a not-so-good-looking used tire, we carried on.

The country sped by, eucalyptus trees and gum trees slowly taking over the grasslands. Jay or Ron explained how the ranchers would set bushfires to herd the cattle together. The cows were drawn to the place of the fire because it was a clean camp, free of ticks, and eventually sprouting new young grass. These firings also scarred and thus stimulated the eucalyptus trees to send up new shoots. Supposedly there were twice as many trees as at the turn of the century. Nothing—drought, fire, or an ax—will get rid of the eucalyptus. There was not a twig of undergrowth save the grass amongst these plains of trees. This might have been a result of low rainfall; this might have been the result of overgrazing, or this area, too, might have suffered from the destructive force of millions of rabbits.

I read many years later that the first rabbits were brought to Australia by an Englishman who released twenty-four bunnies on his property so he'd have something to shoot for sport. I also read that the first fleet of settlers brought them in 1788. However they came, the rabbits devastated Australia. A variety of attempts to contain or destroy them included a rabbit-proof fence, shooting them, and destroying warrens. The introduction of a myxomatosis virus in the 1950s severely reduced the population, but those who survived bred immune offspring, and so the population was again on the rise.

The cane toads and rabbits were only some of the invasive species. Over one hundred thousand wild camels populate Australia, eating 80 percent of the vegetation available to them. There are also large populations of wild horses, goats, and deer all introduced by the first settlers, decimating the vegetation in a country that had been so isolated from the rest of the world, it had spawned strange animals that exist nowhere else in the world, like the platypus, the egg-laying, duck-billed, beaver-tailed, otter-footed mammal that is also venomous. Crazy animal, eh? We never saw one. Nor a kangaroo.

The cathedral termite houses bulged up everywhere, tall red ten-to-fifteen-feet-tall pinnacled mounds. Jay and Ron both insisted they get easily thirty feet tall. Ron told us that if the stumps are crumbled down to almost a powder and watered then rammed and tamped down, they form a floor as hard and solid as cement. I love learning those sorts of things indigenous to a particular area. Stranded in the outback of Australia, I think, I could build a rammed-termite-brick house that would be a strong, cool shelter with a broad overhanging roof so the walls didn't disintegrate during the torrential monsoon downpours.

Heading to Cooktown, we suffered the muggy humidity of the coastal lands and enjoyed the expanse of the dry wastelands as we went inland. We saw marshlands reminiscent of the lowlands of Maryland with its tributaries branching off smaller and smaller from the Chesapeake. In the highlands going through Mt. Molloy, Margeba and the Head of Kuranda, the scenery was a bit more like New Zealand, pasturelands and forests constellated with small towns. One-horse towns like Kuranda held the same good vibration and pulchritude as areas like Santa Cruz, California, in the '60s with rain forests and evergreens predominating with only a few fields cutting through the thick forest and only a few neatly tended shacks and small houses dotting the scenery. From Kuranda, with impressive vistas, the road descended seven miles from the rain-forested mountain to the cane fields and eventually back to Cairns.

Though I've met many fine Australians since then, at that time, I did not have a favorable impression of Australia. I've been told since then that Queensland and Cairns were considered the backwoods of Australia, equivalent to our conservative redneck areas of America. It was a sexist, racist, male-dominated, small-minded area where Aborigines were spit on, and I myself felt treated like a secondhand citizen.

But we were there and, again, back in the civilized world, we were caught in the vortex where we needed to find work, so we would be there a while. Living near a town meant spending money. If you didn't have money, you desired it just so you could spend it, the very circle of insanity I never adapted to well. But I did enjoy eating a meal out once in a while or being able to buy real shampoo and fresh vegetables. There's always a middle way to balance the extremes.

It was always easier for Dave to find work in any port not only because he was a man (in a very sexist society in Australia) but also because my only skill, since age eight, had been typing. Back in Cairns, Dave obtained work at a boat works right across from our anchorage. Being back in an English-speaking country, I also went in search of work. After a week, I secured a casual job, taking on overload work in a printing office in town using Varitype and an IBM composer, the same machines I'd worked on—what?—seven years earlier when I worked in my father's publishing company that published journals on experimental psychology.

Upon hiring me, the director made it clear they (meaning his company and the union) did not care to hire women. He spoke of the woman lino-operator with disdain, clearly not wanting her to be working there, but there were no men for the job. It was a strange process to be interviewing for a job where I was being told how much they didn't want to hire me because I was a woman, but darn, they were going to have to because there were no men for the job. I would earn $2.75 an hour, close to $22 a day. I resolved that I would save it, hoard it, and use it as I saw fit, and not let Dave squander it—a term that was often irrationally applied depending upon my mood.

Up to the point when I joined Dave, I never had been in a long-term relationship where I commingled money or was dependent on another. Being dependent on Dave created a lot of unfamiliar conflict for me, at times feeling like I'd given up any control I had over my life. I had actually not been in even short-term relationships since my first year at university, eight years before, where I'd met a handsome Chilean exchange student. I, fairly quickly after meeting him, had moved in with him. Besides going to college full time and working part time, I fell right into the role of the domestic housewife, mimicking my mother's every move, anticipating what my Chilean liked to eat, fetching whatever he might need. He was ten years older than I was, worldly, educated, an artist, and an activist. After three months he, in as gentle way as possible, told me I had to leave. His argument was, "You must learn to have your own life and *share* it with a man. You should not make a man the center of your life."

I was devastated, to say the least, but I hardened my heart, finished out the semester, and went back to Santa Barbara for the summer, and it's from there I decided to move even farther away from family and all those who didn't love me. I moved to Hawai'i. Though it was so deeply painful at the time, fifty years later, I have always been thankful to Olman for setting me free. Because of him, I had some memorable adventures, starting with that auspicious move to Hawai'i.

But there I was in Cairns, Australia, still not standing up for myself as an individual. Having a job and my own financial independence was a cover-up for the emotional prison I'd put myself in. It was the same diversion that working on the *Follies Bergeres* had been. Again, my perception of the lack of commonality between Dave and I seemed to get exacerbated when we were in ports. It was in ports that I criticized how he spent money, how he drank too much, how he didn't work hard enough, how he was too sociable in the pubs. I hadn't discovered anything about myself because I was focused on blaming him for what wasn't working in my life. I was quick to criticize, but I had no communication skills to be able to identify my needs or request what I needed to make the relationship functional. I had attached myself to the first person who had declared he loved me since Olman had set me free. I hadn't a clue about love or loving or what being in a relationship was about, and yet I had inextricably bound myself to Dave. Though I'd had brief affairs with men over the previous eight years, I had never fallen in love again, and I'd never shared or commingled money and everyday living until I sailed away from New Zealand. Somehow, without seeing it coming, I had once again usurped my freedom and autonomy. Yes, Dave had his baggage, but mine was much heavier. And I kept picking it up to carry instead of realizing it just wasn't serving me.

The outgoing river current, bolstered by a twenty-one-foot tide, made it virtually impossible to row to shore without being swept downriver a mile unless it was slack tide. In Cairns, without an engine any longer, we anchored farther away from shore so we'd have an easy sail out, either in an emergency or when we pulled anchor to sail on to new horizons. Within several days of being anchored in Cairns, we figured out the trick of going to shore only at the slack tide.

Heavy rains and the fast-flowing outgoing tides can play havoc on boat anchors too. One afternoon, sitting on deck reading, I looked up to see a forty-foot fishing boat drifting broadside down the river at a rapid pace. Dave was working at the boat dock within my sight though across the river at least a quarter mile away. Before I even had time to send out a signal to him via a unique call we had developed, other boats were setting off their horns in alarm. I saw Dave jumping into his employer's twelve-foot motorboat and, full throttle, speeding out into the river mouth, trying to intercept the boat before it slammed into any of the two dozen sailboats at anchor. The adrift boat was moving probably twelve knots with the outgoing tide and the river's outflow.

The fishing boat missed our boat by several feet and was about to slam broadside into a small thirty-five-foot cruising yacht when Dave reached it. He jumped onboard the drifting boat, rushed to the bow, and quickly kicked the anchor wench free to drop more anchor, which apparently was still attached but aweigh. Amazingly, the anchor caught. The boat swung around, bow upriver, as the anchor held, but as it swung, it clipped off the bow stay of the sailboat it was about to ram. Luckily that was all the damage that it did. As Dave had not bothered to secure the runabout he'd powered out there, just leaping off it, the boat had drifted out with the tide. Another yachtie had, in the meantime, jumped into his rubber Avon and captured the runabout, bringing it back to rescue Dave from his adventure. I was impressed with Dave's quick thinking and action. He really was far from a flawed human being.

No argument, there's a need for anchors in life. When they're set, they need to be set deeply into the sand or mud or rock or coral with lots of line played out so they cannot lift free. Then you can come to a stop, rest, find safe harbor, have time to look at the scenery in more detail. Beware of where you set it though. The chain could get snagged and entangled where, in the end, one may not be able to get free of that anchor.

Anchors aweigh, boats adrift, anchors down, calmly moored. Lines and moorings and attachments, resting places, and open seas. Winds and doldrums, rushing rivers, and stillness flowing. Frayed ropes, spliced ropes. Constant change. The line that bound Dave and I frayed, and then we'd splice it together, and then it frayed, and then we spliced it together.

Tides turned, winds shifted like moods changing hour by hour, week by week. Dave got word his father was ill, and his parents were sending him money to return to the States.

Through all of this, Dave had me taking my temperature to see when I was ovulating. We were like rabbits before he left, and maybe it was the calm afterward, after he flew back to California, that allowed the embryo to lay hold in my inverted uterus, but I was clearly showing signs of pregnancy within weeks of his departure with morning sickness and an aversion to the smell of cucumbers.

Anchor down, grabbing hold, swinging and facing into the wind. "Oooh, I'm going to have a baby. Oooh, how sweet."

Working as a typesetter in the small shop where only one other woman worked and the sexism of the Australian male reigned, I took the time to typeset an attractive card that I made specially to send to my father announcing that "I have happily conceived out of wedlock. You are going to be a grandfather." This would have been the first grandchild in the family. I'm not sure why it was necessary to include that "I've conceived out of wedlock." Maybe I was still trying to scream in his face for all his failures and the pain he'd caused. I figured he couldn't be too judgmental because he had left my mother for my mother's sister after twenty-two years of marriage.

I did not get a response from my father. On the assumption that my letter, by small chance, had gotten lost in the oceanic space between Australia and Texas, I created another fanciful and happy note that he was going to be a grandfather and that I was happy about my pregnancy.

That was in March 1975. My father never replied. I vowed to never speak to him again. I never did.

Dave returned, and in June, we left Cairns, Australia, to find a welcome place to have our baby. I was three months pregnant. I had seen one male obstetrician in Cairns. He was a horrible dominating, sexist man. I literally felt like a piece of meat on his examination table. Combining that with the visible racism and sexism, I was not, under any circumstances, going to have a baby in Australia. With no specific destination in sight, we headed north toward Papua New Guinea.

I was very seasick even in the calmest of seas all the way to the first anchorage in Papua New Guinea.

CHAPTER 5

If you don't know where you are going, any road will get you there.
—Lewis Carroll

We were in search of a nesting site to have our baby. After a rough, windy seven-day-long passage from Cairns, we arrived at Talewewai, which turned out to be an unprotected anchorage at which we violently rolled for two days before deciding to make the short sail to Wari. How beautiful to be back in the turquoise lagoons filled with fish and shellfish and peace and tranquility, away from the port of Cairns.

Walking slowly through the pathed village of thatched huts, I heard an almost indiscernible *tap-tap* of metal on metal. Sitting peacefully in the shade of their houses or under the coconut trees, I noticed people tapping a small knife on the edge of a small flat tin and then put the knife in their mouths. This was my first introduction to the ritual of chewing betel nut. More metal tapping metal. It was a sound that, over the months, became part of the under-hum of life in Papua New Guinea, coming from inside of huts or from women sitting on the ground weaving mats or from men in their fishing canoes. Betel nut, the areca nut was chewed by the youngest child. I often saw babies teething on pieces of the nut. It was only later as people entered their teens, that it was mixed with the slaked lime and betel leaf. Betel leaf is a stimulant (as is the areca nut). The mixture of both has had both ceremonial and symbolic value in many Asian and Hindu cultures for several thousand years. In Papua New Guinea, it was chewed any time, all the time just as one would smoke a cigarette. Young and old, man or woman.

They put a bit of areca (a nut the size of a walnut coming from a palm tree but looking very similar to a young coconut) into their mouth, and they start chewing; the nut activates salivation. Then they wet the end of their knife and dip it into their little tin of lime, a tin that might have once held chewing tobacco or breath mints. On other islands, I found the islanders, possibly not having had access to chewing tobacco, carried their lime in small dried hollowed-out gourds closed with a whittled-down stick, the sound of the knife tapping off the excess lime being more muted but still discernible wherever we went.

Tapping off the excess on the side of the tin, they'd lick off the lime, being careful to keep it on the same side as the nut in their mouth or else the lime would burn the gums and lips. And then they'd stuff in a bit of what locally they called *luga*, which was the actual betel leaf (of the *Piperacea* family, which also includes pepper and kava). The mixture turns the saliva red in color. All of this paraphernalia of chewing of betel nut was kept in small baskets that everyone carried. It was usually the only thing carried in the baskets, their little "drug kits." Though it's been used for millennia, doctors are finding it's a major cause of oral cancers.

Of no concern to them, they smiled brightly though shyly, their mouth edged faintly with red; their teeth darkly stained, some almost to the point of blackness, from the betel nut.

Wari had clay, and they were famous for their beautifully made clay pots that looked like they'd been thrown on a wheel but were made completely by hand, pressing and shaping the sides to a thin perfection and a perfect roundness that seemed impossible to achieve. I'm not sure how they fired them, but I believe they built hot fires in the ground and buried them. There have been archaeological studies of the pottery trade from Wari, Goodenough, and some islands in the Trobriands, tracing the trade back more than a hundred years. I know I was impressed enough that I spent my last few dollars on a bowl from Wari though I ended up selling it for four times the amount a few weeks later to a sailboat who had heard of the pottery but hadn't made it to Wari and talked me into selling it. It was a sensible trade, for, one, I quadrupled my money, but more realistically, that fine thin pot would not have made it long on our sailboat without eventually getting broken.

On Wari, the children were watching and awaiting our arrival, which ended up being at a little wooden wharf. After the normal routine of securing the boat, we went into the village, surrounded by a buzz of children. It was a pristine village of thatched huts with not a leaf left lying on the ground. The main path of the village was lined with a low sword-leafed plant, similar to the New Zealand flax plant and hibiscus bushes; all the rest of the area was shaded by coconut trees and banana groves. The jungle crept in at the base of the mountain though the hills themselves were only grass covered. It was mostly sand on which the village huts themselves stood though the jungle edge revealed rich soil from the volcanic hills. I could see small square patches of yams and melons in several places on the hills. Along the coast, intermingled in the coconut trees, were patches of manioc, pineapples, papayas, melons, and bananas, most of which seemed laden with bunches of bananas of varying development.

Wari was a picturesque village. Though not as colorful as the Polynesian islands we'd visited, it was completely traditional. There were no plywood shacks. I was enchanted that all the structures were thatched. There were few flowers, and what was blooming were mostly hibiscus. I saw frangipani trees but without flowers. The people themselves were dressed in dirt-stained, drab clothes, the color of the thatched huts instead of the vibrantly colored prints found in Tahiti, the Cook Islands, or Hawai'i. We were now distinctively in Melanesia, a different ethnicity altogether.

The Melanesians were an attractive people, dark bronze in color with Negroid-wiry hair, none of the waist-length long hair like in Polynesia. There were almost no fat or overweight people here unlike Polynesia where fat was a sign of wealth and being well provided for. Few people stood taller than five-foot-nine whether from genetics or lack of nutrition.

After their initial curiosity wore off and after they learned we had no money to buy their wares, they pretty much left us to our privacy, which was very nice because it was exceedingly trying to have so many little faces clambering on the boat, forever peering in the portholes and hatch, though their invasiveness was always with a degree of consideration mostly because they were shy.

We befriended Eddie and Delma, the schoolteachers who could speak good English. The other inhabitants spoke little English, speaking only Police Motu or Hiri, one of several official pidgin languages of Papua New Guinea. John, the Society chairman (the Society was the local cooperative store of which he was in charge), visited us almost every day. We traded. We gave him fishhooks and rope and red feathers. He gave us betel nut, fish, oranges, pineapple, kumara. Dave ended up chewing betel nut almost daily after that to the enjoyment of John and the locals. Delma, the teacher, gave me a beautiful big basket. She said she'd like to give us a mat, but all hers were too big, but she invited me to go to the school to learn how to weave mats and baskets, which I did.

I noticed many women wearing grass skirts and no tops though most of the women wore knee-length skirts with blouses. Delma said all women, including herself, wore their grass skirts often. Most of the islanders had little money; grass skirts were free but for the time it took to make them from the sago palm. In the week there, I spent peaceful days in the village. Besides little tidbits of life on Wari, watching mats be woven and clay pots be created from a blob of mud, I learned a few Motu words: *waila* (water), *keno* (sleep), *korau* (you go), *kulauma* (you come), *kagutoki* (hello and thank you). A dog was *bowwa* of course. "Give me a betelnut"—"Sala kuyeyama ya tun."

On June 29, we sailed to Samarai, an island about three miles off the coast of mainland Papua New Guinea. Once the administrative center for Milne Bay Province, it was located on the southeastern tip of the China Strait. Samarai conjured up visions of samurai swordsmen, disciplined, educated martial artists, and of Japanese fighter planes committing hari-kari in the name of the empire. Samarai—not samurai—was destroyed during World War II, but not by the Japanese. The Australians destroyed it to prevent the wharves and buildings from falling into Japanese control. One of the first major battles of World War II in which the Allied troops defeated a Japanese invasion happened in Milne Bay, not far from Samarai.

Samarai was at one time the second biggest "city" next to Port Moresby in Papua New Guinea. It was originally a significant stopover point for trading ships between Australia and Asia since its "discovery" by Captain John Moresby in 1873. On the 56 total acres of the island, there were 1,500 local people and 34 Europeans. It was a port of dirty warehouses, a dirty anchorage, and a dirty disappointment. There was a little fenced-in marketplace, selling the areca nut and betel leaves, much like the marketplace in Suva, Fiji, that had been filled with kava root. But you could also buy a few limes, smoked fish, and kumara. The town also had a small library and a "colonialist's club." Otherwise, it was an ugly dirty rusted-tin town in decline, much of which had been more rapid in the seven years before our arrival when the administrative center was moved to Alotau in Milne Bay, a few miles around the bend on the mainland.

The sail over from Wari was an 8:00-to-5:00 day sail. Cloudy. Not too hot, a few rain squalls. While I steered, my quiet thoughts circled and circled around how much I really disliked sailing now. Because of my pregnancy, I was constantly sick when at sea even in the calmest of waters. I was well past the morning sickness stage, but as soon as we pulled anchor, I was nauseous.

We caught four fish sailing from Wari, and on arriving in Samarai, Dave was able to sell three of them (about 40 pounds of fish) for $8.40, or 8 kina 40 toya as their money was called. With our 8 kina 40 toya, we bought aerograms, 400 fishhooks for trading, a bunch of limes, and 2 new chimney glasses for the Coleman lantern.

After we cleared customs the day after we arrived (a very slack procedure), we again walked about. We went to the local library and read a little in books about New Guinea, but too much of it was about the missionary influence. I had grown to resent the missionary influence wherever I went in the islands. I was incredibly closed minded about them all, forever thinking who did they think they were to come to remote islands with people living in harmony with their gods? They come and tell them it was sinful to be naked and that they must adopt the belief that some white dude from some faraway country they've never heard of can save them when they go to a heaven, a place of which they'd never conceived? I recognized that maybe convincing these primitive peoples that, like on other islands, cannibalism wasn't the best idea was a benefit, but otherwise, the destruction of the culture of peoples around the world was abhorrent to me from my very one-sided perspective.

We met an Aussie there, John, who did write-ups of sailing yachts for *Pacific Island Monthly*. He invited us to the local pub-club to interview us. Dave guzzled a few beers on John's money, and afterward, the three of us walked around the island, sauntering as slowly as we could. It still only took us half an hour. I dreaded having to be in Samarai for two weeks as I couldn't envision there being much to keep me occupied. I had really liked Wari, spending a couple hours each day fishing and exploring the reef in the dinghy and the rest of the time enjoying the village life. Delma had taught me the technique of weaving mats there; I hoped to get to some place where there was a lot of pandanus to weave a mat that would fit the floor of the boat.

But Samarai offered nothing to satisfy my needs of the moment. The little bay in which we anchored, right off the wharf of warehouses and dirt, provided no privacy for us. There was a filthy, greasy film of gasoline and oil on the water. Ten degrees from the equator, the oppressive heat with little breeze was torturous, especially when I couldn't dive into clear waters to cool off. The few Europeans that lived there were rude, nosy, imperious. I felt their pompous pretentiousness, their racist manner toward the locals and wanted nothing to do with them. The local people were not at all friendly and averted their eyes when we met on the streets. It was not surprising that again discontent ruled most of my thoughts.

It was through the expats who'd lived in the area long enough to learn—and probably reconstruct to fit their own biased reasoning with an air of authoritative veracity—some of the cultural ways of the local peoples. It was sitting in the white-man's club—to which local people were not invited nor permitted and in which I was the only woman—that I learned the story of One Talk or Wuntok in pidgin English. I sensed a bit of condescension in the telling as to why "these people" would never "succeed in the real world."

In a village—say, the one village on Wari—all of a man's *relatives* are his Wuntok. If that same man was on the other side of his island in another village and he confronted someone, not necessarily a relative but someone from his village, the two were automatically Wuntok. It blossomed further. If you traveled to another island, anybody from your same island, not necessarily even your same village, now automatically became your Wuntok. Being Wuntok, you were responsible to help him or her if in need. By slim chance, if two people from anywhere in Papua New Guinea were to find themselves, say, in New Zealand or Australia, they now were Wuntok and again culturally obligated to take care of each other.

So Dave was my One Talk because we were partners together on our sailboat. We were family and responsible for each other as it should be. If another American came, *if* we were part of this cultural sense of responsibility, he'd be our One Talk, and if he was down and out or needed help, we would be *obligated* culturally to help him. It didn't matter that we didn't know him or that he was from the other side of the United States or that we had nothing in common politically, spiritually, or economically; we were from the same "larger village," and hence One Talk.

In one breath, it was a beautiful human way of taking care of each other when away from your home. But the situation, in the terms described by this expat, was it didn't work well in the modern white man's economic community. Most of the cooperative society stores were always broke and unable to procure goods because of Wuntok. Say, a man goes to Samarai to get supplies for his store on another island, and he has $10. If he runs into a Wuntok, and this Wuntok is broke, the custom of Wuntok code declares he must give him money. So now, the first man has no money or insufficient money to buy supplies for his store, so he would return with little or nothing that he'd gone there for. Or in the situation of the main cooperative store warehouse in Samarai: A Wuntok comes in, and the storekeeper happens to be from his island. The man says, "Gimme one sack rice, one sack sugar, one box . . . and I'll pay you when the copra comes in." The Wuntok storekeeper cannot deny him the advance. Of course, the warehouse never gets paid. The only stores that seemed to flourish were European run because, of course, they controlled their credit giving and they made a point of collecting. Most importantly though, their cultural rules were capitalism; they weren't governed by the law of Wuntok.

We did leave Samarai to go to Magalkarona Bay, Sariba Island, on July 4 to await the arrival of mail in two or three weeks. Though we could see Sariba from Samarai—maybe fifteen miles away—without an engine, the sail took a long time. The lack of wind combined with strong currents through these islands in Papua New Guinea contributed in part to the reduced number of sailing yachts and the continued isolation of the area. We spent a long time trying to beat into the light wind to get to Sariba. We had tried to go through the China Straights so as to enter Liiki Bay, the giant lagoon that was the lacuna of the *U* forming Sariba, but the tidal currents were too strong to allow progress. We turned around, making giant tacks between the land mass of Samarai and Sariba until we finally arrived in Magalkarona Bay in the late afternoon.

We dropped anchor on the southeast corner of the large bay in front of a slipway and large colonial house that seemed strangely out of place. I immediately insisted on more privacy, especially after being at Samarai, so we pulled anchor and simply allowed the boat to drift deeper into the beautiful little peaceful bay, the head of which was dressed with a picturesque village of thatched huts lining its beach shore.

Though the day had begun sunny, the first we'd had in a week, it quickly turned to a pluvial downpour. I managed to get the rain catcher set up right as the rain ended. Had I been quicker, we would have been able to collect fifty gallons of freshwater at least. Not to worry missing out on that downpour though. We found, in the days and months to come, there was no lack of water falling out of the sky.

CHAPTER 6

Thousands have lived without love, but not one without water

—W. H. Auden

After the dirt and bustle of New Caledonia followed by Cairns, we re-immersed ourselves in the more peaceful island life I'd experienced in my first year of sailing. Soft, quiet sunrises yawned into daily life at anchorage, moving slowly through the day, not rushing to do much. And not much to rush to do. In Papua New Guinea, life revolved around the daily rain showers that started around noon and often continued for most of the afternoon. We geared ourselves to accomplishing certain things in the mornings when it wasn't raining: laundry, exploring on shore, dinghy sailing around bays, diving, and snorkeling.

As a rule, at sea, where we needed to conserve water, we used about a gallon a day per person for staying hydrated and cooking. At sea, we bathed only in saltwater, using Joy dish detergent to wash our hair and body as it sudsed up well in saltwater; no other body soaps or shampoos would lather. The *Paz del Mar* carried about 200 gallons of freshwater. There were days on end, even weeks on end, when we would have no rain or appreciable precipitation to replenish our water tanks. With conservative use, the two of us could be at sea for 100 days without rain or needing to reach a water source on land. The longest I was ever at sea without seeing land was six weeks, forty-five days.

At anchor, we had an awning up, suspended across the boom, tied off to the rigging, which we maneuvered in such a position that the runoff from the rain would channel into large funnels set into five-gallon jugs. Without the awning, the deck of the cabin was our catchment. Dave had installed one-inch-tall trim on the edges of the cabin deck that ended at half-inch copper tubing to which we attached short pieces of hose that dumped into two five-gallon jugs, one on each side of the cockpit.

Showers at sea were accomplished in the simplistic manner of standing at a secure point on deck (usually one arm around a shroud) and tossing a standard two-gallon bucket into the ocean to which a half-inch line was attached to the handle. Pull it up. Dump the water over your head. Suds up with Joy. Throw the bucket back in and haul up enough water to pour over your head and body until the soap was washed off. This occurred whether we were sailing north from Hawai'i to the mainland United States, where the ocean and air could be quite chilly, or in the lovely tropics, where in some places the ocean was like a bathtub. I'm sure there were a few big, rich-man's fancy sailboats that had showers below deck, but I never saw one. This method was the sailor's shower.

I had one very painful bath on the passage from Hawai'i to the Marquesas on *Westward Ho*. I had finished washing my hair and body, and with my eyes shut to keep the detergent out, I tossed in the bucket and pulled up the water, pouring it over my head. One bucketful was not sufficient to get the soap out of my hair, and hence, I again tossed the bucket in. As I tossed it in, I felt strings trailing from my body to the bucket. *Maybe the rope is beginning to fray*, I thought, a bit puzzled. I pulled in another bucketful and again poured it over my head and body. Upon opening my eyes, I found that I was draped with the blue tentacles of a Portuguese man-of-war jellyfish, tentacles that I'd been rubbing across my face, chest, arms as I was rinsing off the soap. And almost simultaneously upon seeing these strings, I began to sting.

I was completely naked with close to every inch of my body burning, and as I ran below, I could see that we were sailing through a fleet of their little blue sails. A few years later, when we were in Queensland, Australia, during box jellyfish season—a jellyfish whose sting can kill you within one minute—I learned that applying alcohol to the sting neutralizes it. Those who dared the box jellyfish in Australia by surfing or diving would always carry rubbing alcohol or vodka or 101-proof rum (some believe urine works; it doesn't). But I didn't know about alcohol then, so I suffered several hours of intense, burning red welts across my whole body. My crewmates laughed; I laughed too in between the tears of pain. It was so bizarre.

As anyone knows who has spent time swimming in the ocean, saltwater leaves you forever feeling sticky as the salt clinging to the body, even if toweled off, absorbs the moisture again. The towels, after multiple uses, might get dry during the day in the sun but feel soaked again in the evenings. Besides its necessity for survival, freshwater for bodies and laundry was truly a luxurious craving, a hidden addiction you don't know you have until you can't have it.

We, as any cruising yacht, had a small sink down below with a spigot worked by a foot pump connected to our freshwater supply used only for cooking and drinking. At sea or at anchorages away from crowded ports where sewerage could be a problem, we always washed all our dishes in saltwater. Dishwashing, as with laundry, was always done in the cockpit, hauling up buckets of saltwater (except, as I said, in nasty dirty moorages like Papeete or Samarai). Laundry at sea waited until we reached port. In the warm tropical South Pacific, there were no clothes to wash upon reaching shore, only sheets and towels, as we were forever naked.

All washing was done by hand with blocks of natural soap, a two-inch rounded stick, and water. Wet the clothes, rub that block of lard-lye soap to lather it up, fold it, hit it with the club. *Thud-thud*. Fold. *Thud-thud*. Fold. *Thud-thud*. Fold. It was a rhythm heard on the river rocks near streams, by watering holes, and even coming from washrooms in some of the small towns throughout the South Pacific as the women, working together, chattered in groups. I was usually alone in the cockpit of our boat, *Paz del Mar*, rubby dub, soap, fold, *thud-thud*, *thud-thud*. Next garment. Soap splattered throughout the cockpit and on me. When done, I'd grab the line, attach the bucket, throwing it into the ocean, open end first. Dump it on the cockpit. Wash down the soap. Another bucketful. Another bucketful. Plop, pull, *swoosh*, *swoosh*, rinse. Toss, plop, pull, *swoosh*, *swoosh*, rinse.

Though I usually washed the laundry in the cockpit on the boat, I went to shore to do a final rinse in freshwater. In populated ports, I'd go to a tap on shore where I'd also take a very public bath in my bikini. On remote islands, like Magalkarona Bay (or in the cavern in Tonga), I loved to go to the streams to rinse the laundry, joining a multitude of local women as they did their laundry, chatting, laughing, maybe telling gossipy stories of their husbands or lovers or children in their native tongue. I might not understand them, but the camaraderie of the women together was warm. It was a pleasant way to while a few hours away in the company of strangers. Several years later, when I finally returned to the States, I felt that lack of community. In our society of walls and houses and our own private laundry rooms, women—people in general—lived in isolation.

Eight months later, when we set sail away from Papua New Guinea with our six-week-old daughter, I had one dozen terrycloth diapers. I'm not sure Pampers had been invented yet in 1975; if they had, they had not made it to Papua New Guinea, nor did I have money to buy something to be thrown away. I washed diapers in the rinse water from the previous days' wash using Joy detergent. I rinsed them thoroughly in saltwater, becoming an expert on wringing every drop of saltwater out of them. Using a scarce one gallon of freshwater to rinse the saltwater from them, I hung them from the rigging to dry. To this day, I have a deep-seated negative loathing about seeing Pampers used, and I have no tolerance for the excuses given by the parents as they use up resources of trees, cotton, and oil while tossing urine and feces and plastic into landfills (though the rest of us must use toilets).

I was a boat wife in many respects. I acquiesced to this role, I suspect, because Dave was the one who could more easily earn the money and because that had been my mother's way, which was modeled to me. If he wasn't earning money, he was the one who did the major work on the boat, repairing rigging, making new spars. But the reality was that even if I was working also or even if I was also making repairs, I unconsciously played the boat wife. There wasn't much to do though as most days spread out each morning like an empty clean sheet to make of it as I would. I'd write in my journal, read books, and cook. As sailors of old, where the art of macramé began, I did a lot of knot tying. One particular project I was proud of involved encircling an empty bottle of rum in tiny knots of crochet thread. I also embroidered shirts with abstract designs or flowers or complete sailing sceneries.

Shortly after anchoring in Magalkarona Bay, a small wiry man paddled up in his wooden dugout canoe with a bowl of oranges and limes. His dirty shorts were the same brown as the canoe, only a little lighter than his bronzed chest. I think he meant to sell them to us and was a bit disappointed when we told him we had no money. He said we should take some anyhow. We ended up giving him some fishhooks, which seemed to brighten him up. His name was St. Francis. I so distinctly remember Dave taking a double take and saying, "Really? St. Francis?"

But his name simply reflected the influence of the missionaries in the area. Dave offered him betel nut, which he had been partaking of since Wari Island. St. Francis took the double take then, finding it quite amusing and enigmatic as Europeans did not chew betel nut—at least none that I'd met—let alone gifting it to the local people.

The next morning, we rowed to shore to visit the small village that lined the beach. It was a storybook village of maybe fifty people. Unlike Wari, it was much more colorful with flowers blooming and decorative bushes planted along walkways and between houses. There were no stores or any form of commerce. I assumed they paddled over to Samarai if they had money to buy from the society stores.

The dense mountainous jungle was oftentimes hung with mist as the early-morning steam would rise up or as a low cloud bringing more rain would caress the jungle, twisting and wisping before finally letting loose. There were rocky streams and cascades every couple hundred yards, carving out their entrance from the jungle to the sea. Seldom did a breeze stir. Silence pervaded but for the hollow echo of birds in the jungle, roosters in the village, the slap of a fish on the water.

All the houses—thatched roofs, sago bark or sago slatted walls—were built six feet or higher up on stilts. Though it was partially to raise the house up above the flooding that would occur with the torrential downpours, the main reason, I believe, was designed to protect against mosquitoes, which besides causing the normal pesty bites and itching, also carried malaria. Under each house smoldered a fire made of damp wood; with no breeze, the smoke went straight up through the cracks in the floors that were made of two-inch round smooth sapling branches. The insides of these thatched huts were almost black from the accumulated soot from these fires. Under each house was also where all the food was cooked, protected from the rains. It was common to see families sitting on logs in the space below their elevated huts, eating their yams or fish or mixtures of wild greens and shredded coconut steamed in banana leaves.

I was enthralled to be experiencing an even less civilized culture than I had in the Marquesas or Fiji. Because of this lifelong pull to less developed areas, I often reflect on the idea that I was meant to live in the 1800s, not in the industrialized age in which I found myself. Something soulful in me resonates with the simple lifestyle.

It was low tide when Dave and I decided to wander around the cove back toward the slipway we had started to anchor in front of the day before. The low tide allowed us to cross the sandflats, thus shortcutting most of the muddy path. The property was, in contrast to the thatched village, a proper colonial home and estate. The slipway operation was quite extensive with two cradles designed to haul out quite large boats. It had a big engine overhaul shop too. At first, it seemed a strange place to come upon in this remote part of the world though in reality it wasn't all that far from Samarai, the main center for this group of islands, and of course boats were the only method of transportation.

The house had manicured lawns and a beautiful white gazebo. On the porch of this well-maintained English-style house, there was an umbrella stand and a rocking horse. I remember passing an immediate judgment about these people being stuffy and racist without having even met them, figuring that since they had all this, living in this style, they were, therefore, aristocratic snobs. After poking around a bit more, never meeting anybody, we returned to the boat where I had bread rising to bake.

Near dusk, which occurred around 5:00 p.m. every day of the year, a gray-haired aged woman in a grass skirt and bare breasted paddled over in her canoe and offered us some foot-long beans and yams. Thanking her, we invited her on board for a cup of tea. She said she was on her way to trade her vegetables to the Europeans at the slipway and would return. Forty-five minutes later, her canoe silently slid out of the blackness up to our boat. She came on board, and I made her tea. Dave and she chewed betel nut; she kept laughing at—or with—Dave. Her name, she said, was Dalego. She drank her tea and talk-talk-talked in broken English and Police Motu; it was almost eight, and we hadn't eaten dinner, so I asked her if she'd like to join us. I was reluctant because, as usual, I wasn't having anything good: beans and rice and, now—with her green beans—green beans. Because beans were not part of the typical islander's diet, I had found few islanders who liked them. She ate with us and ate it all.

Dave made plans to go to her house the next day to learn how to make lime from the coral for chewing his betel nut. We had a bright-red strip of carpet down below on our cabin floor; by our standards, it was old and ragged, stained and ugly, but Dalego kept commenting on how beautiful it was. After she left, we talked about maybe trading it with her in exchange for her making a pandanus mat that would fit into that space.

The next day, during a brief break in what seemed to be constant rainfall, we went to shore again and indeed made arrangements to trade for the carpet. Then it rained solidly for two days, never letting up. Dave and I were stuck below in the sweltering thick humidity. With the rain seeming to never stop, with the daytime light so dark it always seemed like dusk, I grew restless and irritated. Many things irritated me easily at that point. It seemed impossible to be content in the moment, just living, just being in the moment. Though forever keeping our goal in sight—that we were in search of a place to give birth to our first baby—irritation hovered on the edge of my daily life as we sat waiting in this rain-drenched bay.

For these people in this quiet village, life just went on. Unlike me, nobody worried about where they were going because these people were in fact going nowhere. Few had ever conceived of going anywhere else, let alone where to sail to next or what the next place would be like or where their baby would be born. For me, my thoughts were almost always on whether the next place would allow me that giant exhale of satisfaction that, finally, I had found the place where I wanted to spend the rest of my life. I kept it way in the background of my thoughts that, wait, I *had* found that place in Hokianga and I'd left. For now, I was just wondering if and when we'd find a place to give birth to my child. I heard the sound of the slightest ripple of the ocean water on the beach. I heard children playing in the background, chickens clucking, roosters crowing, machetes hacking at the jungle, a cooking pot clanging somewhere. Dogs barked. Pigs, roaming freely, grunted. Life kept going on with not a bird, not an animal, not any other human worrying about anything. Except me sitting in my discontent, wondering when and where we were going.

From the boat, particularly early in the morning when the birds were most vocal, a cacophony of bird calls drifted across the bay. They came from deep inside the jungle that grew up the side of the mountain behind the village. I held the magic of each bird call, suspended in that crisp silence of the enshrouding jungle. These were the moments I captured and held close as another point of meditation, allowing me to find my solitude, in spite of Dave, on the trills and warbles. They joined with all the moments of finding peace in my childhood on the creeks in Maryland or the calm found lying in a field of grass staring at the sky. Each bird call became a physical object, a ball pinging against an encompassing jungle of silence, here, there, deeper, higher, *ping, ping*, hidden in the trees, dotting the hillside. It suspended my body in a lightness of being, and if I had any grumbles or complaints about Dave or the heat and the rain or the lack of stimulation, all got carried away on each bird call. A tiny shift of focus. Briefly.

We finally met the owners of the slipway and were invited over for morning tea. They were an elderly couple, Grace and Bunny Burrows who had been there for over fifty years. Bunny was a very pleasant sparkling man (so much for my prejudgment!). Grace was slower to show her warmth or to warm up to. For most of my visits, I never saw her smile, and I felt that everything I said was scrutinized, categorized, and criticized silently in her mind. I decided she wasn't the type of woman with whom I'd want to talk freely or spend a lot of time with. For whatever reason, she didn't open up until shortly before we left, at which time she shared stories of her many years there, stories that made me wish I too had lived during those times.

In the beginning though, Dave and Bunny talked "man talk," and I felt stuck talking banalities with the old lady though a common interest was chatter about her garden. Otherwise, I deemed her to be a *Women's Weekly* or *Reader's Digest* sort of woman, and in contrast, I was an unmarried twenty-five-year-old sailing around on a funky sailboat with not a dime to my name in search of a remote place to have my first child. Though she did make a few comments about my choice of where to have my baby, overall she in fact did not speak words of judgment. She was very generous and gracious with the overabundance of her garden, giving us endless amounts of foot-long beans and lemons, eggplant, and other vegetables. I was sure she felt pity for me, but oh my, I was so grateful for what she shared!

Bunny offered Dave a few days' work to help build a small twelve-by-twenty-foot engine house. Since we'd sold the fish for $8 a week ago, it was an unexpected godsend. We were very cognizant that we were not in the midst of capitalist enterprises, and our ability to earn any money would be extremely limited. We were forever hoping we'd receive money from Gabin Marques for the engine we'd left with him, which he was using to haul out boats, we'd heard—money we never did receive. I also had a tax return that I should eventually be getting from Australia from my typesetting job.

We asked Bunny and Grace what they knew of outlying islands or places where we might go to have the baby. They made mention of an island called Woodlark or Muyua where they had a friend, Don Neats, and family who had a plantation and sawmill there. It was about 120 miles from Sariba, against the no'westers of the Louisiades, seventy miles from Misima toward the Trobriands. The island was about forty miles long, sixteen miles wide, most of it never surveyed. There were 2,500 natives at Kalamadeo, the principal and only settlement. Grace also added that it was "too far away from anything; there are no white people there save Don Neats and family." She did express only that one time that she thought I was foolish to go up there in "my condition." She thought I should be staying near Alotau. She was the type of woman one couldn't explain things to, so I'd just nodded and made her think I was paying heed to her concern. But Muyua sounded perfect to us.

While Dave worked, if it wasn't raining, I'd row around in the dinghy. Often in new bays, we would put up the little sailing mast on our eight-foot pram instead of row. But there was so little wind, nary the exhale of a sleeping baby's breath, so I rowed. When I got to exceptionally colorful stretches of coral reef, I'd stop and just drift, barely dipping an oar in the water, looking at the colorful parrotfish and other reef fish. I tried dropping a hook a couple times, but I couldn't get any of the parrotfish to bite. Days drifted by like the rain. In most third-world countries, particularly lush tropical places that don't suffer drought or lack of food, time doesn't have a lot of meaning to the individuals living there. There are no deadlines to meet, no time clocks to stamp. Food grew year-round, and though I couldn't catch them, the fish were in the sea.

It was no surprise that nine days after making arrangements with Dalego, she had not yet started work on our mat as I discovered when I visited her at her home. She was inside with her older sister who was tattooed from her head to at least below her belly where her grass skirt covered her down to her knees. There were two young men there, Savano and another one who apparently, at times, worked at the slipway. Smoke wafted up through the flooring from below, keeping the malarial mosquitoes away and blackening the walls. Everything smelled like a wet campfire. The four of them sat chewing betel nut and talking, talking.

Occasionally they'd direct a question to me without any of the shyness exhibited by so many of the other people. Though there was difficulty in communicating, I felt incredibly comfortable sitting with these people, much more comfortable than sitting under the judgmental eye of Grace. To these local people, my pregnancy was natural and not something I should fear or worry about like the white people did. Women and young girls thought nothing of reaching out and touching my belly, which was always bare as I wore only short, short skirts or pareos and a bikini top.

I feel blessed to have been surrounded by these less-educated, less-"medicalized," more-natural peoples during my pregnancy though I was definitely not ignorant of all the complications of childbirth. My feeling then, as it remains today, was that though doctors and modern medicine are needed and have saved many lives, I believe they have also complicated childbirth at every level, most particularly in taking away its naturalness.

Years later, after the birth of my third child at home in Oregon City, I began to study midwifery. I attended three-day medical conferences once a month as well as lay midwifery workshops, practicing giving pelvic exams and checkups. After almost a year, I participated in two births. One was a triple-cord wrap, the baby, blue and lifeless, needed intubation, and the mother hemorrhaged. All survived thankfully. The second was a breach delivery where the arms were trapped in utero like wings, taking almost seven minutes to deliver the head. Though I recognized this was uniquely unusual to have two out of two births go bad, I realized I didn't want the responsibility that it entailed, and there ended my midwifery career.

Like the breezeless hours, time continued to stand still. If Dave wasn't working at the slipway, we would lie around and read books as the rain pounded on the deck, turning the silky gray, oftentimes muddy, bay pimply and rough from the pounding drops. Though the listless humid-hot days pressed us down, hanging on us as limp as wet laundry, we did find energy to focus on the future and preparations that needed to be made. With a baby coming, we modified one of our settees, adding a railing that could be hooked up on either end to keep the baby from falling out. Back in

1975, there were no chemical toilets on board sailboats; the head, as the foot-pump toilet was called, pumped right into the ocean via a through-hull fitting. To make more room, we threw out the head and built an area for a bassinet to be secured in. From then on, we used a designated bucket of saltwater for our toilet needs (when we were in port) or the well-named poop deck. I believe nature can handle a small amount of effluent, but there was a tipping point at which time chemicals and treatment facilities become necessary. We had not quite reached that point yet. Nor had the islanders: Their toilet was the high-tide line. A few had wooden latrines built out over the water. The fish took care of the rest.

Not to continue to discuss the rain, but New Guinea knew how to rain in all of its varieties from torrential cloudbursts, violent but short, to exhaling drizzling misty breaths, to a simple steady rain. The rain and gray had slowed everything to a snail's pace. My journals reveal the monotonous sameness of how little was happening. Every day was inky gray; the water smooth silk when it wasn't raining as not a baby's breath of wind stirred a ripple tickle.

My pregnancy was causing food cravings. Though we had stocked up with food in Cairns, Australia, that had been over seven weeks now, and we were almost completely out of anything except beans and rice. My body was screaming for something it was lacking. For Dave's work on Bunny's slipway, he would earn close to $100. We ate beans, rice, fresh fish we caught. We got fresh vegetables from Grace. But I needed meat. Red meat. And peanut butter.

Bunny Burrows sent one of his boats over to Samarai regularly for supplies and mail. After seventeen days in Magalkarona, I caught one of his boats over in the pouring rain. Besides me towing along, he generously took quite a few locals over with him too. It was only a twenty-minute trip on the small twenty-foot wooden vessel spewing out diesel fumes, quite different from us spending almost all day trying to sail to Sariba with little wind and a strong current. By the time we returned, the sun was actually shining.

Stacks of letters from my mom, my brothers, four of my best friends, and Jack and Irene from New Zealand lifted me out of my reoccurring depression and the general emotional misery that I had periodically returned to. I was elated to read long newsy letters from home. I was even happy to read a letter from Jean-Pierre and where his ship was taking him. Jean-Pierre had been a good-looking young Frenchman whom Dave had invited to live with us for several weeks in New Caledonia. He was studying to take his captain's exam, which he passed eventually. I had complained so much about his presence and my lack of privacy that he finally moved over to Joe's boat *Intrepid*. I was happy to hear from him and know all was working out well with him.

Letters were a lifeline to the world I left behind.

My outward-bound letters, depending on which island I was on, could take up to a month to get to the States. Letters back could take that long or longer, so letter exchanges could take up to two months at the most. Often, after first arriving at a port of call where we'd mail out letters announcing our arrival, we'd sail out to more-remote and less-populated islands within the archipelago as we were doing over in Magalkarona Bay. We would eventually return, three to six weeks later, to get our exit documents to sail on to another archipelago, and it would be then that we'd finally receive a letter or letters that had been sitting there waiting. We would always take the time to reply to them before setting sail for a new port with, of course, the suggestion that their next letters should be sent to this port or that port. It wasn't unusual for other yachts in any particular port to gather letters that had been sitting in general delivery for yachts never to have arrived or known to have left long before for other islands, and they'd bring them along when they followed weeks or months later.

After my mother's death in 1992, sorting through her things, I found all the aerograms I'd sent home. I retrieved two shoeboxes full of rubber-banded bundles of letters folded back to their original compact blue squares, stored in chronological order, detailing almost seven years of sailing adventures. Almost everything I wrote home about was recorded there and preserved. So today, sitting in those two shoeboxes of letters written forty-five or more years ago were the sights and sounds experienced and people I'd met, the reflections at sea, the adventures on land, all recorded—for me now—to reread or for my children or their children or their children's children to reread. It would be a treasure trove for future descendants doing genealogy or just wondering about where they came from, who their ancient relatives were, what kind of lives their great- and great-great- and great-great-great-grandparents lived. I'm saddened to think that today with email being the predominant means of communication—or, worse, only Facebook or Instagram—and few people writing letters, there will be little to pass down to a future generation of how life was before.

The letters I sent home, written to the very edges of each aerogram, conveyed a different insight than what I recorded in my journals by hand. In the silence of my journals, I recorded more of my intimate reality, things never expressed to friends or family or even to Dave, I guess. I could never write home that I was forever sad, forever angry, forever discontent, sometimes lonely, that I had made the biggest mistake of my life by sailing away with Dave and, now, pregnant by him. Those thoughts peppered my journals, but I did not write home about any of that. I wrote of the adventures, the details of new places, new cultures.

Receiving a packet of letters from family and friends pulled the past to my present and filled me with some moments of joy and happiness with news from home. An occasional nudge of homesickness and nostalgia would pass over me, like a ghost, but it never stayed long. Sadly, I no longer have any of the letters I received from family and friends through the years. Though I don't remember ever throwing any away, I can fantasize that they're floating on seas sailed, like the crumbs left behind by Hansel and Gretel, attaching me to my past, bringing forward mostly the good memories and unfinished dreams I'd left behind.

I would occasionally go over to visit Grace at the slipway, breaking the monotony of sewing, writing, reading, fishing, cooking, cleaning, sleeping, and feeling altogether quite unhappy and not quite knowing why. It was on one of my visits there that we finally found what we thought would be where we would go to have our baby: Fergusson Island (Kaluwawa) in the D'Entrecasteaux Group, farther south of the Trobriands than we had thought we'd need to sail and not too far from Samarai. Dave was working that day, but Bunny insisted he quit and come meet Kate and Andy and their six kids who were visiting.

An Australian family, they owned and ran the Kedidia Plantation, a copra plantation at the head of the bay on the south side of Fergusson, facing Esa-Ala on Normanby Island. They said they'd be leaving in December for New Zealand because of the forthcoming independence of Papua New Guinea from Australian control. Most of the white people had the understanding that white Europeans would no longer be welcome in PNG after the independence though it might have just been that Andy thought that things would change so much that they didn't want to stay, and admittedly, they were ready for a change.

They owned—or controlled—most of that area, all the way out onto Sebulogomwa Point, a wide peninsula a couple hundred yards wide. There was a deserted thatched hut previously used by some missionaries that Andy offered for us to live in if we wanted. There was a Catholic mission at Budoya nearby, he said, with an old Dominican sister who was supposed to be "the super midwife" for the area. It all sounded perfect. I was very cognizant of the deep animal instinct that needed a nest. Though I was still over four months from my due date, Mother Instinct had reared its head, silently inspecting and searching for and needing to know where her cub would be born. It had to be safe, and safe was not in the hands of that doctor in Cairns. Though always traveling on a faith that all would work out, I immediately felt a sense of relief in having a better sense of where we were headed.

Not too long after meeting Andy and Kate, I spent an afternoon listening to Grace recount her earlier years in Samarai from when they had arrived in 1925. She spoke of the days when they'd dress up in gowns and white jackets and go to the balls at the private club in Samarai. I could easily envision a high-browed colonized atmosphere back then before the war came. Years later, when I saw the movie *Out of Africa* with Meryl Streep and Robert Redford, my thoughts, imagination, and memories would always return to that afternoon sitting with Grace, imagining a colonial Samarai and these few hardy white pioneers who had created a semblance of a high society in these humid islands near the equator.

She spoke of the war years when Samarai, across the bay, was bombed by the British and Australians to keep it from the Japanese who had invaded Milne Bay not so far away. In a more cheerful tone, she told stories of the later years after the war. Sitting on her porch, sipping tea, the afternoon filled with her stories, she opened up and told me about her life, bringing the past alive. Sadly, our time was coming to a close at Sariba, and that was our first and last long conversation together. I failed to record any of her stories; I simply have held that moment in time.

Sundays were the worst of days for me. The fish seemed to leap everywhere, knowing that that day alone they were safe. The missionaries taught the locals that it was a sin to fish on Sundays let alone swim or paddle their canoes. Memories of Tonga. I see the villagers walking up and down the beach with their hands clasped behind their backs. Church bells—what I think was just an old barrel ring—clanged three times a day, and the people gathered to sing and listen to someone preach. All this happened on the one day that the sun was shining down Bible rays from heaven, and the wind was actually blowing perfectly to go dinghy sailing. It was the best day in three weeks to actually get the laundry washed and dried. My lesson learned in Tonga, I accepted that even though we were not of these people's faith, not only would it be offensive, but it might also be illegal if we were to blatantly fish or sail or do our laundry in front of them. There were no police in the village of Magalkarona, but at the very least, I was not going to risk being offensive to these villagers who had all been kind, friendly, and generous to us in the almost month we'd been there. We would be gone soon. I could wait. "Sunday morning, please be gone. I'm tired of you."

Leaving port for the next destination took preparation. A boat's bottom needs to be as smooth as a baby's bottom, clean of moss and barnacles, so as not to slow the boat down. Ideally, a fresh coat of bottom paint, containing copper and other toxic ingredients, slows the growth of algae, barnacles, and mussels. Since we were generally so broke we could barely buy food, paying for a haul out or for bottom paint was often not in the budget. With the right kind of beaches, you could do the poor-man's haul out: careening the boat on a beach at low tide, doing one side first, working quickly to scrape and scrub off the whole bottom, allowing it to dry enough to apply a coat of bottom paint if we had it, all before the tide rushed in. And then we'd situate the boat to careen it on the other side for the next tide. You needed the perfect beach that came up quickly from deeper water, and it also worked best when you had friends to help as you were, in fact, racing against the tide. We had last done this on a beach a few weeks after arriving in New Caledonia, almost a year before. In Magalkarona, we had neither the paint nor the place to beach the boat. Dave and I both jumped overboard with mask and snorkel and scrub brushes at moments when the clouds had thinned and rays of sun were able to penetrate into the water to give us more light.

We also needed to double-check all our sails, pulling them out and inspecting the seams for wear and tear or weakening threads, for small tears or holes that we wouldn't see when the sail was up and set. We had a hand crank, heavy-duty sewing machine for seam stitching, a palm and needle for the heavy stitching around grommets and elsewhere. We double-checked the rigging again—stanchions, turnbuckles, deck fittings, anything that might end up meaning the difference between life and death. We securely tied off the twenty-foot rowing oars and the nine-foot surfboard.

Below decks, stowing all the loose items in their bins can be extra time consuming, especially if the anchorage you've sat at for weeks or months was protected and calm and there were no swells that rolled in and tossed you from side to side or even from bow to stern. Everything has a secure place on a boat. Nothing can be left to rock, roll, move, or jiggle. A photo on a bulkhead was not hung by one hanger to rock back and forth but was nailed in place.

Under every settee seat were bins and tubs and jugs and cans of stored-food supplies. Time was taken to label the top of every container, every can with indelible ink in the slim—and God forbid—chance that items would get wet (which would probably mean we had almost sunk). If wet, labels would wash off, and we wouldn't know what was in the can. If there was even a half inch—even a quarter inch—of space between containers, something was wedged in to solidify them so there would be no shifting and clinking and clacking while sailing mostly for our sanity to not have that repetitive sound. There's enough ambient sound of water on the hull, clanking rigging, fluttering sails when at sea or at a rough anchorage as it was not to add to it with the clank of cans. All the plates, bowls, cups, pots, and pans were secured in railed bins with no cupboard doors. Because the tropics are humid and damp, it was good to have as much air circulating through areas as possible, especially when the dishes were washed in saltwater.

With the bottom scrubbed and the boat prepared, we rowed over to Grace and Bunny's house to return books they had lent us and to thank them for all their help: giving Dave some work, sharing the fruits and vegetables from their gardens. In the four weeks of sharing time with her, I had released my prejudgment of Grace; she was quite the pioneering woman who probably had had quite a hard life living in a Papua New

Guinea way less civilized than when we had arrived. I felt jealous of never being able to experience those same moments in history. She gave me a baby's bath, which I was quite tickled to get though Dave made it clear that he felt it was just another bulky thing to have on the boat.

We pulled anchor around noon on August 4, a month after arriving, to sail back to Samarai to finish stocking up on whatever we could afford and prepare for our trip to Fergusson Island. With the brief morning sun returning to clouds, I sculled away with one twenty-foot oar while Dave set the sails. It seemed that all the villagers from Magalkarona stood on the beach and shouted *kaiijon* from the beach; we waved back as the wind caught our sails and steadily increased. We made it back to Samarai in one and a half hours, arriving in a steady drizzle.

Making a mad rush to get to the post office before it closed, we checked mail and posted letters announcing where our next stop would be for receiving mail: Esa-Ala on Normanby, Milne Bay District, Papua New Guinea. This was the closest civilization, three miles across a channel from Sebulogomwa on a neighboring island. I rushed from shop to shop, first checking and comparing prices and then buying moderate quantities of all we needed with the hundred-plus dollars to our name.

This was when I got talking to a new cruising boat that had arrived. They mentioned the clay pots of Wari and how they wished they had seen them. I told them I had bought one and brought it up from below. Envious and clearly wanting one, they asked if I would sell it to them. Relatively poor and knowing it would probably eventually get broken, I agreed, and we settled on $20, four times more than I'd paid for it.

Dave had run off to get the propane tank refilled, which we used only for cooking. He was carrying it back to the boat and thought he heard it leaking, hissing. He put the tank on the ground and put his ear down by the valve, and it almost blew his head off. A loud pop sent him flying straight up in the air, he said—I wasn't clear if it was the physical force or the surprise—but the main blast hit him on the inside of his knee. A giant red surface bruise formed, looking more like a burn. We watched it for several hours, fearing an air embolism might form and kill him.

Returning to the boat carrying half of our shopping, we were informed that we needed to move our anchorage because a ship was coming in, and in the event it missed its mark—their description of the hypothetical problem—we needed to move. Anchorages can be tricky, especially when crowded. At anchor, boats swing and move around with the currents and wind. We had originally anchored in a good spot that gave us the room we needed, but being forced to move did not leave us a lot of options. We ended up spending the best part of the night kedging around to avoid hitting boats that had come in and anchored seemingly on top of each other. Then the tides changed, and we feared running aground. We were up at 6:00 a.m. only to find out that the ship was late coming in, and when it did, it ended up having no problems. We could have rested peacefully all night.

I stopped by the hospital and picked up some more iron pills (the only dispensary of such items as there was no such thing as a pharmacy in Samarai), and we finished up shopping. We ended up leaving a few minutes before we were planning when our anchor dragged, and we were forced to quickly hoist sails, sailing away with the anchor aweigh but luckily with a good breeze moving us away from the shoreline. With the anchor finally pulled up and secured, we pulled the dinghy up on board and secured it on top of the cabin deck.

We had a beautiful and an almost uneventful sail to East Cape. The currents were with us all the way through the China Strait. At times, the eddies and the chop produced very strange effects with incredible cross-currents. One tense moment occurred when Dave was confident we could squeeze past a spit of land jutting out without another tack, and I was confident we would shipwreck on it. He refused to tack, holding the bow of the boat as tight as possible into the wind to the point of losing forward motion and luffing the mainsail, slowing us even further. We were sailing parallel to the shore fifteen feet away *within the surf line* of four-foot breaking waves with Dave refusing to tack. I think in hindsight, by the time he realized he'd completely misjudged the situation, we really could not have changed course. We squeaked by on the skin of our teeth. I admit there needs to be only one captain to a boat. The rest are crew who need to keep their mouths shut and take orders. Being a strong-headed, self-sufficient woman, this was a good source of many of our disagreements even in less-than-dangerous situations. The emotions brought up during close calls were often not a pretty picture.

We made anchorage at East Cape right before nightfall with the help of all the villagers, it seemed. After Samarai and Sariba, it was a beautiful anchorage: beautiful secure, crystal-clear waters showing exquisite coral gardens. For over an hour after anchoring we were inundated by canoes, the boat crawling with both curious children and adults. Finally, they dispersed, and we ate. I thought we would get some much-needed sleep, but John (there were a lot of men named John), the local man who helped us anchor and spoke quite good English, came back, wanting to talk until late. I had to laugh when he asked Dave whether he had fought in World War II. John didn't look much older than Dave who was about to turn thirty-four, but John himself thought Dave might be fifty or fifty-five years old. Time was a hard concept to grasp in the South Pacific. No one had a calendar. No one knew the day they were born. A birth was marked by burying the placenta in the ground on which a fruit-bearing tree was planted, a tree that would always be the property of that individual. Time was simply marked by the growth of the tree and the person.

CHAPTER 7

If you're going through difficult times today, hold steady.
It will change soon. If you are experiencing smooth sailing
and easy times now, brace yourself. It will change soon.
The only thing you can be certain of is change.

—James C. Dobson

I was almost five months pregnant when we set sail from East Cape, Papua New Guinea, on August 8, 1975 on our last stretch to Fergusson Island, my nesting site. It was a distance of less than fifty miles, but with the notoriously light winds and strong currents of the area, it was very slow sailing across an almost-glassy-smooth pondlike ocean.

With Fergusson Island in sight with the day approaching midafternoon, we finally pulled out our twenty-foot oars. We had to get to a shoreline to at least drop anchor before nightfall as we were too precariously close to land in all directions to be floating in the sea with the coming nightfall. Setting them in their oar locks, the port one more forward than the starboard one so that the giant sweeps wouldn't hit in the middle, Dave and I stood on each side of the cockpit and started rowing the six-ton *Paz del Mar* for the point of Sebulogomwa. The first several strokes felt like trying to push a steamroller, but the boat slowly gathered momentum, and each stroke eventually kept us cutting through the water at about three knots. We were naked in the hot, humid equatorial sun, rowing steadily across the glassy-smooth seas until dusk. The mainland was on the far horizon behind us; Sebulogomwa was coming closer ahead of us. My belly was distinctly rounded and visible. I felt my strength. I liked sculling this heavy boat even in the hot sun.

As dusk was approaching, realizing we couldn't reach the further point at Sebulogomwa, we turned the boat farther west and headed for a nearer shore toward what appeared to be a thatched village. We dropped anchor in front of Salamo, the site, as we learned later, of the Protestant mission. We were exhausted, and luckily it was dark enough that the locals did not greet us as normal though we woke at dawn to hear the fishermen in their canoes talking to each other as they paddled circles around our boat, and we could hear the children on the shore shouting with curiosity.

We rowed to shore briefly to say hi, but knowing we still needed to get across the bay to Sebulogomwa, we soon lifted anchor and rowed away from shore toward the southeast point of the island. Eventually a breeze picked up enough to set the sails, and by noon, we were anchored stern to the palm-fringed shoreline. A small colorful coral reef, not much wider than thirty or forty feet, fringed the shore about sixty feet off the line of coconut trees, creating a miniature shallow turquoise lagoon. A passage existed, probably created by Andy at some point, in which to enter the lagoon. The anchor was set out in the coral reef, and the two stern lines tied us off to sister coconut trees. We were close enough to tie a long line off on either end of the dinghy so we could just pull it back and forth between the boat and shore without having to get the oars out.

Andy, the plantation owner that we had met at Bunny Burrows' place on Sariba, had seen us sailing over, and not too soon after we anchored, he motored up in his twenty-five-foot work boat, *Two-Bob*, to greet us. He showed us the thatched hut nestled on stilts in the coconut grove where we could live. He owned a small trading store on this point, run by a native family. They were within sight of our house, and we walked over to meet them; they would be our closest neighbors. Though we lived next to them for five months, nowhere do I have their names recorded though I do know they had named their four-year-old daughter Maria.

The trading store seemed to mostly sell tobacco plugs, canned mackerel, processed white rice, sugar, candies, all of which I was forever angered at seeing brought in to these indigenous cultures. And fishing hooks. I noticed some colored pieces of terrycloth on a shelf; though I thought they were dishtowels at first, I was informed they were in fact diapers. Ah, yes, diapers. Only then did it dawn on me that I would be needing diapers. It hadn't registered until that point that I had none. Silly me.

Andy showed us where there was a shallow five-foot-wide watering hole that filled with water from the torrential rains where we could bathe. We were free to put in a garden anywhere we wished. He said he'd be back the next day to pick us up in his boat to take us to his plantation home, Kedidia, at the head of the bay around noon to come spend the day and have dinner.

He did return and motored us down to Kedidia, to his comfortable home where they had resided for over fifteen years. Kate was homeschooling the kids when we first arrived. She greeted us briefly but returned to teaching in a side room set off for that purpose while Andy gave us a tour of his property. Among the work sheds and other aspects of his running a copra plantation, he proudly showed us the vanilla plants he had growing all around his home. A variety of orchid, vanilla plants must be hand-fertilized to produce the long vanilla beans that I saw hanging waiting to be picked, one reason vanilla is expensive to buy.

They also grew their own peppercorns. Since pepper was the largest spice crop in the world and was such a common household item that was always on our table since my earliest memory, I'd never thought of its origin or how it was processed. Black pepper (*Piper nigrum*) was a flowering vine in the family *Piperaceae*, the same family that kava and the betel leaf comes from (the betel leaf, too, having a peppery flavor). I learned that it was the different processing of peppercorns that created the different kinds of powdered pepper. Black pepper is made from cooked and dried unripe fruit. White pepper is made from ripe fruit seeds. There is something called green pepper that I've never used that's made from uncooked dried unripe fruit.

Andy pointed up toward the mountains and talked about the big logging operations that used to exist in the area, cutting the teak forests. Without aid of Caterpillars or helicopters, the people built wooden flumes to carry the logs down on the rushing waters from the mountains to the ocean to be loaded on boats. He gave other snippets of history of the area, pointing out how gold had been found both on Fergusson and over on Normanby years before, but it too had petered out as with the logging. Sadly, I have recently learned that commercial gold mining operations are returning to the area, portending great destruction. But at that time, copra was the main export product (as it was on most of the islands I'd visited), producing a small amount of income to an otherwise subsistence society.

Copra is simply mature coconuts that have been halved and dried. Copra boats came through periodically and bought the dried coconut meat for pennies on the dollar to be later turned into cosmetics and cooking oils. The current price today averages about $300 per hectare of coconut trees. A standard plantation could have approximately 130 trees per hectare, each tree bearing approximately 65 nuts a year. I can't imagine how little the people must have been earning back in the mid-'70s. In Papua New Guinea, because of the high rainfall, all the nuts, after being husked and the white meat popped from the hard shells, had to be smoke dried, laying the halved nuts up on covered racks with a fire burning below it for five or six days. So besides the collection, husking, and splitting of the coconuts, they also had to collect firewood and tend to the fires to earn their pennies on the dollar.

In many of the other South Pacific islands, cooperatives had been created for the copra industry where each person probably earned more for their effort. Here, the local people worked for Andy. Though Andy showed great generosity to us, I have no idea how fair he was to the locals. I know he never seemed to exhibit a sense of superiority over or discrimination toward any of the locals.

Kate finished teaching the kids who were set free to play and/or do chores. She joined Dave and me in their spacious and comfortable living room, offered us drinks and snacks, and we chatted for quite a while before Kate headed to the kitchen to start cooking for a late afternoon dinner. A baked ham! Real ham, not out of a can! Brown sugar and fresh pineapples on top! That's all I can remember eating though I know it was a full-course meal. Oh, sweet ham. Oh, meat!

Andy had a pool table, and now he had a pool partner. Dave and he, continuing to drink, played pool for several hours after the meal while Kate and I talked. Out of numerous topics covered (how did she like living there, homeschooling, et cetera), I asked her if all her kids were born here on the island. "Oh, no," she said almost as if that was a ridiculous option.

She would leave and return to Australia to give birth, stay six to eight weeks, and then return to Kedidia. Although that seemed the logical way to have her children, she seemed to hold no judgment about the fact that I left Australia to find Budoya. Indeed, I would be the first white person to ever give birth there.

They seemed to have no regrets about their lives there though with the forthcoming independence of PNG from Australia, they were planning on moving back to New Zealand. Kate said the things she missed were having conversations, like ours, with white people where you could share abstract and worldlier ideas than what she could share with the local people. And though her children seemed well educated and well mannered and in many ways were receiving an education far superior to what any civilized school could offer, Kate worried that her children needed more than what they were getting on this remote island.

We explored my reasons for wanting to come to a remote place to have my child. I had to honestly tell her that it had to do with the visceral response to the Cairns doctor whom I saw when first pregnant. In my gut, I could not subject my body to such a man during such an important moment in my life. That's the only explanation I could give. And that we didn't like towns or cities, and we wanted to find a place just like what we had found there on Fergusson Island.

It became clear that we were not returning to our boat that night, and Kate, quite used to visitors staying overnight, made up a bed for Dave and me, setting out clean towels for a nice hot shower. It was the first hot shower I had had for at least two years when my mother and I had toured New Zealand and stayed in nice hotels! Even though we were within degrees of the equator, and it was hot and humid day and night, it felt so good to stand under that hot shower. Languishing under the warm stream of water, I remember so clearly noticing for the first time how large my breasts were getting. I squeezed a drop of milkish fluid from my nipple. I rubbed my belly slowly with sweet-smelling soap, marveling at the miracle of it all.

I awoke in the middle of the night. The house was very quiet. All I could think about was the leftover ham in the refrigerator. I snuck into the kitchen and cut myself off a small slice, savoring every nibble. And then I cut myself off another hunk of it. And then just one more. When I was done, I was sure someone would notice that the next day's sandwich makings weren't quite sufficient for all those sandwiches anymore. I felt guilty, horribly guilty. I felt like a thief.

In the morning, as we were preparing for Andy to take us back to our little hut and home, Kate handed me a small wrapped-up package. She squeezed my hand while giving it to me and said quietly, "Enjoy."

When I unwrapped the bundle, it was what looked to be all of the rest of the ham meat trimmed from the bone.

Sebulogomwa became our new home for the next five months. The morning sun rose and greeted us across the eastern waters each morning, rising up through the coconut grove, and it bid us good night across the western bay each night, a tranquil, majestic spectacle every day. Thankfully, most days shared just enough breeze to cool us even in the heat of the day. I rejoiced to be off the boat and having more room.

We put in a garden in soil that was made up of pumice and coconut roots. Our seeds sprouted quickly enough but then sat without growing. We finally realized the soil, if it could be called that, was too leeched out by the 200 inches of rain a year to have any nutrition in it. (Well, after all, it *was only pumice and coconut roots*, no soil.) Our solution was we built a wooden stand onto which we put a toilet seat, and it was there that we would meditate once or twice a day. Adding to our humanure, we would throw in the fish heads, guts, and skeletons of all the fish we caught, layering in the nutrition, and then move our toilet bench down the row, transplanting the young tomatoes, cucumbers, cantaloupes, and bean plants into each mound. I built up separate mounds of strictly fish compost for lettuce, radishes, carrots, and other foods I did not want contaminated with our humanure. With the heat, sun, rain, and added nutritional supplements to the soil, we had an abundant garden. Cantaloupe turned out to be a new food to the local, though they were actually more interested in the seeds for stringing into lovely necklaces. So we'd eat the fruit and save the seeds for them.

On first arriving, we realized the roof of the cook shack needed some repair. The locals in Papua New Guinea wove coconut fronds in a different method than I had done for my house in New Zealand. As our house was on the path to the trading store on the point, we always had a steady line of locals walking by. We were something new and interesting to look at. Noticing me weave the fronds as I was doing, they stopped to watch, just sitting down on the path near our house, staring and laughing amongst themselves, something that, I guess, was not considered rude to do in their culture. Feeling a bit self-conscious, I waved one of the women over, who comfortably sat herself down after packing her mouth with betel nut and showed me how they wove the fronds into roofing mats. Their way was much simpler and quicker, so I adopted it. After repairing the roof, we moved a two-burner propane stove, our pots and pans, and cooking gear to the eight-by-ten thatched cooking shack.

In the evenings, we'd sit on the little four-foot-wide porch of our thatched hut on stilts in the middle of a coconut grove, playing Scrabble. A lantern hung from a nail away from the thatching. The only onlookers were the geckos, attracted by the army of moths and other insects homing to the lantern's light. While contemplating our Scrabble moves, we'd watch the geckos gorge themselves, their throats and bellies bulging. It was quiet in the dark coconut grove. No clinking of rigging or ripples on the hull. Beautiful silence. When the moon grew fuller, we watched it rise on the eastern side of our peninsula, peeking through the coconut trunks, rising higher to be almost hidden by the ceiling of coconut fronds, and if we were awake in the wee morning hours, we could watch it set into the ocean on the west side.

Several days after we got settled in at Sebulogomwa, Andy returned on *Two-Bob*, his Sebulogomwa–Esa-Ala transport boat, and gave us a water taxi ride the several miles down to the Budoya Mission where we met Sister Angelica for the first time (the super midwife) who gave us a tour of the dispensary and hospital area. Sister was maybe sixty years old. Thin, sweet, draped in the habit of her sect, she was nevertheless a bundle of energy.

The mission hospital was a small wooden house with one main room with four beds in it, a delivery room, and a small private room. Everything was extremely clean and smelling like a hospital. The delivery room was small with a high wooden table. That was it. No fancy adjustable hospital bed, just a tall flat hard table. Comfort aside, I felt an innate confidence in Sister and her nurse trainees: two sixteen-year-olds and two eighteen-year-olds who, I was told, had about second-grade educations before they learned the more-important skills of nursing.

The main ward was most generally used as the maternity ward, if it could be called that. That day, there were three local women there; two were breastfeeding their newborns. Small bassinets stood by each bed. There was no such thing as the nursery—thank God—or incubators or neonatal intensive care units (which I was cognizant could be useful). Just a simple wood room with four beds, four bassinets. Besides new mothers, this was also the room where the nun and nurses would stitch up deep cuts and wounds or treat malaria and pneumonia patients, the two other great illnesses that brought the people to the hospital.

The windows were square holes with sticks propping open wooden shutters. There was electricity for lights only when a generator was turned on. The windows were always open—open to the air, the mosquitoes, the moths in the evening light of kerosene lanterns—unless rain and wind caused them to be closed.

Sister Angelica gave me a prenatal exam, announcing that all was normal. My only previous exam had been done by the arrogant, sexist Australian doctor in Cairns. I hadn't put on any weight for which I was naïvely proud, not knowing that good weight gain also reflected good nutrition to my growing baby.

That first day, we stayed long enough to be included in lunch, which we shared with the Sister, the Sister's cousin visiting from Australia, and Father Howard who had just been transferred to Budoya from Alotau where he had been head of the secondary school mission there for four years. Luncheon talk mostly centered around gardening though Father Howard and Sister Angelica also shared stories of their years at missions throughout Papua New Guinea.

After lunch, before leaving, they had showed us their gardens, their chicken and egg coops, their pig pens. There was one cement-block structure painted white, which housed their perishable stores, keeping them safe from rodents and insects. We viewed the small schoolroom, which was a long thatched structure with half walls and woven mats that could be dropped for inclement weather, not unlike the *fales* of British Samoa. The house in which the Sister dwelled was a blend between a tropical colonial ranch house and local thatched construction. Rough-hewn, twisted support logs could be seen supporting the roof, which was made of smooth tree poles covered with a tight thatch. They had a lovely hardwood floor, comfortable Western furniture, and shelves of books. The student nurses were housed in a separate small building between the

Sisters' house and the hospital. In all the time I was there, I never was sure where Father Howard slept and lived. He could have actually been sharing the house where Sister Angelica lived for all I knew.

I spent many hours talking with Father Howard though. He was the first—and possibly the last—Catholic priest I ever had long conversations with; we covered the esoteric aspects of Christianity as well as why he was compelled to do missionary work as he had so devoted his life to. Though I had a distrust and actual abhorrence of organized religion, the conversations I had with Father Howard were the first that transported me beyond the dogma and into the mystic aspect of Father Howard's belief system where I was actually able to get a glimmer of something related to what I constantly experienced in my meditations at sea, devoid of the trappings of a dogma. In many talks with him through the months, he also shared his insights into the local customs and beliefs. Never did he or the Sister Angelica attempt to convert us or preach to us for which I was thankful.

Eventually, Dave and I walked home, meandering down a single narrow footpath through the thick jungle for three or four miles. There being no vehicles on the island with speedometers, I never knew exactly how far the mission was from Sebulogomwa, but it took well over an hour to walk at a steady pace. As with all roads first traveled and new to the eye, the first day walking back from Budoya Mission to our house and boat anchored at the point of the peninsula seemed a long way. A long, long way. I wondered how I could do it very frequently, but it turned out that I walked down to Budoya Mission at least once a week during the next four months, enjoying every step of the way. I became familiar with the landmarks on the path, each village, and with the villagers themselves. Small villages would appear every 100 to 300 yards, the cleared hard-packed ground stolen from the jungle. Five or six or sometimes ten huts on stilts would be spaced about the clearing, all with fires smoldering under them. As I usually walked alone, I would wave and smile and exchange brief hellos with the women who were often bent over tending their cooking fires smoldering under their houses, protected from the torrential rains that would come daily at some point while toddlers would sit playing in the dirt nearby as older children would be scurrying about playing or doing small chores.

There was not a blade of grass that grew around the village houses (though the mission grounds had lovely lawns). The ground was hard-packed dirt. Not a leaf lay strewn. Children could be seen collecting fallen leaves and carrying them off; grass-skirted, bare-breasted women would sweep with brooms made of tangled twigs. The women cooked, tended to the children, collected firewood. They tended their gardens that were always away from the villages down thin paths barely discernible, leading into the jungle out of view of the main path. The men would wander away into the jungle with a spear in search of an animal or, more likely, would be silently gliding across the bay in their canoes, fishing. I made note that it was the women who carried the load of hard work. It was the women who carried everything.

We fell into a routine. We actually had grass around our shack, which I intended to keep, so I spent some time each day leaning over, belly getting more in the way, cutting grass with a hand sickle. I sowed more tomato, capsicum, eggplant, and chive seeds in a seed box. What I had planted when we first arrived seemed to be growing well with the help of our fertilizing method. I transplanted 120 pineapple seeders though we never stayed long enough to see them bear fruit as it was a two-year cycle.

There were, of course, no businesses or ways of earning any money here. It was, and still is forty-five years later, a subsistence society. The people grew their vegetables, mostly starch vegetables like taro, yams, and manioc, harvested the fruits and other wild greens nature provided, and fished and hunted. The little money the locals earned came from harvesting and making copra. Any chance of us making any money would only come from Andy and his family.

Andy did end up giving Dave a couple odd jobs, fixing things on *Two-Bob*, and a couple small projects around his plantation. Otherwise, we lived on the food stores of beans and rice we had on board and on our vegetable garden. We also set a fishing net every evening near shore. The net was about thirty feet long that we'd stretch from the inner edge of the reef toward shore. We learned not to leave it out more than a couple hours, or else the reef sharks would rip holes in it, trying to get the fish that had been caught.

Usually within an hour, we'd have a good-sized fish to cook up for dinner. Invariably the next day, Dave would have the net hanging and would be mending any tears made by sharks or on the reef. Andy's employee (our neighbor) that ran the little trading store had a pack of seven or eight dogs, looking thin and emaciated much like Mexican dogs, that would come sneaking around our perimeter at night. They came daily for a feast of leftover fish and other scrapings, but they would never truly befriend us. I could commiserate with these dogs, though, with the cravings I experienced.

We were invited to share meals with Andy and Kate every couple of weeks: roast beef one night, roast pork another. We always spent the night. I know they craved the opportunity for visitors like I craved the food they served. Invariably, I would sneak back to the refrigerator in the middle of the night for more. I think Kate always knew I was doing this. Of course, she did: she'd had six children! Six pregnancies.

Cravings aside, I felt I was healthy. I got plenty of exercise working in the garden, swimming and snorkeling for hours on our little coral reef, walking to Budoya, rowing to Esa-Ala. Overall, we ate a balanced diet: fish, coconuts, fresh vegetables, sprouts (I still had alfalfa seeds and mung beans), beans, and rice if we caught no fish. As I had on other islands, I asked the local people what wild greens they collected and how they prepared them. Most had similar dishes, whether in Polynesia or Melanesia, comprised of blending the gelatinous starch of manioc (from which tapioca was made) with shredded coconut and some wild greens wrapped in banana leaves and steamed, usually on hot rocks in the ground oven or *umu*.

Oh, but I continued to crave meat. Red meat. There were flying fox where we lived. Not as many as in Cairns, Australia, when the evening sky would blacken as thousands would rise up from the mangrove swamps along the Trinity River every dusk and head off in search of fruit and nectar. Their exodus would also trigger the mosquitoes to leave the swamps and search out other blood sources—us on our boat. The bats are of the genus *Pteropus* and are the largest bats in the world. They are also known as fruit bats. They do not possess echolocation, but instead rely on smell and eyesight to locate their food, which can range up to forty miles away. When it locates food, the flying fox "crashes" into the foliage and grabs for it. It will hang upside down on a branch with its hind feet and will draw food to its mouth with one of its hind feet or with the clawed thumbs at the top of its wings.

These same bats were at Sebulogomwa. At times, I would see the flying fox hanging upside down from fronds in nearby coconut trees, sleeping during the day. One day when I was particularly craving some red meat, and seeing a flying fox, I asked Dave if he would shoot it for me so I could eat it for dinner. As with so many of the more exotic foods—lizard, frog legs, iguana, alligator—it was said to taste like rabbit or chicken. Dave refused. He didn't understand a pregnant woman's need for what she craved.

After being quite angry with him, I got out the .22 rifle, and I shot it. Though I'm not happy with the power of the NRA today, I had taken sharp shooting training when I was eleven, and I was an excellent shot. Thinking it would drop to the ground and "job done," I was quite stupefied when instead it died clutching the coconut frond thirty feet above my head. I then asked Dave to go up the coconut tree and get it for me. He again refused and stated his unhappiness in my having shot it to begin with.

I was desperate. Though eight months pregnant, I planted the bottoms of my feet on the trunk as I had climbing nikau trees in New Zealand, and with my legs splayed out on each side, my hands barely able to reach around the trunk because of my belly, I climbed the thirty feet up the tree and dislodged the bat. Though it has a wingspan of almost six feet, the animal itself only weighed about three pounds. I skinned it, gutted it, and put it on a spit over the fire. I ate the whole bat and shared not a bite with Dave. It was excellent.

Years later, I read now that the bats are nearing extinction in many areas where they live because of man overharvesting them for their delicate flavor. They have been placed on the CITES list of endangered animals. I try not to think that the one flying fox I took to soothe my maternal cravings might have contributed to their demise.

I was abiding in the same waiting game as every other pregnant woman but with less frenzied activity to occupy my week. I tended the garden, snorkeled on the reef, rowed the dinghy someplace, read, cooked, washed dishes, took naps, set the fish net for dinner. We played Scrabble in the evenings. Out of this sense of sameness and boredom, we briefly discussed the idea of pulling anchor and leaving before the baby was born. We had also been influenced by the number of people contracting malaria daily while we were there. We pondered the prudence of staying there. But if we were to leave, where would we go? Eight then seven then six weeks before I was due, the reality was I could not just sail off to any island. I had found the perfect place. I had confidence and a connection with the Sister and the nurses at the Budoya Mission. We weren't leaving till after the baby came. Breastfeeding would immunize it for at least the first six weeks. Decision made.

We, along with all Europeans, took a prophylaxis weekly to prevent contracting malaria, a parasite spread by the *Anopheles* mosquito. If it bites a person with an active case of malaria and then comes and bites you, you can contract the malaria parasite. While taking chloroquine (the prophylaxis we took), you never have an active case yourself. If all of the locals were given prophylaxis and no one ever had an active case of malaria, then malaria could eventually get wiped out as it did in the southern states of the United States, as it did in the Panama Canal area or in Australia. The mosquitoes would die off, or if they survived, there was no malaria parasite to transmit.

We asked Sister Angelica why there was so much malaria when there were drugs to take. She said they could not get the local people to come to the hospital once a week to take the pill; most had no concept of time or days of the week or calendars to know when to come. For the same reason, she couldn't send the pills home to stay in whatever medicine cabinet they'd have in their thatched huts to safely store multiple-month supplies of prophylaxis for a family to take weekly. So someone was always sick with malaria, spreading it on to everyone else. They came to the hospital only when they were very ill, took medicine to knock back the parasite in their blood, regained their health, and returned home only to repeat the process every six to eight weeks for their whole life. Since then, I've also learned that taking prophylaxis for long periods of time was not healthy either.

CHAPTER 8

There, in the shimmering distance, was a sail. I stared in momentary
disbelief, but there it was, one of the most beautiful sights the Pacific can
ever offer—a ship in full sail edging her way through the blue waters.
                                                                    —Tom Neale

I was surprised by the number of sailboats that actually visited our
area. Most only stayed a day or two on their way to the Trobriands, bringing
their stories and their dreams and plans for future adventures. It broke the
monotony and slothlike sameness of the days. One day in October, sitting
on the porch reading, I heard anchor chain dropping. Excitedly, I jogged
my heavy belly over to the tree line to meet Tom and his girlfriend Sally
on the *Lazy Be*. The next day, *Koko* sailed in, on which were Jason and
Elena and their two daughters, Lily and Jenny. Each boat had stopped only
because they had seen our boat tied stern to the coconuts. They stayed
almost ten days.

While they were there, with Dave successfully catching fish with the
net every night, we feasted on fish de Sebulogomwa. Sally would contribute
canned hams and munchies. Andy came down more than ever before,
always bringing lettuce and cheeses and roast chickens, and we'd have
great buffet-type lunches. Andy kidnaped Lily and Jenny, the kids from
the *Koko*, to come play with his children at Kedidia early one morning,
a welcome relief to children and parents alike, and it was arranged that
we should all come down later in the day for dinner for what turned into a
good-time party: Tom, Sally, Jason and Elena, Andy and Kate, Dave and

I, and now eight children running and screaming around the house, inside and out. The beer flowed; the snooker table was occupied nonstop by the competitive men, hooting and boasting. Women relaxed, talking: Sally going on about women's lib, Kate secure in her role in life, Elena mostly sitting and listening. My eye and nose stayed focused on the roast leg of pork in the oven.

Everyone spent the night, sleeping on couches, floors, spare beds. Somewhere during talk the night before, it had been decided that we must go see the hot springs and steaming pools, which were about halfway between Kedidia and Budoya Mission. So after a great breakfast of pancakes and eggs, we set off. As we walked along the path single file, two girls, maybe ten or twelve years old, joined us as we passed their village. I bring it up only because they thought nothing of joining into a group of people like us though it's clearly not something we'd do within our own culture. That sense of privacy and boundaries was very different than ours.

Coming to the hot springs after traipsing several miles through the jungle, we spent several hours picking our way through bubbling mud holes, empty steaming cracks, boiling spouting geysers. It was like a miniature Yellowstone yet undiscovered. But when we arrived at the main pools, on the bottom of the crystal-clear turquoise pools lay several human skeletons. Pure white skulls looked up from five or ten feet below; other bones lay scattered across the bottom, some bouncing and wiggling, moved by the hot steam bubbling out of the ground into the pool. Andy explained that, when healthy, the locals knew the pools were close to the boiling point; but in their fever-driven delirium, they would jump into the pools to try to cool the malarial fevers. (I had also read though in one of the pamphlets from the mission that before the missionaries came, cannibalism was prevalent, and this was a place that they would take their victims to cook the flesh, and after eating their meal, they would discard the skeleton in these pools.) Both versions made me cringe.

We stayed for a while. I sat in silence, staring into the boiling pools while the others explored and scurried about. More poignant than a gravestone, death stared out at me from this clear water. An elbow pushed out on my side. I put a hand on my bare round belly—as was my usual attire, I was only wearing a bikini top and a short, short skirt that came below my belly—feeling the nudge of my baby inside. I was seven and a half months pregnant. Life and death.

I hung out on *Lazy Be* and *Koko* sharing stories. We had potlucks on our little porch. Sally chattered on about women's lib. Though a topic different than the weather or food, it was only refreshing for the first hour. Soon her complaints became more focused on Tom's faults. Sally clearly was growing tired or had grown tired of Tom—a mirror for my own plight?—and on the day they were to leave, she announced that she had arranged to ride with Andy to Samarai because she and Tom just couldn't get along.

I'm not sure why I thought it was my place to intervene, but I reminded Sally that she had sort of left Tom in a bad situation, having no place to recruit new crew and leaving him to single-hand his boat through fairly treacherous waters. Eventually they made up and left together to return to Cairns and not to continue on whatever adventures they had set off on. Before leaving though, they gave us quite a quantity of canned foods and coffee and shampoo and conditioner—oh, glory be—saying they had way more than they would or could use, especially since now they were going to return to Cairns.

The night before *Lazy Be* left, with animosities settled, Sally made a huge pot of spaghetti, and we all motored down to Kedidia on the *Lazy Be* and shared a great feast with Andy and his family. The men stayed up late, drinking ouzo and then switching to Galliano drunk with garlic (introduced by Andy). The next morning, Andy dropped us off at Sebulogomwa before motoring on to Samarai and Alotau for supplies. Tom and Sally sailed away, back from where they came; the *Koko* carried on to where they were going. We were again left to our solitude, and for a few days, it was actually pleasant: no more women's lib and the cries of another discontented woman. No more hours of preparing huge though quite scrumptious meals for crowds.

When Andy returned from Samarai, Dave started building a new exhaust to air Andy's engine room, working several days on that. Then he got himself in gear to plane our new spars. Andy had given us two trees that we had barked and left to season and dry and from which Dave made a new gaff and spinnaker pole to replace ours that were rotting. I worked on mending the spinnaker and finished making a big black square sail. Every day around eleven, the wind would begin to blow off the sea from the northeast-east with the seeming sole purpose, I fantasized, to try to shove, push, and hasten the sun off to the west and bring the relative coolness of darkness. Sometimes it gave me relief, but not often. It was on that light, light breeze that other sailboats arrived, stopped and visited, and sailed on.

If we could stay stationary and have the world keep moving past our boat step, bringing change and newness occasionally, possibly that would satisfy me. If every week a new boat with new people would drop anchor and tell new stories, I *think* I would be happy. I realized why Andy and Kate were so gracious with their invitation for us to come stay there. We were their stimulation. They invited us down to their plantation two, three, four times a month over the months we were there, picking us up in *Two-Bob* and bringing us back. They invited other sailors down. I wondered how I would have ever survived had it not been for roasts of beef, hams, pork, and the cheeses and fresh whole wheat breads. There were several times when we stayed for two or three days, sleeping in real beds. Kate would share with me stories of childbirth in between homeschooling her six children.

I also realized why Andy and Kate were somewhat glad that Papua New Guinea's coming independence was forcing them to leave. They, too, had lived with this still, quiet sameness for over fifteen years. Andy was forecasting complete disaster after independence because, he said, even the sharpest best-educated of the local people could not grasp the world as we knew it. They had no business acumen. They had no push to plan for the future. They were much like blind men, not knowing the colors of red or yellow, the light of day, the depth of vision; they, in essence, could not perceive the same world we see and couldn't comprehend that which they'd never experienced. Kate voiced her worry that her children needed more than their plantation life.

Another yacht arrived one morning, about three weeks before my child was born. We helped them anchor stern to the shore alongside *Paz del Mar*. The gal, Robin, was a nurse and luckily so. Several hours after their arrival, I walked over to the house of our neighbors, the couple that tended Andy's small trading post. Unbeknownst to me, they weren't home, but their dogs were, the pack of seven or eight dogs that we had fed every night with our fish and rice scraps. There was no such thing as dog food in Papua New Guinea. They lived off scraps of yams, coconuts, and what they could scavenge, a dead fish washed up on the beach. Though I would never pet them, I thought of them as my friends, that they knew me, and that they would never bite the hand that had been feeding them. I did not factor in territoriality.

Our neighbors weren't home, and as I approached the house, this pack of dogs attacked. I was wearing the same short, short skirt that came halfway up my thighs and hung below my bulging belly and a bikini top. My reaction was to run. In that timeless moment, I saw them dragging me to the ground and ripping out my baby, so I ran.

I ran. But one of the dogs bit me in my lower calf. Another one caught me deep—deep—in the cheek of my buttocks. My running wasn't saving me. I had the presence of mind though to stop, turn around, and with all my anger and all the viciousness I could conjure up, roar at them, raising my arms out and up, making myself bigger. It worked; they ran away. The bite to my leg was a puncture wound, but the bite to my ass ripped deep from near my anus outward and needed stitches. As blood trickled down my leg, I returned to the new yacht, to these people we'd barely met, and spent the next hour leaning over, cheeks spread, and having Robin the nurse put stitches in my ass. She then prepared a wonderful meal for all of us from their ship's stores. She gave me a whole jar of peanut butter, which I took back to our hut and ate spoonful by spoonful the next day all on my own.

Two days later, Andy motored up on *Two-Bob*. We told him of the dog biting me; at that point, it almost seemed funny. I recognized the dogs were simply being territorial and protecting their master's property. But Andy was not going to accept that any dog attacked anybody. After asking me which dog it was, he marched over to his storekeeper's house with a noose of rope which he put around that dog's neck and dragged the dog to his boat. Without saying a word to us, he threw off his mooring line and motored out into the bay. Standing on shore, we watched him throw the dog overboard and proceed to drag it behind his boat until it had drowned. In his silent rage, he motored back to Kedidia; we didn't see him for several more days.

A few days later, we were visited by a missionary from Dobu. He was a bit tedious, not at all as interesting as Father Howard. Arriving with Bible in hand, I felt he was stiffened with his dogma. I struggled to feel the love I felt from Sister Angelica and Father Howard. Luckily he didn't stay long before he carried on down the path toward Budoya.

Feeling that we were quite off the beaten path of anyone, we were surprised when a couple days later an English couple came tramping through. He was a biology professor, out collecting specimens on Normanby, Fergusson, and possibly, he said, carrying on to Goodenough Island. He was the perfect cartoon professor character, tall and thin with floppy silvery hair, overly large hands, his pants pulled too high up around his waist, sloping shoulders. He taught biology in England, he said. His wife had quite an attractive face but a sad body, fat and marbled with cottage cheese showing through her sweat-drenched clothes that hung on her. She was a medical instructor. They actually were quite fascinating, and I really enjoyed the stimulation of their visit and hoped to see them again. Of course, we never did. The only thing that returned was the next day. And the next. Each day came and slipped away. Slipped by. Just slipped like the sun coming up on one side of the peninsula and going down on the other side.

Several times a month, we rowed across Dawson Strait to Esa-Ala to pick up mail. Several times, I rowed the three miles over and back by myself, enjoying the exercise, though usually it was something we did together. The water was always smooth without a ripple; I felt I was rowing on a sheet of glass, awed that my oars did not shatter the glass with each dip.

I got a letter from my mother saying my maternal grandmother had died, my sweet Grandma B who, as I was told later, had fallen in love with my Grandpa Sam, my father's father. I so loved my Grandma B. We shared the same birthday, but more than anything, I believe it was her radiant unconditional love that saved my very soul while growing up. She was sunshine and warmth. Though born into a financially stable home and marrying a Harvard business graduate in 1916, her husband (a grandfather I'd never met, dying several years before I was born) had been severely ill for many years of their marriage, and she had had to work most of her life, unusual for a woman of her generation and of her social standing. She had opened and run a rest home in Massachusetts, which was also a public restaurant serving lunch and dinner. Because she was the sole proprietor and she could never close the doors, we always went to visit her in my younger years. I got so much attention there from all the old women that resided there. Love. Sustenance. Validation. Besides my soul food, she made twenty loaves of fresh oatmeal molasses bread every night and always served lime sherbet after the meals.

My memories returned to her house in Bridgewater that had been built during the time of horse and buggies. There was a long tall passageway that connected the main house to the stables in the back. In my childhood, that room was equipped with a giant rope hung from the upper rafters, and we spent endless hours swinging on that rope; it was a slow-motion swing, being so long from one end of the barnlike connection to the other. It smelled fully, deeply, completely of old cedar timbers, a smell I would pay money to bottle as it holds such dear memories. In my mind's eye, I swing slow-motion through the air. My grandmother was gone. I smell the cedar timbers. I smell the lavender soap in her bathroom with the big claw-foot bathtub. I smell oatmeal molasses bread baking. I swing back, holding the memories, good memories. Pure child's joy.

Friends wrote. Some had had babies. Another letter announced that my younger brother had married. Life out beyond our remote equatorial island was continuing on.

My baby brother got married! I hadn't seen either of my brothers for almost six years now. In many respects, I hardly knew them. As happened on occasion, like this one, news could drop me into a fog. Wispy threads of thought whispered that something was definitely broken in me but wasn't broken in my brothers. I pondered what made me so different from them; why could they find love? My mother hadn't yet revealed my first six weeks of life to me, those pivotal weeks in my life where I was taught I didn't matter, that I wasn't loved enough to be picked up or comforted. At that point, I blamed my parents' twenty-two years of marriage, expressed through ugly anger and fighting, as being my only model. I never ever witnessed any sort of affection or love between my parents—not one day—only my mother kowtowing to please her husband. Spinning in circles, I remember distinctly hovering on the edge of some deep truth or knowledge, trying to see through what was clouding my vision. Could it be that I was broken because I was the girl; they weren't broken because they were the boys? Could it be . . . The view through the window stayed clouded for many years to come.

As my body now aches from arthritis and my hair thins and lines crease my face, I will state emphatically that I would not substitute my youthful body for the wisdom and knowledge I now know. One of those pieces of knowledge is that each set of conditions produces yet another set of conditions ad infinitum, and there is no blame for the choices made under whatever set of conditions. Until the window is washed clean, you just can't see clearly. To think that I felt my brothers had escaped unscathed was a delusion that supported my tainted belief that I was irretrievably broken. When letters were slipped into my closed-off world of dirty windows and thick walls, my only thought was *that* world was out of my reach. It was many years later before I learned my attitude and perception could change—and did indeed change—when I washed the windows, opened the door, and knocked down the walls.

For all the unknown dysfunctional reasons that had led me to this very point in time, here I was on a remote island in Papua New Guinea about to have a baby with a man I didn't love. Meanwhile others find love and marry. What was wrong with me? Circling back again, my hope was having a baby would make me happy. Would make *us* happy. Oh, how we delude ourselves. Dave was and is a good man. It was *my failings* that I couldn't or didn't love him. I'm sorry I wasn't conscious enough to know my feelings or to have been able to communicate them. I could fantasize about what my life would have been if I'd remained living alone in New Zealand. What children would we not have had? What lessons would I have never learned? Yes, I could fantasize a million ifs. But in the end, I was being pushed forward by forces much greater than myself.

Blame, ponder, retract blame, bow to greater forces, think whatever. The reality was I *was* pregnant, weeks from delivering a baby on a remote island in Papua New Guinea with grass-skirted, bare-breasted, betel nut-chewing natives. Though I didn't love Dave as I "should," through arguments and making up, through a few candid talks, through being able to get away from each other, through daily diversions, we generally got along. I was able to find a peaceful place to reside in most of the time. I wrapped myself in the cosmic maternal energy of creation and new life with all its proclivity to protect—to protect the very process of creation. Maternal instinct usually usurped moments of discontent.

I wanted to do this differently than my parents; *we* were going to do it differently than our parents. I sometimes could convince myself, though briefly, that this was a child of love and would be brought up in love, surrounded by love, and loved. Then the fearful reality would creep in, shading things gray: how could I achieve this when I didn't love Dave, when my journals were filled with my discontentment? The thoughts would spin in circles, chasing their own tail. I was only beginning to have glimpses of no matter where I sailed to, there I was. I could move from one place to another, but this unhappiness and discontent kept being there. No one had yet given me that roadmap, so it took me many years to learn that simple truth.

I was an introvert and really needed time to myself. Those moments of peace and clarity I experienced at sea were the moments I aligned myself with my soul, my spirit. Even though confined to a small boat, we both respected our hours gazing at the horizon in states of meditation as a holy place; it was our altar, and we knew not to disturb each other. It was home. It was my wisdom place, and if I stayed still and listened to the voice, the same voice that witnessed the immensity of the endless universe, I could easily sit in a joyful, peaceful awe. In those months at Sebulogomwa, Fergusson Island, Dave and I found our way; we found a way to not focus on our problems. Respite came with visitors. Respite came with us being visitors. Refuge for me came in my moments alone when I could quiet the hollow sound of my own steps in flight. Respite would come with our baby being born.

CHAPTER 9

The difference between school and life? In school, you're taught a lesson and then given a test. In life, you're given a test that teaches you a lesson.
—Tom Bodett

The heaviness of pregnancy started to restrict my adventures more and more. I ended up with a severe ear infection, requiring me to take antibiotics, which kept me from swimming for almost three weeks. Each night, Dave set the net and caught a fish I'd cook for dinner. In the mornings, we tended the garden. We read books. We visited with Andy and Kate and their children. An occasional yacht would ghost through, stopping a day, a week, and then move on.

The liquid air of the jungle hung still most days with the same slight breeze recycled from the day before, I'm sure, beginning to blow around 11:00 a.m. Occasionally we'd hear a motorboat crossing over to or from Asa-Ala, maybe Andy's boat or a boat from Salamo, the other mission. We never heard a plane in the sky. Of course, there was no roar or hum of traffic in the background. Just a soft, comforting silence. Small breaks in the silence were noticeable: the faint sounds of lapping water on the bay's edge, more noticeable on the flood tide, a coconut dropping with a thud to the ground with no warning, the afternoon rains coming. You could hear the downpour approaching, slapping the forest leaves as it came closer and closer. The low murmur of people walking down the path blended in with the intermittent under-hum of a verdant quietly pulsing world. Always returning to the sound of silence, I searched for the words of the prophets.

Our house was situated fifty feet from that path. Multiple times a day, single files of people walked by quietly on their thick-padded bare feet out of the jungle into our coconut grove. Always single file because that's as wide as the path was, the width of one body. A man would lead, carrying a stick or spear. Maybe two men, just wearing dirt-colored shorts or sago penis covers. Several women, each carrying three-foot-wide baskets on their head—which they would load up with whatever they found, bought, or traded—and often a baby strapped to her back in a stretch of cloth and a toddler on her hip would follow single file. They wore old grass skirts or drab-colored cotton skirts. Usually no blouses or tops.

At the point where the path came closest to our house, especially in the first month we were there, they would stop and sit down. From our perch on the porch, we would stop reading or knot-tying and watch. A few times I'd wave, but in the beginning, there was no response. They pulled their little woven bags into their laps and retrieved a slice of nut. Slipping a piece in their mouths, they'd start chewing. They'd dampen their knives with the saliva formed from chewing the nut and then dip it into their gourds, tap-tapping off the excess on the side of the gourds, licking the lime powder off; then they'd break off a piece of betel leaf and stuff it in, repeating the ritual we had first witnessed months ago on Wari Island. Baskets and implements were passed between them. It reminded me of hippies in the '60s meeting on the streets and stepping to a discreet corner to pass a joint. As they chewed and spit, they would grow more talkative. Chattering away, they'd laugh; they'd often point at us, laugh some more. Others passing in either direction might stop and join them. Now it reminded of hippies who had just smoked a joint and had completely forgot what they had been in the middle of doing before they got stoned. Dave and I shared this thought and would end up laughing with/at them in return.

These were generally not noisy people. Not like the Greeks who are a very loud people. As are Italians and New Yorkers. People in cities—or the things of cities—are loud. Here even laughing or talking was done quietly. They seemed to live on the undercurrent hum of life. It was like they were always a bit stoned, which with the amount of betel nut they chewed, I suppose they were. It was a stimulant but also a psychotropic.

I tried chewing betel nut once on Wari. The drug was absorbed sublingually while chewing; it was not swallowed. I was suddenly overwhelmed with the sensation of all the blood rushing thickly and rapidly to the ends of my hands and legs. I found it very unpleasant; maybe like a person's first time smoking a cigarette or drinking too much and feeling that sense of lack of control. I never tried it again although Dave chewed it off and on, mostly with the local people, throughout the time we were there.

Eventually these little gatherings on the path would end, and they would rise and walk on through the still, dense liquid air. The completely empty quiet returned. Eventually I might hear in the distance a motorboat heading back from Esa-Ala, another coconut dropping with a thud to the ground, another group of two or three might come walking quietly down the path. They might stop and stare or just keep walking. As time went by, as we stayed and became a regular fixture on their trip to and from the trading store, we were no longer something to stop and stare at. And for us, they too blended into the under-hum, a silent group of people walking by. We'd raise our hands in greeting. They waved back.

I walked once a week from the tip of Sebulogomwa to the Budoya Mission to meet with Sister Angelica. There were no pelvic exams or blood tests or all the other complicated tests that Western medicine does with pregnant women. She felt my baby from the outside with her age-wrinkled skilled hands of experience. She listened with a stethoscope. She put her ear to my belly. All was well always.

My baby was due December 19. Sister Angelica was leaving December 15 for a Christmas retreat in Australia. As my due date approached, she geared up the nurse trainees to deliver my baby, two sixteen-year-olds and two eighteen-year-olds. She assured me that though they all had basically a second-grade education, they were skilled midwives. There was never a fleeting whisper of a doubt in my mind that there would be any problems.

I often walked down and back to the mission by myself while Dave stayed behind to mend the fishing net or write in his journal. Or sleep. I don't know what he did. I often would spend most of the day down at the mission, talking with Father Howard or Sister Angelica. I enjoyed the walk. Nearing villages, I'd hear children playing or the quiet murmuring of adults. I'd peek in and grab a glimpse of their simple lives as I'd walk by, so often the same scene of women bent over the cooking fires situated under the houses, babies strapped to their back, or toddlers sitting in the dirt nearby.

On one trip, three young girls joined me on my way home. They came out of a little pod of houses with some papayas to give me. One had a baby crow perched in her tightly curled Melanesian hair. They were feeding it papaya. It couldn't fly yet; its eyes bulged behind the skin of its sockets with only three featherless quills protruding from its black downy body. These girls were maybe only five years old, but they walked with me back to my house—at least a mile from their homes—and ended up being a helpful audience to my scrubbing clothes by the edge of the water hole dug in the pumice and coconut roots. The baby crow, sitting on the thick nest of black hair, watched it all. Squawking, it was fed by one of the little girls more papaya, its mouth gaping open on reflex. Though we had no means of communicating and we said little to each other, pregnancy created a common bond with the island children and this pregnant woman.

Sister Angelica explained to me that she could treat most things needing medical intervention: pneumonia, malaria, and childbirth. She explained though that the one thing she could not cure was a curse or witchcraft. Several people a year came to her mission hospital who were dying; they all said they'd been cursed; she said they all died within two days. There was nothing medicine could do. She assured me though that the white man could not be cursed because the people believed that the white man's magic and power was greater than theirs, so no one would ever attempt to put death spells on the white man. My baby was to be the first white baby born on this island. Sister Angelica told me with a comforting smile she'd heard it was rumored I must have very strong powers.

Speaking of curses, I shared with her the incident in Rarotonga several years before. Realizing the power of suggestion I had suffered from, I asked her if she believed they died because they believed they'd been cursed. It was a possibility, she pondered. She said that even if they had not heard the curse delivered straight to them, if they were sick, they believed they were sick because they had been cursed, and therefore, they would die. She spoke about it as if it was just a matter of fact, it was a truth, an event that happened at her mission, and it just was. She couldn't save these people. Sometimes they had no symptoms, and there was nothing to treat, but they'd come to the hospital, announcing they were cursed, hoping the white man's powerful medicine could save them. They died because they believed they would.

Though most of my life I'd held an antipathy to churches, I was very comfortable with Sister Angelica and Father Howard who had devoted their lives to missionary work. Our conversations spanned the gamut, but they never preached to me. There was a peacefulness about Father Howard that I was attracted to; he reflected a quiet acceptance of a father I wish I'd had. He had found a deep inner peace in which he joyfully and quietly dwelled. I was aware, I think for the first time, of feeling wrapped in this authentic sense of spirituality when I was around him, but I didn't really understand what I was experiencing. I made a note, tucking it away for many years, that I had met a holy man. I had touched a holy space. To this day, I don't remember what he looked like at all; it was his presence that remains in my mind.

One day, walking back from the mission, a seemingly crazy local man followed me and talked with me the whole way back. He wore the typical brown-drab rag shorts. He was barefoot as almost every villager was. His hair was long, almost dreadlocked, clearly having not been pick-combed or cut for a very long time. I could see the dust and pieces of twigs in it. His fingernails were dirty; in fact, his body was streaked with dirt-cut rivulets of sweat. He hadn't bathed for quite a while. This was unusual for any local person to be that dirty.

I had moments of feeling that he might be dangerous, but he seemed only to be manic and extremely eccentric. And well educated. His English was good though he lacked the ability to follow one track of thought for long. Partly from him and partly from inquiring of Sister Angelica later, I learned he was one of the few islanders who had actually left the island for the equivalent of a high school education in Port Moresby. He had returned quite mentally ill. The Sister, of course, could not or would not attribute this to the education or the cultural shock of leaving his village or whether in fact he might have been cursed for achieving more than others. But she acknowledged that he was indeed mentally ill.

He followed me down the narrow jungle path, talking incessantly the whole way back to the house where Dave was when we arrived. On arriving back at the hut, Dave felt very threatened by the man and angrily and forcefully ordered him to leave. The man became quite agitated and clearly more mentally unstable. I had had no problem with talking with him and walking with him down the isolated jungle path; treating him gently and with compassion. Dave's angry threats did drive him away. It was only then that I was more concerned about him than all the while that I had walked with him. I imagined, now angered by Dave treating him so poorly, that he might sneak back and harm us. I seldom worried about any kind of harm from anyone in the years I was in the South Pacific.

Several weeks later, we rowed our eight-foot dinghy across Dawson Strait to Esa-Ala on Normanby where the mail came for those on the immediate islands. It was about three miles between the tip of Sebulogomwa and Esa-Ala. It was always a lovely row; the water was almost always glassy smooth, and the dinghy moved quickly through it, only the sound of the oars dipping in the water and the rattle of the oarlocks breaking the silence. Walking to the post office that one day, I saw the very same man enclosed in a caged pen about twenty-foot square in what I would call the center of town though Esa-Ala was not much of a town. When he saw me, he leapt at the side of the ten-foot-tall fence, clinging to it a bit like a monkey in a cage with his feet and his hands, clearly happy to see me. I approached him, again with compassion and kindness, but Dave again angrily warned me away from him. The man responded to Dave much like a caged animal would, almost snarling.

The man has haunted me for many years. I've pondered whether he was indeed the product of Western education crossing its wires with his cultural ground or whether their society, like all societies, just have mental illness. The one truth I knew was they seemed to have no humane way of dealing with him except to lock him in a caged area with a small hut to sleep in in the middle of a tiny island port village for everyone to stare at. I never rowed back to Esa-Ala after that last time; Dave went by himself, or Andy would bring any mail over to us on *Two-Bob*. There are times I see the mentally ill and homeless on our streets, and I'm reminded of that man.

On our first meeting with Sister Angelica and Father Howard, they had lent me some interesting books and booklets about Papua New Guinea anthropology. One dealt with education and the issues of trying to bring Western education to these people. It explored the fact that this was a society not yet ready for such education. The reasons were twofold: one, simply, there was so little they could do once they were educated; and, two, excelling educationally produced men and women who were better than others.

Sister Angelica voiced this frustration. Culturally, to these people, it was bad or evil (and would bring on a curse) if one were better than another or possessed more than the other, and this applied to education as well as having more food or the biggest yam. There were many rituals—created on the spur or part of ceremonial exercises—that existed to give away and redistribute an individual's wealth in this region, hence balancing out having more than others. They of course could not conceive of how one could redistribute one person's education to another. To Sister's frustration, if it appeared that one was excelling in school and was becoming better educated than others, then the student would quit. Few students went past the basics of learning the alphabet and learning to read primers. They would then return to the real life of living in the villages.

In one of the books I had borrowed, a learned anthropologist discussed the cultures of the New Guinea people with those of the Western world. Speaking in anthropological terms, the local people viewed the world as animistic, needing to be controlled by correct ritual with truth being relative. Westerners viewed the world as governed by concrete physical laws that were fixed truths by which world economics and trade agreements were forged. For the people of Papua New Guinea, their correct ritual mandated that no one have more than others; that wealth, gained by luck or hard work, needed to be redistributed.

I learned this early upon our arrival at Sebulogomwa. Andy had taken us over to a near island to visit another old-timer, Doug Mills. Many of the locals had come down to the beach with yams and other food crops to trade (I think). One yam in particular was monstrous; it must have been 100 pounds at least. I exclaimed, "Wow, what a huge yam!" lavishing praise and wonder, but Doug, who wasn't far from me, quickly turned as if to walk behind me.

While passing, he stopped and whispered in my ear quite urgently, "Say you've seen bigger. Say you've seen bigger!"

Not understanding why, I immediately announced, "Oh, but I've seen bigger. I've seen wayyyy bigger!!"

The air relaxed again.

Over the time we were there, I saw this cultural truth expressed in other ways. Our neighbors chose to redistribute their wealth through Maria's fifth birthday party. We were invited. I remember we scrambled to provide some sort of present—*our* cultural practice—though I have no idea what it might have been since we had no store to go shopping. I vaguely remember presenting it and them not really knowing what to do with it because, unbeknownst to us, the party was for *them* to be giving their wealth away.

We came early afternoon and were led to the back area of their house, which was a "proper house," in that it had a concrete floor and half walls of wood, opened wooden windows, and a thatched roof. On entering a room that was possibly thirty feet long and ten feet wide, it was already filled with people. Two long mats stretched the length of the floor. On either side of one mat sat the women, mostly in their grass skirts, bare breasted, a baby at a nipple; on either side of the other mat, the men sat. On both mats, food was piled high: yams and greens and cooked chickens. It was a feast. Dave and I separated and joined our appropriate mats, but I noticed no one seemed to be eating much. I sat uncomfortably, wondering what the social rules were. We waited for a prayer or benediction or someone to say, "You may begin."

Eventually a few people began to slide small amounts of this abundance onto their slivers of banana leaves, a common plate used by local people throughout the South Pacific and other areas where bananas grow. I finally started to fill my banana leaf with food, but as I ate, I noticed that the women were, one by one, leaving the feast and not returning. I could only think how strange. I decided no one would notice if I too rose up from the floor and headed outside. What I witnessed was the redistribution of wealth. The women were lined up at the cookhouse out back with their two- and three-foot-wide baskets onto which they piled yams and bananas and whatever other assortment of food was being distributed, and they sauntered home. The men remained behind, sitting on the floor on either side of the mats, continuing to eat. Being forever hungry, I returned to the women's side as the only woman who remained.

This reminded me of the almost lost ceremonies of the First Nations people of the United States and Canada. At potlatch gatherings, a family or hereditary leader hosted guests in their family's house, holding a feast.

A main purpose of the potlatch for these peoples too was the redistribution and reciprocity of wealth. Potlatching was actually made illegal in Canada in 1884 in an amendment to the Indian Act and in the United States in the late nineteenth century, largely at the urging of missionaries and government agents who considered it "a worse than useless custom" that was seen as wasteful, unproductive, and contrary to civilized values. Missionary William Duncan wrote in 1875 that the potlatch was "by far the most formidable of all obstacles in the way of Indians becoming Christians or even civilized." I detest the atrocities committed in the name of religion. But the hypocrisy of the Christians to think that sharing was an unchristian or uncivilized practice!

Father Howard acknowledged in our talks that, for any culture, real education must be internal to the culture: the passing on of accumulated wisdom of that society was essential for the full development of the child within that particular culture. To introduce a Western education on these people was "at best instruction, at worst indoctrination." Unlike the missionaries in the nineteenth century who took the Native American children from their homes and sent them to boarding schools, stripping them of their language, their heritage, their tribe's stories and myths, their very identities, Father Howard acknowledged not only the dangers of a child being taught completely Western things but also the innate cruelty of taking the child from the soul of their village. Their rituals and myths were essential to who they were.

I respected that Father Howard and Sister Angelica seemed to simply minister to the basic needs of the people, bringing healthcare and some education. They left the main education to the village, an education in harmony with the land that took lifetimes of listening to hear, absorb, and truly learn.

CHAPTER 10

Vast tracts of ocean, whether Polynesia, Micronesia or Melanesia,
contain island populations that remain outside the modern world.
They know about it, they may have traveled to it, they appreciate
artifacts and medical help from it, but they live their daily
lives much as hundreds of generations of ancestors before them,
without money, electricity, phones, TV or manufactured food.

—Andrew Rayner

On September 16, 1975, Papua New Guinea gained its independence from Australia. We didn't follow the politics of Papua New Guinea afterward, but the upheaval and expulsion of foreigners and white men that Andy and Kate both dreaded and looked forward to never happened. After being ruled by three external powers since 1884, after Japan invaded it and wars were fought on its soil, and after gaining its independence from Australia, it chose to remain a member of the Commonwealth, realm of Her Majesty Elizabeth II, Queen of Papua New Guinea. It joined the United Nations.

We were there for this historic event although their blastoff into nationhood presented an interesting perception of the significance (or lack thereof) independence meant to these people, at least on this island where we were living. Though the event was held on the grounds of the Budoya Mission, I'm not sure how much the mission influenced how they would ritualize this momentous moment in history. I'm unaware of how or why the particular ceremony was chosen to represent their independence: It was their *funeral* ceremony. It was apparent to us and to Sister Angelica and Father Howard that the villagers had little concept of why or what they were celebrating.

Much of the actual presentation was performed by the schoolchildren, which made me think that the folks at the mission or mission school had had some input into what would happen. There were also a few dances performed by the elders. Otherwise, for us the only thing to witness of interest was the hundreds of islanders who came as mere onlookers, standing on the perimeter, waiting for something to happen but not participating. They did come dressed for the occasion. The men wore new sago penis covers. All the women and young female children had on their new grass skirts. A few had seeded necklaces adorning their naked torsos. I looked for delicate necklaces made of cantaloupe seeds.

For weeks, as I had walked past the villages back and forth from the mission, I had witnessed numerous women working on making new skirts at different stages. I didn't know at the time that they were destined for this celebration. I would stop and watch how they would strip the green sago palm leaves into thin strips and hang them over a line to dry. After being dried, they would weave and loop the strips on to a string of twisted coconut husk that would become the waistband. Fresh new skirts were still the color of golden wheat; as they aged, they became the drab-brown color of the sago palm huts and every piece of cotton clothing. Some here, for this event, had been dyed a deep purple in contrasting vertical sections.

There were sports events—or some similarity to them—that seemed to act mainly as a filler. They were a bit pathetic from our point of view because, again, these people did not seem to be competitive by nature. Again, education, capitalism, or even socialism, and general betterment of living conditions seemed to fail because of the people's fear—fear, more than abhorrence—to being better than the next man. So even in the sports events, we didn't witness an aggressive competition of spirit or skill.

But at this "great" festival of independence, we saw for the first time the wearing of the *bagi*, the strange ornamental necklaces of exchange that were part of the Kula ring. We had heard of the Kula ring through Andy, Father Howard, and the other old-timer Australian, Doug Mills, who had made Papua New Guinea his home for many decades. As Doug Mills explained to us, the bagi was not owned by anyone but was exchanged at least every two years between members of the Kula District that encompassed the Trobriand Islands, farther north of where we were, as well as the Milne Bay District. When it was time to exchange, it was paddled by canoe to the next island in a clockwise direction. It was transferred with great ritual and ceremony. That person would keep the bagi or *mwali* (bracelets) for a time and then take it to another island to share.

Years later, in researching it, I discovered the Kula ring, according to learned anthropologists who studied such things, involved much more complex history, much more complicated ritual, and more powerful members of a community and more power plays than was conveyed to me then. Through Doug Mills, I was led to understand that there was only one bagi necklace exchanged every two years; I learned decades later there were in fact many bagi or mwali. Rules varied within different island groups, and it seems there was a lot of power play involved. But almost like a child clinging to the belief in Santa Claus, I have clung to Doug Mills' description of the Kula ring all these years: a ritual of sharing wealth, a ceremony of redistribution, ignoring any idea that it was also wrapped in prestige and power structures.

Witnessing the independence festivities as foreign onlookers, Doug pointed out the young ten- or eleven-year-old girl standing out from all the others. She was wearing only her new wheat-colored grass skirt, and the bagi that hung down her back was striking. Its main shell was a *kina*, a rare, fine large red oyster shell bored with holes and strung with other assortments of shells. (Kina, because it was the symbol of wealth, was also the name for the money of Papua New Guinea.) At the ends of the bagi were white cowry shells, pearly shells, and what looked like colored beads. This ornamental necklace appeared to be quite heavy and uncomfortable as the girl usually had her hand at her throat, pulling it away from her neck.

In spite of the new grass skirts and armbands of greenery, the Papuan celebrations were not particularly colorful. As a rule, we had not found the culture from Wari to Fergusson to be a particularly colorful people as were the eastern Polynesians. Everything was a shade of brown or natural green. No leis were ever made or worn here as in Tahiti and the Cook Islands. No bright-colored pareo wraps. Most of the villages did not even boast hedges of colorful hibiscus or frangipani.

The lack of color seemed to enhance the fact that the ceremony they had chosen to depict was their funeral ritual. The primitive and uneducated peoples here knew nothing of a "new freedom" they had been given. All the dances depicted the death of Australia's motherhood. The men drummed on long hollow wooden drums stretched taut with lizard skins. They danced as they drummed, hopping first on one leg while thrusting their other leg out and forward, and then switching, they hopped on the other. All the while, a woman blew on a conch shell, one note repetitively. This lasted for what seemed like hours.

We sat politely watching. Sister Angelica and Father Howard joined us at times though they would leave on occasion to tend to other matters. Doug Mills sat with us much of the time, telling stories of his years living there. He spoke of the Kula ring. He spoke of how the people made soap from the "soap ginger" plant, and they used coconut cream, grated and squeezed from mature nuts, to condition their hair. I had in fact seen women on the beach one day where their hair was wet with whiteness; yes, Doug said, they were probably wearing their conditioner for the day. We would have all died of boredom watching this independence day celebration had we not been interacting with Doug Mills, Father Howard, and Sister. Andy and Kate and all six kids came over to Budoya for a few hours but didn't stay long.

Finally, after long, repetitious, and quite boring hours of this display, what they called the feast finally took place. Over the previous days and weeks, the people had erected a giant platform or stage, lashing long poles together to form the frame, lashing more bamboo poles across to form the platform. For several days, all the village people had been bringing yams, bananas, plantains, and sweet potatoes from their gardens, piling them onto this platform. On this day of independence, the platform was heaped high. We were under the impression, as were even the sisters at the mission, that great fires would be built, and the evening would be spent in feasting as truly would have been the case had this happened in Polynesia or any other country.

But instead, upon some cue, all of the schoolchildren mounted the platform and proceeded to hand out the yams and bananas to everyone present, including us. After about fifteen frantic minutes of yelling and outstretched arms, passing the food out to everyone present (the one time I can remember these people getting noisy), the stage was empty. The broad baskets that the women balanced on their heads were piled with fifty or sixty pounds of food, and with their babies wrapped on to their backs, their toddlers on their hips, and the other children following, they headed back to their villages with the men carrying nothing but a spear or a long stick. I ended up with about thirty pounds of yams to take home on my shoulders and back for our own solitary feast.

No *dimdim* (white man) there had an explanation for why there had been no feast, and of course, none of the locals present could comprehend the question because it was natural not to have a feast. My theory propounded to Sister Angelica, with which possibility she concurred, was there was always the fear among these people that someone might be poisoned or murdered by eating the food prepared by someone else, so it was safer to eat the food prepared only by those you knew and trusted. (Was that why few had eaten at Maria's birthday? I will never know.) If that was true, it was interesting watching this underlying hum of distrust and sorcery control these people's lives: it encouraged people to share, and it encouraged people to keep to themselves, all driven by the power of a sorcerer's curse.

Prince Charles, along with the Australian prime minister and other high officials, officiated in the main ceremony in Port Moresby. Papua New Guinea became another member of the British Commonwealth. But with independence day over, there was nothing that changed—that we witnessed while we were there anyhow. Michael Somare addressed the United Nations in October, and PNG became the 142nd member. A villager had heard his speech on the radio and told Dave, "Now the Americans will come here." We didn't follow the logic at all. We just nodded our heads in agreement, "Oh, yes, it must be so."

Sometimes their innocence was sweet. Sometimes it seemed a little precarious.

A few days after these activities, Andy came by on *Two-Bob* with a letter he'd received from the ADC (Administrative District Council), which proved to be an almost illegible copy of a letter the ADC had received from the Dobu Government Council (the adjoining island of Normanby or Dobu) announcing that it had asked for a government loan because it was going to buy Sebulogomwa and Kedidia, Andy's plantation. They hadn't even approached Andy. They had no idea what Andy might sell it for or whether in fact he was actually going to sell it. It reflected, as Andy had argued, that even the local government didn't know how to approach business dealings.

Here was a newly formed independent country that was, at that time, contemplating kicking out all the Europeans who had money and enterprises to be replaced by their own people who had no money, let alone any knowledge as to how to earn money, manage money, or run a business, and whose cultural instinct was to abhor or at least fear being richer or better than anyone else. They practiced Wuntok; they would never collect the debts of their Wuntok. On these islands, there was nothing resembling a bank. No one understood the basics of economics and business management. It was fascinating to be present during this transition and watch the innocent ignorance of these people coming into the twenty-first century.

Forty years later, while taking a course in Bogota, Colombia, I met an elderly gentleman who said he had lived in the highlands of mainland Papua New Guinea for twenty years. He told me of how after the ATM machine first came to his town—it was constantly broken. He said the locals would watch white people go up to the machine, insert a card, and pull out money. So figuring they also could perform such magic too, they were forever slipping pieces of cut cardboard into the card slot, which of course would jam the machine.

Today, as of this writing, Papua New Guinea is still one of the most culturally diverse countries on Earth. There are over 800 separate languages spoken there. It is also one of the Earth's least explored regions, both culturally and geographically. Out of over six million in population, only 18 percent live in the few urban areas like Port Moresby or Lae. Interestingly, as of 2011, Papua New Guinea had the seventh fastest-growing economy in the world mostly because of the mining and resource sectors, which, sadly, from my perspective was, once again, the taking and raping by the rich corporations and the enslavement of a culture and its people. Close to 80 percent of the population continue to live their traditional lifestyles, practicing subsistence-based agriculture as we witnessed on Fergusson Island.

After their independence, as they worked out how they wanted to be in the world, the PNG constitution actually expressed the wish for "traditional villages and communities to remain as viable units of Papua New Guinean society" and for active steps to be taken in their preservation. Many people live in extreme poverty, with about one-third of the population living on approximately $1 a day though I must say that though they are not rich in money, they never seemed to have a lack of food or a place to live or a sago skirt or penis cover to wear. Possibly learning how to read a calendar and tell time might allow them to eradicate malaria, but otherwise, I commend them to their simple communities and periodically redistributing their wealth.

As the occupation of Wall Street grew in momentum several years ago, not only in the streets of New York but also in other American cities and around the world, I found myself reflecting on the simpler times of my life. I thought of the generosity of the islanders, especially in the Marquesas and Tahiti. Even New Zealand. I thought of rituals of exchange and commodities of value, prestige, wealth, necessities such as food and clothing, and how such rituals of exchange and what was valuable have evolved, changed, and morphed in different cultures.

In Papua New Guinea, the Kula ring continues on though other forms of trade have changed and maybe caught up with the rest of the world as they mine their wealth from the ground and sell it for not even gold, not even paper cash representing its value in gold, but a virtual wealth somewhere in the bowels of a computer representing the wealthy, the big banks, the stock exchanges of the world. For those now having the wealth, it was no longer in their culture to redistribute it and share it. There are a few, maybe the Bill Gateses and Warren Buffets of the world. But overall, the societal and cultural safety net to ensure that all have what they need seems lost.

In the seven years I sailed in the South Pacific, we lived each day as it came, much like the islanders. I didn't have a bank account. I didn't have a credit card with which I could buy something today and pay for it some time in the future somehow. And as I've repeated before, we seldom had even a dime to our name. In the seven years I was gone, I earned approximately $1,500 total. We had no health insurance. Somehow, even at age twenty-five partly because I had been living such an alternative lifestyle, I was quite oblivious to the idea that there was such a thing as medical insurance or that one needed it. It didn't exist in 1975 in Papua New Guinea.

The stir of independence day settled like a leaf nudged by a breeze, and then all came to a rest.

Dave got a letter from Tom Neale from Anchorage, Suwarrow Atoll. He had visited Tom Neale after reading *An Island to Oneself*, an autobiography by Neale about living alone on a small island for three different lengths of time from 1952 to 1977. Enamored that Tom Neale was actually living Dave's dream, Dave had ended up sailing to Suwarrow to stay there for several weeks several years before. I'm sure wanting to see yet another sail on the horizon moving toward his island, Tom was inviting him to return to Suwarrow anytime Dave desired.

And I got a letter in which my mom had sent me $79 Australian. And as it seems to be always feast or famine, Andy snuck me $100 in payment for Dave's work. He wouldn't pay Dave as he claimed Dave would argue about receiving it. Having spent our last 40 cents one day, we were rich with $179. I was still waiting for my $92 tax return from the Australian government. We ate fish and wild greens the locals taught me to find and harvest; we had our garden food. Dave eventually took a multiday trip to Lae with Andy, a much larger center of commerce, and stocked up on other foods we'd need for when we left.

My due date came and went. Sister Angelica left for her retreat in Australia.

CHAPTER 11

*The knowledge of how to give birth without outside
interventions lies deep within each woman.*

—Suzanne Arms

My waters broke several hours before dawn on December 29, 1975.
Ten days past my due date, asleep in our thatched hut, under the protection
of mosquito netting, I was content to lie there, holding the magic of that
moment all to myself. I had asked somebody—I can't remember who—to
send me *Spiritual Midwifery*, a book written only that year by Ima May
Gaskins. I hadn't received it and didn't until a week later. In spite of having
read nothing, I knew I had lots of time to lie there and not to rush. I lay
there and waited for the next contraction. And then the next.

The soaked sheets began to give me discomfort, so I finally nudged
Dave in the darkness. "Hey, my waters just broke."

Surely having watched too many movies, Dave seemed to panic. He
jumped up in the darkness, lit the lantern, and began gathering a bag of
clothes and our precious dozen diapers to rush down to the mission.

I lay there, Mother Wisdom residing deeply within me. I informed him
calmly that I was not going anywhere until it was light out, at least another
two hours. I did ask that he get some clean sheets and change our bed,
which was made up of the boat's Naugahyde settee cushions that lay on the
floor of the thatched hut, draped with a mosquito net. After he complied,
I lay back down quietly marveling that this long-awaited day had finally
arrived.

Sister Angelica had informed me that I should give myself an enema, something I later regretted doing and which I never did again though, with all that pushing going on, I understood the logic behind it. So as soon as it was light enough to see what I was doing, I followed through with heating some water, filling our hot water/douche bottle. I self-administered the enema, lying down for as long as I could to retain it before rushing out to our little latrine seats in the garden. In the meantime, Dave went to hang the fish net, something he did every morning, this morning no different. The net, as usual, needed mending in small places where it had been torn on coral or by a reef shark.

When I finally felt that the activity of the enema had settled down and the sun having finally come up over the sea's horizon through the coconut trees, we set off down the foot path through the jungle to Budoya Mission. The baby was pressing down low. I was distinctly waddling. In all the previous months, I had never walked down to the mission so early in the morning. At this early hour in that exquisite morning silence, the older women were all out tending early-morning cook fires where they would boil up the yams that would be eaten all day. The men were out in their canoes fishing, gliding silently over the glassy-smooth waters.

As I waddled past the first village, a woman looked up. She cooed, "Oh, sìnabada, sìnabada," bowing slightly and reverently in knowing acknowledgment.

Another woman by another fire heard her and looked up, smiling her redtoothed smile. "Oh, sìnabada, sìnabada," also bowing in acknowledgment of motherhood.

For many years, I thought they were saying, "Oh, Mother. Mother." In researching for this book, I found that sìnabada in Police Motu means "white woman," but its literal translation is "mother-big." This translation does not refer to the fact that I had a big belly, and I was waddling down to join the sacred club of motherhood, but it means a "woman of senior standing" (like the wife of an official), again in keeping that my being a white woman put me in a senior standing above them, in their minds, with greater sorcerer's power. In searching for this translation, I came across the words of sinána vada, which is translated as "mother"—sinána—and "to be born"—vada. I didn't ever like being considered senior to any of these people, but it was clearly sìnabada that I heard. Interestingly, the women of the villages had never before called me sìnabada in all my walks to Budoya before, so I would prefer to assume that it was a colloquialism for the senior position I was now taking on as mother. Whatever its meaning, though, it remains the most welcoming of sounds that morning that I have kept close to my heart since.

I was walking slowly, stopping completely when a contraction would come. As I passed each village, women would notice me, and the cooing would start again. To this day, the magic of that quiet morning's welcome into the circle of Universal Mother resides deep within me. Those women had seen me walk the four miles to the Budoya Mission many times before, but this morning, they knew I was walking to become a mother. No anonymity. No secrets. I was participating in the universal ritual of motherhood.

I think it was that very one early-morning experience that colored all my future thoughts about childbirth. Though I recognized the times and places when medical intervention was necessary, childbirth as a whole was such a natural process. Witnessing the birth of my two granddaughters, twenty-five years later, with all the wires and monitors and painkillers and contraptions and interferences with the natural process, I am so thankful to have participated in the natural beauty of that spiritually and physically amazing moment.

Several times on the walk to the mission, it became clear that the enema still had its work to do. There was no such thing as a toilet on that island. The local natives would walk down to the water's edge and do their duty. If the tide had not yet come in, one could witness a line of red stools (so colored from the betel nut they chewed) along the beach near the water. The high tide would wash it out, and the fish would have their fill. This sounds very gross, I'm sure, to readers, but this has been the universal toilet for oceanic communities for millennia, at least in the primitive sparsely populated areas. I could not bare my bottom to the world, so as the enema hit me, I was scurrying for the cover of the jungle foliage. These episodes were the only uncomfortable thing I remember about walking four miles to the mission.

It being a slower walk than normal, we arrived at the mission hospital somewhere close to midmorning. One of the nurse trainees greeted us. Sister Angelica had long ago left for Australia as this was now December

29. I was given a private room (the only one), separate from the main hospital ward. It was about eight by eight, containing a single bed and a chair and a bassinet. The nurse took a stick and propped open the wooden window, bringing in light. A young local girl was giving birth in the birthing room when we arrived. As Monica, the eighteen-year-old student nurse in charge, gave me a pelvic and checked my progress, I heard this young woman screaming for her mother. Screaming. Wailing. All I could think was there was no way I would scream and cry like that during childbirth. Maybe it was their way, I thought, but it wasn't going to be my way.

After doing a pelvic exam, Monica informed us that I would probably have the baby that evening some time, and then she left to attend to the young screaming woman. After sitting with me for a while, Dave decided that he would leave and walk back to Sebulogomwa and mend the fishing net and get the boat squared away to bring up to Budoya in a day or two. He felt there was nothing he could do for me there. He left, leaving me alone to labor. In one breath, I was fine with that because really there was nothing he could do. This was *my* labor, *my* work of love. But on the other hand, I couldn't understand why he would want to leave at such a milestone of his life.

Again, the history of our dysfunctional past served up its leftovers as I labored alone that day. A part of me did understand why Dave couldn't stay, didn't stay. We all have our secrets, our demons, our dysfunctional pasts. And Dave had his. There was no blame. I circled my thoughts and beliefs about this: I was in labor with his first child, and yet he walked away. To mend a fishing net, no less. And then I'd let my whining criticism lie down, putting it aside, recognizing again that it served nothing constructive and that there was in fact nothing much he could do for me at that moment. My body labored on alone in a solidarity and quiet strength.

I walked out on to the mission grounds, on to the large green where the independence day celebrations had been held several months before, a space that had previously been filled with hundreds of people. Down on the water stood two rickety wooden buildings built on stilts twenty feet from shore. Sagging foot-wide planks led from the shore to the buildings. These were the latrines for all who visited the mission: the sisters, the nurses, the teachers, the students. It was an open outhouse seat that dumped directly into the water below. I was told emphatically not to use it (I'm sure for fear that I might give birth there). Instead, I had been given a portable bedpan in my little room. Quite modern, I thought.

I walked around the edge of the green, a green I had explored many times before on my visits to the mission. I walked and walked. I stopped for contractions. I walked. I went up to the dispensary and drank water. The girl was still screaming. I walked more. Somewhere around one-thirty in the afternoon, I was aware that the girl had finally given birth, a baby girl I was told. She was in the dispensary exhausted and sleeping. Her mother, in a grass skirt, sat holding the baby next to the bed.

Alone, I continued walking until about three when the contractions had become closer and closer together and lasted longer. It finally got to the point where I felt I needed to go up to my bed and lie down. To my relief, Dave joined me right as I was heading up there, and I told him he should probably go and get Monica or Josita to let them know that it was seeming to be almost one endless contraction. Dave actually wanted to argue with me that, no, we shouldn't bother them, that I wasn't going to have the baby, they said, until that evening. One can imagine I wasn't accepting his response as I gritted my teeth, and I told him he'd better damn well go get the nurses.

I was lying on the bed when the two older nurses (eighteen years old) rushed in. I explained my situation, and they quickly helped me into the small delivery room to that hard wooden table. It was a little after three when I climbed onto that incredibly uncomfortable table.

Dave settled into a chair next to me, holding my hand. Monica checked me and said that soon I would have the urge to push. Everything up to this moment had seemed so natural, but I then realized I was so unprepared. I had ordered some books to read about childbirth, but they had not arrived. The contractions were long with shorter and shorter breaks between. I had intense back labor, making the wooden table even more uncomfortable to find relief though I did manage to laugh and joke with the nurses in between contractions. They were incredibly calm and professional through most of the delivery though Sister Angelica did confide that there was a general nervousness because I was the first white woman (ah, sìnabada) to give birth there.

Time does not exist for a mother in labor. Maybe forty-five minutes later, the pushing began. It was difficult to govern how to push when delivering a baby for the first time. Years later, I assisted my daughter-in-law and then this very same daughter in childbirth, and I could tell them, "Do not push from your chest. All the energy needs to push down there."

But for my first time, I had to discover how to do that. I gritted my teeth and pushed into my chest. Again. And I'd laugh and joke between contractions. Dave would stand up and look down between my legs and then get faint and have to sit down again.

Another contraction. Another push into my chest. There was a lot of pushing and wasted energy—I know now—so the baby's passage down was slow, but she did start moving down, and I slowly became aware of where I needed to direct my energy. I would lose awareness of Dave being there as all concentration centered on this life moving down my birth canal, moving toward the light and first breath of air. My teeth gritted. I pushed. I laughed and joked between contractions. They brought me ice. Ice! Where did that come from? Ice. Cold ice. I was drenched with sweat both from the work I did and because I was in a ninety-degree, humid, tropic rainforest.

The head began to crown, and without asking, without notice, Monica gave me a double episiotomy. Most babies born there are no bigger than five pounds, a result of, first, small-statured people but also probably lack of nutrition to grow bigger babies. Neither Monica nor Josita had ever seen such a large head crown; they apparently couldn't conceive of how it could be delivered without making double incisions. This was the only part of the delivery I would have liked to undo.

Dave got woozy, and *I* had to direct him to put his head between his legs. Then I forgot about him again, and I pushed. The contraction passed, and my awareness would again focus back with Dave, and then the contraction would begin again, and my awareness would be on Monica and Josita and what they were telling me to do. I was feeling very confident in their abilities, and I kept thinking I should let them know that they didn't need to be nervous about me being a dimdim, that no matter what they did, I would not curse them with my great white power. I didn't bring it up.

Dripping with sweat, they put long white cotton boot leggings on my legs. I remember thinking that was interesting. It was necessary with the young women who came in with grass skirts, a sanitary precaution for them, but—oh, yeah, I realized—such silly thoughts in times like this that, oh, my gosh, I might not have been wearing a grass skirt, but I had walked the whole distance in rubber flip-flops, so I'm sure my feet weren't quite the cleanest.

Dripping with sweat, I was brought a cool rag and ice water. With each contraction and each push, I was surprised at how unaware I was of the progress down the birth canal without Josita informing me. Dripping with sweat. Dave finally, at my request, got some pillows so that I could sit up more and let gravity help me a bit with the last final pushes. Dripping with sweat. The wooden windows, though propped open, brought no movement of air though I could see the blue sky and the tops of coconut trees. I'm dripping with sweat.

Finally, half sitting, I saw the head come out, dark and wet. I saw Josita struggling to get the cord unwrapped from her neck, and at the same time, I heard her warn me not to push while telling one of the younger, sixteen-year-old nurse trainees to keep suctioning her mouth. A little tube was up the nose or mouth or both of my baby with one of the teenage nurses gently sucking on the other end with her mouth.

This was the one point at which I was slightly worried as I could feel another contraction coming. Trying to keep from pushing would be like trying to stop a sneeze from coming. Or trying to alter the path of a tornado. Or trying to stop a fast-moving car whose brakes are locked on an ice-packed highway before it hits a snow-blanketed wall. Or trying to stop—

And then suddenly, the body of my daughter just slid out, *slurp*, and I said, "Wow." I saw it was a girl as Josita lifted her upside down while the teenage nurse continued sucking through the tube and the other younger nurse trainee, without warning, stuck a needle in my leg to cause the uterus to contract, and Dave ran off to check the chronometer for the birth time—4:30 p.m. PNG time—and Monica kept pulling gently and patiently on the blue twisted umbilical cord that had been tied and cut, separating my daughter from me forever. And then suddenly, *slurp*, the placenta slid out with one more big rush and one more big wow. And it was over. Wow. Dripping with sweat.

A bedpan was stuck under me, and Josita started stitching me up, nine stitches altogether, most of them falling out within the first few days. Someone was tending to Heidi, our daughter, while I was being stitched up. I started shaking violently, and I was told it was natural. Finally, Dave wheeled Heidi over next to me. She lay quietly in a little bassinet with a fist in her mouth. Dave likened her to a little Winston Churchill, which I did not see as a compliment as in my eyes she was beautiful. She was perfect. Her head was round and perfect. She was not a Winston Churchill. We had almost no film left in our camera. We took one picture.

The girls finally walked me over to my small private room. My legs were wobbly and unsteady. My stomach felt flat and flubbery and empty. They wouldn't let me nurse right away, which later, in hindsight after having had several more children, I thought was a bit odd. But one of the girls sat in my room all night, feeding her sugar water when she fussed and changing her diapers. My first feeding was awkward and unsuccessful, but by the end of the day, with my cow udders huge and dripping, soaking everything constantly, Heidi attached to my nipple naturally.

Dave slept on a cot in the room the next four nights, bringing me food cooked in the convent cookhouse. I ate wonderful meals those days with lots of eggs and cabbage and vegetables. Eventually Dave managed to bring the boat up to Budoya from Sebulogomwa, rowing with the giant sweeps on his own for the lack of wind. After that, he stayed on the boat, cooking my meals there and bringing them to me.

They were insistent that I stay at the mission hospital for ten days and recuperate. I argued that I was not an invalid, but in the end and in hindsight, what a blessing to be there with the nurses doing everything for me: washing my dozen diapers, helping to change my baby, taking her away in the evenings if she was fussy to let me sleep a bit more, feeding me the first few days before Dave finally brought the boat down and anchored it out beyond the two latrine shacks. They had a shower out back, which consisted of a two-gallon bucket of water that you hoisted up on pulleys and then opened up a shower head hanging from a tube. It was all quite luxurious for sure.

On the third day, on the night of January 1, 1976—not New Year's Eve, but the night of January 1—right after it had gotten dark, the two younger nurses came to my room. They told me to get up and come with them. "Why?" I asked.

"Just come," they said.

A torrential monsoon rain was falling in the darkness. One picked up Heidi and swaddled her tightly, carrying her out. I followed with the other girl holding an umbrella for both of us. I had no idea where I was going. We walked from my little room over toward the white cement storehouse. It was very, very dark, and I could not see anything though I could hear the murmuring of a lot of low voices around me. Upon arriving to an area near the white storehouse, they seated me in a chair and handed me my baby Heidi. One girl continued to stand by me, holding the umbrella over both of us. I still had no any idea what was going on.

The generator started in the background, and then several feet next to me under cover of a large umbrella, the lights of a movie projector lit up, projecting first a white light then a bull's-eye counting down 5, 4, 3, 2, 1 against the white wall of the storehouse before suddenly Julie Andrews was dancing across the mountains singing, "The hills are alive with the sound of music." That song and that moment is forever burned into my memory.

From the light of the projector and the movie on the screen, I could see that I was surrounded by maybe a hundred or more locals, all holding banana leaves over their heads against the pounding rain. As the movie played, they were all singing the whole musical score of *The Sound of Music*. Sitting in the rain on a remote island off of the Papua New Guinea mainland, surrounded by people wearing sago penis covers, grass skirts, cotton skirts, chewing betel nut, hunkered under banana leaves while the rain pounded everything and everyone—people who could barely speak a word of English—sitting here with my newborn baby, I felt that the *jungle* was alive with the sound of music. Everyone seemed to know every song of the musical. I marveled that this movie was being played but also thought that any movie would be a magical wonder, let alone a film that depicted other worlds of Austrian castles and big cities, mountains covered with snow, automobiles, armies, so many places and things unknown to these people.

The cost of the birth of our daughter in Papua New Guinea was the repair of a bread oven that Maria von Trapp had had built when she had been a lay missionary at the mission. Maria Agatha Franziska Gobertina von Trapp (born on September 28, 1914 in Austria) was the second-oldest daughter of Georg Ludwig von Trapp and Agatha Whitehead von Trapp. She was a member of the Trapp Family Singers whose lives were the inspiration for the musical play *The Sound of Music*. She was the last surviving sibling, having died a few months before her hundredth birthday in Vermont. The von Trapps fled Austria after the German annexation of Austria, fearing reprisals resulting from declining to sing at Hitler's birthday party and Georg von Trapp's refusal to accept a commission in the German navy. They came to the United States in 1938, settled in Vermont in 1942, and performed throughout the country. Baron von Trapp died in 1947. The family continued to tour and perform concerts until 1955.

As the history melds with this moment of me sitting in the rain watching *The Sound of Music*, in 1956, the Trapp Family Singers had been touring Australia, New Zealand, and the South Pacific. Their Sydney host was Archbishop Carboni, the Vatican's representative in the area of Papua New Guinea. The archbishop was reportedly very much concerned about the great success communist agents were having all over that vast territory, and the von Trapps promised him they would go to the islands and start lay missionary work.

In 1957, Maria von Trapp toured PNG with her friend Franz Wasner (who had accompanied the von Trapps across the Alps into Italy) to scope out the project. Maria visited Budoya, or Bwaioia as it was then known, on Fergusson Island, along with Rabaul, Wewak, the Sepik, and the Highlands. She later returned to Budoya and served as a missionary there until the mid-60s, tending to the sick and helping to teach the young ones. During that time, she had had built a domed ferro-cement bread oven. It had since fallen into disrepair, and no one knew how to fix it. Through Andy, I believe, Dave obtained some cement, patched the oven, and brought it back to a condition by which the mission could again enjoy bread.

When *The Sound of Music* was produced, someone—and I never did find out who (I doubt that it was Maria von Trapp herself as she had never been happy with the Hollywood version of her family's life)—thought to send a projector and the movie to Budoya Mission where it was played the evening of January 1 of each year in celebration and remembrance of Maria von Trapp.

I stayed in the hospital for ten days. At the time, I thought it was ridiculous. I wasn't sick or an invalid. Because the young nurses did everything for me, it became boring except, after I returned to the boat and I was on my own doing everything, I wished I was back in the little hospital being taken care of. I was inundated with washing diapers, along with all the dirty laundry that Dave hadn't done, and making order of the boat, which Dave also hadn't done. What had he been doing?

I remember feeling overwhelmed and exhausted. Heidi would wake up several times during the night wanting to be fed. I would get up, get her from her little box we used as a bassinet, and I'd nurse her. Though I was tired, they were magical moments as she always stared right above my head in fascination. I'm confident she could see my aura and was fascinated by it. She was a really good eater; in fact, too good. Almost every feeding resulted in her projectile-vomiting with her burp, which involved cleaning up puddles of milk, something I did alone in the middle of the night while Dave slept.

Somehow, I found the rhythm of motherhood: beating my dozen terrycloth diapers (along with the other laundry) with a stick in the cockpit, *thud-thud* turn, *thud-thud* turn, rinsing, hanging it from the rigging to dry. I cooked, cleaned, nursed, washed, cooked, clean, nursed, washed, nursed, nursed. Sister Angelica finally returned from Australia. She came out to our boat and shared her secrets of burping and soothing colicky babies, secrets I pass on to other young mothers now.

We slowly made plans to leave, to sail north. We finished up all the loose ends needed to get done on the boat. Andy and Kate brought us an old and a bit frayed woven basket from Bukas Island that had served as a bassinet to Kate's six children. I restitched the worst of the worn areas with sturdy sail thread, and we replaced it for the box we had been using, setting it in the small space created when we threw out the marine toilet.

CHAPTER 12

Only later did I come to understand that to be a mother is to be an illusion. No matter how vigilant, in the end a mother can't protect her child—not from pain, or horror, or the nightmare of violence, from sealed trains moving rapidly in the wrong direction, the depravity of strangers, trapdoors, abysses, fires, cars in the rain, from chance.
—Nicole Krauss

Several weeks after our daughter was born, we managed to move the boat back to our moorage at Sebulogomwa, again anchoring stern to the coconut trees: two stern lines tied off to two coconut trees and a bow anchor stretched out toward the reef.

Before Heidi had been born, I realized that I needed some way to carry her and, at the same time, to be able to get in and out of the dinghy or to even be able to row the dinghy by myself. The local women, as they'd walk through the jungle with fifty pounds of yams and food in their baskets on their heads, would have their babies strapped to their backs with a length of cloth. In all honesty, I tried, practicing by using sacks of rice or other inanimate objects, to put a baby on my back like they did, but I could not successfully maneuver even a sack of rice safely to my back. I didn't like the idea of the baby behind me; I wanted her in front of me where I could see her face, throw a protecting arm around her if need be, or easily breastfeed.

I took a two-yard length of plain white fabric, sewing in large darts to taper down the two ends, one end less tapered than the other to fit her head and shoulders, the foot end narrower. I tied the ends together. It mimicked a miniature cloth hammock put over one shoulder to hang in front. After Heidi was born, I found I had to tweak it here and there to fit her more perfectly, more comfortably, and safely. It was plenty deep with room to throw in a couple diapers too. Once she was snuggled in, I could maneuver freely with hands free when necessary to climb up onto the boat from the dinghy and vice versa. In the beginning, I was nervous about this tiny baby literally hanging, swinging, suspended in the air as both of my hands would reach for the cockpit railings to pull myself up, leaning from the dinghy to the boat, hoisting one leg and the other up to the boat. But after a few transitions, I knew Heidi was safe and secure, and I moved easily.

Wanting to get my stomach flat and hard again, I would go off in the early mornings before the sun was high and hot, sometimes alone but usually with the baby securely in her carrying hammock strapped to me. When sitting in the dinghy, she would basically be lying in my lap though snugly contained in her carrier. My hands were free to row. I would brace my feet on the little stern seat of our eight-foot dinghy, and I'd stroke hard across the smooth, crystal-clear reefs in the mornings while Heidi would sleep. I eventually managed to learn to breastfeed her and row at the same time, holding her head up toward my breast with a bent knee while I rowed in shorter, gentler strokes. The motion of the dinghy would put her quickly back to sleep though.

In the following weeks after her birth, we adjusted to life with a baby. She was almost always attached to me in the sling while I cooked food in our thatched hut, worked in our little garden, harvesting the last of the food. I walked down to Budoya Mission several more times for checkups and to share some final hours with Sister Angelica, Father Howard, and the nurses who could not help but come and goo-goo over this little fat white baby.

But it was growing time to leave. Heidi would be immune to malaria through my breastmilk for up to six weeks according to what we had learned. We didn't want to risk her contracting malaria, which was the main reason we had decided to leave. Also, in all honesty, we were dying from a lack of stimulation.

We prepared the boat for sailing, bringing our kitchen gear back from the thatched cooking shack, the spices, the plates and bowls, silverware, and pots and pans. Our small stacks of clothes and bedding were given a final wash, dried, folded, and stashed in their respective places on the boat. Most of the clothes were held in open-netted hammocks tied to the side of the hull in the bow above the extra sleeping bunks. Dave built a framework to secure the bassinet that Andy and Kate had given us in the small three-foot-wide space where the marine toilet had once been. It fit perfectly. I wove another netted hammock to swing above the bassinet, which held the baby's meager dozen diapers and few items of clothes that I had finally received in a care package from my mother a week after she was born. Until then, the mission had donated swaddling blankets and clothes for her. I seldom had her in clothes or even wrapped in a blanket as it was always a stifling ninety degrees-plus most of the time. Holding her securely in the carrier I'd made kept her warm to the point of sometimes sweating.

On February 11, we took the last of the items back to the boat and ensured that they were all secure, that nothing would be flying through the air as the sails caught wind, the boat heeled, and we sailed away. We slept on board that night.

Upon awaking at dawn's light, I found I had a series of deep holes seemingly burned into the back of my right arm at the shoulder joint. It looked like someone had taken a cigarette and burned holes in me a quarter of an inch deep in six or seven places. It hurt like hell. I could see them awkwardly by holding up a mirror. Dave and I were both baffled by what had caused this. We made coffee and ate breakfast and sort of waited and watched to see if this, whatever this was, was going to have any further concerning effects on me. We finally decided that other than the intense pain, I was having no other effects and that we would be safe to sail away. It wasn't until I returned to the States that I learned it was more than likely the bite of a brown recluse spider.

On February 12, 1976, with Heidi being just six weeks old, we set sail from Papua New Guinea, heading somewhere north, possibly the American Trust Territory of Micronesia. Possibly somewhere else. As Heidi slept in her bassinet, we released and readied one of our two twenty-foot oars into the sculling oarlock mounted on the stern of the boat. Dave took the dinghy to shore and released the two stern lines tied to the coconut trees and rowed quickly back to the boat, tying the dinghy to the stern and climbing back on board. There was not even a whisper of a wind yet, so we decided we'd row out into the strait between Fergusson and Normanby Islands toward

Esa-Ala before we hoisted the sail and hauled the dinghy up onto the boat to secure.

As Dave pulled up the anchor, I began to scull the boat forward in huge figure-eight sweeps, steering the boat through the passage in the coral by pushing the tiller with the shin of my leg. There was no current or wind, and slowly the boat gathered momentum to inch out of the passage and into the open waters. After getting the anchor up, Dave hurried back to where I was, and we quickly switched my sculling oar into the port oarlock, and Dave picked up the starboard sweep, and we again in tandem rowed out into the glassy early-morning bay. The water was so smooth; the only sound was that of the sweeps dipping into the sea.

Once we were well away from the shore, we secured one sweep, and I again took up sculling the boat while Dave secured the anchor firmly to the stanchions and stored the anchor chain and line. Grabbing the dinghy line, he pulled the trailing dinghy midships. I left the sculling sweep long enough to help him pull the eight-foot plywood dinghy up over the stanchions and onto the top of the cabin where we secured it to the cabin railings. Five or six lines crossed back and forth across the overturned hull, lashing it down securely. The dinghy's bowline was tied securely to a mounted eye hook on the front of the cabin. Shoving the dinghy hard, we could not budge it, and we knew it was secure against any rough seas.

I went back to sculling the boat, heading north through the passage between the two islands. Dave hoisted the mainsail. I pulled on the sheet, tightening it up as there was yet no wind to fill the sails. He prepared the mizzen and jib but decided to wait until there was at least a breeze. In the meantime, the mainsail would stabilize us against the tiny swell that was starting to roll through as we got into the pass.

Anchor secured, dinghy secured, sail set. We were on our way north. Somewhere. Not really sure where and, as the wind wasn't giving us any help at the moment, it wasn't important. We were just about ready to again set the sweeps for both of us to row when Heidi started to stir below, whimpering and then crying.

Though obviously having a baby changes things, it was at this point that sailing with a baby, or even a small child, became a reality. There were clearly going to be things in which I might not be able to participate in the moment-by-moment activities of sailing. Some things could be easily adapted to and postponed as in this case where, instead of us both rowing with all our bodies as we had almost exactly six months previously, Dave was on his own.

He took up the sculling oar. I went and fetched Heidi and brought her up to the cockpit, sitting in the morning sun to nurse her. Dave sculled in a steady, quiet rhythm. Oh, if I could bottle that silence where not one engine or human sound penetrated my bliss, just a barely discernible swooshing motion inching us forward at maybe a knot and a half. We slowly moved out beyond the pass heading due east, starting to get a bigger view of Fergusson Island with its jungled mountains rising up beyond. A tiny breeze finally grabbed the sail and helped move us forward. Sanaroa Island came into view. Fergusson then Sanaroa slowly, ever so slowly, grew smaller. Muyua Island appeared off to port in the distance, and after passing it, we finally turned north.

I sat with Heidi in my arms in the cockpit, feeling the shift from being in a small environment hemmed in by a close-to-impenetrable jungle with even the water itself being a barrier to now penetrating that very barrier and becoming one with it again, floating silently in the expansive, endless environment of the ocean and sky. Heidi slept. Dave sculled. I eventually took Heidi below and put her back in her bassinet and came back topside to take over sculling while Dave set the big jib and the mizzen sail. The boat's sails grabbed enough wind that we actually heeled a tiny bit, and I could hear the water slapping the hull.

The wind picked up enough that we heeled more, enough to allow the plates and bowls to shift in the galley below. Each time we'd set sail after being in port, there was always the adjustment and solidifying anything that could shift. Normally I would go below and slip a towel into the half-inch loose space so that as the boat heeled and released and heeled and righted, we wouldn't hear the constant shifting of objects. This time, though, when the boat heeled enough to shift things below, I experienced for the first time an absolute panic attack. I stared at the dinghy lashed tightly to the deck. It was our life raft too. It was what would save us if a storm were to threaten the boat and we were to have to abandon ship.

Though I am more compassionate in my older years of people who have unfounded obsessive fears or paranoias, realizing the power of the mind to create just such a scenario, at that point, that very moment when *Paz del*

Mar heeled, my only reality was that we were suddenly in the throes of a wicked gale, monstrous waves washing over the deck. We were secured by our life harnesses to the rigging, and Dave was shouting to me to cut the ropes of the dinghy. I was shouting back at him, "But I don't have the baby! I don't have the baby! The baby is down below! I have to get the baby!"

He struggled to release the dinghy on his own as I fought to open the closed hatch to get below. As I released my life harness so I could actually reach her bassinet, I was thrown into the settee. Pushing myself up, I searched for my hammock carrier. Twenty-foot swells tossed the boat like a cork as I struggled to get the hammock carrier underneath my drenched foul-weather gear. I managed to grab my little six-week-old baby and slip her into the hammock, but I couldn't get my foul-weather gear to close over her bulk underneath. I gave up and again struggled back to the closed hatch. It was only five or six steps from the bassinet to the hatch, but each step left me momentarily suspended in air as the boat plunged into a trough, rocked violently to port, rose up to breach the next wave. One hand protecting Heidi who was then screaming in fear, her little arms reaching frantically upward through the sling, I was barely able to stay on my feet. I managed to get the hatch open and find my life harness trailing across the cockpit.

Pulling myself up into the cockpit, a wave swept across the deck and cabin. Dave had released the dinghy from its lashings on deck but almost lost it completely with the wash of the wave. The dinghy slammed down between the cabin and the stanchions. I was of little help at this point because I had one hand on the ship and the other hand protecting my tiny baby's head. The tsunami-size wave drenched us both as it washed completely over the whole boat, and the shock of the cold seawater drenching Heidi through the opening of my weather gear stopped her crying for only one second but a second long enough for me to look down and make sure she hadn't in fact inhaled the water. Her screaming immediately returned at full-lung capacity.

Meanwhile, Dave was screaming at me over the roar of the wind and the flapping of the sails that had been dropped and were lying loose untied. He was screaming at me to help him get the dinghy over the stanchions and into the boiling sea.

"Edie. Edie." Louder, "Edie."

Coming out of the nightmare of that storm that took my daughter's life because I couldn't save her and myself, I looked at Dave blankly as I returned to the present: an almost-glassy sea with just a ripple of a wind starting to heel the boat gently and moving us forward north through the Solomon Islands. The wind was barely blowing five knots.

"Edie. Can you make some coffee?"

I couldn't tell him of my fears, the fears of motherhood having just sunk deep into my gut. My life of sailing, the freedom, and challenge and spirituality that it had brought had, in that moment, come to an end. Now there was only the survival of my baby to think about. How would she survive this dangerous ocean, this monstrous force of nature? How could Dave even understand my fears? They were unreasonable. They were silly, I'm sure, to him. Somehow, I had to get through this on my own. My not being able to share that moment with him was also the repetitive, reoccurring proof of how disconnected our relationship truly was.

I returned to the beauty of the day. As Dave sat at the tiller, settling into the joy of again being at sea, I went below and lit the propane stove and put water on to boil. I ground some coffee with a heavy hand-cranked wheat grinder. I pulled out the wire-rimmed sock we used to make our drip coffee, scooped in several spoonfuls of fresh-ground coffee, and when the water was boiled, I poured the water through the sock until the cup was full. I made another cup for myself and then went back up to the cockpit and was able to return to the beauty of once again being at sea. Heidi slept soundly to the rocking of the boat and the sibilant sea caressing the hull at her head, which inside the boat was technically underwater.

For the first day or two, we had to avoid large logs that were floating in the sea, being swept down from the highlands of mainland New Guinea in rushing floods from tropical storms. Because we were sailing through a maze of islands making up the Solomons, stretching from the infamous Guadalcanal in the southeast to Bougainville and Rabaul, all sites of Japanese occupation and conflict during World War II, we stood watch every night. Several times during the first two nights, our hull slammed into a floating log invisible to our eyes, again triggering me to revisit my imaginative end of life.

Though we had passed the bigger island of Bougainville where there might have been medical help, it wasn't until several days later, as we were getting closer to Nukumanu, that I became concerned that Heidi had failed to poop. I was terrified that something was dangerously wrong, and here we were at sea with no contact with the world and no medical help. My concern grew grave enough that, as we were getting closer to Nukumanu, I insisted that we stop there and seek out some help.

Nukumanu, the Big Bed, was the most distant of PNG's islands, being 432 kilometers northeast of Bougainville. Located in the path of the Polynesian migration to Oceania some five thousand years ago, the Nukumanu Islands were settled by the Polynesians, so the peoples retained their Polynesian character though they were geographically and politically part of the Melanesian archipelago of Papua New Guinea and the Solomon Islands. Comprising a ring of more than twenty islets on a reef surrounding a large lagoon, the islets and islands of Nukumanu remain largely unchanged to this day. They are located on a sandy strip of coral no more than a meter above sea level just four degrees south of the equator.

I was never much interested in history in school. Back in the '60s, teachers had not yet brought history alive. They were requiring only that you learn the date, the key person, and a one-line sentence as to the historical event. It was pure memorization. I vaguely knew that great parts of World War II had been fought in these islands though their importance remained unknown to me, only that many of these islanders, living their simple subsistence lives, were thrown into the middle of bombs and guns and a war between nations of which they hardly knew existed beyond the horizon of the ocean.

Just as I learned Maria von Trapp had been a missionary at Budoya, I also learned that Nukumanu was the last place on the path of Amelia Earhart before she and her copilot disappeared forever into the vast Pacific Ocean. On July 2, 1937 at 0000 Greenwich Mean Time, Amelia Earhart and her navigator, Fred Dave Noonan, departed Lae, New Guinea, for the next leg of her 29,000-mile around-the-world flight. The intended destination of this leg was tiny Howland Island. At 07:20 hours GMT (about 800 miles into the flight), Amelia provided a position report placing her about 20 miles southwest of Nukumanu. The atoll has little economic activity to speak of to this day, but its claim to fame was perhaps that it was the island Amelia Earhart never reached.

CHAPTER 13

It takes a village to raise a child.

—Old African proverb

Sailing into the anchorage near the north entrance of Nukumanu, we found it was clear that there were no frequent visitors to this most remote of the Solomon Islands. The beach was lined with the villagers having stopped all that they might have been doing (which often isn't a very busy schedule) to watch us sail in.

We dropped the sails, dropped the anchor, and put the dinghy in the water. Whether it was my now hypervigilant mother energy or just my sailor's premonition, I felt nervous about where we were anchored, and we agreed to reset the anchor a bit farther from shore. Not having an engine, we accomplished this by pulling up the anchor, putting it into the dinghy, and Dave rowing hard and crazily away from shore to redrop it while I played out as much line as possible. With the anchor dropped, I hauled in the anchor line, pulling the boat farther out from shore. While I was doing this, Heidi had begun to cry below, and by the time we felt securely anchored, she was screaming.

I took a few minutes to nurse her in the cockpit and settle her down, and then we climbed in the dinghy and rowed to shore. As we pulled the dinghy up onto the beach, the villagers quickly surrounded us. The younger children stood silently with hordes of small flies crawling in the corners of their eyes. They never attempted to brush them away. They just stared at us. Most anybody who had reached puberty showed varying degrees of beautiful geometric tattooing on their bodies from their knees to their heads. I saw no grass skirts; though even more remote than Fergusson, clearly "civilization" had gained a stronger footing though the images that remain in my mind, even to this day, are the flies in eyes and the beautiful tattoos.

As we started walking along the main path cum dirt road through the village, we were approached by an English-speaking woman who was the schoolteacher. The villagers were talking amongst themselves, and she conveyed the question they all seemed to have: did I have my baby at sea? I laughed. "Oh, no; she was two months old, and she was born on Fergusson Island."

"Aahh," they seemed to sigh in relief.

But I did convey that I was concerned that my daughter had not pooped for many days—two weeks to be exact—and if there was someone I could consult.

We were approaching what might be considered the center of the village, and she offered for us to sit on some logs. She told someone to bring us water nuts while we waited. Teenage children and women surrounded me, peeking into my carrier to peer at the now-sleeping Heidi. One woman asked if she could hold her, reaching her arms for her. I pulled her out of the carrier and passed her over to the tattooed woman; more women surrounded her, all with big smiles on their tattooed faces.

In the flurry of the villagers surrounding us and us talking with the schoolteacher, she asking us questions and sharing with us information about their small village and island, I suddenly realized that Heidi had been carried away; she was no longer within the group in the center of the village. I stood and asked, "Where is my baby?"

Looking down between the thatched huts, I could see a gathering of women. The teacher said, "Oh, she is okay. She is with the mothers."

I felt lucky that I had begun motherhood in a kinder, gentler society, in a more natural society. Though this was only the second place we'd been besides Sebulogomwa and Budoya Mission since having Heidi, I had already spent almost five years in the environs of indigenous peoples, and I knew that children were loved and cherished. Every child truly had a whole village to raise him or her with many mothers in the forms of aunts and grandmothers, cousins, siblings. You seldom heard a baby cry, and you never saw anybody frustrated or upset with a crying baby maybe because a crying child was always ministered to. It was also noted, not just by me but other expats or professionals as well, that babies in the islands were slow to learn to walk because they were always held and cuddled.

Children were so revered, were so valuable to the heart of society that in some of the South Pacific cultures, the firstborn of a firstborn child went to the paternal grandparents; the second-born of the firstborn child went to the maternal grandparents. It was the third child and subsequent children that the couple kept and raised as their own. A grandmother had no purpose but to raise and nurture children and not because they were forced to take in their grandchildren because their own children had become drug addicts as seems to be a growing condition in our society today.

Heidi was eventually returned to me, completely content. She wasn't hungry for a long time even as my milk dripped, and as I came to discover was not uncommon, she had been fed by others while out of my sight, passed from breast to breast. I had become "native" enough to absolutely accept this societal mothering.

The universal nurturing mother was always present in the South Pacific. A year later in Ponape, we were living in a small tin-roofed cement house, providing solid ground and space for Heidi. The tiny shack was nestled in a local community of other small shacks under coconut trees and surrounded with frangipani and hedges of hibiscus. One night, Heidi would not stop crying. Neither Dave nor I could find a source of her tears and angst. She wouldn't nurse, and though she'd been eating solid food for months, she wasn't hungry. No temperature, nothing that led to thinking she was sick. She was simply in a horrible mood, with no means of communicating why. And being a young unskilled mother with no loving parenting skills ever shown to me while growing up, I was extremely frustrated.

I finally walked out into the night with her. She continued to cry and cry. I held her. I jiggled her. I tried to nurse her. Dave was of no help; he was in a sense emasculated in his ability to help only because he had no breasts. But out of the darkness of the night through the quiet of the coconut grove came an old, old woman who lived in the shack 200 feet from us. Coming quietly on her bare feet, she approached, arms outstretched, reaching for Heidi. I handed my baby to her. The woman, wearing no top, no blouse but only a skirt, held Heidi in one experienced eighty- or ninety-year-old arm and with the other reached down close to her waist and gathered up the nipple hanging at the end of a depleted breast, which really was only a long bag of skin. She gathered up that nipple and that skin and placed the nipple into Heidi's mouth.

Heidi stopped crying and began to suck, not on this woman's milk as she had none, clearly, but on this woman's deep motherhood, her deep calm and connection to baby, to child. A part of me, of course, was so relieved that Heidi had finally stopped crying. Another part of me, my ego, my image of my own mothering, was crushed. How inadequate was I that I could not accomplish what this unknown ancient stranger could?

We stood together outside in the silence of the coconut trees until Heidi was sleeping soundly, after which she quietly, gently returned her to my arms and padded silently back to her shack, having never said a word.

Another exquisite joy for a young mother in the islands was a "babysitting service" that came with your restaurant service that we first experienced in Ponape. Ponape was developed to the point of having a small community college. While living there for almost a year, Dave developed a course to teach celestial navigation at the community college. I, in the meantime, had also gotten a part-time job being a "secretary" to several teachers from the Teacher Corps who were there teaching teachers to teach. With us both working and having money for the first time, we had money to actually go out to any of the several restaurants in the town. Upon arriving at any restaurant whatsoever with our six-month-old or one-year-old, the first thing that happened, sometimes even before a menu was presented, was a waitress would whisk Heidi away, and we would not see her until the end of our meal.

After Heidi was returned to my arms by the women of Nukumanu, I was finally led to a large communal thatched hut where the medicine woman waited for me. She was elderly, rounder than many of the islanders who lived on diets of fish, taro, manioc, and coconuts. As with just about any adult her age, except for the schoolteacher who, we had learned, was from another island, she was beautifully tattooed in Polynesian/Maori pattern from her head, down her neck and arms, bare chest and breasts, and belly and back, and I could see the tattoos again reappear around her knees below the ragged cotton skirt she wore. The schoolteacher explained that she was the village healer, and she would attend to my daughter, and then she left us alone.

We sat on a large woven mat in the center of the hut. The only light came in from the window openings. It was much like a Samoan *fale* with half walls and woven shutters that would be closed only to keep out rain. She took Heidi and laid her on the mat. Stirring momentarily, Heidi immediately relaxed when the woman touched her gently, prodding her abdomen. Scooping up some semi-hardened coconut oil, the woman began to massage Heidi's abdomen in a round circular fashion while she spoke in very broken English about how beautiful my baby was.

I asked her about her tattoos, how they did that, and she gestured to an assortment of objects on the far wall. I never got close to look at them, but they were not the sterile tattoo needle guns used in tattoo parlors of today. Though the thought had crossed my mind that it would be pretty cool to get a bracelet or anklet tattooed by these people, the thought disappeared quickly as I shooed flies away from Heidi's face as the woman continued to massage her belly.

After about a half hour, the woman lifted my daughter and handed her to me and told me in no uncertain terms that my baby would have a bowel movement within a half hour. I should be prepared, she said. As I walked out into the hot sun and glaring sandy paths to find Dave, I was suddenly aware of a change in the ambient sound of the island. The roar of pounding waves on the shore signaled that our boat might be in some peril. I quickly located Dave who seemed to be oblivious to the distinct change in ambient sound, and we hurried back to our dinghy. Most of the bay was blocked by huts and coconuts, so we didn't have a clear view of the bay till we neared the beach where we'd left the dinghy.

As we looked out, we could see the *Paz del Mar* pitching and rolling violently. Very violently. Though we were aware this wasn't the best of protected anchorages when we first set the anchor, there was no sign that we would be this unprotected by the shift of the wind, nor had we any warning that indeed the wind would shift. The sea was rolling in with nothing slowing it down. Where we had beached the dinghy, it was now pounding with surf and swells large enough to swamp it easily. It was going to be difficult to row out past the breakers. Without a two-month baby in my arms, I would have loved the challenge. But warrior had been usurped by mother who chose different paths of protection than confrontation. We argued about whether he should go out alone, but we both decided it would be difficult for him to deal with the boat on his own.

So with Heidi nestled as securely as possible in my hammock carrier, reminiscent of Omoa in the Marquesas, we waited for a lull in the breakers. Seeing the best bet of an opportunity, we scooted the little eight-foot dinghy out and climbed in, which with a baby in arms was difficult enough from high-thigh-deep water. Dave grabbed the oars and started pulling as hard as he could. We hit the first wave that had already broken and was roiling in; it was maybe only a three-foot wave, and we managed to plow through it safely though it almost brought us to a dead stop. Dave rowed harder yet to beat the cresting of the next wave, which was two feet bigger. The bow of our little dinghy was pointing skyward at about seventy degrees as we crested the wave before it broke. We managed to get beyond the shore breakers.

Rowing quickly to the boat, we found ourselves confronted with the next danger of trying to board the boat while it was rocking and heaving. Dave tried to steady the dinghy against the boat as I tried to climb up over the cockpit railings, but I was thrown backward, almost over the side with Heidi. I did manage to stay in the dinghy, and we finally both managed to get on board and tie the dinghy off. I quickly went below to lay Heidi in her bassinet as Dave ran forward to check the anchor line that seemed to be holding.

The tide had gone out quite a bit, and the coral heads were much shallower than before. Luckily we had re-anchored farther from shore earlier. Dave climbed up into the rigging and looked out toward the pass through which we had come hours earlier and from which the wind was coming now. Without an engine, we were in a predicament of being able to sail away from our anchorage safely or not. He scanned the area for the dark coral heads to see how much maneuver room we would have to tack out safely. It was almost three o'clock, and we didn't have much more light. Near the equator, the days are only twelve hours long no matter what season.

In the end, we decided that we could probably not safely exit with the low tide, the shallow coral heads, and the wind blowing from the direction it was. We were going to have to stay anchored there that night at least and hope the wind and sea changed during the night. We were anchored in a bizarre situation with the wind coming from one direction but the swell coming in from a ninety-degree angle through the pass. Most of the time, we were rolling horribly from side to side while occasionally pitching bow to stern. There was a great need to steady the boat.

Being tossed about on the deck of the boat, we set about rigging what we called flopper stoppers. On one side of the boat, we secured a bucket to the end of the main boom and then pulled the boom out almost perpendicular to the hull, securing it fore and aft. The bucket was set so that it would dip into and below the water and, once filled, would stay submerged. The upward rocking of the boat would pull against it, steadying the rocking. We rigged our self-steering pole from the other side in a similar manner. Amazingly, the two flopper stoppers worked miracles in steadying the rolling.

Heidi had had a massive bowel movement during our maneuverings above. I was a happy mother as I changed her diapers and cleaned up the flood.

The village was a pretty sight from the boat that evening with dim kerosene lights shining from the huts. Sometimes we'd see someone walking along with a flashlight or lantern. The surf break started to quiet some as the tide came in, and somewhere during the night, the rolling stopped. We could hear the roosters crowing, a few dogs barking, and the village stirring to life as we too awoke at dawn. Without even making coffee, we took apart our flopper stoppers and hoisted the sails, letting them flop loose as Dave pulled on the anchor. When we were just above the anchor, he yelled for me to tighten up the mainsail and the jib, and as the wind caught the sail, he pulled the anchor free, and I steered in the general direction of the pass.

Dave quickly got the anchor on deck, and he scurried up the rigging to look for and steer me clear of any coral heads that I might be heading toward, and when we were safely in deep water with the water again slapping the hull in its gentle dance with the sea, Dave came down from the rigging. The routine repeated as we secured the anchor to the stanchions; setting the self-steering, I helped him again pull the dinghy up onto the boat, turn it over on top of the deck, and lash it down securely.

We headed north toward the Caroline Islands. It did not take long for Nukumanu to disappear from our sight. It has only 1.8 square miles of habitable land surrounding a 138-square-mile lagoon. Even at the highest points, elevation was barely more than six feet above sea level. The island probably hasn't changed much since we visited it forty-five years ago. It has a population of 730 people. But with so little land to support a growing population, many young people go away to high school on the mainland where they find jobs to support their family back on the atoll. Over the years since I was there, they have attempted to set up an export business for sea cucumbers and trochus shells, valued for making pearl buttons. Weather and sea conditions and transportation determine success. Also because of overharvesting, these enterprises are sometimes shut down by the government to allow stocks to return to sustainable levels.

On February 28, we sailed from Nukumanu. Amazingly, for sailing in the equatorial belt, which generally has not a puff of breeze, we had good trade winds. Six days later, at about five degrees north of the equator, Kusaie—now known as Kosrae—came into view. With a minimum amount of problems tacking into the harbor, we dropped anchor and hoisted our flag, giving notice that we were needing to come to shore for immigration and customs.

CHAPTER 14

Madame, all stories, if continued far enough, end in death, and
he is no true story teller who would keep that from you.

—Ernest Hemingway

On March 6, 1976, we arrived in Kusaie, a tin-can shambles town.

That was my last journal entry for over a year. But that day and the days that followed were easy to remember.

After securing our anchorage and getting our papers in order to present to Immigration, we untied the dinghy and got it in the water. I put Heidi into my carrier, along with a few changes of diapers, and rowed to shore. Upon tying off our dinghy and climbing up onto the dock, I was quite surprised when the island administrator greeted us with, "Are you Edie Snow?"

Ominous dread, like a 2:00 a.m. phone call, immediately piqued my attention. We had only a general direction we were heading. I acknowledged that, yes, his guess was correct and, "How did you know?"

He replied that he, as well as most of the islands in the general area, had been on the lookout for us. He had some bad news for me. I knew that my mother's sister had been very ill, so I asked, "Did my aunt die?"

The man said, "Well, yes, your aunt has died, but also your father."

Whoa. "When?"

"February 12."

I looked at Dave and said, "That's the day we set sail from Papua New Guinea." And I remember distinctly thinking also, *That was the day something bit me on the back of my arm.* My father's kiss goodbye? Funny where the mind takes us in these moments.

I stood there quietly for a moment, thinking how I'd blocked him out of my life. I'd never written him about my daughter's birth—his first grandchild's birth. I'd given up on trying to reach out to him because he never ever responded to me. I had cut him out of my life permanently. As my throat started to tighten and the tears clouded my eyes, a storm of emotions swept through me: Why was anyone even bothering to tell me that he died? Do I care? Did he care?

And then: Oh, what if he did care? What if his last thoughts were how he knew I'd had a baby, but he regretted not taking the time to write? Even in my anger that shut him out a year ago, I had kept in the back of my mind and heart that I would have time someday in the future to make up for it, to maybe return to the States and get to know him as an adult—two adults talking and sharing as two equals, not a domineering brilliant psychologist scientist correcting and reprimanding and criticizing his daughter. Maybe he'd even tell me he was proud of me or that he envied my decision to live a less-cluttered life than he had.

The island administrator was droning on about how my mother had, via international ham radio operators and the office of United States senators, sent out the word to be on the lookout for our yacht. The *Paz del Mar* was red hulled with a white cabin; it wasn't hard to miss as there were few red yachts sailing; most were white. Something Dave said to the island administrator jostled me out of my reverie; I forced myself to breathe, relaxing my constricted throat that was trying so hard not to feel a grief I thought impossible to feel for this man. The IA was letting us know that they had a ham radio operator who would be ready to try to make a call to the States, to Texas, where my mother now was.

My parents had separated nine years previously with the family scandal being that my father left my mother for my mother's sister, the very aunt who had also just died. My father had refused to divorce my mother for reasons unknown to any of us but instead had bought her a nice condominium in Hawai'i, a new car, sent her a more-than-sufficient stipend to live on each month, and paid for a month-long trip anywhere in the world once a year like the month she came to New Zealand to visit me. She took advantage of this freedom to not have to work but instead volunteered full time for the American Red Cross with all her heart and soul. One of her biggest accomplishments through those years had been helping Vietnamese refugees situate in the States, finding them homes and jobs for which services she was honored and recognized as the Red Cross Volunteer of the Year. But now she was in Texas where my father and her sister had been living.

We were in fact able to contact her through a ham radio operator. Now that she knew where I was, she was going to arrange to get a plane ticket and some money sent to Ponape (now Pohnpei) where the closest planes infrequently flew through. I was set up with the name of another ham radio operator in Ponape through which I would contact her again when I finally reached there. It would probably take another three weeks for me to get to Ponape via a small interisland cargo ship that came every seven to ten days.

My mom told me they'd had a great memorial service for him that lasted eight hours. Eight hours! Not only had many of his colleagues from Harvard and Yale, Rochester, UCSB, the University of Texas, and the University of Wisconsin come in his honor, either in person or sending their thoughts and eulogies for others to read in their stead, but Dixieland jazz musicians locally and from around the country had also come to play Dixieland jazz all day.

Dixieland was the only thing I witnessed that made my father laugh and smile and come alive and actually hint that he was human inside. He had sponsored the formation of Dixieland jazz societies in most places where we'd lived, getting a monthly jam session together at a local restaurant, and then being unable to quit the fun, would bring everybody to our house to keep playing and drinking and singing and dancing till the wee hours of the morning. Over the radio, my mother described how the musicians jammed almost all day, ending as was appropriate to carry his soul onward with "When the Saints Go Marching In" with all the mourners following the band out of the tent, singing in unison. Strange to think others had so revered him.

The island administrator and his family were Americans. Kusaie, and all of this stretch of islands, was still under the trusteeship of the United States at the time, then known as the Trust Territory of the Pacific Islands. They have since gained their independence and formed several different political jurisdictions, the main one being the Federated States of Micronesia. In the ten days it did indeed take for the ratty cargo ship to arrive, the IA made us very welcome. We were invited to their lovely comfortable tropical home in paradise frequently for meals and to do laundry, a true luxury instead of my soap-and-stick *thump-thump-thump* method. One of their children would coo over Heidi while I could sit and relax in the clean comfort of their home.

I myself wasn't on Kusaie long enough to get to know the island or the people or the town. I remember the town of Kusaie itself was rundown and dirty. It was a tin-can shanty town. The few expats living there were men who had married local women, many much younger than them. My biased generic assessment was they all appeared to be alcoholics, living a chauvinistic, male-dominated sort of style that I didn't care to know.

While I waited on this remote island in the Eastern Carolinas, I was wrapped in mourning for my father, clothed in remorse that I had in fact cut him out of my life. There was no undoing my shunning of my father. In the days that I waited for the interisland cargo boat to arrive, the grief revisited me like ghostly tentacles encircling my heart and thoughts. Other than my grandparents dying, I had so far been isolated from death. I was quite astounded how each layer of grief seemed to expose yet another layer beneath it and another beneath it, revealing itself in guises of bitterness and self-pity and anger. I was quite astounded that I had any of these feelings at all.

Dave, meanwhile, spent a lot of time on shore, socializing, getting to know people, and in the end, setting up some work to earn some money. John and Liz would lend me enough money for passage on the cargo boat to Ponape. After arriving in Ponape, it would still be close to a week before the plane would arrive that flew to the States via Hawai'i, so I would be staying in a little hotel in Kolonia. John and Liz knew the owners of the hotel and had talked them into letting me stay until I was able to receive the money that was being wired by my mother from Texas.

Throughout my years of sailing and traveling, I had received so much generosity and help from strangers, but for some reason, the fact that I was at the mercy of all these people helping me get to the States also sent me into tears. I was an emotional wreck for that period of time. My facade of being so free and self-sufficient was blown apart.

Heidi stirred in her bassinet, awaking from her nap. Three months old. I lifted her up, and I hugged her tight, and I rocked her, and I told her how much I loved her, how precious she was, that I would give her everything she would need, that she would never need to earn my love. It was free, unconditioned. It had an anchor that would find ground, and love would grow. And the whole world would love her back softly, smoothly without judgment, without conditions attached. She would have such love. She would always have such love.

The cargo ship arrived. It was maybe 120 feet long, a rusty dirty blue. While slings of copra were loaded on board, slings of supplies for the stores were offloaded: cartons of mackerel and sacks of rice, cartons of sweetened condensed milk, beer, and cigarettes. The cargo ship would be in port only as long as it took to offload and load. John said I should get in line and save a place on deck where I would sleep for the two-day passage to Ponape, along with what looked like at least another fifty islanders. I had taken one of our raggiest cotton blankets, thick gray cotton, for my bedding. Dave helped me carry my things onto the deck, and I found a spot up against the deck house to claim as my space. Several hours later, the lines were cast off, the diesel fumes from the smoking, noisy engine filled the air, and we pulled away from the docks. As mothers do, I grabbed Heidi's small arm out of her sling and waved it to her father as she slept snugly in my arms.

I had packed a meager supply of food that would be edible and keep during the trip. We did not have prepackaged food; everything was cooked fresh: beans, rice, salads. I did have some dried fish to gnaw on, and I'd baked some biscuits. I had a can of yucky canned cheese and some fruit. I ate meagerly for two days.

I struggled with tending to Heidi, changing the few diapers I had as infrequently as I could, knowing I could not wash diapers for two days. I waited till they were sodden with pee before I'd change them; I'd let her poop and then poop again before I'd change her out of her poopy diapers. There was, of course, freshwater available on the ship with which I could clean her up, but the heads—the toilet facilities—were filthy and reeking within half a day. The men peed off the deck near the stern. But the women did use the toilets though many were used to squatting, so I would find the toilet seats filthy with footprints. For two days, I ventured into the putrid heads with Heidi in her sling, washing out the diapers the best I could, attempting to dry them on deck. With no place to hang them, I would lay them out flat on the dirty, rusty deck, pinned down on the corner by my bags.

I don't remember a lot about that passage from Kusaie to Ponape. I remember the stench of the diesel fumes that at times the wind seemed to grab and toss right into my face. It was a smell that can also make me nauseous. There was little chance to escape it but for the wind taking it into a different direction. I remember the putrid stench of the toilets. I remember the islanders being curious of me, a young blonde white woman with a small baby sleeping on the deck of a rusty interisland ship for two days with fifty other bodies. I do remember that most of the islanders on deck were seasick for most of the passage. Only one woman ever offered to take Heidi from me, an offer I took her up on to run into the reeking bathroom to wash out diapers.

Two days later, I arrived in Ponape.

CHAPTER 15

Coming back is the thing that enables you to see how all the dots in your life are connected, how one decision leads you to another, how one twist of fate, good or bad, brings you to a door that later takes you to another door, which aided by several detourslong hallways and unforeseen stairwellseventually puts you in the place you are now.

—Ann Patchett

The boat docked out on the island of Deketik, which was connected by a manmade causeway to the main island and the town of Kolonia, the capital. The water was a deep dirty green surrounding the flat dirt expanse that made up the port dock and received the copra ships and fishing vessels. Deketik was also where the small airstrip was.

Walking down the dirty gangplank, I was greeted by the hotel owner and taken to a quaint small hotel, one of the first on the island, at that time used mostly to house visiting administrative officials as tourism had not yet gotten established. Exhausted and filthy from the trip, the first thing I did was wash eleven diapers and hang them out to dry on the railing of my very small hotel room. They hung limp in the humidity in the shade of the thick tropical growth. (Ponape is one of the wettest places in the world, receiving upward of 300 inches of rain a year in some areas.) I showered myself and then bathed Heidi. It was late afternoon when I had arrived at the hotel. After getting cleaned up, the hotel owner took me to what was considered the local bank to see if any money had arrived from my mother.

Sadly, now, I didn't record anything in my journals during this period of time. Through most of this time—or up until the time of Heidi's birth—I had kept detailed accounts of people and places, events, and happenings. Having Heidi changed all of that, where I no longer had the uninterrupted time to write my thoughts as they came to me to record the details of life happening around me. I had a baby. I took care of a baby. That was my center. When we sailed into Kusaie, I was suddenly swept up into a flurry of activity around my father's death. I moved through each day filled with grief and regret and remorse and fear that I might somehow inflict the same wrongs upon my daughter. So I held her closer, tended to her. I didn't look out on to the world and around me quite as much. The world was very small: it was wrapped into this little hammock sling I had sewed together in which my baby rested at all times.

In other words, I don't really remember the bank in Ponape. I only have a vague memory that there was no such thing as a real bank there because there was a problem with me getting the money my mother sent. This was a time before electronic ticketing of plane flights and electronic transfers of money. She was wiring me $1,000. This was to pay for my plane ticket to fly first to Honolulu where she wanted me to stop and take care of her condominium, which she had quickly abandoned when she had heard my father had died. Because she was technically still married to him, she was in fact the beneficiary of all that he had left behind. My father had not rewritten his will since my childhood in Maryland. My mother was going to need to stay in Texas for quite a while to work out his estate.

I was to stop in Honolulu and go to her condominium. I was to contact a property manager, and through a power of attorney she would send to her condominium address, she was authorizing me to put her condominium up for rent, fully furnished. She needed me to box up all her personal possessions, her clothes, her books, her letters, family photos—all the personal effects that would not be rented with the condo and put them in long-term storage. She was hoping that the $1,000 she was wiring me would be sufficient for the plane ticket, a taxi to her condominium, and sufficient to pay for me to live for the week or two or however long it would take for me to secure her condo, get it rented, and then fly on to Austin, Texas.

I'm dredging images out of a thick fog that seemed to hang over me in that week I was in Ponape. I remember the main street of Ponape, wide, made of dirt, thick with dust when it was dry, sodden and thick with mud when it was wet. Small four-stroke Suzuki cars seemed to be the main vehicle on these roads, most being in varying degrees of disrepair, spewing varying shades of gray smoke out of their tailpipes. I distinctly remember being driven up a jungled, bumpy dirt road somewhere above the town of Kolonia to the home of an American ham radio operator. There I again had a fairly long conversation with my mother. It was disjointed as I'd forget to say "over" after each segment of my speech. Releasing the button, I'd be sitting in silence, waiting to hear something from her end, before the ham radio operator would remind me that I needed to say "over." I'd click on the microphone again, say, "Over," and then unclick and wait. In the end, she assured me the money had been sent, and I should be able to get it. We worked out the details of what she wanted me to do in Honolulu, and we basically left it that I would call her from Honolulu when I arrived.

For another day, I remember changing Heidi into clean, though still damp, diapers until I was finally able to get this $1,000 my mother had sent. Apparently, the problem had been "the bank" had been unable to accumulate $1,000 in bills to give me though the wire transfer had been complete. I did eventually get the money. The first thing I did was buy another dozen diapers and a good meal at a local restaurant.

Somebody (of whom I have no memory) had been assigned by somebody (again, I know not who) to help me get around. I vaguely remember it was someone who worked for the hotel. Because the airport was not open often because there were only flights once every ten to fourteen days, this someone took me out to that little airport when they knew it would be open so I could actually purchase this ticket to fly to Hawai'i.

My biggest memory is yellow and quiet days spent in this small hotel room. Everything was yellow in the room, pleasant shades of yellow: yellow bedspreads, yellow curtains hanging from a sliding glass door that went out on to a narrow balcony where the jungle pressed in and surrounded me, yellow flowers in the jungle, yellow towels. Some say yellow is a healing color. It was a small room though, not very much bigger than the double bed in it with a small cubicle where my raggedy duffle bag sat before entering the tiny bathroom. But it was a real bed. It was a real shower. There was a real toilet that I could use instead of pulling up a bucket of water in ports or "hanging it out" on the poop deck when we had the privacy of the immense sea.

There was no telephone to the outer world. There was no television station or television to watch. It was hot and humid. Ponape was only 6.5 degrees north of the equator, but in spite of all that, I felt I was living in luxury for that week while I waited for a plane to take me to Honolulu. I was feeling slightly overwhelmed with the tasks my mother was requesting me to do. It had been almost five years since I'd been back in the States, in the hustle and bustle of the churning city life. At least I was familiar with Honolulu, and it would be warm and sunny. My mother's car would be there for me to use. I don't think I had a valid driver's license any longer, but I didn't even think about that. I'd have the comfort of her condominium, a telephone. A television! Wow. As I sat waiting for the plane to arrive in five days, four days, three days, I bolstered my spirits with some of the positive changes that I'd be experiencing, and I began to actually feel excited about returning to the States and seeing my mother and my brothers, introducing them to Heidi, and taking care of my father's ashes. Maybe yellow is a healing color.

I paid for my hotel room and was given a ride to the airport. The terminal out on Deketik seemed little more than a large plywood hut with a tin roof, crude and rough. I don't remember that it even had real windows or just the island shutters, which they had hoisted open for that one day of the one arrival and one departure. There were wooden plywood benches and a few plastic seats inside. I was quite surprised to see so many people traveling. I checked my one duffel bag as luggage and carried with me a well-worn backpack, stuffed with a dozen diapers, some baby clothes, and luckily, a change of clothes for myself.

I say "luckily" because as I was waiting to board the plane, Heidi filled her diaper to overflowing. Soft and sweet baby poop oozed all over inside her hammock carrier, soaking through on to my little skirt and blouse. The plane was on the runway, and they were close to beginning to board. I jumped up and rushed for the little cubicled-off plywood bathroom facilities. Of course, it was not equipped with a changing table, not even a counter. Only a dirty washstand—did I say dirty?—and an unpainted cement floor with one toilet stall set off by a peeled-paint plywood wall but no door.

With Heidi still in her hammock sling, I laid her on the dirty floor and began to quickly peel off my shit-covered clothes, careful not to spread it any further than it already existed. I took a clean corner of my skirt and dampened it with water and washed down my legs and stomach where I could feel the mess had soaked through. I quickly put on my fresh outfit, another short skirt, and tank top. I remember my hands shaking, scared to death I was going to miss the plane because of this mishap. With Heidi still lying on her sling, I quickly undressed her completely, and suspending her over the sink, I ran cold water over her back, bottom, and legs, washing her. I found a corner of my dirty shirt that was in fact still clean and dry and I dried her, and then I sat on the toilet seat and dressed her in clean diapers, a plastic diaper cover, and a new little onesie.

Right as I was going to try to figure out how I would juggle her and gather up the shit-soaked clothes and wash out my sling, a big Ponapeian woman pushed into the small bathroom. She looked at me knowingly and reached for Heidi. I passed her over quickly, and I proceeded to wash out my clothes and Heidi's diaper and clothes—and my precious hammock sling—in the sink until the water ran clear. I wrung them out as tightly as I could and buried all but the sling in the bottom of my small carrying bag. I took Heidi's other backup plastic diaper covers and laid them across these sodden clothes and then replaced all the other dry things on top. I took Heidi back into my arms as the woman rushed into the tiny cubicle, almost too tiny for her massive frame, before coming out to join me in the line that was now boarding the plane.

I reflect now on the large baby bags young parents carry around today filled with two dozen disposable pampers, five or six outfits, colorful plastic rattles and toys and teething rings as well as fancy car seats with such complicated fastening devices you need to be a physicist to figure out how to get the baby in or out of it, three-wheel jogging baby buggies, backpacks with sun bonnets and plastic windows and storage compartments to carry supplies to hike the Appalachian Trail. I carried a tiny faded, ragged old single-opening backpack with a dozen new diapers and now only one change of baby clothes. No toys, no gadgets.

We boarded the plane. I shoved the bag under the front of my seat and laid Heidi across my knees, playing with her bare feet. As the plane prepared for departure, I strapped myself in and turned her around to face forward, wrapping my arms around her.

For the second time since she was born, since that first day we had set sail and I had panicked that I would not be able to save her in the midst of a storm that sunk the boat, I spun through a whole scenario of how this plane, in taking off, foundered and plummeted into the sea at the end of the runway and how I could not free myself from my seatbelt and hold on to her while I busted out the window of the plane to swim to the surface to save her life.

I closed my eyes as the plane flew down the runway. Only after I heard the wheels being pulled up into the belly and the plane made its steep turn, revealing the island of Ponape below, setting course for Honolulu, did I rest assured that at least for now, my daughter was safe.

It was a long and grueling flight. We landed sometime after midnight, but we had crossed multiple time zones. I believe we had flown for over ten hours nonstop. It was 2:00 a.m. when I shuffled up to the immigration line in Honolulu International Airport. I handed them my passport. They asked for my daughter's passport. I looked at the man with a blank stare and replied, "She's a baby. She doesn't have a passport."

There began an almost four-hour ordeal of me trying to bring my daughter into the United States. It was a question—a fact—a little bit of an essential element of international travel that I had never even considered. Hmm. Nobody had asked for me to show a passport for her when I left Ponape. Why not? Why now? I had with me a blue piece of paper, smaller than an index card, not at all official looking, from the Budoya Mission signed by somebody who had been given some tangential right to sign the paper, verifying that my daughter had been born to two Americans, me and Dave. That was the piece of paper I had with me. I had no passport for her. I had no U.S. citizenship documents for her. I had me, exhausted, tired, dirty, after ten hours of flying. I had my ragged bag of dirty diapers, loading down my arm with its wet weight. I had my baby. I had a dead father. I had a mother who wanted me to take care of her condominium. I had nothing else. They were not going to let me enter Honolulu, Hawai'i, the gateway to the United States!

I continue to want to live in the fairytale world that would have no boundaries, no immigration, no citizenship, no illegal aliens. I feel the barriers and separation are what cause the problems that create the haves and have-nots of the world; it creates people who are in a sense enslaved in their country, by their country because of environmental or economic reasons that might keep them there or by corrupt political power structures. Just like an open market free of monopolies, in my world with no walls, creativity, freedom, communication, and understanding flourish. Call me naïve; try to shut me off from singing John Lennon's "Imagine" in endless loops, but that's what I want to hold tight as my ideal world.

Having just spent five years, at that point, sailing from island to island with the freedom of a dandelion seed in the wind, I very much wanted to scream in the face of that immigration officer that his little requirements were *rubbish, just rubbish.* "This is my baby. My father has died. My mother has just sent me money to come and take care of a few things for her at her condominium, and then I am flying to Texas. What part of this don't you understand?"

It seemed/seems so simple to me. It wasn't so simple to them.

It was dawn, 6:00 a.m. before they had worked things out where they would finally release me to enter the United States with my daughter. My mother later told me that she had received a call about the problem and that she had contacted the U.S. congressman or senator, the same high-flying person who had assisted in finding me in Micronesia; and it was through this elected official's credentials—a man whose name I didn't know and don't know today—that I was released into the United States with the knowledge that I would not be able to leave back to Micronesia or any foreign country until my daughter had a passport.

Finally released and freed from Immigration, I took a taxi to my mother's condominium. It was well over twenty-four hours since I'd left Ponape. I could see the air moving in patterns. I was so exhausted. I found the office of the condominium association, but I had to wait another frustrating length of time before someone arrived where I was able to get a key to my mother's home. I showered. I put Heidi in the first bathtub in her life and washed her in warm water. We climbed in my mother's queen-size super-comfortable bed, and I slept, waking just enough to nurse Heidi, and falling asleep again until Heidi's own continued wakefulness forced me to get up. My mother's condominium was 1,500 square feet of plush pure-white carpets on the thirteenth floor with a large lanai looking out toward Diamond Head in the distance. Luxury.

I found my mother's car keys and drove to the grocery store, laying Heidi on the passenger seat next to me, performing the maneuver of my parents before me, reaching out to steady her each time I came to a stop. It didn't even dawn on me that there were such things as car seats. I'm not sure that there were at that time in early 1976. I wasn't fully aware of them until my third child was born in 1980. Silly me. To me, the only dangers from which I needed to protect my daughter were hurricanes in port, storms at sea, and planes crashing from the sky.

Once I was caught up on sleep, the time spent in Honolulu went quickly. I contacted the necessary people to manage renting my mother's home. I collected and bought storage boxes, and while Heidi lay on the plush white carpet, I boxed up books and memorabilia, art objects, personal things, taping the boxes shut, inscribing on them what was in which box. I then called a small moving company to come and collect them, haul them down the elevator, and take them to a storage facility.

I had made an appointment with the proper authorities to begin the process of getting a Certificate of Birth Abroad for Heidi and a passport. The whole process, I was told, would take at least two months if not more because, first, they had to receive the legal Certificate of Birth Abroad, and then they could process the passport. I eventually booked a flight to fly from Honolulu to Texas to confront my demons.

I had arrived in Kusaie exactly three weeks after my father had died. It took ten days before I caught the cargo boat to Ponape along with two days to get there. I was eight days in Ponape, waiting for the plane to fly me to Honolulu. I flew for a day, and I was almost two weeks in Honolulu before I flew to Texas, arriving just short of two months after my father had passed.

My mother and younger brother picked me up from the airport, and we drove out to my father's lake house. It was on the cliffs overlooking Lake Austin, a place my father had built as his country hideout for revising his books. He also had another house just down the road from his publishing company in Austin, which also wasn't too far from his office at the university where he taught graduate classes in psychology. It was on the floor of that house, "the town house," where they had found my father's body. When he hadn't shown up for work all day, the journals' manager finally sent someone down to check on him. There they had found him sprawled on the floor in the foyer within reach of the front door. He'd lain there alone for almost eighteen hours after suffering a massive heart attack.

My mother, of course, goo-gooed over her first grandchild as I got settled into the spare room. She had had a closet full of Hawai'ian muumuus in Honolulu and had asked me to bring some back for her and had offered that I take any that I might want. I had grabbed a couple that zipped down the front, which made breastfeeding easy. I had changed into this muumuu right before dinner was ready, and as I sat down for dinner, my milk suddenly dropped, a wrenching feeling that starts up in the pectoral muscles, pulling milk down into the breasts. I instinctively clasped my hands together as I pressed my forearms against my breasts to keep them from leaking, looking much like a pose of prayer. My mother stopped and stared at me almost in horror and asked, "What? Have you started to pray and say grace now, have you?"

I laughed and said, "No, Mom, my milk just dropped."

She said, "What does that mean?"

Before Heidi had been born, my mother had wanted to send me a care package of bottles and powdered formula. I, with actual horror, had replied to her, "Why? Why would I need that? I have breasts."

She replied with a bit of innocence that she had never breastfed. She had never considered breastfeeding. She just assumed I would use bottles and formulas. Remembering that she had never nursed me, probably barely held me in her arms or performed the most natural of motherly tasks, I unzipped the muu, baring both of my breasts. Two streams of milk shot almost completely across the table.

"Oh, my!" she exclaimed as I zipped up the muu and again pressed my forearms to my breasts with my hands clasped together. "I never knew. I didn't know such a thing could happen!"

I was suddenly a bit embarrassed over my less-civilized act of letting milk shoot across the table though in hindsight, it was a humorous scene. At least at that moment, it also accentuated the great differences between the woman who had raised me and the young mother that I was. Feeling snagged in a time capsule, cut off by the changes spanning generations, I felt so estranged from this woman who had borne me and mothered me.

At least at that moment. Though both mothers, at that moment, I felt we were not sharing, nor would we share the same experiences. She had not nurtured and mothered me as I did my daughter. It seemed strange that I felt more closely connected to all the women in the islands, like the strangers who whisked away my baby on Nukumanu, than I did to my own mother.

I'd left a rebellious teenager; I returned a young mother. Though my father was dead, the scars remained of his rejection, his anger, and from the emotional and physical abuse he wreaked upon his family, his inability to love or be emotionally present. I was an onion, unwillingly peeling back complex layers of the family from which I had come. Here I sat with my mother in a house my father had built after he'd left her for her sister. At least at that moment, I hardly knew what to think.

The coroner's report was that his heart—his physical heart—was small and thick walled, the result of alcoholism as was the cirrhosis of the liver. In my mind, his heart reflected his inability to love. Its thick walls reflected his own screams of hurt and anguish that he never chose to explore and find a cure for. He'd tried to find happiness in his work, his fame, his notoriety, in changing partners, and in a fifth of Tanqueray gin each night, numbing any feelings he might have ever had. Yes, I sailed to the far ends of the world to get away from all that reminded me of my father. And here I was back in his midst.

The next morning my mother and I, with baby Heidi securely nestled in her hammock carrier, went to the offices of the publishing company my father had started in the early 1960s. With his own funds and time, he'd started the journals to provide a venue for experimental psychologists to publish refereed papers to abide by many universities' "publish or perish" rule. He pioneered new ways of publishing. I had in fact worked there from age thirteen on five days a week, five hours a day after school, typesetting, skills that had gotten me the job in Cairns. After he got the company up and running and out of the red, he donated it and all its value to an organization he had been instrumental in creating. He remained the managing editor of the journals until his death. (Since then, the journals were sold to a German publishing group for a sum in the millions.)

When I arrived at the offices, all work stopped. Some employees were new and knew not who I was, but several of the office people had been working there long before I'd left. They greeted me with hugs and, of course, swept Heidi out of my arms.

Ann and Sharon led me into my father's offices quietly, only with the hint that they had something they wanted to show me. Arriving at his desk, they stepped back and then pointed to the wall opposite his desk on which was a world map. Colored pins were stuck on all the islands I had visited with strings attaching the routes I had sailed. The last string ended on Fergusson Island in the Milne Bay District of Papua New Guinea. Both women told me simply and quietly how proud my father was of me, how he had followed my path across the ocean, being kept informed by letters I'd written home to my mother and brothers. They told me that when he found out I was pregnant, he'd asked them, "Should I grow a beard now that I'm going to be a grandfather?"

Tears poured down my cheeks as I stared at that map, my throat tightened in pain and anger, thinking of the two or three letters I'd received from him over the past five, six years. As the women saw me crying, they tried to comfort me, but I could only repeat how angry I was that he couldn't have been bothered to ever let me know. Even as of this writing, forty-five years later, I mourn that fact. The tears flow. Why the hell could he never ever tell me that he loved me, that he cared about me? Why couldn't he have ever told me whether I was good enough at anything, whether I had done good enough in school or in setting the crab line, in swinging the baseball bat, in the school play? Well, of course, he wouldn't be able to tell me that: he never went to a school play. Nor did he go to any of my swimming competitions. One match I came in third place, inches behind the girl that went to the Olympics the following year, but he was never there to cheer me on to tell me how good I was. I was almost a straight *A* student in school, but I remember no acknowledgment of that or interest. Sure, sure, he was busy with his life, but what about me?

I traveled a long way with anchor aweigh. Sadly, learning after the fact the simple knowledge of how proud he was of me could not undo the years of always feeling unloved, unimportant, and wanting to run as far away as I could from any reminder of how miserable my childhood had been. In reality, it only made me sadder to think he, for whatever reasons he had—his own miserable upbringing, I'm sure— could not express the simple words "I love you. You are beautiful and precious and so perfect in my eyes. I will do everything in my power to raise you up with love and support all your dreams so that you can grow into a loving, wonderful adult."

The next day, one of my cousins (the son of my father's lover, my aunt) took my mother, my two brothers, myself, and baby Heidi out onto Lake Austin in a small sixteen-foot motorboat. We motored along until we had found a place away from other boaters, away from houses along the lake. Just a quiet, still, calm place. We opened up the coffee can–like container that had been provided by the crematorium containing his ashes. It was a quiet, still day until the very moment my younger brother reached in for a handful of ashes to sprinkle onto the lake. The wind whipped up, and the ashes blew in our faces. My other brother turned to the downwind side of the small boat and grabbed a handful of ashes, but the wind swirled around again and tossed the ashes back in our faces. My mother reached quickly for a handful of ashes in what she thought was a lull, and again the wind whipped up. I kid you not. My father had waited months to cause his last bit of havoc.

As I took the can and reached for the ashes, trying so hard to be meditative and solemn and prayerful, the wind blew hard and the finer ashes blew into my eyes and stuck to the tears running down my face. I took the can and threw it into the lake, angry. But for a few of the lighter ashes, the can sunk quickly out of sight into the algae-green river.

Nobody said anything to me. There was no quickened outburst like, "What are you doing?" For me, what I did was appropriate. He had brought a lot of pain to everybody in that little boat. Everybody. It was my cousin's mother whom he had taken for a lover on the night of his father's funeral. It was my mother's sister whom he took to his bed and left my mother, his wife of twenty-two years, sitting on the outside while he explained that he was "helping her sister with her grieving process." He mistreated my aunt in the same drunken rages that he mistreated my mother, and my cousins were witness to this. My older brother had been drafted and sent to Vietnam to witness atrocities no man should witness in a war that should have never been fought all because my father, though he was close to a millionaire, would not pay for him to get into university to get an educational deferment from the draft. And me? Me, he had almost killed me with an ice pick when I was fifteen years old in one of his drunken rages when I had tried to keep him from beating up my mother.

But my younger brother was familiar now with a slightly different father than we had all experienced of which he told me later that night after dinner, after my older brother and his wife had gone home and my mother had gone to bed. First, in the empathic way of my younger brother, he told me he understood why I dumped my father's ashes into the lake as I had, that he understood my anger and hurt, but he wanted to tell me something profound that had happened the night our father died.

My younger brother had a small house in Bastrop, a small town fifty miles outside of Austin. He was heading home after a long day's work at his own budding small printing company. He was well out of town when he had a strong—strong, he reiterated—premonition to go visit our father. He tried to ignore it because there was never a good reason or time to visit our father, especially in the evening as he was more than likely well into his fifth of Tanqueray gin by then. But the sense that my brother should turn around and visit him was so strong that he finally heeded it and turned the car around and drove almost twenty-five miles back into Austin to my father's house close to his office.

Upon knocking on the door, my brother tells me, my dad answered with a warmth and a welcome and a smile my brother could not remember having ever experienced before. He said it almost seemed like my father was expecting him and was very, very happy to see him. We had all grown up to tiptoe around Dad for fear that we would disturb him. My mother's role as his wife was to make sure she kept us children out of his hair; he literally did not want to hear that we existed, whether it be the laughter of children playing or the anger of children fighting or the tears of a child needing comfort. When I was a teenager, he sat endlessly in a brown leather chair, running his hands from front to back through his close-cropped hair, thinking. Thinking. Thinking. And we were not to interrupt that thinking. We'd learned to avoid him as much as possible though we kept trying to be good enough to be recognized. I became an overachiever. "Do you see me now? Do you see me now?"

But that night, my father welcomed my brother into his home. He had in fact not been drinking—at least enough that my brother could tell. He offered my brother a seat, and they began to talk. My father began to talk, sharing thoughts and *feelings* about his life and our life living on the farm in Maryland. He spoke of how much he loved the solitude of Maryland and had preferred to stay but that it had been our mother who had insisted she didn't want her children growing up as country bumpkins; our mother kept driving him toward a different lifestyle than what he wanted.

Some of my earliest memories of the Maryland farm were of my father and mother having horrible arguments late into the evenings that would wake me up. I would creep to the top of the stairs and peek down through the banisters and listen to my father rage at my mother and my mother cry and beg. I was too young to know what they fought about. I saw my mother as weak and badgered and my father as angry and badgering. These arguments seemed to get worse after we moved to Madison, Wisconsin, for three years, and in Santa Barbara, they started to get physical where my father would strike my mother.

I can't remember all that my brother told me of that last conversation he had with our father. He conveyed to me that he felt that our father was very, very sincere and candid in the things that he disclosed. He spoke of his frustrations being torn between his work and this woman, our mother, with whom he had little in common, who wanted different things than what interested him. He also spoke of his long love for our mother's sister, a love that had existed even before our parents had married when he had met my aunt through a colleague, a social psychologist, to whom she was already married. All these family secrets he revealed to my brother in a sober, candid, honest fashion.

My brother felt it was both an apology and confession. He also felt a mild confusion as to why this unique moment had occurred, why he'd felt this need to turn back that evening to our father's house, why our father was baring his very soul and feelings that night for the very first time ever. My brother said his last words were a resigned, "Well, I guess I have to start over now."

Eventually my brother drove away, back to his home in the country, feeling very, very blessed, he said, to have had this wonderful frank talk with our father. For the first time, my brother had seen a different side to our father, a more-human side, a humble side, a side that had a heart and had suffered a lot of pain on his own, not only meting out the pain to those he touched, which was all we, his children, had ever known.

My brother left his house around 10:00 p.m. that night. My father was found 4:00 p.m. the next day. He was lying near the front door, facing in the general direction back toward his living room, they said. The coroner estimated that he had died about eighteen hours beforehand. My younger brother felt in his heart of hearts that after farewells at the door, thanking my brother for stopping by, he'd closed the door behind him, turned to walk back to the living room, and was struck dead by a massive heart attack, dropping him to the floor right there.

My older brother isn't so metaphysical, but my younger brother and I believed in our hearts that our father, as I think many people do, knew his time was near; he'd put out that last soulful call to the only person who heard it and bared his heart to my brother. Me, I was bit by a brown recluse spider at the time of his death. I'll never know what that was about, but my thought has always been that was his kiss goodbye. And that he didn't mean it to hurt so much; he just wanted to make sure I knew he'd kissed me goodbye.

I believe in the reality of that mystic force or energy that brought my brother to his house that night. I do believe also, not in his scientist mind, but in his soul, that my father knew this would be his last chance to bare his soul and let his secrets out, and his soul flew out to my brother's car speeding out of Austin and urged him to return, to return, to come and listen to his side of the story. To his side of the story. One last chance to say, "I'm sorry. Behind the monster you've witnessed, I am a man of heart and dreams and stories untold."

My brother heard his plea and went back. Hearing his story helped to heal my seeping wounds, to close the cracks, to soften the hardened shell, to find the truth that had driven me to pull anchor and sail away, to stay away.

After staying over three weeks in Austin, I was notified that my daughter's passport would be ready within a week in Honolulu. My mother had since decided that she would be remaining in Austin, at least while sorting out my father's will, and had asked that I take care of a few other things for her in Honolulu before flying back to Ponape. She took me shopping and bought Heidi cute little outfits and paid for a couple new things for me. She also paid for me to go to the dentist and have my teeth cleaned and checked, something I hadn't done for many years.

My mother continued to do the job my father had assigned to her a quarter of a century before: take care of the children through mostly only physical actions that showed her love. I still struggle to remember cuddly moments with my mother, warm moments, loving moments. I have none, no memories of any warm moments, though she was physically present at the swim meets and track meets, always cheering me on and she took me to piano lessons and to the country club to keep me out of my father's hair. She visited me in New Zealand.

I flew back to Honolulu and took care of my mother's things for her. I picked up Heidi's passport, showing a fat, bald little three-month-old baby in a little flower-printed dress with lacy frills. The picture was of her whole body; you can see my fingers peeking through the frills of her dress, holding her propped up, supporting her completely for the photographer.

With a newer backpack containing several dozen cotton diapers, a change of clothes for me, several changes of clothes for Heidi, toys and rattles and teething rings, and a couple plastic bags for dirty diapers, I boarded the flight from Honolulu, presenting two passports, to fly back to Ponape, Caroline Islands, Micronesia, to reunite with Dave.

CHAPTER 16

Do not let your fire go out, spark by irreplaceable spark in the hopeless swaps of the not-quite, the not-yet, and the not-at-all. Do not let the hero in your soul perish in lonely frustration for the life you deserved and have never been able to reach. The world you desire can be won. It exists . . . It is real . . . It is possible . . . It's yours.

—Ayn Rand

When we were little (I was between the ages of four and eight), we lived on a farm in Maryland. It was a twenty-six-acre parcel of land, half of it being sowed in corn and soybeans in rotation (my father leased out the land to other farmers), an almost equal portion in a mixed pine forest, and the remainder in low-lying land barely holding in the boundaries of Smith Cove, a creek tributary of the Little Choptank River, which broke into the Big Choptank, which flowed into the Chesapeake Bay. He commuted to Baltimore several times a week to teach psychology to both graduate students and undergrads, but he had bought the farm as a quiet and restful place to write and revise his textbooks on psychology. My most enduring memory is of him closeted away in his downstairs office and us walking on eggshells at all times. But there are some good memories too.

We were three, my brothers and me. We were three inquisitive, energetic, not-to-be stopped youngsters living in the countryside without the restrictions that busy roads and cars and strangers placed on young children playing freely. My father showed us the woods, the pine forest. He walked us back through the lower marshland, past the cattail groves, into the woods. He carried a hatchet and showed us how to notch out small chips out of the trees to show the direction back to the farmhouse. He showed us how not to get lost.

We also spent a lot of time on the creeks and rivers by our home. We often went out and laid a trotline in the evenings. They were magical times when the water was smooth as silk, reflecting the blues or grays of the sky. As a whole, it was a quiet, contemplative endeavor. With great coils of half-inch line, about every four feet, we'd wedge a piece of salted eel into a twist of the rope. That was our job to be completed before my father finished working in his office. And then we'd motor out, out past the sandbar, and drop a buoy and anchor and play out the line for its half-mile length. Sometimes we'd go over to the sandbar, pulling our runabout up on to the sand—my father would sit while we three would dig for clams or just swim off the bar—and then we'd motor back out to the buoy and hoist it on board. Turning off the engine, we would quietly pull the trotline up and into the boat. We would take turns with the net held out over the edge into which the Chesapeake blue crabs would drop as they came up out of the water, still clinging to the salted eel, dumping them into the bottom of the boat. We had to wear hip boots as the crabs would be knee deep in the boat by the time we were done.

On other days, we had creeks to explore, dinghies to row out to sandbars, forests to scout, neighboring farmers' corn silos and hay barns to play in. There were logging camps nearby still using mules and wagons. There were chain gangs, men in striped pajamas chained together, that worked cleaning the ditches out every summer. There was wild asparagus in those ditches that we'd harvest when they were in season. There was the old 200-year-old graveyard to explore. The world was there for our exploration, giving us freedom and a sense of self-confidence.

I realize the moments that stay locked in time that I easily pull into the present are those moments where I was fully present, totally in that moment. I wasn't cowering and trying to shut out the world. I was the watcher and the watched, the doer and the experience itself. There were times as a child I would lie in the wheat fields and leave my body, being transported away into a moment of spiritual awe, one with the sky, the clouds, far out of my body. That was the same sense of awe I experienced sailing as I felt back to my experiences when I was a child. The days crabbing, the freedom to explore the waters and the land, were all gifts from my father.

Something had shifted after I came back to Ponape from the States. My head and heart were twisting around and around, analyzing the ideas of family and family relationships. Thin threads of very ephemeral ideas were fraying apart; I kept trying to bring them to a consolidated point so I could fit them through the needle's eye. If I could only do that, then I would be able to sew together all the loose ends and long stretches of openings and pull it all into a tight package called family, called love and security. But I wasn't quite able to do it. My ends wouldn't come together; I couldn't thread me into that tiny eye. I couldn't make myself be totally present in that singular task because I was distracted by my questions and criticisms of myself and my choices. I kept missing the entrance to understanding it all.

I was returning to Dave in Ponape, having been gone over three months, not really knowing who he was or why I was with him or why I was returning to him or who we were together. And I realized that I probably would not be returning to him at all had it not been that we were now a family—and there I was, trying to thread myself into the eye of the needle to sew together family. I *wanted* us to work out because we were family, because we had promised ourselves we would do it differently than our parents had done.

Dave had worked at several different projects in Kusaie while I was in the States. He was in Ponape waiting for me when I flew back. I had felt enthusiastic and excited until the reality of returning to life on a thirty-foot sailboat with a crawling six-month old took a two-handed grip on my shoulders and shook me. I struggled to juggle the continuing sense of adventure and exploring a new place with day-to-day survival, which seemed more pressing than ever now that I had a baby that was crawling and climbing everywhere on our thirty-foot sailboat. It became pressing that we baby-proofed the boat, and we set about making a fishnet weave to attach between the deck and the lifelines so that Heidi would be safer and less likely to fall overboard.

In one respect, childrearing was easier. Feeding, for example. Instead of using high chairs and bibs, I'd put Heidi in the cockpit, naked, and feed her. The food that inevitably would dribble down her front and be flung across the cockpit was easily cleaned up by hauling up a bucket of saltwater and dumping it over Heidi's head and the cockpit, washing everything down quickly. Heidi loved it.

But overall the rest of my day-to-day life became harder. Part of what made it harder was I knew my true traveling days were over. I could see no more adventures on the horizon. I was just surviving. And surviving was often just that: doing laundry by hand, *thump-thump-thud*, hauling a toddler—now out of protective baby carrier—and laundry to shore to rinse in freshwater. But here, freshwater was not close at hand. It was a mile trek down the causeway to town. I grew increasingly unhappy. I was never alone. I grew to understand my dad's ferocious need for silence and alone time to think, to be creative. I didn't have it. Ever.

I didn't write in my journal at all anymore. I had no time. I had no silence. I had no aloneness. I was seldom fully present, fully anchored in the moment. I was always wanting to be somewhere else under different circumstances. Being a mother was an immense burden whose weight most of the time, thank God, was indeed alleviated by all the joys associated with my daughter. Another metamorphosis was underway, a settling in to a more responsible way of being in the world.

We bought a little squat fat-tired motorcycle. Heidi traveled in a backpack whether I was with Dave or riding alone. After a lot of complaining and insistence to move off the boat, we eventually found a place to stay on shore where there was more space for Heidi to move around in and a water tap at hand to make daily chores easier. We house-sat a large and beautiful and fully furnished three-bedroom house owned by Americans for two months while they were on the Mainland. I dreaded having to return to the boat and its cramped quarters, so afterward, we found a little squalid tin hut to move into. Again, we brought the settee cushions to shore that became our bed on the hard concrete slab. Dave built a rough counter space in the room meant to be the kitchen, which consisted of a two-burner stove. The shower was outside as was the tap for washing the dishes and laundry. It was nestled in coconut trees, close to other little squalid huts with neighbors, one being the old lady who comforted Heidi that one night, where little neighbor girls would come and play with Heidi for hours on end, fascinated by her blonde hair and white skin.

There was an assortment of expats living in Kolonia, Ponape. Most of them were teachers connected to the small community college or the high school there. Dave had made contact with several of them and had managed to create himself a teaching position teaching a class on celestial navigation, something no islander knew about. He set about writing a textbook from which to teach the class. The $100 a month he would receive was not sufficient to live on. Shortly after my return to Ponape, several men with the Teacher Corps arrived, a government organization that sent teachers off to less-civilized areas to teach people to be teachers. They had secured a small office and were in need of a secretary to type up their reports, letters, and to perform other secretarial duties. Desperate for money, I applied for and got the job (there not being many other qualified persons on the island who knew how to type and spell and perform secretarial duties). I worked three days a week.

This became a time when the differences between Dave and I became even more pronounced. I think the differences in how we were raised and what we expected in a family unit accentuated the conflagrations that had smoldered beneath the surface since he arrived in New Zealand. Admittedly, motherhood had changed my perspective of what was needed for financial security, and the idea that coursed through my veins was completely different than Dave's idea. So to appease my need to have more money to provide for our daughter, I found a job. Though I had expected Dave to take care of our daughter on the days I worked, he didn't feel that he could. In the end, I hired a babysitter.

I hired the wife of John Johnny to babysit. John Johnny was one of the student teachers in the Teacher Corps program, and they lived several houses from us in a not-quite-as-squalid tin hut. I paid one-fifth of what I earned for Heidi to be taken care of by John's wife. I know she received lots of love. She also came home with head lice repeatedly, and though I repeatedly secured lice shampoo for John Johnny's household, my habit after returning from work was to pore through Heidi's short, fine hair, looking for critters before bringing her into my home. In spite of my frustrations that I should have to pay for her daycare, I'm thankful for the love and doting attention I know she received in the nine months I worked.

I think we stayed in Ponape as long as we did because of the expat community there where we made a lot of friends. We ended up meeting a wonderful couple, another young family, who was my saving grace. My days off from work were often spent with Jill and her two young children, one just a month younger than Heidi. Her husband was a schoolteacher as well as his father before him who had been a schoolteacher on Ponape for twenty years previously. We had a lot in common age wise, socially, and spent a lot of time together. Jill was a quiet, mellow woman, six-foot tall and thin; Dan was a bear of a man, five-foot-nine and thick as a bull. Several years later, they ended up leaving Ponape and returning to the States where they lived only ninety miles from where we ended up settling in Oregon. It was Jill's third child I helped deliver years later (the precarious cord wrap) when I trained as a midwife.

We stayed in Ponape until the following May. Fishing boats came in every afternoon. I bought a five- or eight-pound tuna for $1, which along with cucumbers and tomatoes and green beans became a regular dinner meal. For variety, I bought five-pound bags of frozen turkey tails for $1 from which I'd make a greasy soup stock with which to cook beans or rice for more flavor. The water of Ponape was very contaminated. For most of our drinking water, I caught water off the rusty roofs. Tap water though would need to be boiled for twenty minutes to kill off the amoebic dysentery that flourished in it. In spite of precautions, Heidi, being a child who would habitually put her hands in water and then in her mouth, ended up with amoebic dysentery.

Not all, of course, was work and toil. There was an old barge that was anchored out near our boat. We took the liberty to row over to it one day and discovered inside its holds a myriad of fish tanks filled with tropical fish. We eventually were introduced to the owner of the barge, another American, who came to Ponape several months out of the year to dive and capture tropical fish that he then imported to pet stores around the United States. I thought what a great little business to have. He did a lot of his diving over on the east side of the island near some old ruins called Nan Madol. One of the expat community college teachers took us out there. Nan Madol was built by peoples from islands south of Ponape in approximately 1100, maybe even as early as the eighth century. They built Nam Madol as an altar to worship their gods. Built of great basalt stones on top of the coral reef off the east coast of Ponape, it was one of those engineering feats anthropologists and archeologists marvel at discovering. The lost city consisted of a series of small artificial islands linked by a network of canals, enclosing an area of about one and a half kilometers by half a kilometer in size within stone walls of massive basalt. The name *Nan Madol* means "spaces between" and is a reference to the canals that crisscross the ruins.

Nan Madol was the ceremonial and political seat of the Saudeleur dynasty, which united Pohnpei's estimated 25,000 people until about 1628 when legend describes a warrior from Kusaie sailing over to drive the Saudeleur rulers away. I learned more about Nan Madol years later, but it fascinated me much like the tikis looming over the cliffs of Fatu Hiva had fascinated Thor Heyerdahl years before me. How did they get there? What was the history? Not a complete secret to all, I guess, as James Rollins' novel *Deep Fathom* and Clive Cussler's *Medusa* both worked the ancient ruins into their fiction.

There were archaic and ugly customs still alive in Ponape too. One was if a man's wife cheated on him, he could legally cut out her eye. There was a very sweet woman working at one of the bars in Kolonia who had a glass eye, the result of that very punishment. The eye was too small for her socket and didn't sit well. It was a permanent statement of a bad choice she'd made. But then maybe it was a better choice. Maybe it was a choice of the lesser of two evils. I heard that her husband had been an abusive man, and maybe she was simply searching for someone to love her. Is that a bad choice? To be loved? To be honored? To be supported?

There was a fairly large American expat community that distracted us regularly with potlucks and parties. Though Dave and I, in the metamorphosis into parenthood, continued to struggle, there were incidents that would bring us together as a unit, as protectors and defenders of each other. One was the attempted "rapes" that happened to me in Ponape. Two of them. I put "rapes" in quotes because to this day, I don't believe the men's intention had the evil behind it as we see in the vicious power-dominated rapes whether it be in our communities or in Africa and war-torn areas of the world though I have been highly criticized by many women for being so forgiving and naïve. As I understand it, the action was culturally "accepted" not only in Ponape but also in various parts of the South Pacific coming out of an old tradition. For centuries, because families all lived and slept together on their floor mats in their small one-room huts, marriage—before the church and white man—consisted of a young man sneaking into the house and sleeping with the daughter. If the father did not kick out the courting man and he came three nights in a row, it was a silent acceptance that his daughter was now married.

This behavior had morphed some over the years, and as was explained by the long-term expats and the local law enforcement folks, similar attempts were culturally accepted. If the advances of the man were rejected, this was the ultimate shame for the man—talk would spread quickly that the man's attempts were rebuffed—but no harm to the woman.

But doubt not that the advance upon my body was quite rattling to me.

The first event happened when we were living in our little hot squalid tin house. As it was hot and humid, we were asleep stark naked on the cushion-bed on the floor. Dave was on the inside; I was on the outside with Heidi between us. I was sound asleep flat on my back when I woke up to a strange sensation. I opened my eyes and I thought I saw a white motorcycle helmet hovering right over my pubic triangle. I closed my eyes. Was I dreaming? Upon opening my eyes again, I still saw a young man on his hands and knees with a white motorcycle helmet on with his face about six inches from the space between my legs. Out of my mouth came, "What the fuck do you think you're doing?" as I started to leap out of the bed.

Of course, my words woke up Dave who bolted out of the bed, almost crushing Heidi. This boy-man was flying out the door, and I was right behind him, but Dave's outstretched arm was grabbing my shoulder and shoving me out of the way as he bolted after this guy. Both of them went running off into the night, Dave, stark naked, chasing the guy down the street.

Heidi had woken up and started to cry, so I comforted her. I grabbed a pareo and wrapped it around me and turned on the lights and walked out to the tiny porch in front of the shack with Heidi to wait. Dave finally returned. He'd failed to catch the kid, but we found his shirt sitting on the front porch. The following day, we went from house to house asking if anybody knew whose shirt it was. We did finally discover who the kid was and reported him to the police, but the police sort of laughed it off that we should let it go. The boy would suffer more shame, they said. He didn't after all, they asked, even touch me, did he? Quite a shock to think that no one would even lift a finger to prosecute this violation. But to them, it was not a violation.

But in the process of going door to door, we also found one of Dave's shirts hanging on someone's clothesline. We reported that to the police also, and the police refused to do anything about that either. Wow.

The second incident happened later, closer to when we were preparing to sail away from that godforsaken island. We were back living on the boat. I was done with my secretarial assignment with the Teacher Corps program. Dave had just finished his last class teaching celestial navigation, and we were gearing up to sail away, south again soon. Dave was contacted by the local hospital staff, asking if he could help navigate a big fishing boat over to an adjoining island where a local man had inadvertently hooked a large fishhook around his jugular vein and they needed to evacuate him to Ponape. Normally they would use one of the cargo vessels, but there were none available close enough. They needed Dave's skill to navigate the 100 miles.

It was supposed to be a one-day turnaround trip. The crew that accompanied him were men from that island, so as they entered the lagoon, Dave was looking at the charts and saying, "So what about these large coral heads here? Do they pose a danger?"

And the men who all paddled shallow outrigger canoes and not fishing boats that drew ten feet of water, all replied, "No, they are no problem. You can go right over them."

It happened to be spring tide; and it happened to be the peak of high tide on spring tide when they went solidly aground on the coral head that was only five feet below the surface. The tide would not be that high again for another month. After much arguing, the village chief apparently ordered all the young men of the island out to the coral head with crowbars and sledgehammers and any other implement they could use that would demolish the coral head around the keel of the fishing boat. After two days of many men working, they were finally able to free the boat. The boat luckily was not damaged, and eventually, they were able to rescue the man with the fishhook in his neck and head back to Ponape.

The medics at the hospital had kept me updated on what had happened, and they let me know that the boat should be returning around ten o'clock that night. At eleven, they had still not come in. I climbed high into the rigging and looked way out to sea with the binoculars to see if I could see a boat returning. I saw no lights. Being exhausted, I went below and set my alarm for an hour later. I woke up, climbed up into the rigging, and again looked out to sea. There were a few cars and some men waiting on the dock, but I could see no boat's lights out on the horizon anywhere. Again, I set the alarm and went back to sleep. Again, I woke up, and I climbed the rigging. There were more cars on the dock, but I still saw no boat coming in. As I started to climb down the rigging, suddenly a hand grabbed my ankle. I looked down, and there was a huge wet islander man below me yanking on my foot.

I kicked at him and yelled, "Let go!"

He said, "Shhhh. Shhh."

I said, "Screw you. Don't shhh me," and I struggled free of him and climbed back up higher in the rigging, and I started screaming, "Rape! Murder! Rape! Murder! Help! Rape, murder!" at the top of my lungs.

The man below continued to "shhh, shhh," and I continued to scream. The people on the shore jumped in their cars and turned their cars around and put their high beams onto the boat. This giant, heavy island man went to the stern of the boat and climbed silently back down into the water and started to swim to shore.

I had worked myself up into a right state at that time just by screaming. The intruder was lucky that our rifles had been stolen in a break-in several months before because otherwise, having worked myself up into a frenzy, I have no doubt that I would have killed someone that night. I heard a motor start up near the dock and head out to me. I ran below and found a crowbar and a giant flashlight. I shined the light on the man swimming to shore, and then I whipped it back around to this motorboat that was powering out to my boat. Four huge men motored out in a small ten- to twelve-foot boat, almost sinking it. I shone the light in their faces, holding the crowbar threateningly raised in my hand. They asked, concerned, if I was all right, and they were wanting to come on board and check on me, but all I could think was they could well be part of this whole plan, that they might be connected to this other man. I raised the crowbar at them and screamed that they were not going to fuckin' come on board my boat, that they needed to go get the police.

They did. They left, and about twenty minutes later, the boat returned with one man bringing one policeman out to the boat. I told the policeman what had happened. I gave him a description of the man, which was very much like a description of half the men on Ponape. It turns out he had left a flip-flop sitting in my cockpit, and it was very much like every flip-flop worn by every man and woman on Ponape. The policeman ended up giving me his can of Mace and giving me instructions that if I spray it, to make sure that I was not downwind.

I thanked him kindly, and he returned to shore. I sat in the cockpit for a while, waiting and hoping that Dave would return, but I eventually went to sleep again. I awakened again to the sound of a boat's motor, bringing Dave out to our boat. It was almost 3:00 a.m. before he returned, four days late. In the morning, we shared stories. Dave told me the story of putting the boat on the coral, the islanders destroying the coral to free the boat. And in the end, the man with the fishhook: The fishhook could have easily been removed by cutting off the eye-hook end and pulling the hook out, which is all that the doctors did in the end. Nobody thought of that solution. They thought they would have to do delicate surgery to remove it.

In spite of taking prophylaxis for the months during and three months after being in Papua New Guinea, I had my first malaria attack in Ponape. One day, several months after taking my last pill, I felt like I was getting the flu. I ached; I was feverish. I lay down below in the boat with chills in ninety-degree weather. Six hours later, it passed, and I thought I was fine. Exactly forty-eight hours later almost to the minute, I again started to ache and have chills and fever and then sweats. My fever was much higher this time. Six hours later, it stopped. Then exactly two days later, I again had the same symptoms, but this time the fever was dangerously high. We carried a *Merck Manual*, and upon investigating the symptoms, we diagnosed it as malaria. I took chloroquine, and the symptoms left. I had relapses of malaria about every six weeks to two months about six more times. My last attack, though weak, was the day my son was born in Tahiti. I've never been affected by it since.

We stayed in Ponape almost a year as we morphed into different beings with life revolving around parenting. The archetype of mother was ruling, and my demands for a greater sense of security reigned strong. Dave didn't seem to have the same sense of responsibility, and those differences and my unfilled expectations created a lot of friction and continued unhappiness though our social life with the relatively large number of expats provided enough diversion that my happiness came in the form of less despair, not necessarily more happiness. As usual, a change of scenery would be the solution to all problems.

We sailed away from Ponape in early May 1977, almost a year after arriving. We were heading south and east, back toward Tahiti. Dave was dead set on taking me to Suwarrow, where he had visited Tom Neale before he had chased me down in New Zealand. Suwarrow Atoll held some sort of utopian ideal that I think Dave blindly felt would solve all our problems. I think, for me too, having been inundated by people and bad people and bad things that bad people do, the idea of a deserted island sounded wonderful. I'd already forgotten the loneliness and lack of stimulation we'd experienced on Fergusson. Memory is short-lived.

CHAPTER 17

*But that's how it is on a sailing ship, and in this respect its
journey parallels that of life: simply knowing where you want to
go isn't enough, because life is a windblown voyage, consisting
mainly of the detours imposed by alternating calm and storm.*

—Carsten Jensen

After leaving Ponape, we spent many days in the equatorial doldrums
where nary a breath of wind blew for days on end. It has its peace. It has
its beauty, where the deep dark blue of the mirror-smooth ocean pulls the
sun's rays down into its depth never to be seen again. We would sit there
barely moving for days, sails set and barely flapping occasionally against
a small rolling sea. Hot. No wind.

Heidi was walking, and the days in the doldrums made sailing with
her easy. I didn't need to worry about her safety as I did when the wind
was pulling us along at a steady clip, and we were heeled and rocking. She
had great sea legs for a young walker, actually maybe better than ours. I
attributed it to her low center of gravity. But luckily for the whole trip from
Ponape to the New Hebrides, where we made first landfall after six weeks
at sea, we had no bad weather and nothing that posed any problems to deal
with. If we had to handle sails, I took the tiller, as usual, and held Heidi
in my lap. The occasional time when I was needed to also be hauling in
on a wench, I would put Heidi on the floor of the cockpit on the leeward
side and tell her to stay. She wasn't able to climb out of the cockpit yet, so
I knew she'd be safe.

She had long outgrown her little bassinet. She slept on the side settee for which we would raise up the crib siding and secure on either end. It was, so far, high enough for her not to be able to climb out of. I could only hope that by the time she could, she would understand the importance of not ever trying to.

There was one particular day in the doldrums where Heidi was taking a nap in the early afternoon. We brought up the settee cushions onto the deck and were lying comfortably in the hot sun. We ended up making love. The moment that I climaxed, two porpoises leapt out of the water a foot from the edge of the boat, two feet from my head, and looked me right in the eye. Right in the eye. *They* knew. They knew not only that we had been making love, but they were also there and rejoicing in the conception of my second child. Several days later, I started getting seasick even when the seas could barely roust up a breeze and a swell. As we eventually moved out of the doldrums and picked up some speed, I was sick every day, most all day. The porpoises knew why.

We arrived in the New Hebrides a month later. We were six weeks at sea total, and as usual, Dave and I sat in that dream space for endless hours at sea. The reverie was definitely interrupted more often with Heidi climbing about and forever demanding attention, but even she would seem to enter the slipstream and touch it.

The New Hebrides, now called Vanuatu, was a condominium government. It was essentially run by three separate governments—one French, one British, and one joint administration. The joint government consisted of both local and European officials. It had jurisdiction over the postal service, public radio station, public works, infrastructure, and censuses, among other things. Local people could choose whether to be tried under the British common law or the French civil law. There were British schools and French schools, and locals chose where they sent their children. There were two forms of currency. Visitors could choose which immigration rules to enter under. Nationals of one country could set up corporations under the laws of the other. In addition to these two legal systems, a third Native Court existed to handle cases involving Melanesian customary law. Oddly, the presiding judge of the Native Court was appointed by the king of Spain, not by the British or the French.

There were two prison systems to complement the two court systems. The police force was supposed to be one, but it consisted of two chiefs and two equal groups of officers wearing two different uniforms. Each group alternated duties and assignments. There were three operating languages, which was a serious barrier to the operation of an already-innately inefficient system. All documents had to be translated once to be understood by one side, then the response translated again to be understood by the other though Bislama creole represented an informal bridge between the British and the French camp. Though we there for almost four months, we were luckily unaware of an undercurrent of change that was just beginning. They gained complete independence in 1980, several years after we left.

There were French hospitals and British hospitals. The hospital where I went for my prenatal checkups was British run. We were befriended by both the French and the English. Invited by British friends, I sat through my first (and last) cricket match while chasing Heidi around, and having high tea with British friends on many an afternoon. French friends would invite us for multicourse dinners and what seemed to me to be high-society dinners, where I again enjoyed the fresh radishes dipped in soft butter. New Hebrides was a strange mixture of old and new, money and simplicity, the French and the English, an island culture trying to move into the twentieth century.

Port Vila was the capital and main town, but we were anchored a fair distance away from there thankfully. We were again anchored stern to some trees, but this time, we were in front of some lovely wealthy colonial homes. Across the bay was a small island on which locals lived in their thatched huts. Early each morning, the sound of babies crying would slide across the water with wisps of morning cook fires ghosting along with the sound, sounding as close as if it was happening next door. Heidi's first words were pronounced there while tugging on my pant leg, "Baby cries. Baby cries."

She earnestly pleaded that I do something about it with her plaintive two words. I would take her up into the cockpit and point across to the island 500 yards away and tell her, "The babies are over there. Their mothers are there. They are okay."

And we would look out across the glassy water, distracted by a small fish here and there occasionally breaking the mirror smoothness. "Fish jumps."

"Yes, that's right. Fish jumps."

Maybe it was childrearing that brought the fog, but I don't have a lot of detailed memories of the New Hebrides in spite of being there for four months. I went to the local hospital for prenatal checkups. Taking Heidi along, the nurse noticed that Heidi looked very pale and anemic and thought maybe she had intestinal parasites. I was shocked that I wouldn't have noticed that. We tested stool samples, and sure enough, she tested positive and was prescribed medicine. For almost a week, Dave and I literally argued over who would be the one who changed her morning diaper. This time I will save the details that are indelibly anchored in my memory.

And I remember French perfume. To this day, I associate French perfume with morning sickness. If I smell French perfume, I feel nauseous. Luckily, so many other scents have flooded the market, most people would not be able to identify a French scent, and I haven't smelled it for years.

Dave picked up a little work doing some boat repairs on other yachts, doing a little carpentry at the homes of different expats we met, doing some sail repairs for boats. I stayed on the boat with Heidi who was eighteen months old when we arrived and twenty-two months old when we sailed away again. My days were the same: doing laundry, forever trying to make an interesting meal out of restrictive ingredients, taking Heidi for walks, going for checkups, cleaning, doing laundry, cooking, cleaning.

Getting pregnant and being forever seasick was the only reason we ended up in the New Hebrides. Well past any time where I would experience morning sickness, we finally decided it was time to again set sail. We would be heading east toward Rarotonga and hopefully, eventually Suwarrow. But I was mistaken to think I would be over any morning sickness. I forgot that, with Heidi also, if I was pregnant and sailing, I was sick whether it's two months' pregnant or six months' pregnant.

It took us over a month to get to Rarotonga. I was sick every day. I checked in with a doctor there. I hadn't gained a lot of weight just like with Heidi, but he deemed me healthy enough and felt that neither I nor the baby I carried were worse for wear in spite of the constant nausea when I was at sea.

It turned out that an old friend of Dave's was living on Rarotonga. She was a retired schoolteacher from California that he had met several years earlier somewhere in his travels. After getting through customs, we went off in search of her, finding her without much trouble as she was a bit of "the eccentric American woman" that gave everyone something to talk about. She was living in a small house outside of Avarua, down by the beach. When we arrived, she was in her yard, wearing a tiny G-string bikini. Mind you, Ruby was probably pushing seventy years old. Gray pubic hairs poked out from wherever it could escape from. Her butt crack was showing—inches of it. Her skin sagged from every point of her body, and her bikini top covering her sagging breasts was closer to belly button level than chest level.

Putting all that image aside, she was indeed a wonderful character. At first. She managed to stay there under the auspices of writing the biography of Prince Albert. This is what she told us. I never saw her write anything, and why she would be writing any of it in Rarotonga, so far from England, did not add credence to what she said, but she had managed to stay in Rarotonga for several years. Dave thought she was the bee's knees maybe because she was such a crazy character, and they stayed in touch for many years later after we had returned to the States.

I was a little over six months pregnant when we arrived in Rarotonga. The immigration folks, with a growing number of sailing yachts needing moorage and anchorage, were insistent that we could only stay for ten days. Storm season was also upon us, where tropical storms and hurricanes were more apt to appear though not to the extent that they happened in the Caribbean, but it was the season for them if they did occur. Dave told the authorities that we had repairs we needed to do, and we managed to squeeze another five weeks out of them. Eventually though, they were finally insistent that we leave. I was actually dreading sailing any farther, dreading the seasickness and the strain of being pregnant and trying to take care of Heidi on the boat, so we decided that I would stay behind and stay with Ruby while Dave single handed the boat over to Tahiti. He would contact me when he arrived.

I was more than ready to join Dave in Tahiti after being almost a month with Ruby. He might have enjoyed her, but I think she wasn't quite screwed together properly. She thought it perfectly okay to pour Heidi an eight-ounce glass of red wine. I wasn't paying attention when Heidi was wanting something to drink. I had no reason to think that a retired schoolteacher and grown adult would give my two-year-old daughter a full glass of wine. I returned from the kitchen right as she finished gulping down the glass, bottom up. Not having seen any grape juice in the house, I asked Ruby what she had given Heidi. "Oh, a glass of wine."

I was like, "Exactly how much of a glass of wine?"

She pointed to the fill line.

A half hour later, my daughter was falling-down drunk. In one breath, it was a little bit funny, but on the serious side of parenting, I was horrified. I did not think she had been given so much as to endanger her health other than having to steady her from falling and hurting herself. She did finally lie down and go to sleep, or maybe it would be called passing out. But she woke me up in the middle of the night complaining of a headache. I was furious. I let Ruby know. But I was sort of stuck, waiting for Dave to arrive in Tahiti and also waiting to get enough money to fly me to Tahiti to join him. I vaguely remember some plan that he would make money in Tahiti and send it to me, but in the end, I called my mother long distance and asked that she send me enough money to fly to Tahiti. It was a hard blow to my ego to ask for that help, but for some reason, my mother acquiesced and sent the money.

I arrived in Tahiti three weeks before our son was born who arrived two weeks early. I had managed to have one appointment with an obstetrician in Papeete before I went into labor. He was a very angry French doctor. I did not like him at all. And he was not happy with me. He had no medical records though I insisted that I had been getting checkups and getting prenatal care through the months. My French was poor, and he knew no English, so our conversations were not well understood. I only knew he was not a happy or nice man.

My mother decided she wanted to come to Tahiti for the birth and help out, and she quickly made plans to join us. She thought she was arriving in Papeete in plenty of time, but her trip was dampened somewhat by the airlines having lost her bags. She arrived with nothing, not even her toothbrush. They admitted it was their problem, and they bought some immediate items for her: toiletries and a couple changes of clothes.

She was staying on our little sailboat anchored out in the bay about eight miles away from downtown Papeete and from the airport. We would row to shore every morning and go to a small hotel that was at the head of the bay to use their phone. They'd call the airlines to see if her bag had come in. I, in the meantime, would sneak through the halls of the hotel to the ice machine and sneak a bucket of ice to take back to the boat to keep things from spoiling. I did this for several months afterward until they finally caught me and banned me from the property altogether. I even offered to buy the ice from them, but they refused; the problem for me was the closest ice was over a mile away, and it would melt by the time I got it back to the boat.

We would go to the beach every day. I was wearing a bikini, and I would dig a hole in the sand so I could lie on my belly. My mom would watch Heidi play at the water's edge. I could relax! There were a few tourists that came to this hotel, and one day, while I was lying on the beach, some tourists came and sat near us after I had settled in. They were from Iowa, I think, and the sweet woman was commenting on what a cute little girl I had. She asked if I was staying in the hotel, and I said, "No, I'm staying out on that red yacht anchored out in the bay."

"Oh," she marveled, "With that young little girl?"

I said, "Oh, yes, indeed, and I rolled over to sit up, and my eight-and-a-half-month belly was revealed."

The woman from Iowa quickly gathered up her things and suggested to her husband that they really needed to go inside now. My mother was walking up as the woman scurried off. It made me chuckle. Apparently, I was just not made for proper society.

My mother's bags finally arrived. Even though my mother had money and could afford a taxi, I insisted that we take the wonderful tropical Tahiti buses—*Le Truck*—in to the airport to fetch her bags. They have no windows—open air—and they're colorful. It would be fun. On the way back, my mom suggested she stop and buy some groceries. The treat was on her. I'm not sure why she hadn't offered beforehand, but maybe she was tired of eating fish and coconuts and rice like we were. So we stopped at a store about a mile away. She bought a lovely little roast beef. I was drooling. I had not had red meat from a cow for I'm not sure how long. The last time I was in the States after my father's death, I think. She bought potatoes and salad fixings. There wasn't going to be a bus for a while, so we set off walking.

Now, mind you, at this point, I've got my mother's suitcase and now a bag of groceries and a two-year-old daughter who could walk but not for a mile. So eventually I found myself with my daughter on my hip and my mother's forty-pound suitcase in my other hand while my mom hobbled along carrying the groceries. I was suddenly hit with that telltale feeling like, hmm, that felt like a contraction. I kept walking. Hmm, that felt like another contraction. As we neared the coconut-groved bay where the boat was anchored, with neatly kept grounds adjoining the hotel, I had what was clearly another strong contractor. I never told my mother. We loaded up the dinghy, and we rowed out to the boat. I helped my mother on board, hoisted Heidi up into the cockpit, lifted up the groceries and my mother's suitcase for her. I climbed on board, tied off the dinghy, and nonchalantly told my mom I was going to take a little rest up in the V-berth and if she could keep an eye on Heidi. Not thinking twice, she happily agreed, and I went up forward and lay down. The contractions continued.

Dave had procured a job at the *Tahiti Bulletin*, an English daily newspaper that was put out to keep the English-speaking tourists informed of what was happening in the world. His job was to monitor AP notices and radio news reports and type up summaries of news happenings. He was due back by five. I suggested that we start cooking that roast beef. I got up and turned on the little tiny propane oven and put in the little four-pound roast. Labor or not, I was going to eat that roast beef that night before I had a baby! Of that I was sure.

Close to five, I heard the tale-tell call Dave and I had developed to tell us apart from every other yachties hailing a boat. I got out of the V-berth and grabbed the dinghy and rowed to shore to pick him up. On the way back, I told him, "I'm in labor."

He was like, "Wow, okay, we've got to go."

I said, "No, we aren't going until I've eaten dinner. I want to eat that roast beef!"

The timing was good, and the meal was ready by six. As we ate it, I told my mom that I was in fact in labor and that we'd be heading in to the little clinic/hospital after dinner. Of course, she too wanted me to drop everything and rush in, but I was content to digest my food. I did take a big slug of rum though, known to slow down contractions a tad, just to be safe.

Dave rowed off in search of the person who had the "yachties' car keys," the keys to an old Peugeot that was just passed on continuously for the yachties to use as they needed. He finally found the keys and returned for me. Right as we got to the car, it started raining. The bad thing about this car is it had only a front windshield but no side windows or rear windows, and the wipers didn't work on the front passenger side. It was dark by now, and the ride to Papeete was a little treacherous in the downpour. But we made it safely to the clinic, a small clinic/hospital in downtown Papeete. It had a large room with ten beds in it for the new mothers, showers down the hall, and a birthing room. That was my first time there; that's all that I saw.

I checked in with the nurse who was very sweet and pleasant. Then the mean doctor came in to check me. He put me on the birthing table, examined me, and told me he needed to give me something to speed up the labor. I argued with him, flashing anger, saying, "No. I don't need anything to speed up labor. I'm doing just fine."

He argued that he didn't want to be there all night waiting for me.

I argued back, "Then go home. I don't need you here. The nurses can deliver."

He argued that wasn't going to happen, that he needed to give me Pitocin. I was horrified at this guy. In my mind, he was just a self-centered, mean man, not at all interested in the beauty and miracle of childbirth.

I felt confident I would have the baby soon, so I finally said, "Okay, I'll make you a deal. If I have the baby after 1:00 a.m., we'll do it your way, but if I have it before then, we'll do it my way."

I'm not sure exactly what time it was then, but possibly nine-thirty. He finally agreed.

I started walking the halls. I stood in hot showers, letting the heat soak into my lower back where I was having back labor. I walked the halls some more. A nurse was walking with me when I had a strong contraction. In French, she said, "C'est mal?"

I thought she was asking if it was bad. I replied, "No, no, it's not bad." I mean, it wasn't really bad-bad yet. I learned later she probably thought I was nuts because "c'est mal" was the obstetric colloquialism for, "Are you having a contraction?" which clearly I was.

Dave in the meantime had gone down the street to some French bar. I remembered how he left to go hang up the fishing net when I was in labor with Heidi. *What is this with him?* I was thinking. But just as before, having some prescience, he returned a few minutes before the doctor wanted to check me again. It was almost eleven-thirty. I went into the labor room. I climbed up onto the table, put my legs up into those stirrups, and he examined me. I remember feeling a flow of water. He said something to the effect, "There, okay. Your water is broke. You will have this baby in one hour."

He removed his gloves and walked out of the room, and my next contraction was a full I-need-to-push-right-now contraction. The only French word I could think of was *pouser, pouser,* "to push, to push."

A nurse ran back in and tried to put a bar across my chest to keep me lying flat while I was struggling to get up into a sitting position. The doctor came running back in while another nurse was putting my feet back up in the stirrups. I was screaming at these people through this contraction, "Leave me alone! I am having a baby! I don't want to lie down, especially with a bar across my chest, and I don't want my feet up in the air! I want to use gravity!"

Dave had managed to get into the room about halfway during the chaos and was telling me to calm down as if he was siding with the doctors and nurses. I was growling throughout the contraction and yelling at these people. As the contraction passed, the mean doctor, in French, told me, "You must be quiet, or the police will come."

I slowly translated what he said in my head, and as the next contraction, thirty seconds later, started to build, I asked him in English with my teeth gritted closed, "The police are coming because I'm having a baby?" adding in my head, *You have got to be fucking kidding me.*

As the contraction came on full force, I closed my mouth, never making another sound, and bore down hard. My son almost shot out onto the floor because the doctor really didn't have an hour before this baby was coming, and damn it, I wasn't going to spend one more minute in this delivery room with this horrible man. He did manage to catch my son before he slithered off the table onto the floor.

The nurses whisked my son away to check his vitals and clean him up. I delivered the placenta, was cleaned up quickly, and returned to my room, which contained nine other beds filled with women and their babies. Everyone was sleeping. They brought our son in and put him in a bassinet next to my bed. He slept. I slept.

The morning after my son was born in Tahiti, I woke early to his stirring whimpers from the bassinet that was next to my bed and to the cries of several other babies in this room containing ten beds. A row of window openings—again, no glass, just wooden shutters that were propped up by sticks along the length of the room—opened out on to the flower gardens of a simple Tahitian neighborhood of small homes with rusted tin roofs. I suppose, I reflected, that if I were making a lot of noise at midnight, the folks in this neighborhood would have heard. Is *that* why the police would have come?

A Chinese woman was tending her screaming baby, wrapping it in yet another blanket. Even in the early-morning hours, it was at least eighty degrees in the room. I wanted to tell her, "The baby is too hot. Take off the covers!" But I didn't. I leaned over and pulled Arlo from his bassinet and gave him my breast, which he took readily and sucked hard. A woman next to me was trying to get her baby to drink a bottle of formula. She was sitting up in bed with a pareo wrapped around her waist and her breasts tightly—tightly—wrapped in white cloth. Later in the day we talked, and she said she did not want the burden of breastfeeding, and she was going to dry up her milk.

I could not understand anybody who did not want to breastfeed. It was so easy, so simple. Milk was always right there, ready to go. No making formulas, purifying water, purifying bottles and nipples. Just breast, nipple, baby's mouth, put them together. I was told later by an American gal who was married to a Tahitian and who'd had a baby a week before mine that there was a new fad with Tahitians that made them feel more worldly and upper class if they bottle-fed their babies. *Ah, back to the '50s they go*, I thought.

Arlo only had diapers on and had been lightly swaddled in a blanket. I loosened it to explore his little body as he ate. Since he was born at eleven-thirty at night, I was exhausted, and he had slept most of the night, so this was the first time I really had a chance to explore and look at him. He was beautiful. Perfect round head, big eyes. He had a birthmark that smudged the side of one eye, wrapping down a bit of his cheek. Very light. I could hardly notice it. It might even go away (though it never did). It wasn't the bright purple kind that seems almost disfiguring but just a light shadow of darker skin kissing his face.

I, like all young mothers, looked at his arms, and lifted his tiny hands and admired his tiny fingers with the minuscule fingernails already needing to be trimmed. My hands went down his legs, and I reached to his feet, and it was only then that I noticed that they were twisted and turned and almost rolled into balls at the ends of his skinny little shins. My hands instinctively tried to straighten them out to be pointing up and out, but they didn't want to be remolded. I was pondering his feet, thinking they had just been extra squished weirdly in my womb when a nurse came in to check on everyone. She saw me looking at Arlo's feet and said something in French, which was hard to understand. Like my school French had not included construction tools, it also never included medical French. She made motions like wrapping up his feet. I later came to understand she was saying his feet would need to be casted to straighten them out.

I didn't worry too much more about his feet at the time. They were quite twisted with his big toes arching inward and sideways toward his heels and the top of his feet bending upside down, again curving toward his heels. I remembered the children I'd seen walking on the tops of their crippled feet on the island of Niue years before. I remembered the woman telling me they used to throw deformed children into the sea. I gently rubbed his feet as he nursed.

I actually had a greater concern at the time. Dave wanted Arlo to be circumcised as he was. I didn't know anything different myself. My brothers had been circumcised. I had never seen an uncircumcised man though I had seen many island babies and young boys who had their foreskin and had not been circumcised. I naïvely thought that maybe they had circumcision performed at an older age as a rite of passage ceremony. I didn't realize that most of the world did not perform circumcision.

I had asked the nurse when she came in, "We would like our son to be circumcised."

A deep frown crossed her face. "Porquoi?" she asked. "Why?"

"Well, because that's normal to do."

"No, we do not have a doctor who does that."

I asked to speak to a doctor. It turned out it was the same mean doctor who had delivered my son. I asked him if he would circumcise my son. In French, with a heightened degree of anger, he replied, "My God, no, I would never do such a thing. What kind of mother are you?"

Friends and families came to visit the other mothers all day. It was, at times, like a great party was going on though nobody brought their ukuleles. Large, fat Tahitian women in their bright pareos and flowers in their hair, wearing leis as a matter of daily attire, would come in and greet the new mothers. The Chinese woman in the corner whose baby never stopped crying was only visited by what appeared to be her mother, a small wrinkled woman. They chattered to each other in Chinese while others spoke Tahitian. Little French was spoken unless it was by me trying to communicate with someone.

I woke up not feeling very good. The nurse determined that my uterus was not seeming to contract as much as it should after birth, and she brought in a vial of liquid and told me to take ten drops now and ten drops at the end of the day. I followed her directions, and within about an hour, I was very happy and joyful and smiling. The Chinese woman's screaming baby was no longer bothering me; the fact that the woman next to me had tightly wrapped her breasts and was bottle-feeding her baby no longer bothered me. The room that was filled with noisy though happy well-wishers, leaving me no privacy, no longer bothered me. I was just very, very happy. I did feel a little feverish and aching though in spite of being, as I said, very happy.

Near the end of the day, the fever and achiness subsided, and it was then it dawned on me that I might be having a malaria attack. I stored the information at the back of my mind behind my happiness. Dave stopped by. My two-year-old daughter apparently was not allowed in the hospital, so my mother had stayed behind on the boat with her. I was telling Dave that the nurses were concerned that my uterus wasn't contracting up quite as much and as quickly as they'd like to see, and that they had given me a vial of medicine to take. He asked, "What is it?"

I said, "Hmm, I don't know. Let me read it."

My memory is the drug given me was methergine, the base ingredient of LSD. I read in the smallest of print, ergot or ergotoline. That's why I'd been so happy all day. I was thinking maybe they should give some to that

Chinese woman so she'd lighten up a bit and unswathe her screaming baby. I took another dose that night but found I didn't sleep very well and never took any more though I saved the vial for many years.

The day I was released from the hospital, I again began to ache and have a fever. They were actually going to keep me another day, but I explained to them that I was confident I was having a malaria attack. I took the prescribed dose of chloroquine. The symptoms stopped, and that is the last malaria attack I ever had.

Dave had brought in the not-quite-as-white sling that I had made for Heidi over two years ago. I slipped Arlo into it, and we prepared to leave with our uncircumcised son whose feet were twisted up in the wrong direction. The nurses explained to me what needed to be done with Arlo's feet. They had written us directions to the big hospital that was on the outside of town and told us that we should go directly there upon leaving the birthing clinic. They gave me the name of a doctor I should see there.

Dave had the yachtie's Peugeot. We loaded into it and found our way to the big main hospital; we found our way to the offices of this orthopedic doctor. He spoke a very tiny bit of English, and he explained that Arlo had a very common congenital deformity called clubfoot that could be corrected with putting casts on his feet. He explained how they would take X-rays of his feet, and then I would go to the casting clinic, that because he was so young and that he would be growing quickly, I would need to bring him back once a week so his casts could be cut off and new ones put on.

Only then did it hit me that my baby was imperfect and that there were problems though I was confident from what the doctor said that we would get these casts and he would be fine. In a fog, with Dave with me, I held my three-day-old baby down and tried to keep him still as they X-rayed his feet. We then took him to the casting clinic where they wrapped his feet in wet gauze soaked in plaster of Paris, and after each foot was wrapped, but still wet, they grabbed his little feet and started pulling his feet up and around and into the position that they should be in. He screamed. He screamed so hard with the pain they were causing that I yelled at the man to stop. He would not stop. It needed to be done, he said. He did the other foot. The casting material was hot as it set up. Arlo's little toes peeked out the end, tiny and red. His little trembling chin and little hiccupping gasps took a long time to quiet.

I wiped the tears from my eyes and slipped Arlo into the carrier. I took the X-rays that had been developed and then put into an envelope, and we drove back to our anchorage. I felt weak, exhausted—from the malaria somewhat, I think, and from the trauma of my baby's tears.

Arriving at the boat, this was the first time I'd seen my mother since I'd gone into labor. She had stayed on the boat the whole time with Heidi. Dave had left her there to go to work at the *Tahiti Bulletin* where he had written a newsflash, "New First Mate Born, First Mate Arlo." My mother was not able to maneuver getting in and out of the dinghy with Heidi on her own, so she had stayed on the little thirty-foot sailboat out in the bay for almost three days. She didn't seem any worse for the experience, though I had missed Heidi, and I was excited to show her baby brother.

I returned to the daily tasks of life on board the boat: tending to twenty-five-month-old Heidi and her needs, nursing Arlo, doing laundry in the cockpit with my soap and stick, *thud-thud*, turn, *thud-thud* turn. I'd rinse most of the soap out in buckets of saltwater, and then with Arlo in my sling, Heidi, and my mother and buckets of wet salty laundry, I would row to shore. Sometimes my mother would hold Arlo and chase Heidi around while I rinsed out the saltwater under a running tap that was provided for both sailors and beachgoers. Sometimes Heidi would squat naked but for her tiny little bikini bottoms I had sewed her and plunge her little hands into the bucket of laundry and help me swish them clean while Arlo would swing in the sling suspended in the air over the bucket. I needed to get used to doing it on my own as my mother stayed only another two weeks before she returned to the States. There would be no one to help me do these tasks.

I remember an interesting conversation I had with my mother several days after returning to the boat. We were on shore, and I'd just finished rinsing out the laundry, wringing it out. It was piled in the bucket, and we were getting ready to return to the boat to hang up the laundry to dry. I think my mother had been wanting to ask this question since I'd returned because she was very hesitant when she did: "Why didn't you get Arlo circumcised?"

I stopped loading up the dinghy and straightened up and looked at her and said, "Because the doctors won't do it here. They think it's barbaric. And as I've thought about it, I tend to agree with them."

My mother replied, "No, you have to get him circumcised."

"Why? I think it's a pretty weird thing to want to slice off the end of a baby's dick. What a way to introduce him into this world."

"No," she said, "your father was not circumcised," which of course was more information than I needed to know, but then she went on to state emphatically that that's why their marriage had failed and that there was no passion in their lives.

I don't think my jaw physically dropped, but I remember responding spontaneously, "Mom, I'm pretty sure there was no passion because there was no love between you."

That ended the conversation. But that was a strange conversation that has stayed with me ever since. I learned later, that circumcision grew in greater popularity during the two world wars where it was thought that circumcision helped prevent the spread of venereal disease. Many soldiers entering the first war were ordered to be circumcised. Later, when they returned and married, remembering the pain they suffered having it done at age twenty or twenty-five, they figured they'd save their baby boy the pain in later years by having it done at birth. The obstetric community also jumped on this bandwagon.

Most Europeans, other than the English, never opted for circumcision of their male babies and thought it was barbaric. The English though had begun major circumcision, like America, in World War I and into World War II, but when the war was over, and they were rebuilding England, it was then that the national health program was developed in England. Doctors, already overstressed with everyday medical necessities, refused to participate in processes that were not medically necessary, and circumcision practices began to die out in England.

But in America, after World War II, with an overabundance of jobs and not enough workers, one of the incentives employers used to entice employees was creating and providing health insurance for those workers. So instead of a national health system being born in the United States, health insurance companies were formed, and their interest was in *making* money and paying for every and all conceivable procedures; they were not interested in *saving* money. So circumcision became an automatic part of childbirth without the mother nor the baby having any rights to say differently. Hence, over 90 percent of American male children continue to be circumcised out of habit and out of the fear of being different.

My mother returned to the States, leaving me to take care of two children on a thirty-foot sailboat. I piled Heidi and Arlo into the dinghy each morning and rowed Dave to shore so he could go off to rewrite news stories for a six-page eight-by-eleven-and-a-half printed English paper for the tourists. I would return to the boat and wash diapers and sheets and towels and pareos, *thud-thud*, turn, *thud-thud*, turn.

Most days I'd get the laundry washed and hung, and we'd return to shore to walk down through the manicured grounds of the adjoining hotel, out to the road, and down to a little Chinese market where I could buy fresh baguettes still warm from the bakery. For another month, I managed to continue to sneak through the halls of the hotel and grab a bucket of ice to bring back to the boat to throw in our small cooler to keep my batch of yogurt that I made every day fresh and growing. When they finally caught on to me, my innocent response was, "Gosh, you have so much ice. I didn't think it was a big deal. I'll pay for it!"

But they said it was only for their hotel guests. With no more ice, I ceased to make yogurt. Heidi drank lukewarm powdered milk or limeade made from fresh limes of which there was always an abundance.

I continued to make alfalfa sprout salads; we ate beans and rice, dried fish from our ship's stores; we bought baguettes and good French cheeses, cheap French red table wine in five-gallon jugs, onions and cabbage, and sometimes chicken or meat. Though Dave made money working at the *Tahiti Bulletin*, I wasn't ever aware of how much; I was just aware that we were always very poor. Money was tight for groceries.

There was one other French couple on a boat anchored near us who had a little girl a year older than Heidi, and we'd get the children together to play occasionally, but they were very typically French and not very friendly, so it was all very strained for me to spend time there. All the other yachties were either old retired folks or younger couples or groups of young men on adventures. None had children, and few were interested in spending time on our boat with children crawling across them in the limited space, and it was almost impossible to relax on their boats if we took the children over there as the danger of Heidi falling overboard or getting into something dangerous was always imminent.

There were so many more yachts sailing now than had been in Tahiti seven years earlier. Some were the same type of adventurous, hardy souls;

many were of a different breed, richer with fancier boats, maybe only sailing for a year, not making a life out of it. We had weekly potlucks on the sandy point near our anchorage, which was fun and interesting. There were some members of boats with which we had a natural attraction, and friendships were quickly made. We had little camaraderie with the newer fancy, rich-man boats with all the latest fancy equipment: nice life rafts in fancy ejection boxes on the stern, radar and radio antennae in their rigging, real running lights, not kerosene lanterns. We gravitated more toward the boats with stuff hanging from it and wooden dinghies propelled only by oars.

We were the old-timers in Tahiti. Some of the newer sailors, just starting the milk run, gravitated to us to hear of our experiences and suggestions as to where would be the next good place to go. We could tell them of where we'd sailed seven years ago, but we always gave them the caveat that things were changing quickly. We talked about the Papeete of before, before Quinn's was destroyed and replaced with a shopping center, before everything had gotten so expensive. Seven years later, it seemed like paradise lost.

We saw these changes as a big negative. But the timing seemed to be such that it was clear, with Arlo's crippled feet, that we were going to need to return to the States to get good medical care. I had continued to take him weekly to the hospital. A loud vibrating buzz saw would cut off his little casts. The sound terrified him, and his screams would start as soon as the saw started up. They promised it was not able to cut through skin even demonstrating how it stopped vibrating when it hit their hand, but nonetheless, they managed to cut his skin one day cutting off one of the casts. He has a scar there to this day. A different week when they put on the casts, they somehow ended up pinching his skin into the hot casting material. Within twenty-four hours, he was screaming and crying nonstop. Clearly there was some sort of problem, but being preverbal, it was hard to diagnose. We finally decided it must have something to do with the casts, so we returned to the hospital, and they removed the casts to find, in fact, he had deep infected pussy sores that had rotted into the corners of both of his ankles.

In order for the sores to heal, that was his only week he didn't have to wear casts. In that week, for the very first time, he got to swim in the ocean with me, feeling the freedom of the warm tropical water, the awe of floating free. That was the week when a retired Canadian doctor and her husband sailed in. We had met on the docks preparing to get in the dinghy, and she had noticed Arlo's feet. Inviting us over for drinks later, she asked about his feet. I told her what I knew, which was only what the doctors had told me: that it was a common deformity and was correctable. She asked to see his X-rays, which I brought over. Her brow was furrowed, and she became very serious and insisted that the kind of medical care we were receiving here was probably not going to correct his feet, that we really needed to return to the States for proper care.

It seemed that all things were coming to a confluence and pointing to us to head back to civilization, at least for a while. The cost of sailing was taxing our abilities, what with fees being demanded by the authorities, restrictions on how long we could stay. With Tahiti becoming more and more expensive, even living on the sailboat, we could afford to buy little of anything extravagant. The local people were not as generous and welcoming with fruits and fish like they'd been seven years ago. Now whatever they offered, they wanted money in exchange. The whole energy of the islands had changed. Further, there was starting to be a lot of political unrest, the Tahitians rebelling against the French and even against the influx of tourism that, though it was bringing in money and jobs, it was also bringing in drugs and crime, prostitution, and greed. It was changing the heart of the people.

It was time to leave. We might have left a bit sooner, but we were waiting for Arlo's Certificate of Birth Abroad. I was informed he could fly back with me without a passport if he had the Certificate of Birth Abroad. My mother sent money to have me and the children fly first to Hawai'i and later on to Oregon while Dave sailed *Paz del Mar* back.

Dave and I continued to struggle as a couple over the next few years. It's not a surprise really because, even before Heidi was born, we were often ships passing in the night. I think in hindsight, after years of personal growth work, Dave was all those parts of me that I had disowned. He was laid back and relaxed and never worried about tomorrow or about money. He was the rooster that crowed loudly and strutted around while, especially after having children, I was mother hen with my wings spread, always in a worried state of needing to protect and provide. Even before we had children, I was always much more security conscious as far as having at least some money for our wants and needs. Dave did not adapt well to working and earning the money necessary to pay for a house and food and heat and transportation and medical care and all the costs of trying to raise a family in the United States, all of which added to my stress and unhappiness. We had yet another son together before we split up.

I set my anchor, laid out a lot of chain. The call of the ocean and its freedom were silenced for the many years while the voice of mother—with her attendant handmaidens of protector, provider, survivor and superwoman—reigned.

ANCHOR DOWN

As Katherine Thanas said, "All of us look out at the same world. And we all see a different version of it, depending on what's already in our minds . . . Notice how the dust of our mind obscures the clear reflection of the world, how our values and preferences determine our interpretations." Clear vision starts with getting out the rag and washing off the first level of dust and dirt, and it often takes many washings and rinsing before the view is clear.

It took forty-five years to write this book. It took forty-five years to *begin* to have a clear perspective on all that occurred inside of me while outwardly having the adventures and experiences that I had. I had great experiences—and many unhappy days too—simply because I was blinded by the driving force that pulled up my anchor and allowed me to drift out to sea. I never knew at the time that my urge to sail or travel or move was my tried-and-true method to avoid emotional pain.

I ended up spending the next forty years transcribing court trials in my home where, as a single parent, I was always available to my kids' needs. Of course, working at home, I learned to appreciate fully the stress my father experienced trying to write his textbooks with young children making noise—happy or sad or angry—in the background. That is also why this book never got written until now. My kids are grown now. I live alone as I do so enjoy.

Dave was and is a kind and loving person. He was and is funny and intelligent and resourceful. He was and is a loving father. We were and are completely different people, carrying too much baggage to be able to be a functional couple. The dirty windows of life that I looked through and the view of the world I saw were completely different than Dave's. Neither of us could see each other clearly, nor find a way to communicate well. Even decades later, when we both became Buddhist practitioners, he chose the Mahayana path and I the Theravada path, a continuation of our disparate views and paths through life.

I am sorry for my inability to have loved him as we all deserve to be loved.

He loved the sea, and he has returned to sailing. His course is charted to go to Fergusson Island and see how he might help deal with malaria there. Now he has solar panels to charge his batteries, GPS navigation, and satellite Internet and a meager monthly social security check. I'm happy for him.

For me, without even standing on its shores or sailing upon its face, the point where the ocean meets the sky remains an object of my meditation.

Ripples on still waters.

Anchor down.

ACKNOWLEDGMENTS

I thank every friend and stranger who, when I'd tell some of these tales, encouraged me to write a book.

I thank Cynthia Russell for her feedback on my very first fledgling draft and encouraging me to explore my emotions deeper. I thank her and the other Tawanda Girls (you know who you are) for teaching me the strength of woman.

I thank Ellen Beckett for proofing and giving me feedback.

I thank Leslie Caplan, writing coach, of Write It Strong, for her encouragement to keep writing.

I thank David Olvera for providing the impetus to return to this story and complete it.

I thank all the characters in my story—all real people hiding behind fictitious names—who helped me along my way.

I thank "Dave" for remaining my friend in spite of our differences.

INDEX

M

Magalkarona, 183–84, 187, 196, 199, 201
Maoris, 108–12, 114
Marques, Gabin, 152, 154–55
Marquesas, 8, 10–11, 34, 48, 53–58, 77, 81, 241, 267
Maurice (bar and store owner), 15–16, 149–52
Maya, 60, 62, 70, 79–80, 85
Mel (retired shop teacher), 53, 65, 67–69, 72, 75, 77, 87–88, 92–93
Mills, Doug, 232, 236–38
mom, 115–17, 126–27, 154, 195, 242, 272, 284, 310–11, 319
Monica (student nurse), 246–49
Moselle Bay, 144–46
Mosquito Island, 79, 86, 90
mother, 32, 117, 124–27, 138, 148, 173, 222–23, 256, 271–73, 276–79, 281–91, 309–11, 316, 318, 320
Mrs. O'Malley (nanny), 125
Mt. Carbine, 162–63

N

Nadi, 80, 83, 86, 90
Neiafu, 71–72
New Caledonia, 92, 133, 138, 143–45, 151, 156, 196, 199
New Hebrides, 304–7
New Zealand, 83, 91–93, 95, 104–5, 108, 113, 116, 118, 122, 128–30, 148, 172, 179, 215, 224, 271, 291, 296, 303
Niue, 67–68, 70, 80, 315
North Island, 94, 111, 116
Noumea, 143–44, 158
Nukumanu, 261–62

O

Omoa, 47–51

P

Palmerston, 65–68
Papeete, 35, 53–57, 152, 309, 312, 321
Papua New Guinea, 176–77, 180, 183, 185, 188, 197, 207, 209, 220, 224, 232, 235–36, 239–41, 251, 256
Patrice (French sailor), 17–18
Pawarenga, 95, 115, 121–22, 128, 148, 157
Paz del Mar, 41, 56, 119, 140, 151, 155–56, 158, 185, 187, 204, 220, 258, 266, 271, 322
Physalia, 79, 85, 90
Pole (New Zealand schoolteacher), 106–7, 118, 129–30
Ponape, 76, 264–65, 272–77, 279, 281, 283, 294, 296–98, 302–3
Prony Bay, 141–43

R

Raphael (Taipivai head honcho), 26–27, 29–31, 33, 35–37
Rarotonga, 60–62, 64, 82, 146, 229, 307–8
Rebel, 90
Red Rose, 40, 70, 85, 90
Restless, 76, 79, 84

S

Salimar, 85–87, 90
Salty, 79, 84–85
Samarai, 180–84, 190, 195, 198, 201–2, 219
Sariba, 183–84, 193, 195, 198, 205
Sea Dancer, 53, 85, 91